To Terry
with love
Elly

S0-BZY-478

SPIRITUALIST PHILOSOPHY

Spiritualist Philosophy

THE SPIRITS' BOOK

CONTAINING

THE PRINCIPLES OF SPIRITIST DOCTRINE

ON

**THE IMMORTALITY OF THE SOUL: THE NATURE OF SPIRITS
AND THEIR RELATIONS WITH MEN; THE MORAL LAW:
THE PRESENT LIFE, THE FUTURE LIFE, AND
THE DESTINY OF THE HUMAN RACE.**

ACCORDING TO THE TEACHINGS OF SPIRITS OF HIGH DEGREE,
TRANSMITTED THROUGH VARIOUS MEDIUMS,

COLLECTED AND SET IN ORDER

BY

ALLAN KARDEC

Translated from the Hundred and Twentieth Thousand

BY

ANNA BLACKWELL

10th Edition

LAKE - Livraria Allan Kardec Editora
(Instituição Filantrópica)
Rua: Assunção, 45 - Brás
Cep: 03005-020 - São Paulo - Brasil
Tel.: (011) 229-1227, 229-0526, 227-1396,
229-0937, 229-0514, 229-4592
Fax: (011) 227-5714, 229-0935
e-mail: lakelivraria@uol.com.br
http://www.lake.com.br

TO

THE DEVOTED WIFE

OF

ALLAN KARDEC

THIS TRANSLATION

IS

AFFECTIONALITY INSCRIBED.

TRANSLATOR'S PREFACE

In presenting to her countrymen a work which has long since obtained a wide acceptance on the Continent, the translator has thought that a brief notice of its author, and of the circumstances under which it was produced, might not be without interest for English readers.

Léon-Dénizarth-Hippolyte Rivail, better known by his *nom de plume* of ALLAN KARDEC, was born at Lyons, on the 4th of October 1804, of an old family of Bourg-en-Bresse, that had been for many generations honourably distinguished in the magistracy and at the bar. His father, like his grandfather, was a barrister of good standing and high character; his mother, remarkably beautiful, accomplished, elegant, and amiable, was the object, on his part, of a profound and worshipping affection, maintained unchanged throughout the whole of his life.

Educated at the Institution of Pestalozzi, at Yverdun (Canton de Vaud), he acquired at an early age the habit of investigation and the freedom of thought of which his later life was destined to furnish so striking an example. Endowed by nature with a passion for teaching, he devoted himself, from the age of fourteen, to aiding the studies of those of his schoolfellows who were less advanced than himself; while such was his fondness for botany, that he often spent an entire day among the mountains, walking twenty or thirty miles, with a wallet on his back, in search of specimens for his herbarium. Born in a Catholic country, but educated in a Protestant one, he began, while yet a mere boy, to meditate on the means of bringing about a unity of belief among the various Christian sects—a project of religious reform at which he laboured in silence for many years, but necessarily without success, the elements of the desired solution not being at that time in his possession.

Having finished his studies at Yverdun, he returned to Lyons in 1824, with the intention of devoting himself to the law; but various acts of religious intolerance to which he unexpectedly found himself subjected led him to renounce the idea of fitting himself for the bar, and to take up his abode in Paris, where he occupied himself for some time in translating *Telemachus* and other standard French books for youth into German. Having at length determined upon his career, he purchased, in 1828, a large and flourishing educational establishment for boys, and devoted himself to the work of teaching, for which, by his tastes and acquirements, he was peculiarly fitted. In 1830 he hired, at his own expense, a large hall in the Rue de Sèvres, and opened therein courses of gratuitous lectures on Chemistry, Physics, Comparative Anatomy, and Astronomy. These lectures, continued by him through a period of ten years, were highly successful, being attended by an auditory of over five humdred persons of every rank of society, many of whom have since attained to eminence in the scientific world.

Always desirous to render instruction attractive as well as profitable, he invented an ingenious method of computation, and constructed a mnemotechnic table of French history, for assisting students to remember the remarkable events and discoveries of each reign.

Of the numerous educational works published by him may be mentioned, *A Plan for the Improvement of Public Instruction*, submitted by him in 1828 to the French Legislative Chamber, by which body it was highly extolled, though not acted upon; *A Course of Practical and Theoretic Arithmetic, on the Pestalozzian System, for the use of Teachers and Mothers* (1829); *A Classical Grammar of the French Tongue* (1831); *A Manual for the use of Candidates for Examination in the Public Schools; with Explanatory Solutions of various Problems of Arithmetic and Geometry* (1848); *Normal Dictations for the Examinations of the Hotel de Ville and the Sorbonne, with Special Dictations on Orthographic Difficulties* (1849). These works, highly esteemed at the time of their publication, are still in use in many French schools; and their author was bringing out new editions of some of them at the time of his death.

He was a member of several learned societies; among others, of the Royal Society of Arras, which, in 1831, awarded to him the Prize of Honour for a remarkable essay on the question, "What is the System of Study most in Harmony with the Needs of the Epoch?" He was for several years Secretary to the

Phrenological Society of Paris, and took an active part in the labours of the Society of Magnetism, giving much time to the practical investigation of somnambulism, trance, clairvoyance, and the various other phenomena connected with the mesmeric action. This brief outline of his labours will suffice to show his mental activity, the variety of his knowledge, the eminently practical turn of his mind, and his constant endeavour to be useful to his fellow-men.

When, about 1850, the phenomenon of "table-turning" was exciting the attention of Europe and ushering in the other phenomena since known as "spiritist", he quickly divined the real nature of those phenomena, as evidence of the existence of an order of relationships hitherto suspected rather than known—viz., those which unite the visible and invisible worlds. Foreseeing the vast importance, to science and to religion, of such an extension of the field of human observation, he entered at once upon a careful investigation of the new phenomena. A friend of his had two daughters who had become what are now called "mediums." They were gay, lively, amiable girls, fond of society, dancing, and amusement, and habitually received, when "sitting" by themselves or with their young companions, "communications" in harmony with their worldly and somewhat frivolous disposition. But, to the surprise of all concerned, it was found that, whenever he was present, the messages transmitted through these young ladies were of a very grave and serious character; and on his inquiring of the invisible intelligences as to the cause of this change, he was told that "spirits of a much higher order than those who habitually communicated through the two young mediums came expressly for him, and would continue to do so, in order to enable him to fulfil an important religious mission."

Much astonished at so unlooked-for an announcement, he at once proceeded to test its truthfulness by drawing up a series of progressive questions in relation to the various problems of human life and the universe in which we find ourselves, and submitted them to his unseen interlocutors, receiving their answers to the same through the instrumentality of the two young mediums, who willingly consented to devote a couple of evenings every week to this purpose, and who thus obtained, through table-rapping and planchette-writing, the replies which have become the basis of the spiritist theory, and which they were as little capable of appreciating as of inventing.

When these conversations had been going on for nearly two years, he one day remarked to his wife, in reference to the unfolding of these views, which she had followed with intelligent sympathy: "It is a most curious thing! My conversations with the invisible intelligences have completely revolutionised my ideas and convictions. The instructions thus transmitted constitute an entirely new theory of human life, duty, and destiny, that appears to me to be perfectly rational and coherent, admirably lucid and consoling, and intensely interesting. I have a great mind to publish these conversations in a book; for it seems to me that what interests me so deeply might very likely prove interesting to others." His wife warmly approving the idea, he next submitted it to his unseen interlocutors, who replied, in the usual way, that it was they who had suggested it to his mind, that their communications had been made to him, not for himself alone, but for the express purpose of being given to the world as he proposed to do, and that the time had now come for putting this plan into execution. "To the book in which you will embody our instructions," continued the communicating intelligences, "you will give, as being our work rather than yours, the title of *Le Livre des Esprits* (*The Spirits' Book*); and you will publish it, not under your own name, but under the *pseudonym* of ALLAN KARDEC.[1] Keep your own name of Rivail for your own books already published; but take and keep the name we have now given you for the book you are about to publish by our order, and, in general, for all the work that you will have to do in the fulfilment of the mission which, as we have already told you, has been confided to you by Providence, and which will gradually open before you as you proceed in it under our guidance."

The book thus produced and published sold with great rapidity, making converts not in France only, but all over the Continent, and rendering the name of ALLAN KARDEC "a household word" with the readers who knew him only in connection with it; so that he was thenceforth called only by that name, excepting by his old personal friends, with whom both he and his wife always retained their family-name. Soon after its publication, he founded *The Parisian Society of Psychologic Studies*, of which he was President until his death, and which met every Friday evening at his house, for the purpose of obtaining from spirits, through writing mediums, instructions in elucidation of truth and duty.

---

[1] An old Breton name in his mother's family.

He also founded and edited until he died a monthly magazine, entitled *La Revue Spirite, Journal of Psychologic Studies,* devoted to the advocacy of the views set forth in *The Spirit's Book.*

Similar associations were speedily formed all over the world. Many of these published periodicals of more or less importance in support of the new doctrine; and all of them transmitted to the Parisian Society the most remarkable of the spirit-communications received by them. An enormous mass of spirit-teaching, unique both in quantity and in the variety of the sources from which it was obtained, thus found its way into the hands of Allan Kardec, by whom it was studied, collated, co-ordinated, with unwearied zeal and devotion, during a period of fifteen years. From the materials thus furnished to him from every quarter of the globe he enlarged and completed *The Spirits' Book,* under the direction of the spirits by whom it was originally dictated; the "Revised Edition" of which work, brought out by him in 1857 (*vide* "Preface to the Revised Edition," p. 19) has become the recognised text-book of the school of Spiritualist Philosophy so intimately associated with his name. From the same materials he subsequently compiled four other works, viz., *The Mediums' Book* (a practical treatise on Medianimity and Evocations), 1861; *The Gospel as Explained by Spirits* (an exposition of morality from the spiritist point of view), 1864; *Heaven and Hell* (a vindication of the justice of the divine government of the human race), 1865; and *Genesis* (showing the concordance of the spiritist theory with the discoveries of modern science and with the general tenor of the Mosaic record as explained by spirits), 1867. He also published two short treatises, entitled *What is Spiritism?* and *Spiritism Reduced to its Simplest Expression.*

It is to be remarked, in connection with the works just enumerated, that Allan Kardec was not a "medium," and was consequently obliged to avail himself of the medianimity of others in obtaining the spirit-communications from which they were evolved. The theory of life and duty, so immediately connected with his name and labours that it is often erroneously supposed to have been the product of his single mind or of the spirits in immediate connection with him, is therefore far less the expression of a personal or individual opinion than are any other of the spiritualistic theories hitherto propounded; for the basis of religious philosophy laid down in his works was not, in any way, the production of his own intelligence, but was as new to him as to

any of his readers, having been progressively educed by him from
the concurrent statements of a legion of spirits, through many
thousands of mediums, unknown to each other, belonging to
different countries, and to every variety of social position.

In person, Allan Kardec was somewhat under middle height.
Strongly built, with a large, round, massive head, well-marked
features, and clear grey eyes, he looked more like a German than
a Frenchman. Energetic and persevering, but of a temperament
that was calm, cautious, and unimaginative almost to coldness,
incredulous by nature and by education, a close, logical reasoner,
and eminently practical in thought and deed, he was equally free
from mysticism and from enthusiasm. Devoid of ambition, indifferent to luxury and display, the modest income he had acquired
from teaching and from the sale of his educational works sufficed
for the simple style of living he had adopted, and allowed him
to devote the whole of the profits arising from the sale of his
spiritist books and from the *Revue Spirite* to the propagation of
the movement initiated by him. His excellent wife relieved him of
all domestic and worldly cares, and thus enabled him to consecrate
himself entirely to the work to which he believed himself to have
been called, and which he prosecuted with unswerving devotion,
to the exclusion of all extraneous occupations, interests, and
companionships, from the time when he first entered upon it until
he died. He made no visits beyond a small circle of intimate
friends, and very rarely absented himself from Paris, passing his
winters in the heart of the town, in the rooms where he published
his *Revue*, and his summers at the Villa Ségur, a little semi-rural
retreat which he had built and planted, as the home of his old
age and that of his wife, in the suburban region behind the Champ
de Mars, now crossed in every direction by broad avenues and
being rapidly built over, but which at that time was a sort of waste
land that might still pass for "the country."

Grave, slow of speech, unassuming in manner, yet not without
a certain quiet dignity resulting from the earnestness and single-
mindedness which were the distinguishing traits of his character,
neither courting nor avoiding discussion, but never volunteering
any remark upon the subject to which he had devoted his life,
he received with affability the innumerable visitors from every
part of the world who came to converse with him in regard to
the views of which he was the recognised exponent, answering
questions and objections, explaining difficulties, and giving in-

formation to all serious inquirers, with whom he talked with freedom and animation, his face occasionally lighting up with a genial and pleasant smile, though such was his habitual sobriety of demeanour that he was never known to laugh.

Amoug the thousands by whom he was thus visited were many of high rank in the social, literary, artistic, and scientific worlds. The Emperor Napoleon III., the fact of whose interest in spiritist-phenomena was no mystery, sent for him several times, and held long conversations with him at the Tuileries upon the doctrines of *The Spirits' Book*.

Having suffered for many years from heart-disease, Allan Kardec drew up, in 1869, the plan of a new spiritist organisation, that should carry on the work of propagandism after his death. In order to assure its existence, by giving to it a legal and commercial *status*, he determined to make it a regularly constituted joint-stock limited liability publishing and bookselling company, to be constituted for a period of ninety-nine years, with power to buy and sell, to issue stock, to receive donations and bequests, etc. To this society, which was to be called *"The Joint Stock Company for the Continuation of the Works of Allan Kardec,"* he intended to bequeath the copyright of his spiritist writings and of the *Revue Spirite*.

But Allan Kardec was not destined to witness the realisation of the project in which he took so deep an interest, and which has since been carried out with entire exactitude by his widow.

On the 31st of March 1869, having just finished drawing up the constitution and rules of the society that was to take the place from which he foresaw that he would soon be removed, he was seated in his usual chair at his study-table, in his rooms in the Rue Sainte Anne, in the act of tying up a bundle of papers, when his busy life was suddenly brought to an end by the rupture of the aneurism from which he had so long suffered. His passage from the earth to the spirit-world, with which he had so closely identified himself, was instantaneous, painless, without a sigh or a tremor; a most peaceful falling asleep and reawaking—fit ending of such a life.

His remains were interred in the cemetery of Montmartre, in presence of a great concourse of friends, many hundreds of whom assemble there every year, on the anniversary of his decease, when a few commemorative words are spoken, and fresh flowers and wreaths, as is usual in Continental graveyards, are laid upon his tomb.

It is impossible to ascertain with any exactness the number of those who have adopted the views set forth by Allan Kardec; estimated by themselves at many millions, they are incontestably very numerous. The periodicals devoted to the advocacy of these views in various countries already number over forty, and new ones are constantly appearing. The death of Allan Kardec has not slackened the acceptance of the views set forth by him, and which are believed by those who hold them to be the basis, *but the basis only*, of the new development of religious truth predicted by Christ; the *beginning* of the promised revelation of "many things" that have been "kept hidden since the foundation of the world," and for the knowledge of which the human race was "not ready" at the time of that prediction.

In executing, with scrupulous fidelity, the task confided to her by Allan Kardec, the translator has followed, in all quotations from the New Testament, the version by Le Maistre de Sacy, the one always used by Allan Kardec.

ANNA BLACKWELL

THE SPIRITS' BOOK.

PREFACE TO THE REVISED EDITION

In the first edition of this work, we announced our intention to publish a Supplement treating of points for which it had been impossible to find room in that edition, or which might be suggested by subsequent investigations; but the new matter proved to be so closely connected with what had been previously published as to render its publication in a separate volume inexpedient. We therefore preferred to await the reprinting of the work, taking advantage of the opportunity thus afforded to fuse the whole of the materials together, to supress redundancies, and to make a more methodical arrangement of its contents. This new edition may consequently be considered as a new work, although the principles originally laid down have undergone no change, excepting in a very few instances which will be found to constitute *complements* and *explanations* rather than *modifications*.

This conformity of the teachings transmitted, notwithstanding the diversity of the sources from which they have emanated, is a fact of great importance in relation to the establishment of spiritist doctrine. Our correspondence shows us, moreover, that communications, identical (in substance, if not in form) with those embodied in the present work, have been obtained in various quarters, and even, in some instances, previously to the publication of *The Spirits' Book*, which has served to systematise and to confirm them. History, on the other hand, proves that most of the ideas herein set forth have been held by the most eminent thinkers of ancient and of modern times, and thus gives to them the additional sanction of its testimony.

Allan Kardec

INTRODUCTION

I

FOR new ideas new words are needed, in order to secure clearness of language by avoiding the confusion inseparable from the employment of the same term for expressing different meanings. The words *spiritual, spiritualist, spiritualism,* have a definite acceptation; to give them a new one, in order to apply them to the doctrine set forth by spirits, would be to multiply the causes of amphibology, already so numerous. Strictly speaking, *Spiritualism* is the opposite of *Materialism*; every one is a Spiritualist who believes that there is in him something more than matter, but it does not follow that he believes in the existence of spirits, or in their communication with the visible world. Instead, therefore, of the words SPIRITUAL, SPIRITUALISM, we employ, to designate this latter belief, the words SPIRITIST, SPIRITISM, which, by their form, indicate their origin and radical meaning, and have thus the advantage of being perfectly intelligible; and we reserve the words *spiritualism, spiritualist,* for the expression of the meaning attached to them by common acceptation. We say, then, that the fundamental principle of the *spiritist theory,* or *Spiritism,* is the relation of the material world with spirits, or the beings of the invisible world; and we designate the adherents of the spiritist theory as *spiritists.*

In a special sense, *"The Spirits' Book"* contains the doctrine or theory of *spiritism*; in a general sense, it appertains to the *spiritualist* school, of which it presents one of the phases. It is for this reasson that we have inscribed the words *Spiritualist Philosophy* on its title-page.

II

There is another word of which it is equally necessary to define the meaning, because it is the keystone of every system of morality, and also because, owing to the lack of a precise definition, it has been made the subject of innumerable controversies; we refer to the word *soul*. The divergence of opinion concerning the nature of the soul is a result of the variety of meanings attached to this word. A perfect language, in which every idea had its own special term, would save a vast deal of discussion; for, in that case, misunderstanding would be impossible.

Some writers define the soul as being the principle of organic life, having no existence of its own, and ceasing with the life of the body. According to this purely Materialistic belief, the soul is an effect, and not a cause.

Others consider the soul as being the principle of intelligence, the universal agent, of which each being absorbs a portion. According to them, there is, in the entire universe, only one soul, which distributes sparks of itself among all intelligent beings during their life; each spark, after the death of the being it has animated, returning to the common source, and blending again with the general whole, as brooks and rivers return to the ocean from which they were produced. This opinion differs from the preceding one, inasmuch as, according to the latter hypothesis, there is in us something more than matter, something that remains in existence after our death; but, practically, it is much as though nothing remained of us, since, no longer possessing individuality, we should retain no consciousness of our identity. According to this hypothesis, the universal soul is God, and each being is a portion of the Divinity. It is a species of Pantheism.

According to others, again, the soul is a moral being, distinct, independent of matter, and preserving its individuality after death. This acceptation of the word *soul* is certainly the one most generally received; because, under one name or another, the idea of a being that survives the body is found as an instinctive belief, and independently of all teaching, among all nations, whatever their degree of civilisation. This doctrine, according to which the soul is a *cause*, and not an *effect*, is that of the *spiritualists*.

Without discussing the value of these opinions, and considering the subject merely under its philological aspect, we say that these three applications of the word *soul* constitute three distinct ideas, each of which demands a different term. "Soul" has, therefore, a triple meaning, and is employed by each school according to the special meaning it attributes to that word. In order to avoid the confusion naturally resulting from the use of the same word to express three different ideas, it would be necessary to confine the word to one of these three ideas; it would not matter to which, provided the choice were clearly understood. We think it more natural to take it in its most common acceptation; and for this reason we employ the word SOUL to indicate the *immaterial and individual being which resides in us, and survives the body*. Even if this being did not really exist, and were only a product of the imagination, a specific term would still be needed to designate it.

For want of such a term for each of the other ideas now loosely understood by the word *soul*, we employ the term *vital principle* to designate the material and organic life which, whatever may be its source, is common to all living creatures, from the plant to man. As life can exist without the thinking faculty, the vital principle is something distinct from independent of it. The word *vitality* would not express the same idea. According to some, the vital principle is a property of matter; an effect produced wherever matter is found under certain given conditions; while, in the opinion of the greater number of thinkers, it resides in a special fluid, universally diffused, and of which each being absorbs and assimilates a portion during life, as inert bodies absorb light; the *vital principle* being identical with the *vital fluid*, which is generally regarded as being the same as the animalised electric fluid, designated also as the *magnetic fluid*, the *nervous fluid*, etc.

However this may be, one fact is certain, for it is proved by observation, viz., that organic beings possess in themselves a force which, so long as it exists, produces the phenomena of life; that physical life is common to all organic beings, and is independent of intelligence and thought; that intelligence and thought are faculties peculiar to certain organic species; and, lastly, that, among the organic species endowed with intelligence and thought, there is one which is endowed with a special moral sense that gives it an incontestible superiority over the others, viz., human species.

It is evident that, being employed according to various acceptations, the term *soul* does not exclude either Materialism or Pantheism. Spiritualists themselves understand the term *soul* according to one or other of the first two definitions, without denying the distinct immaterial being, to which, in that case, it would give some other name. This word, therefore, is not the representative of an opinion; it is a Protean term, defined by each after his own fashion, and thus giving rise to interminable disputes.

We might also avoid confusion, even while employing the word *soul* in the three senses defined above, by adding to it some qualifying term that should specify the point of view from which we consider it, or the mode in which we apply it. It would be, in that case, a generic word, representing at once the principles of material life, of intelligence, and of the moral faculty, each of which would be distinguished by an attribute, as is done, for example, with the word *gas*, by adding the words *hydrogen*, *oxygen*, etc. Thus we might say—and it would, perhaps, be the best plan to adopt—*vital soul* for the principle of material life, *intellectual soul* for the principle of intelligence, and *spiritual soul* for the principle of our individuality after death; in which case the *vital soul* would be common to all organic beings, plants, animals, and men; the *intellectual soul* would be the peculiar property of animals and men; and the *spiritual soul* would belong to men only.

We have thought it all the more important to be explicit in regard to this point, because the spiritist theory is naturally based on the existence in us of a being independent of matter, and that survives the body. As the word *soul* will frequently recur in the course of this work, it was necessary to define the meaning we attach to it, in order to avoid all misunderstanding.

We now come to the principal object of this preliminary explanation.

III

Spiritist doctrine, like all new theories, has its supporters and its opponents. We will endeavour to reply to some of the objetions of the latter, by examining the worth of the reasons on which they are based, without, however, pretending to be able to convince everybody, but addressing ourselves to those who, without prejudices or preconceived ideas, are sincerely and honestly desirous of arriving at the truth; and will prove to them that those objections are the result of a too hasty conclusion in regard to facts imperfectly observed.

Of the facts referred to, the one first observed was the movement of objects, popularly called "table-turning." This phenomenon, first observed in America (or rather, renewed in that country, for history proves it to have been produced in the most remote ages of antiquity), was attended with various strange accompaniments, such as unusual noises, raps produced without any ostensible cause, etc. From America this phenomenon spread rapidly over Europe and the rest of the world. It was met at first with incredulity; but the movements were produced by so many experimenters, that it soon became impossible to doubt its reality.

If the phenomenon in question had been limited to the movement of inert objects, it might have been possible to explain it by some purely physical cause. We are far from knowing all the secret agencies of nature, or all the properties of those which are known to us. Electricity, moreover, is not only multiplying, day by day, the resources it offers to mankind, but appears to be about to irradiate science with a new light. It seemed, therefore, by no means impossible that electricity, modified by certain circumstances, or some other unknown agent, might be the cause of these movements. The fact that the presence of several persons increased the intensity of the action appeared to strengthen this supposition; for the union of these might not inaptly be regarded as constituting a battery, of which the power was in proportion to the number of its elements.

That the movement of the tables should be circular was in no way surprising, for the circular movements is of frequent occurrence in nature. All the stars move in circles; and it therefore seemed to be possible that in the movement of the tables we had a reflex on a small scale of the movement of the universe; or that some cause, hitherto unknown, might produce, accidentally, and, in regard to small objects, a current analogous to that which impels the worlds of the universe in their orbits.

But the movement in question was not always circular. It was often irregular, disorderly; the object moved was sometimes violently shaken, overthrown, carried about in various directions, and, in contravention of all known laws of statics, lifted from the ground and held up in the air. Still, in all this, there was nothing that might not be explained by the force of some invisible physical agent. Do we not see electricity overthrow buildings, uproot trees, and hurl to considerable distances the heaviest bodies, attracting or repelling, as the case may be?

The rappings and other unusual noises, supposing them to be due to something else than the dilatation of the wood, or other accidental cause, might very well be produced by an accumulation of the mysterious fluid; for does not electricity produce the loudest sounds?

Up to this point everything might be considered as belonging to the domain of physics and physiology. Without going beyond this circle of ideas, the learned might have found in the phenomenon referred to matter well worthy of serious study. Why was this not done? It is painful to be obliged to make the confession, but the neglect of the scientific world was due to causes that add one more proof to the many already given of the frivolity of the human mind. In the first place, the non-glamour of the object which mainly served as the basis of the earliest experimentations had something to do with this disdain. What an influence, in regard to even the most serious matters, is often exerted by a mere word! Without reflecting that the movement referred to might be communicated to any object, the idea of *tables* became associated with it in the general mind, doubtless because a table, being the most convenient object upon which to experiment, and also because people can place themselves round a table more conveniently than round any other piece of furniture, was generally employed in the experiments referred to. But men who pride themselves on their mental superiority are sometimes so puerile as to warrant the suspicion that a good many keen and cultivated minds may have considered it beneath them to take any notice of what was commonly known as "the dance of tables." If the phenomenon observed by Galvani had been made known by some unlearned person, and dubbed with some absurd nickname, it would probably have been consigned to the lumber-room, along with the divining-rod; for where is the scientist who would not in that case have regarded it as derogatory to occupy himself with the *dance of frogs?*

A few men of superior intellect, however, being modest enough to admit that nature might not have revealed to them all her secrets, conscientiously endeavoured to see into the matter for themselves; but the phenomena not having always responded to their attempts, and not being always produced at their pleasure, and according to their methods of experimenting, they arrived at an adverse conclusion in regard to them. The tables, however, despite that conclusion, continued to turn; and we may say of them, with Galileo, "Nevertheless, they move!" We may assert, still further, that the facts alluded to have been multiplied to such an extent that they have become naturalised among us, so that opinions are now only divided as to their nature.

And here let us ask whether the fact that these phenomena are not always produced in exactly the same way, and according to the wishes and requirements of each individual observer, can be reasonably regarded as constituting an argument against their reality? Are not the phenomena of electricity and chemistry subordinated to certain conditions, and should we be right in denying their reality because they do not occur when those conditions are not present? Is it strange, then, that certain conditions should be necessary to the production of the phenomenon of the movement of objects by the human fluid, or that it should not occur when the observer, placing himself at his own individual point of view, insists on producing it at his own pleasure, or in subjecting it to the laws of phenomena already known, without considering that a new order of facts may, and indeed must, result from the action of laws equally new to us? Now, in order to arrive at a knowledge of such laws, it is necessary to study the circumstances under which those facts are produced; and such a study can only be made through long-sustained and attentive observation.

"But," it is often objected, "there is evident trickery in some of the occurrences referred to." To this objection we reply, in the first place, by asking whether the objectors are quite sure that what they have taken for trickery may not be simply an order of facts which they are not yet able to account for, as was the case with the peasant who mistook the experiments of a learned professor of physics for the tricks of a clever conjuror? But even admitting that there has been trickery in some cases, is that a reason for denying the reality of facts? Must we deny the reality of physics because certain conjurors give themselves the title of physicists? Moreover, the character of the persons concerned in these manifestations should be taken into account, and the interest they may have in deceiving. Would they do so by way of a joke? A joke may amuse for a moment, but a mystification, if kept up too long, would become as wearisome to the mystifier as to the mystified. Besides, a mystification carried

on from one end of the earth to the other, and among the most
serious, honourable, and enlightened people, would be at least as
extraordinary as the phenomena in question.

IV

If the phenomena we are considering had been limited to the
movement of objects, they would have remained, as we have
already remarked, within the domain of physical science; but so
far was this from being the case, that they speedily proved to be
only the forerunners of facts of a character still more extraordinary. For it was soon found that the impulsion communicated
to inert objects was not the mere product of a blind mechanical
force, but that it revealed the action of an intelligent cause, a
discovery that opened up a new field of observation, and promised
a solution of many mysterious problems. Are these movements
due to an intelligent power? Such was the question first to be
answered. If such a power exists, what is it? What is its nature?
What its origin? Is it superhuman? Such were the secondary
questions which naturally grew out of that first one.

The earliest manifestations of intelligence were made by means
of the legs of tables, that moved up and down, striking a given
number of times, and replying in this way by "yes" or "no" to
the questions asked. Even here, it must be confessed, there was
nothing very convincing for the incredulous, as these apparent
answers might be an effect of chance. But fuller replies were
soon obtained, the object in motion striking a number of blows
corresponding to the number of each letter of the alphabet, so
that words and sentences began to be produced in reply to the
questions propounded. The correctness of these replies, their
correlation with the questions asked, excited astonishment. The
mysterious being who gave these replies, when questioned as to
its nature, declared itself to be a "spirit" or "genius," gave itself
a name, and stated various particulars about itself. This is a
circumstance of noteworthy importance, for it proves that no one
suggested the idea of spirits as an explanation of the phenomenon,
but that *the phenomenon gave this explanation of itself*. Hypotheses are often framed, in the positive sciences, to serve as a
basis of argument; but such was not the case in this instance.

The mode of communication furnished by the alphabet being

tedious and inconvenient, the invisible agent (a point worthy of note) suggested another, by advising the fitting of a pencil to a small basket. This basket, placed upon a sheet of paper, was set in motion by the same occult power that moved the tables; but, instead of obeying a simple and regular movement of rotation, the pencil traced letters that formed words, sentences, and entire discourses, filling many pages, treating of the deepest questions of philosophy, morality, metaphysics, psychology, etc., and as rapidly as though written by the hand.

This suggestion was made simultaneously in America, in France, and in various other countries. It was made in the following terms, in Paris, on the 10th of June 1853, to one of the most fervent partisans of the new phenomena—one who, from the year 1849, had been busily engaged in the evocation of spirits:—"Fetch the little basket from the next room; fasten a pencil to it; place it upon a sheet of paper; put your fingers on the edge of the basket." This having been done, the basket, a few moments afterwards, began to move, and the pencil wrote, quite legibly, this sentence:—"I expressly forbid your repeating to any one what I have just told you. The next time I write, I shall do it better."

The object to which the pencil is attached being merely an instrument, its nature and form are of no importance, convenience being the only point to be considered. The instrument known as the *planchette* has since been generally adopted.

The basket, or *planchette*, will only move under the influence of certain persons gifted with a special power or faculty, who are called *mediums*,—that is to say, *go-betweens*, or *intermediaries* between spirits and men. The conditions which give this power depend on causes, physical and moral, that are as yet but imperfectly understood, for mediums are of all ages, of both sexes, and of every degree of intellectual development. The faculty of mediumship, moreover, is developed by exercise.

V

It was next perceived that the basket and the *planchette* only formed, in reality, an appendix to the hand. The medium, therefore, now held the pencil in his hand, and found that he was made to write under an impulsion independent of his will, and often with an almost feverish rapidity. In this way the communications were not only made more quickly, but also became more easy and more complete. At the present day, this method is the one most frequently employed, the number of persons endowed with the aptitude of involuntary writing being very considerable, and constantly increasing. Experience gradually made known many other varieties of the mediumistic faculty, and it was found that communications could be received through speech, hearing, sight, touch, etc., and even through the direct writing of the spirits themselves,—that is to say, without the help of the medium's hand, or of the pencil.

This fact established, an essential point still remained to be ascertained, viz., the nature of the medium's action, and the share taken by him, mechanically and morally, in the obtaining of the replies. Two points of the highest importance, and that could not escape the notice of the attentive observer, sufficed to settle the question. The first of these is the way in which the basket moves under the influence of the medium, through the mere laying of his fingers on its edges, and in such a manner that it would be impossible for him to guide it in any direction whatever. This impossibility becomes still more evident when two or three persons place their fingers at the same time on the same basket, for a truly phenomenal concordance of movements and of thoughts would be required between them, in order to produce, on the part of each, the same reply to the question asked. And this difficulty is increased by the fact that the writing often changes completely with each spirit who communicates, and that, whenever a given spirit communicates, the same writing re-appears. In such cases, the medium would have to train himself to change his handwriting an indefinite number of times, and would also have to remember the particular writing of each spirit.

The second point referred to is the character of the replies given, which are often, and especially when the questions asked are of an abstract or scientific nature, notoriously beyond the scope of the knowledge, and even of the intellectual capacity, of the medium, who, moreover, is frequently unaware of what he is made to write, since the reply, like the question asked, may be couched in a language of which he is ignorant, or the question may even be asked mentally. It often happens, too, that the basket, or the medium, is made to write spontaneously, without any question having been propounded, and upon some subject altogether unexpected.

The replies thus given, and the messages thus transmitted, are sometimes marked by such sagacity, profundity, and appropriateness, and convey thoughts so elevated, so sublime, that they can only emanate from a superior intelligence, imbued with the purest morality; at other times, they are so vapid, frivolous, and even trivial, that they cannot be supposed to emanate from the same source. This diversity of language can only be explained by the diversity of the intelligences who thus manifest themselves. Do these intelligences reside in the human race, or are they beyond the pale of humanity? Such is the next point to be cleared up, and of which the complete explanation will be found in the present work, such as it has been given by the spirits themselves.

The facts referred to, as being of an order beyond our usual circle of observation, do not occur mysteriously, but in broad daylight, so that every one can see them and ascertain their reality; they are not the privilege of a single individual, but are obtained by tens of thousands of persons every day at pleasure. These effects have necessarily a cause; and as they reveal the action of an intelligence and a will, they are evidently beyond the domain of merely physical effects.

Many theories have been broached in relation to this subject; these we shall presently examine, and shall then be able to decide whether they can account for all the facts now occurring. Let us, meanwhile, assume the existence of beings distinct from the human race, since such is the explanation given of themselves by the intelligences thus revealed to us, and let us see what they say to us.

VI

The beings who thus enter into communication with us designate themselves, as we have said, by the name of *spirits* or *genii*, and as having belonged, in many cases at least, to men who have lived upon the earth. They say that they constitute the spiritual world, as we, during our earthly life, constitute the corporeal world.

We will now briefly sum up the most important points of the doctrine which they have transmitted to us, in order to reply more easily to the objections of the incredulous.

"God is eternal, immutable, immaterial, unique, allpowerful, sovereignly just and good.

"He has created the universe, which comprehends all beings, animate and inanimate, material and immaterial.

"The material beings constitute the visible or corporeal world, and the immaterial beings constitute the invisible or spiritual world, that is to say, the spirit-world, or world of spirits.

"The spirit-world is the normal, primitive, eternal world, pre-existent to, and surviving, everything else.

"The corporeal world is only secondary; it might cease to exist, or never have existed, without changing the essentiality of the spiritual world.

"Spirits temporarily assume a perishable material envelope, the destruction of which, by death, restores them to liberty.

"Among the different species of corporeal beings, God has chosen the human species for the incarnation of spirits arrived at a certain degree of development; it is this which gives it a moral and intellectual superiority to all the others.

"The soul is an incarnated spirit, whose body is only its envelope.

"There are in man three things:—(1.) The body, or material being, analogous to the animals, and animated by the same vital principle; (2.) The soul, or immaterial being, a spirit incarnated in the body; (3.) The link which unites the soul and the body, a principle intermediary between matter and spirit.

"Man has thus two natures: by his body he participates in the nature of the animals, of which it has the instincts; by his soul, he participates in the nature of spirits.

"The link, or *perispirit*, which unites the body and the spirit, is a sort of semi-material envelope. Death is the destruction of the material body, which is the grossest of man's two envelopes; but the spirit preserves his other envelope, viz., the perispirit, which constitutes for him an ethereal body, invisible to us in its normal state, but which he can render occasionally visible, and even tangible, as is the case in apparitions.

"A spirit, therefore, is not an abstract, undefined being, only to be conceived of by our thought; it is a real, circumscribed being, which, in certain cases, is appreciable by the senses of *sight, hearing*, and *touch*.

"Spirits belong to different classes, and are not equal to one another either in power, in intelligence, in knowledge, or in morality. Those of the highest order are distinguished from those below them by their superior purity and knowledge, their nearness to

God, and their love of goodness; they are "angels" or "pure spirits." The other classes are more and more distant from this perfection; those of the lower ranks are inclined to most of our passions, hatred, envy, jealousy, pride, etc.; they take pleasure in evil. Among them are some who are neither very good nor very bad, but are teazing and troublesome rather than malicious, are often mischievous and unreasonable, and may be classed as giddy and foolish spirits.

"Spirits do not belong perpetually to the same order. All are destined to attain perfection by passing through the different degress of the spirit-hierarchy. This amelioration is effected by incarnation, which is imposed on some of them as an expiation, and on others as a mission. Material life is a trial which they have to undergo many times until they have attained to absolute perfection; it is a sort of filter, or alembic, from which they issue more or less purified after each new incarnation.

"On quitting the body, the soul re-enters the world of spirits from which it came, and from which it will enter upon a new material existence, after a longer or shorter lapse of time, during which its state is that of an *errant* or *wandering* spirit.[1]

"Spirits having to pass through many incarnations, it follows that we have all had many existences, and that we shall have others, more or less perfect, either upon this earth or in other worlds.

"The incarnation of spirits always takes place in the human race; it would be an error to suppose that the soul or spirit could be incarnated in the body of an animal.

"A spirit's successive corporeal existences are always progressive, and never retrograde; but the rapidity of our progress depends on the efforts we make to arrive at perfection.

"The qualities of the soul are those of the spirit incarnated in us; thus, a good man is the incarnation of a good spirit, and a bad man is that of an unpurified spirit.

"The soul possessed its own individuality before its incarnation; it preserves that individuality after its separation from the body.

"On its re-entrance into the spirit world, the soul again finds there all those whom it has known upon the earth, and all its former existences eventually come back to its memory, with the

---

[1] There is, between this doctrine of re-incarnation and that of metempsychosis, as held by certain sects, a characteristic difference, which is explained in the course of the present work.

remembrance of all the good and of all the evil which it has done in them.

"The incarnated spirit is under the influence of matter; the man who surmounts this influence, through the elevation and purification of his soul, raises himself nearer to the superior spirits, among whom he will one day be classed. He who allows himself to be ruled by bad passions, and places all his delight in the satisfaction of his gross animal appetites, brings himself nearer to the impure spirits, by giving preponderance to his animal nature.

"Incarnated spirits inhabit the different globes of the universe.

"Spirits who are not incarnated, who are errant, do not occupy any fixed and circumscribed region; they are everywhere, in space, and around us, seeing us, and mixing with us incessantly; they constitute an invisible population, constantly moving and busy about us, on every side.

"Spirits exert an incessant action upon the moral world, and even upon the physical world; they act both upon matter and upon thought, and constitute one of the powers of nature, the efficient cause of many classes of phenomena hitherto unexplained or misinterpreted, and of which only the spiritist theory can give a rational explanation.

"Spirits are incessantly in relation with men. The good spirits try to lead us into the right road, sustain us under the trials of life, and aid us to bear them with courage and resignation; the bad ones tempt us to evil: it is a pleasure for them to see us fall, and to make us like themselves.

"The communications of spirits with men are either occult or ostensible. Their occult communications are made through the good or bad influence they exert on us without our being aware of it; it is our duty to distinguish, by the exercise of our judgment, between the good and the bad inspirations that are thus brought to bear upon us. Their ostensible communications take place by means of writing, of speech, or of other physical manifestations, and usually through the intermediary of the mediums who serve as their instruments.

"Spirits manifest themselves spontaneously, or in response to evocation. All spirits may be evoked: those who have animated the most obscure of mortals, as well as those of the most illustrious personages, and whatever the epoch at which they lived; those of our relatives, our friends, or our enemies; and we may obtain from them, by written or by verbal communications, counsels, information in regard to their situation beyond the grave, their thoughts in regard to us, and whatever revelations they are permitted to make to us.[1]

"Spirits are attracted by their sympathy with the moral quality of the parties by whom they are evoked. Spirits of superior elevation take pleasure in meetings of a serious character, animated by the love of goodness and the sincere desire of instruction and improvement. Their presence repels the spirits of inferior degree, who find, on the contrary, free access and freedom of action among persons of frivolous disposition, or brought together by mere curiosity, and wherever evil instincts are to be met with. So far from obtaining from spirits, under such circumstances, either good advice or useful information, nothing is to be expected from them but trifling, lies, ill-natured tricks, or humbugging; for they often borrow the most venerated names, in order the better to impose upon those with whom they are in communication.

"It is easy to distinguish between good and bad spirits. The language of spirits of superior elevation is constantly dignified, noble, characterised by the highest morality, free from every trace of earthly passion; their counsels breathe the purest wisdom, and always have our improvement and the good of mankind for their aim. The communications of spirits of lower degree, on the contrary, are full of discrepancies, and their language is often commonplace, and even coarse. If they sometimes say things that are good and true, they more often make false and absurd statements, prompted by ignorance or malice. They play upon the credulity of those who interrogate them, amusing themselves by flattering their vanity, and fooling them with false hopes. In a word, instructive communications worthy of the name are only to be obtained in centres of a serious character, whose members are united, by an intimate communion of thought and desire, in the pursuit of truth and goodness.

"The moral teaching of the higher spirits may be summed up, like that of Christ, in the gospel maxim, 'Do unto others as you would that others should do unto you;' that is to say, do good to all, and wrong no one. This principle of action furnishes mankind with a rule of conduct of universal application, from the smallest matters to the greatest.

---

[1] **Vide,** in connection with the statements of this paragraph, the qualifying explanations and practical counsels of **The Mediums' Book. — TRANS.**

"They teach us that selfishness, pride, sensuality, are passions which bring us back towards the animal nature, by attaching us to matter; that he who, in this lower life, detaches himself from matter through contempt of worldly trifles, and through love of the neighbour, brings himself back towards the spiritual nature; that we should all make ourselves useful, according to the means which God has placed in our hands for our trial; that the strong and the powerful owe aid and protection to the weak; and that he who misuses strength and power to oppress his fellow-creature violates the law of God. They teach us that in the spirit-world nothing can be hidden, and that the hypocrite will there be unmasked, and all his wickedness unveiled; that the presence, unavoidable and perpetual, of those whom we have wronged in the earthly life is one of the punishments that await us in the spirit-world; and that the lower or higher state of spirits gives rise in that other life to sufferings or to enjoyments unknown to us upon the earth.

"But they also teach us that there are no unpardonable sins, none that cannot be efaced by expiation. Man finds the means of accomplishing this in the different existences which permit him to advance progressively, and according to his desire and his efforts, towards the perfection that constitutes his ultimate aim."

Such is the sum of spiritist doctrine, as contained in the teachings given by spirits of high degree. Let us now consider the objections that are urged against it.

VII

Many persons regard the opposition of the learned world as constituting, if not a proof, at least a very strong presumption, of the falsity of Spiritism. We are not of those who affect indifference in regard to the judgment of scientific men; on the contrary, we hold them in great esteem, and should think it an honour to be of their number, but we cannot consider their opinion as being, under all circumstances, necessarily and absolutely conclusive.

When the votaries of science go beyond the bare observation of facts, when they attempt to appraise and to explain those facts, they enter upon the field of conjecture; each advances a system of his own, which he does his utmost to bring into favour, and defends with might and main. Do we not see every day the most divergent systems brought forward and rejected, one after the other; now cried down as absurd errors, and now cried up as incontestable truths? Facts are the sole criterion of reality, the sole argument that admits of no reply: in the absence of facts, the wise man suspends his judgment.

In regard to all matters that have already been fully examined, the verdict of the learned is justly held to be authoritative, because their knowledge of them is fuller and more enlightened than that of ordinary men; but in regard to new facts or principles, to matters imperfectly known, their opinion can only be hypothetic, because they are no more exempt from prejudice than other people. It may even be said that scientific men are more apt to be prejudiced than the rest of the world, because each of them is naturally inclined to look at everything from the special point of view that has been adopted by him; the mathematician admitting no other order of proof than that of an algebraic demonstration, the chemist referring everything to the action of the elements, etc. When a man has made for himself a specialty, he usually devotes his whole mind to it; beyond the scope of this specialty he often reasons falsely, because, owing to the weakness of human reason, he insists on treating every subject in the same way; and therefore, while we should willingly and confidently consult a chemist in regard to a question of analysis, a physicist in regard to electricity, a mechanician in regard to a motive power, we must be allowed, without in any way derogating from the respect due to their special knowledge, to attach no more weight to their unfavourable opinion of Spiritism than we should do to the judgment of an architect on a question relating to the theory of music.

The positive sciences are based on the properties of matter, which may be experimented upon and manipulated at pleasure; but spiritist phenomena are an effect of the action of intelligences who have wills of their own, and who constantly show us that they are not subjected to ours. The observation of facts, therefore, cannot be carried on in the latter case in the same way as in the former one, for they proceed from another source, and require special conditions; and, consequently, to insist upon submitting them to the same methods of investigation is to insist on assuming the existence of analogies that do not exist. Science, properly so called, is therefore incompetent, as such, to decide the question of the truth of Spiritism; it has nothing to do with it; and

its verdict in regard to it, whether favourable or otherwise, is of
no weight. Spiritist belief is the result of a personal conviction
that scientific men may hold as individuals, and independent of
their quality as scientists; but to submit the question to the
decision of physical science would be much the same thing as to
set a company of physicists and astronomers to decide the question
of immortality. Spiritism deals exclusively with the existence
of the soul, and its state after death; and it is supremely unreasonable to assume that a man must be a great psychologist
simply because he is a great mathematician or a great anatomist.
The anatomist, when dissecting a human body, looks for the soul,
and, as he does not find it under his scalpel as he finds a nerve,
or see it evaporate as does a gas, he concludes that it does not
exist, because he reasons from an exclusively material point of
view; but it by no means follows that he is right, and that the
opinion of the rest of the world is wrong. We see, therefore,
that the task of deciding as to the truth or falsity of Spiritism does
not fall within the scope of physical science. When spiritist beliefs
shall have become generalised, when they shall have been accepted
by the masses (and, if we may judge by the rapidity with which
they are being propagated, that time can hardly be very distant),
it will be with those beliefs as with all new ideas that have
encountered opposition; and scientific men will end by yielding to
the force of evidence. They will be brought, individually, by the
force of things, to admit ideas that they now reject; and, until
then, it would be premature to turn them from their special studies
in order to occupy them with a matter which is foreign alike to
their habits of thought and to their spheres of investigation. Meanwhile, those who, without a careful preparatory study of the
matter, pronounce a negative verdict in regard to it, and throw
ridicule upon all who are not of their way of thinking, forget that
such has been done in regard to nearly all the great discoveries
that honour the human race. They risk seeing their names added
to the list of illustrious proscribers of new ideas, and classed
with those of the members of the learned assembly which, in 1752,
received Franklin's paper on lightning-rods with peals of laughter,
and voted it to be unworthy of mention among the communications
addressed to it; or with that other one which caused France to
miss the advantage of taking the lead in the application of steam
to shipping, by declaring Fulton's plans to be impracticable: and
yet these subjects lay within their competence. If those two

assemblies, which numbered the most eminent scientists of the world among their members, had only contempt and sarcasm for ideas which they did not understand, but which were destined to revolutionise, a few years later, science, industry, and daily life, how can we hope that a question foreign to their labours should meet with any greater degree of favour at their hands?

The erroneous judgments of learned men in regard to certain discoveries, though regrettable for the honour of their memory, do not invalidate the title to our esteem acquired by them in regard to other matters. But is common-sense only to be found associated with an official diploma, and are there only fools and simpletons outside the walls of scientific institutions? Let our opponents condescend to glance over the ranks of the partisans of Spiritism, and see whether they contain only persons of inferior understanding, or whether, on the contrary, considering the immense number of men of worth by whom it has been embraced, it can be regarded as belonging to the category of old wives' fables; whether, in fact, the character and scientific knowledge of its adherents do not rather deserve that it should be said:—"When such men affirm a matter, there must at least be something in it?"

We repeat that, if the facts we are about to consider had been limited to the mechanical movement of inert bodies, physical science would have been competent to seek out the physical cause of the phenomena; but the manifestations in question being professedly beyond the action of laws or forces yet known to men, they are necessarily beyond the competence of human science. When the facts to be observed are novel, and do not fall within the scope of any known science, the scientist, in order to study them, should throw his science temporarily aside, remembering that a new study cannot be fruitfully prosecuted under the influence of preconceived ideas.

He who believes his reason to be infallible is very near to error. Even those whose ideas are of the falsest profess to base them on reason; and it is in the name of reason that they reject whatever seems to them to be impossible. They who formerly rejected the admirable discoveries that are the glory of the human mind did so in the name of reason; for what men call reason is often only pride disguised, and whoever regards himself as infallible virtually claims to be God's equal. We therefore address ourselves to those who are reasonable enough to suspend their judgment in regard to what they have not yet seen, and who,

judging of the future by the past, do not believe that man has
reached his apogee, or that nature has turned over for him the
last leaf of her book.

VIII

Let us add that the study of such a theory as that of Spiritism,
which introduces us at once to an order of ideas so novel and so
grand, can only be fruitfully pursued by persons of a serious
turn of mind, persevering, free from prejudice, and animated by
a firm and sincere determination to arrive at the truth. We could
not give this qualification to those who decide, in regard to such
a subject, *à priori*, lightly, and without thorough examination;
who bring to the work of study neither the method, the regularity,
nor the sustained attention necessary to success: still less could
we give it to those who, not to lose their reputation for wit and
sharpness, seek to turn into ridicule matters of the most serious
import, or that are judged to be such by persons whose knowledge,
character, and convictions should command respect. Let those
who consider the facts in question as unworthy of their attention
abstain from studying them; no one would attempt to interfere
with their belief; but let them, on their part, respect the belief of
those who are of a contrary opinion.

The characteristics of serious study are the method and the
perseverance with which it is carried on. Is it strange that
sensible answers are not always obtained from spirits in reply
to questions which, however serious in themselves, are propounded
at random, and in the midst of a host of others, unconnected,
frivolous, or foolish? Besides, a question is often complex, and
the answer to it, in order to be clear, needs to be preceded, or
completed, by various considerations. Whoever would acquire any
science must make it the object of methodical study, must begin
at the beginning, and follow out the sequence and development
of the ideas involved in it. If one who is ignorant of the most
elementary facts of a science should ask a question in regard to
it of the most learned of its professors, could the professor,
however excellent his goodwill, give him any satisfactory answer?
For any isolated answer, give under such conditions, must necessarily be incomplete, and would, therefore, in many cases,
appear unintelligible, or even absurd. It is exactly the same in
regard to the relations which we establish with spirits. If we

would learn in their school, we must go through a complete course
of teaching with them; but, as among ourselves, we must select
our teachers, and work on with steadiness and assiduity.

We have said that spirits of superior advancement are only
attracted to centres in which there reigns a serious desire for
light, and, above all, a perfect communion of thought and feeling
in the pursuit of moral excellence. Frivolity and idle curiosity
repel them, just as, among men, they repel all reasonable people;
and the road is thus left open to the mob of foolish and lying
spirits who are always about us, watching for opportunities
of mocking us and amusing themselves at our expense. What
becomes of any serious question in such a gathering? It will
certainly be replied to, but by whom? It is just as though, in the
midst of a convivial dinner-party, you should suddenly propound
such questions as—"What is the soul? What is death?" or others
equally out of harmony with the tone of the company. If we
would obtain serious answers, we must ourselves be serious, and
must place ourselves in the conditions required for obtaining them;
it is only by so doing that we shall obtain any satisfactory and
ennobling communications. We must, moreover, be laborious and
persevering in our investigations, otherwise the higher spirits will
cease to trouble themselves about us, as the professor ceases to
occupy himself with the hopelessly idle members of his class.

IX

The movement of inert bodies is a fact already proved by
experience; the point now to be ascertained is, whether there is,
or is not, a manifestation of intelligence in this movement, and,
if there is, what is the source of this intelligence? We are not
speaking of the intelligence displayed in the movement of certain
objects, nor of verbal communications, nor even of those which
are written directly by the medium: these manifestations, of which
the spirit-origin is evident for those who have thoroughly investigated the matter, are not, at first sight, sufficiently independent of the will of the medium to bring conviction to an observer
new to the subject. We will therefore only speak, in this place,
of writing obtained with the aid of an object of any kind provided
with a pencil, such as a small basket, a *planchette*, etc., the fingers
of the medium being placed upon the object in such a manner
as to defy the most consummate skill to exercise the slightest

influence on the tracing of the letters. But let us suppose that, by some wonderful cleverness, the medium succeeds in deceiving the most keenly observant eye, how can we explain the nature of the communications, when they are altogether beyond the scope of the medium's knowledge and ideas? And it is, moreover, to be remarked, that we are speaking not of monosyllabic replies, but of many pages, dashed off, as frequently happens, with the most astonishing rapidity, sometimes spontaneously, and sometimes upon a given subject; of poems of elevated character, and irreproachable in point of style, produced by the hand of an utterly illiterate medium. And what adds to the strangeness of these facts is, that they are occurring all the world over, and that the number of mediums is constantly increasing. Are these facts real or not? To this query we have but one reply to make: "See and observe; opportunities of doing so will not be lacking; but, above all, observe often, for a long time, and according to the conditions required for so doing."

To the evidence adduced by us, what do our antagonists reply? "You are," say they, "the dupes of imposition or the sport of illusion." We have to remark, in the first place, that imposition is not likely to occur where no profit is to be made; charlatans are not apt to ply their trade gratis. If imposition be practised, it must be for the sake of a joke. But by what strange coincidence does there happen to be an understanding between the jokers, from one end of the earth to the other, to act in the same way, to produce the same effects, and to give, upon the same subjects, and in different languages, replies that are identical, if not in words, at least in meaning? How is it that grave, serious, honourable, and educated persons can lend themselves to such manœuvres, and for what purpose? How is it that the requisite patience and skill for carrying on such a piece of deception are found even in young children? For mediums, if they are not passive instruments, must posses a degree of skill, and an amount and variety of knowledge, incompatible with the age and social position of many of them.

"But," urge our opponents, "if there be no trickery, both parties may be the dupes of an illusion." It is only reasonable that the quality of witnesses should be regarded as an element in deciding the value of their evidence; and it may fairly be asked whether the spiritist theory, whose adherents are already to be counted by millions, recruits these only among the ignorant? The phenomena on which it is based are so extraordinary that we admit the reasonableness of doubt in regard to them; but what is not admissible is the pretension of certain sceptics to a monopoly of common sense, and the unceremonious way in which, regardless of the moral worth of their adversaries, they tax all who are not of their opinion with infatuation or stupidity. For the affirmation of enlightened persons who have, for a long time, seen, studied, and meditated any matter, is always, if not a proof, at least a presumption in its favour, since it has been able to fix the attention of men of mark, having no interest in propagating an error, nor time to waste upon worthless trifles.

X

Among the objections brought forward by our opponents are some which are more specious, at least in appearance, because they are made by thoughtful minds.

One of these objections is prompted by the fact that the language of spirits does not always seem worthy of the elevation we attribute to beings beyond the pale of humanity. But, if the objector will take the trouble to look at the doctrinal summary we have given above, he will see that the spirits themselves inform us that they are not equals, either in knowledge or in moral qualities, that we are not to accept everything said by spirits as literal truth, and that we must judge for ourselves of the value of their statements. Assuredly, those who infer from this fact that we have to deal only with maleficent beings, whose sole occupation is to deceive us, have no acquaintance with the communications obtained in the centres habitually frequented by spirits of superior advancement, or they could not entertain such an opinion. It is regrettable that they should have chanced to see only the worst side of the spirit-world, for we will not suppose that their sympathies attract evil, gross, or lying spirits, rather than good ones. We will merely suggest that, in some cases, the inquirers may not be so thoroughly principled in goodness as to repel evil, and that, taking advantage of their curiosity in regard to them, imperfect spirits make use of the opening thus afforded to come about them, while those of a higher order withdraw from them.

To judge the question of spirits by these facts would be as little reasonable as to judge of the character of a people by the sayings and doings of a party of wild or disreputable fellows, with whom the educated and respectable classes of the population have nothing to do. Such persons are in the position of the traveller who, entering some great capital by one of its worst suburbs, should judge of all its inhabitants by the habits and language of this low quarter. In the world of spirits, as in our own, there are higher and lower classes of society. Let inquirers make a study of what goes on among spirits of high degree, and they will be convinced that the celestial city is not peopled solely by the ignorant and vicious. "But," it will be asked, "do spirits of high degree come among us?" To which question we reply, "Do not remain in the suburbs; see, observe, and judge; the facts are within reach of all but those alluded to by Jesus, as having eyes, but seeing not, and ears, but hearing not."

A variety of the same objection consists in attributing all spirit communications, and all the physical manifestations by which they are accompanied, to the intervention of some diabolical power— some new Proteus that assumes every form in order the more effectually to deceive us. Without pausing to analyse a sup- position that we regard as not susceptible of serious examination, and that is, moreover, refuted by what we have already said, we have only to remark that, if such were the case, it would have to be admitted either that the devil is sometimes very wise, very reasonable, and, above all, very moral, or else that there are good devils as well as bad ones.

But, in fact, is it possible to believe that God would permit only the Spirit of Evil to manifest himself, and this in order to ruin us, without giving us also the counsels of good spirits as a counter- poise? To suppose that He cannot do this is to limit His power; to suppose that He can do it, but abstains from doing it, is incompatible with the belief in His goodness. Both suppositions are equally blasphemous. It must be observed that, to admit the communication of evil spirits is to recognise the existence of spirit manifestations; but, if they exist, it can only be with the permission of God, and how then can we, without impiety, believe that He would permit them to occur only for a bad purpose, to the exclusion of a good one? Such a supposition is contrary alike to the simplest dictates of religion and of common sense.

XI

One strange feature of the matter, urge other objectors, is the fact that only the spirits of well-known personages manifest themselves, and it is asked why these should be the only ones who do so? This query is suggested by an error due, like many others, to superficial observation. Among the spirits who present themselves spontaneously, the greater number are unknown to us, and, therefore, call themselves by names that we know, and that serve to characterise them. With regard to those whom we evoke, unless in the case of relatives or friends, we naturally address ourselves to spirits whom we know of, rather than to those who are unknown to us; and as the names of illustrious persons are those which strike us most forcibly, they are, for that reason, those which are most remarked.

It is also considered as strange that the spirits of eminent men should respond familiarly to our call, and should sometimes interest themselves in things that appear trifling in comparison with those which they accomplished during their life. But there is in this nothing surprising for those who know that the power and consideration which a man may have possessed in this lower life give him no supremacy in the spirit-world. Spirits confirm the gospel statement that "the last shall be first, and the first shall be last," as regards the rank of each of us when we return among them. Thus he who has been first in the earthly life may be one of the last in that other world; he before whom all bowed their heads during the present life may then find himself beneath the humblest artisan, for, on quitting the earthly life, he leaves all his grandeur behind him; and the most powerful monarch may be lower than the lowest of his subjects.

XII

A fact ascertained by observation, and confirmed by the spirits themselves, is the borrowing of well-known and venerated names by spirits of inferior degree. How, then, can we be sure that those who say they were, for example, Socrates, Julius Cæsar, Charlemagne, Fénélon. Napoleon, Washington, etc., were really the men they claim to have been? This doubt exists among many fervent adherents of spiritist doctrine. They admit the reality of the intervention and manifestation of spirits, but they ask themselves what certainty we can have of their identity? This certainty it is, in fact, very difficult to obtain; but though it cannot be settled as authentically as by the attestation of a civil register, it may, at least, be established presumptively, according to certain indications.

When the spirit who manifests himself is that of some one personally known to us, of a relative or friend, for instance, and especially if of one who has been dead but a short time, it is generally found that his language is perfectly in keeping with what we know of his character; thus furnishing a strong presumption of his identity, which is placed almost beyond reach of doubt when the spirit speaks of private affairs, and refers to family matters known only to the party to whom he addresses himself. A son could hardly be mistaken as to the language of his father and mother, nor parents as to that of their child. Most striking incidents often occur in evocations of this intimate kind—things of a nature to convince the most incredulous. The most sceptical are often astounded by the unexpected revelations thus made to them.

Another very characteristic circumstance often helps to establish a spirit's identity. We have already said that the handwriting of the medium generally changes with the spirit evoked, the same writing being reproduced exactly every time the same spirit presents himself; and it often happens that, in the case of persons recently deceased, this writing bears a striking resemblance to that of the person during life, the signatures, especially, being sometimes perfectly exact. We are, nevertheless, very far from adducing this fact as a rule, or as being of constant recurrence; we merely mention it as a point worthy of notice.

It is only when spirits have arrived at a certain degree of purification that they are entirely freed from all corporeal influences; and as long as they are not completely *dematerialised* (to employ their own expression), they retain most of the ideas, tendencies, and even the *hobbies*, they had while on earth, all of which furnish additional means of identification; but these are especially to be found in the vast number of small details that are only perceived through sustained and attentive observation. Spirits who have been authors are seen to discuss their own works or views, approving or blaming them; others allude to various circumstances connected with their life or death; and from all these indications we obtain what may, at least, be regarded as moral presumptions in favour of their identity, the only ones that can be looked for under the circumstances of the case.

If, then, the identity of the spirit evoked may be established, to a certain extent and in certain cases, there is no reason why that identity may not exist in others; and although we may not have the same means of identification in regard to persons whose death is of more distant date, we always have that of language and character, for the spirit of a good and enlightened man will assuredly not express himself like that of a depraved or ignorant one. As for inferior spirits who assume honoured names, they soon betray themselves by the character of their language and statements. If some one, for instance, calling himself Fénélon gave utterance to remarks at variance with common sense or morality, his imposture would at once become evident; but if the thoughts expressed by him were always noble, consistent, and of an elevation worthy of Fénélon, there would be no reason to doubt his identity, for otherwise we should have to admit that a spirit whose communications inculcate only goodness would knowingly be guilty of falsehood. Experience shows us that spirits of the same degree, of the same character, and animated by the same sentiments, are united in groups and families; but the number of spirits is incalculable, and we are so far from knowing them all, that the names of the immense majority of them are necessarily unknown to us. A spirit of the same category as Fénélon may therefore come to us in his name, and may even be sent by him as his representative; in which case he would naturally announce himself as Fénélon, because he is his equivalent, and able to supply his place, and because we need a name in order to fix our ideas in regard to him. And, after all, what does it matter whether a spirit be really Fénélon or not, if all that he says is excellent, and such as Fénélon himself would be likely to say? For, in that case, he must be a spirit of superior advancement; and the name under which he presents himself is of no importance, being often only a means of fixing our ideas. This sort of substitution would not be acceptable in evocations of a more intimate character; but, in these, as just pointed out, we have other means of ascertaining the identity of the communicating spirit.

It is certain, however, that the assumption of false names by spirits may give rise to numerous mistakes, may be a source of error and deception, and is, in fact, one of the most serious difficulties of practical spiritism; but we have never said that this field of investigation, any more than any other, is exempt from obstacles, nor that it can be fruitfully explored without serious and persevering effort. We cannot too often reiterate the warning that spiritism is a new field of study, and one that demands long

and assiduous exploration. Being unable to produce at pleasure
the facts on which Spiritism is based, we are obliged to wait for
them to present themselves; and it often happens that, instead of
occurring when we are looking for them, they occur when least
expected. For the attentive and patient observer, materials for
study are abundant, because he discovers in the facts thus presented
thousands of characteristic peculiarities which are for him so many
sources of light. It is the same in regard to every other branch
of science; while the superficial observer sees in a flower only an
elegant form, the botanist discovers in it a mine of interest for
his thought.

XIII

The foregoing remarks lead us to say a few words in relation
to another difficulty—viz., the divergence which exists in the
statements made by spirits.

Spirits differing very widely from one another as regards their
knowledge and morality, it is evident that the same question may
receive from them very different answers, according to the rank
at which they have arrived; exactly as would be the case if it were
propounded alternately to a man of science, an ignoramus, and a
mischievous wag. The important point, as previously remarked,
is to know who is the spirit to whom we are addressing our
question.

But, it will be argued, how is it that spirits who are admittedly
of superior degree are not all of the same opinion? We reply, in
the first place, that there are, independently of the cause of
diversity just pointed out, other causes that may exercise an
influence on the nature of the replies, irrespectively of the quality
of the spirits themselves. This is a point of the highest importance,
and one that will be explained by our ulterior study of the subject,
provided that this study be prosecuted with the aid of the sustained
attention, the prolonged observation, the method and perseverance
that are required in the pursuit of every other branch of human
inquiry. Years of study are needed to make even a second-rate
physician; three-quarters of a lifetime to make a man of learning:
and people fancy that a few hours will suffice to acquire the
science of the infinite! Let there be no mistake in regard to

this matter. The subject of Spiritism is immense. It involves all other subjects, physical, metaphysical, and social; it is a new world that opens before us. Is it strange that time, and a good deal of time, should be required for becoming acquainted with it?

The contradictions alluded to, moreover, are not always as absolute as they may seem to be at first sight. Do we not see every day that men who are pursuing the same science give various definitions of the same thing; sometimes because they make use of different terms, sometimes because they consider it from different points of view, although the fundamental idea is the same in each case? Let any one count up, if he can, the different definitions that have been given of grammar! It must also be remembered that the form of the answer often depends on the form under which the question has been put; and that it would be childish to regard as a contradiction what is often only a difference of words. The higher spirits pay no heed to forms of expression; for them, the thought itself is everything.

Let us take, for example, the definition of *soul*. That word, having no fixed meaning, spirits like ourselves may differ in the meaning they give to it. One of them may say that it is "the principle of life;" another may call it "the animic spark;" a third may say that it is internal; a fourth, that it is external, etc.; and each may be right from his own special point of view. Some of them might even be supposed to hold materialistic views; and yet such is not the case. It is the same with regard to the word *God*. According to some, God is "the principle of all things;" according to others, "the creator of the universe," "the sovereign intelligence," "the Infinite," "the great Spirit," etc.; and nevertheless it is always "God." And so in regard to the classification of spirits. They form an uninterrupted succession from the lowest to the highest; all attempts at classification are therefore arbitrary, and they may be regarded as forming three, five, ten, or twenty classes, without involving error or contradiction. All human sciences offer the same variations of detail; every investigator has his own system; and systems change, but science remains the same. Whether we study botany according to the system of Linnæus, of Jussieu, or of Tournefort, what we learn is none the less botany. Let us then cease to attribute more importance than they deserve to matters that are merely conventional, and let us devote ourselves only to what is really important; and we shall often discover, on reflexion, a similitude of meaning in statements that appeared to us, at first sight, to be contradictory.

XIV

We should pass over the objection of certain sceptics in relation to the faulty spelling of some spirits, were it not that this objection affords us an opportunity of calling attention to a point of great importance. Spirit-orthography, is must be confessed, is not always irreproachable; but he must be very short of arguments who would make this fact the object of serious criticism, on the plea that, "since spirits know everything, they ought to be well up in spelling." We might retort by pointing to the numerous sins against orthography committed by more than one of the lights of science in our own world, and which in no wise invalidate their scientific authority; but a much more important point is involved in the fact alluded to. For spirits, and especially for those of high degree, the idea is everything, the form is nothing. Freed from matter, their language among themselves is as rapid as thought, for it is their thought itself that is communicated without intermediary; and it must therefore be very inconvenient for them to be obliged, in communicating with us, to make use of human speech, with its long and awkward forms, its insufficiencies and imperfections, as the vehicle of their ideas. They often allude to this inconvenience; and it is curious to see the means they employ to obviate the difficulty. It would be the same with us if we had to express ourselves in a language of which the words and locutions were longer, and the stock of expressions more scanty, than those we habitually employ. The same difficulty is felt by the man of genius, impatient of the slowness of his pen, which always lags behind his thought. It is therefore easy to understand that spirits attach but little importance to questions of spelling, especially in the transmission of serious and weighty teachings. Should we not rather wonder that they are able to express themselves equally in all tongues, and that they understand them all? It must not, however, be inferred from these remarks that they are unable to express themselves with conventional correctness; they do this when they judge it to be necessary; as, for instance, when they dictate verses, some of which, written, moreover, by illiterate mediums, are of a correctness and elegance that defy the severest criticism.

XV

There are persons who see danger in everything that is new to them, and who have therefore not failed to draw an unfavourable conclusion from the fact that some of those who have taken up the subject of Spiritism have lost their reason. But how can sensible people urge that fact as an objection? Does not the same thing often happen to weak heads when they give themselves up to any intellectual pursuit? Who shall say how many have gone mad over mathematics, medicine, music, philosophy, etc. But what does that prove? And are those studies to be proscribed on that account? Arms and legs, the instruments of physical activity, are often injured by physical labour; the brain, instrument of thought, is often impaired by intellectual labour, to which, in fact, many a man may be said to fall a martyr. But, though the instrument may be injured, the mind remains intact, and, when freed from matter, finds itself again in full possession of its faculties.

Intense mental application of any kind may induce cerebral disease; science, art, religion even, have all furnished their quota of madmen. The predisposing cause of madness is to be found in some tendency of the brain that renders it more or less accessible to certain impressions; and, where the predisposition to insanity exists, its manifestation takes on the character of the pursuit to which the mind is most addicted, and which then assumes the form of a fixed idea. This fixed idea may be that of spirits, in the case of those who have been deeply absorbed by spiritist matters; as it may be that of God, of angels, the devil, fortune, power, an art, a science, a political or social system. It is probable that the victim of religious mania would have gone mad on Spiritism, if Spiritism had been his predominant mental occupation; just as he who goes mad over Spiritism would, under other circumstances, have gone mad over something else.

We assert, therefore, that Spiritism does not predispose to insanity; nay, more, we assert that, when correctly understood, it is a preservative against insanity.

Among the most common causes of cerebral disturbance must be reckoned the disappointments, misfortunes, blighted affections, and other troubles of human life, which are also the most frequent causes of suicide. But the enlightened spiritist looks upon the things of this life from so elevated a point of view, they seem to

him so petty, so worthless, in comparison with the future he sees
before him—life appears so short, so fleeting—that its tribulations are, in his eyes, merely the disagreeable incidents of a
journey. What would produce violent emotion in the mind of
another affects him but slightly; besides, he knows that the sorrows
of life are trials which aid our advancement, if borne without
murmuring, and that he will be rewarded according to the fortitude
with which he has borne them. His convictions, therefore, give
him a resignation that preserves him from despair, and consequently
from a frequent cause of madness and suicide. He knows,
moreover, through spirit communications, the fate of those who
voluntarily shorten their days; and as such knowledge is well
calculated to suggest serious reflection, the number of those who
have thus been arrested on the downward path is incalculable.
Such is one of the results of Spiritism. The incredulous may
laugh at it as much as they please; we only wish them the consolations it affords to those who have sounded its mysterious
depths.

Fear must also be reckoned among the causes of madness.
Dread of the devil has deranged many a brain; and who shall say
how many victims have been made by impressing weak imaginations
with pictures of which the horrors are enhanced by the hideous
details so ingeniously worked into them? The devil, it is sometimes said, frightens only little children, whom it helps to make
docile and well-behaved. Yes; but only as do nursery-terrors and
bugaboos in general; and when these have lost their power, they
who have been subjected to this sort of training are apt to be
worse than before; while, on the other hand, those who have
recourse to it overlook the risk of epilepsy involved in such disturb-
ing action upon the delicate child-brain. Religion would be weak
indeed if its power could only be sustained by fear. Happily
such is not the case, and it has other means of acting on the mind.
Spiritism furnishes the religious element with a more efficient
support than superstitious terror. It discloses the reality of things,
and thus substitutes a salutary appreciation of the consequences
of wrong-doing for the vague apprehensions of unreasonable fear.

XVI

Two objections still remain to be examined, the only ones really
deserving of the name, because they are the only ones founded

on a rational basis. Both admit the reality of the material and moral phenomena of Spiritism, but deny the intervention of spirits in their production.

According to the first of these objections, all the manifestations attributed to spirits are merely effects of magnetism, and mediums are in a state that might be called *waking somnambulism,* a phenomenon which may have been observed by any one who has studied animal magnetism. In this state the intellectual faculties acquire an abnormal development; the circle of our intuitive perceptions is extended beyond its ordinary limits; the medium finds in himself, and with the aid of his lucidity, all that he says, and all the notions transmitted by him, even in regard to subjects with which he is least familiar in his usual state.

It is not by us, who have witnessed its prodigies and studied all its phases during thirty-five years, that the action of somnambulism could be contested, and we admit that many spirit-manifestations may be thus explained; but we assert that sustained and attentive observation shows us a host of facts in which any intervention of the medium, otherwise than as a passive instrument, is absolutely impossible. To those who attribute the phenomena in question to magnetism, we would say, as to all others, "See, and observe, for you have certainly not seen everything;" and we would also ask them to consider the two following points, suggested by their own view of the subject. In the first place, we would ask them, What is the origin of the hypothesis of spirit-action? Is it an explanation invented by a few individuals to account for those phenomena? Not at all. By whom, then, has it been broached? By the very mediums whose lucidity you extol. But if their lucidity be such as you declare it to be, why should they attribute to spirits what they have derived from themselves? How can they have given information so precise, logical, sublime in regard to the nature of those extra-human intelligences? Either mediums are lucid, or they are not; if they are, and if we trust to their veracity, we cannot, without inconsistency, suppose them to be in error on this point. In the second place, if all the phenomena had their source in the medium himself, they would always be identical in the case of each individual; and we should never find the same medium making use of different styles of expression, or giving utterance to contradictory statements.

The want of unity so often observed in the manifestations obtained by the same medium is a proof of the diversity of the

·sources from which they proceed; and as the cause of this diversity is not to be found in the medium himself, it must be sought for elsewhere.

According to the other objection, the medium is really the source of the manifestations, but, instead of deriving them from himself, as is asserted by the partisans of the somnambulic theory, he derives them from the persons among whom he finds himself. The medium is a sort of mirror, reflecting all the thoughts, ideas, and knowledge of those about him; from which it follows that he says nothing which is not known to, at least, some of them. It cannot be denied, for it is one of the fundamental principles of spiritist doctrine, that those who are present exercise an influence upon the manifestations; but this influence is very different from what it is assumed to be by the hypothesis we are considering, and, so far from the medium being the mere echo of the thoughts of those around him, there are thousands of facts that prove directly the contrary. This objection is therefore based on a serious mistake, and one that shows the danger of hasty judgments; those who bring it forward, being unable to deny the reality of phenomena which the science of the day is incompetent to explain, and being unwilling to admit the presence of spirits, explain them in their own way. Their theory would be specious if it explained all the facts of the case; but this it cannot do. In vain is it proved by the evidence of facts that the communications of the medium are often entirely foreign to the thoughts, knowledge, and even the opinions of those who are present, and that they are frequently spontaneous, and contradict all received ideas; the opponents referred to are not discouraged by so slight a difficulty. The radiation of thought, say they, extends far beyond the circle immediately around us; the medium is the reflection of the human race in general; so that, if he does not derive his inspirations from those about him, he derives them from those who are further off, in the town or country he inhabits, from the people of the rest of the globe, and even from those of other spheres.

We do not think that this theory furnishes a more simple and probable explanation than that given by Spiritism; for it assumes the action of a cause very much more marvellous. The idea that universal space is peopled by beings who are in perpetual contact with us, and who communicate to us their ideas, is certainly not more repugnant to reason than the hypothesis of a universal radiation, coming from every point of the universe, and converging in the brain of a single individual, to the exclusion of all the others.

We repeat (and this is a point of such importance that we cannot insist too strongly upon it), that the *somnambulic theory*, and that which may be called the *theory of reflection*, have been devised by the imagination of men; while, on the contrary, the *theory of spirit-agency* is not a conception of the human mind, for it was dictated by the manifesting intelligences themselves, at a time when no one thought of spirits, and when the opinion of the generality of men was opposed to such a supposition. We have therefore to inquire, first, from what quarter the mediums can have derived a hypothesis which had no existence in the thought of any one on earth? and, secondly, by what strange coincidence, can it have happened that tens of thousands of mediums, scattered over the entire globe, and utterly unknown to one another, all agree in asserting the same thing? If the first medium who appeared in France was influenced by opinions already received in America, by what strange guidance was he made to go in search of ideas across two thousand leagues of sea, and among a people whose habits and language were foreign to his own, instead of taking them in his own immediate vicinity?

But there is yet another circumstance to which sufficient attention has not been given. The earliest manifestations, in Europe, as in America, were not made either by writing or by speech, but by raps indicating the letters of the alphabet, and forming words and sentences. It is by this means that the manifesting intelligences declared themselves to be spirits; and therefore, even though we should admit an intervention of the medium's mind in the production of verbal or written communications, we could not do so in regard to raps, whose meaning could not have been known beforehand.

We might adduce any number of facts proving the existence of a personal individuality and an absolutely independent will on the part of the manifesting intelligence; and we therefore invite our opponents to a more attentive observation of the phenomena in question, assuring them that, if they study these without prejudice, and refrain from drawing a conclusion until they have made themselves thoroughly acquainted with the subject, they will find that their theories are unable to account for all of them. We will only propose to such antagonists the two following queries:—

1. Why does it so often happen that the manifesting intelligence refuses to answer certain questions in regard to matters that are perfectly known to the questioner, as, for instance, his name or age, what he has in his hand, what he did yesterday, what he intends to do on the morrow, etc.? If the medium be only a mirror reflecting the thought of those about him, nothing should be easier for him than to answer such questions.

If our adversaries retort by inquiring why it is that spirits, who ought to know everything, are unable to answer questions so simple, and conclude, from this presumed inability, that the phenomena cannot be caused by spirits, we would ask them whether, if an ignorant or foolish person should inquire of some learned body the reason of its being light at noonday, any answer would be returned to his question? and whether it would be reasonable to conclude, from the derision or the silence with which such a question might be received, that its members were merely a set of asses? It is precisely because they are at a higher point than ourselves that spirits decline to answer idle and foolish questions; keeping silence when such are asked, or advising us to employ ourselves with more serious subjects.

2. We have also to ask them why it is that spirits come and depart at their own pleasure, and why, when once they have taken their departure, neither prayers nor entreaties can bring them back? If the medium were acted upon solely by the mental impulsion of those around him, it is evident that the union of their wills, in such a case, ought to stimulate his clairvoyance. If, therefore, he do not yield to the wishes of those assembled, strengthened by his own desire, it is because he obeys an influence which is distinct from himself and from those about him, and which thus asserts its own independence and individuality.

XVII

Incredulity in regard to spirit-communication, when not the result of systematic opposition from selfish motives, has almost always its source in an imperfect acquaintance with the facts of the case; which, however, does not prevent a good many persons from attempting to settle the question as though they were perfectly familiar with it. It is possible to be very clever, very learned, and yet to lack clearness of judgment; and a belief in one's own infallibility is the surest sign of the existence of this defect.   Many persons, too, regard spirit manifestations as being only a matter of curiosity.   Let us hope that the reading of this book will show them that the wonderful phenomena in question are something else than a pastime.

Spiritism consists of two parts: one of these, the experimental, deals with the subject of the manifestations in general; the other, the philosophic, deals with the class of manifestations denoting intelligence. Whoever has only observed the former is in the position of one whose knowledge of physics, limited to experiments of an amusing nature, does not extend to the fundamental principles of that science. Spiritist philosophy consists of teachings imparted by spirits, and the knowledge thus conveyed is of a character far too serious to be mastered without serious and persevering attention. If the present book had no other result than to show the serious nature of the subject, and to induce inquirers to approach it in this spirit, it would be sufficiently important; and we should rejoice to have been chosen for the accomplishment of a work in regard to which we take no credit to ourselves, the principles it contains not being of our own creating, and whatever honour it may obtain being entirely due to the spirits by whom it has been dictated. We hope that it will achieve yet another result—viz., that of serving as a guide to those who are desirous of enlightenment, by showing them the grand and sublime end of individual and social progress to which the teachings of Spiritism directly tend, and by pointing out to them the road by which alone that end can be reached.

Let us wind up these introductory remarks with one concluding observation. Astronomers, in sounding the depths of the sky, discovered seemingly vacant spaces not in accordance with the general laws that govern the distribution of the heavenly bodies, and they therefore conjectured that those spaces were occupied by globes that had escaped their observation. On the other hand, they observed certain effects the cause of which was unknown to them; and they said to themselves, "In such a region of space there must be a world, for otherwise there would be a void that ought not to exist; and the effects we have observed imply the presence in that seeming void of such a world as their cause." Reasoning, then, from those effects to their cause they calculated the elements of the globe whose presence they had inferred, and facts subsequently justified their inference. Let us apply the same mode of reasoning to another order of ideas. If we observe the series of beings, we find that they form a continuous chain from brute matter to man. But between man and God, who is the alpha and omega of all things, what an immense hiatus! Is it reasonable to suppose that the links of the chain stop short with man, that he can vault, without transition, over the distance which separates him from the Infinite? Reason shows us that between man and God there must be other links, just as it showed the astronomers that between the worlds then known to them there must be other worlds as yet unknown to them. What system of philosophy has filled this hiatus? Spiritism shows that it is filled with the beings of all the ranks of the invisible world, and that these beings are no other than the spirits of men who have reached the successive degrees that lead up to perfection; and all things are thus seen to be linked together from one end of the chain to the other. Let those who deny the existence of spirits tell us what are the occupants of the immensity of space which spirits declare to be occupied by them; and let those who scoff at the idea of spirit-teachings give us a nobler idea than is given by those teachings of the handiwork of God, a more convincing demonstration of His goodness and His power.

ALLAN KARDEC

PROLEGOMENA

PHENOMENA which are inexplicable by any known laws are occurring all over the world, and revealing the action of a free and intelligent will as their cause.

Reason tells us that an intelligent effect must have an intelligent force for its cause; and facts have proved that this force is able to enter into communication with men by the employment of material signs.

This force, interrogated as to its nature, has declared itself to belong to the world of spiritual beings who have thrown off the corporeal envelope of men. It is thus that the existence of spirits has been revealed to us.

Communication between the spirit world and the corporeal world is in the nature of things, and has in it nothing supernatural. Traces of its existence are to be found among all nations and in every age; they are now becoming general and evident to all. Spirits assure us that the time appointed by Providence for a universal manifestation of their existence has now come; and that their mission, as the ministers of God and the instruments of His will, is to inaugurate, through the instructions they are charged to convey to us, a new era of regeneration for the human race.

This book is a compilation of their teachings. It has been written by the order and under the dictation of spirits of high degree, for the purpose of establishing the bases of a rational philosophy, free from the influence of prejudices and of pre-conceived opinions. It contains nothing that is not the expression of their thought; nothing that has not been submitted to their approbation. The method adopted . in the arrangement of its contents, the comments upon these, and the form given to certain portions of the work, are all that has been contributed by him to whom the duty of publishing it has been entrusted.

Many of the spirits who have taken part in the accomplishment of this task declare themselves to have been persons whom we know to have lived at different epochs upon the earth, preaching and practising virtue and wisdom. Of the names of others, history has preserved no trace; but their elevation is attested by the purity of their doctrine and their union with those who bear venerated names.

We transcribe the words in which, by writing, through the intermediary of various mediums, the mission of preparing this book was confided to the writer :—

"Be zealous and persevering in the work you have undertaken in conjunction with us, for this work is ours. In the book you are to write, we shall lay the foundations of the new edifice which is destined to unite all men in a common sentiment of love and charity; but, before making it public, we shall go through it with you, so as to ensure its accuracy.

"We shall be with you whenever you ask for our presence, and shall aid you in all your labours; for the preparation of this book is only a part of the mission which has been confided to you, and of which you have already been informed by one of us.

"Of the teachings given to you, some are to be kept to yourself for the present; we shall tell you when the time for publishing them has come. Meanwhile make them the subject of your meditations, that you may be ready to treat of them at the proper moment.

"Put at the beginning of the book the vine-branch we have drawn[1] for that purpose, because it is the emblem of the work of the Creator. In it are united all the material elements that most fitly symbolise body and spirit: the stem represents the body; the juice, the spirit; the fruit, the union of body and spirit. Man's labour calls forth the latent qualities of the juice; the labour of the body develops, through the knowledge thus acquired, the latent powers of the soul.

---

1 **Vide** p. 59, the facsimile of the branch drawn by spirits.

"Do not allow yourself to be discouraged by hostile criticism. You will have rancorous contradictors, especially among those whose interest it is to keep up existing abuses. You will have such even among spirits; for those who are not completely dematerialised often endeavour, out of malice or ignorance, to scatter abroad the seeds of doubt. Believe in God, and go boldly forward. We shall be with you to sustain you on your way; and the time is at hand when the truth will shine forth on all sides.

"The vanity of some men, who imagine that they know everything, and are bent on explaining everything in their own way, will give rise to opposing opinions; but all who have in view the grand principle of Jesus will be united in the same love of goodness, and in a bond of brotherhood that will embrace the entire world. Putting aside all vain disputes about words, they will devote their energies to matters of practical importance, in regard to which, whatever their doctrinal belief, the convictions of all who receive the communications of the higher spirits will be the same.

"Perseverance will render your labour fruitful. The pleasure you will feel in witnessing the spread of our doctrine and its right appreciation will be for you a rich reward, though perhaps rather in the future than in the present. Be not troubled by the thorns and stones that the incredulous and the evil-minded will place in your path; hold fast your confidence, for your confidence will ensure our help, and, through it, you will reach the goal.

"Remember that good spirits only give their aid to those who serve God with humility and disinterestedness; they disown all who use heavenly things as a stepping-stone to earthly advancement, and withdraw from the proud and the ambitious. Pride and ambition are a barrier between man and God; for they blind man to the splendours of celestial existence, and God cannot employ the blind to make known the light."

"JOHN THE EVANGELIST, ST AUGUSTINE, ST VICENT DE PAUL, ST LOUIS, THE SPIRIT OF TRUTH, SOCRATES, PLATO, FÉNÉLON, FRANKLIN, SWEDENBORG," etc., etc.

THE SPIRITS' BOOK.

BOOK FIRST — CAUSES

CHAPTER I

GOD

1. GOD AND INFINITY—2. PROOFS OF THE EXIS-
TENCE OF GOD—3. ATTRIBUTES OF THE DIVINITY—
4. PANTHEISM.

God and Infinity

1. What is God?

"God is the Supreme Intelligence—First Cause of all things."[1]

2. What is to be understood by infinity?

"That which has neither beginning nor end; the unknown: all that is unknown is infinite."

3. Can it be said that God is infinity?

"An incomplete definition. Poverty of human speech incompetent to define what transcends human intelligence."

God is infinite in His perfections, but "infinity" is an abstraction. To say that God is **infinity** is to substitute the attribute of a thing for the thing itself, and to define something unknown by reference to some other thing equally unknown.

---

[1] The passage placed between inverted commas after each question is the reply made by the communicating spirits, whose very words are given textually throughout the whole of this book. The remarks and developments occasionally added by the author are printed in smaller type wherever they might otherwise be confounded with the replies of the spirits themselves. Where the author's remarks occupy an entire chapter or chapters, the ordinary type is used, as, in that case, no such confusion could occur.

Proofs of the Existence of God

4. What proof have we of the existence of God?

"The axiom which you apply in all your scientific researches, 'There is no effect without a cause.' Search out the cause of whatever is not the work of man, and reason will furnish the answer to your question."

To assure ourselves of the existence of God, we have only to look abroad on the works of creation. The universe exists, therefore it has a cause. To doubt the existence of God is to doubt that every effect has a cause, and to assume that something can have been made by nothing.

5. What is to be inferred from the intuition of the existence of God which may be said to be the common property of the human mind?

"That God exists; for whence could the human mind derive this intuition if it had no real basis? The inference to be drawn from the fact of this intuition is a corollary of the axiom. 'There is no effect without a cause.'"

6. May not our seemingly intuitive sense of the existence of God be the result of education and of acquired ideas?

"If such were the case, how should this intuitive sense be possessed by your savages?"

If the intuition of the existence of a Supreme Being were only the result of education it would not be universal, and would only exist, like all other acquired knowledge, in the minds of those who had received the special education to which it would be due.

7. Is the first cause of the formation of things to be found in the essential properties of matter?

"If such were the case, what would be the cause of those properties? There must always be a first cause."

To attribute the first formation of things to the essential properties of matter, would be to take the effect for the cause, for those properties are themselves an effect, which must have a cause.

8. What is to be thought of the opinion that attributes the first formation of things to a fortuitous combination of matter, in other words, to chance?

"Another absurdity! Who that is possessed of common sense can regard chance as an intelligent agent? And, besides, what is chance? Nothing."

The harmony which regulates the mechanism of the universe can only result from combinations adopted in view of predetermined ends, and thus, by its very nature, reveals the existence of an Intelligent Power. To attribute the first formation of things to chance is nonsense ; for chance cannot produce the results of intelligence. If chance could be intelligent, it would cease to be chance.

9. *What proof have we that the first cause of all things is a Supreme Intelligence, superior to all other intelligences?*

"You have a proverb which says, 'The workman is known by his work.' Look around you, and, from the quality of the work, infer that of the workman."

We judge of the power of an intelligence by its works ; as no human being could create that which is produced by nature, it is evident that the first cause must be an Intelligence superior to man.

Whatever may be the prodigies accomplished by human intelligence, that intelligence itself must have a cause ; and the greater the results achieved by it, the greater must be the cause of which it is the effect. It is this Supreme Intelligence that is the first cause of all things, whatever the name by which mankind may designate it.

Attributes of the Divinity

10. *Can man comprehend the essential nature of God?*

"No; he lacks the sense required for comprehending it."

11. *Will man ever become able to comprehend the mystery of the Divinity?*

"When his mind shall no longer be obscured by matter, and when, by his perfection, he shall have brought himself nearer to God, he will see and comprehend Him."

The inferiority of the human faculties renders it impossible for man to comprehend the essential nature of God. In the infancy of the race, man often confounds the Creator with the creature, and attributes to the former the imperfections of the latter. But, in proportion as his moral sense becomes developed, man's thought penetrates more deeply into the nature of things, and he is able to form to himself a juster and more rational idea of the Divine Being, although his idea of that Being must always be imperfect and incomplete.

12. *If we cannot comprehend the essential nature of God, can we have an idea of some of His perfections?*

"Yes, of some of them. Man comprehends them better in proportion as he raises himself above matter; he obtains glimpses of them through the exercise of his intelligence."

13. *When we say that God is eternal, infinite, unchangeable, immaterial, unique, all-powerful, sovereignly just and good, have we not a complete idea of His attributes?*

"Yes, judging from your point of view, because you think that you sum up everything in those terms; but you must understand that there are things which transcend the intelligence of the most intelligent man, and for which your language, limited to your ideas and sensations, has no expressions. Your reason tells you that God must possess those perfections in the supreme degree; for, if one of them were lacking, or were not possessed by Him in an infinite degree, He would not be superior to all, and consequently would not be God. In order to be above all things, God must undergo no vicissitudes, He must have none of the imperfections of which the imagination can conceive."

God is **eternal.** If He had had a beginning, He must either have sprung from nothing, or have been created by some being anterior to Himself. It is thus that, step by step, we arrive at the idea of infinity and eternity.

God is **unchangeable.** If He were subject to change, the laws which rule the universe would have no stability.

God is immaterial, that is to say, that His nature differs from everything that we call matter, or otherwise He would not be unchangeable, for He would be subject to the transformations of matter.

God is **unique.** If there were several Gods, there would be neither unity of plan nor unity of power in the ordaining of the universe.

God is **all-powerful,** because He is unique. If He did not possess sovereign power, there would be something more powerful, or no less powerful, than Himself. He would not have created all things ; and those which He had not created would be the work of another God.

God is **sovereignly just and good.** The providential wisdom of the divine laws is revealed as clearly in the smallest things as in the greatest ; and this wisdom renders it impossible to doubt either His justice or His goodness.

Pantheism

14. Is God a being distinct from the universe, or is He, according to the opinion of some, the result of all the forces and intelligences of the universe?

"If the latter were the case, God would not be God, for He would be effect and not cause; He cannot be both cause and effect."

"God exists. You cannot doubt His existence, and that is the one essential point. Do not seek to go beyond it; do not lose yourselves in a labyrinth which, for you, is without an issue. Such inquiries would not make you better; they would rather tend to add to your pride, by causing you to imagine that you knew something, while, in reality, you would know nothing. Put aside systems. You have things enough to think about that concern you much more nearly, beginning with yourselves. Study your own imperfections, that you may get rid of them; this will be far more useful to you than the vain attempt to penetrate the impenetrable."

15. *What is to be thought of the opinion according to which all natural bodies, all the beings, all the globes of the universe, are parts of the Divinity, and constitute in their totality the Divinity itself; in other words, the Pantheistic theory?*

"Man, not being able to make himself God, would fain make himself out to be, at least, a part of God."

16. *Those who hold this theory profess to find in it the demonstration of some of the attributes of God. The worlds of the universe being infinitely numerous, God is thus seen to be infinite; vacuum, or nothingness, being nowhere, God is everywhere: God being everywhere, since everything is an integral part of God, He is thus seen to be the intelligent cause of all the phenomena of the universe. What can we oppose to this argument?*

"The dictates of reason. Reflect on the assumption in question, and you will have no difficulty in detecting its absurdity."

The Pantheistic theory makes of God a material being, who, though endowed with a supreme intelligence, would only be on a larger scale what we are on a smaller one. But, as matter is incessantly undergoing transformation, God, if this theory were true, would have no stability. He would be subject to all the vicissitudes, and even to all the needs, of humanity ; He would lack one of the essential attributes of the Divinity —viz., unchangeableness. The properties of matter cannot be attributed to God without degrading our idea of the Divinity ; and all the subtleties of sophistry fail to solve the problem of His essential nature. We do not know what God is ; but we know that it is impossible that He should not be ; and the theory just stated is in contradiction with His most essential attributes. It confounds the Creator with the creation, precisely as though we should consider an ingenious machine to be an integral portion of the mechanician who invented it.

The intelligence of God is revealed in His works, as is that of a painter in his picture ; but the works of God are no more God Himself than the picture is the artist who conceived and painted it.

CHAPTER II

1. KNOWLEDGE OF THE FIRST PRINCIPLES OF THINGS—
2. SPIRIT AND MATTER—3. PROPERTIES OF MATTER—
4. UNIVERSAL SPACE.

Knowledge of the First Principles of Things

17. Is it given to mankind to know the first principle of things?

"No. There are things that cannot be understood by man in this world."

18. Will man ever be able to penetrate the mystery of things now hidden from him?

"The veil will be raised for him in proportion as he accomplishes his purification; but, in order to understand certain things, he would need faculties which he does not yet possess."

19. Cannot man, through scientific investigation, penetrate some of the secrets of nature?

"The faculty of scientific research has been given to him as a means by which he may advance in every direction; but he cannot overstep the limits of his present possibilities."

The farther man advances in the study of the mysteries around him, the greater should be his admiration of the power and wisdom of the Creator. But, partly through pride, partly through weakness, his intellect itself often renders him the sport of illusion. He heaps systems upon systems; and every day shows him how many errors he has mistaken for truths, how many truths he has repelled as errors. All this should be a lesson for his pride.

20. Is man permitted to receive communications of a higher order in regard to matters which, not being within the scope of his senses, are beyond the pale of scientific investigation?

"Yes. When God judges such revelations to be useful, He reveals to man what science is incompetent to teach him."

It is through communications of this higher order that man is enabled, within certain limits, to obtain a knowledge of his past and of his future destiny.

Spirit and Matter

21. Has matter existed from all eternity, like God, or has it been created at some definite period of time?

"God only knows. There is, nevertheless, one point which your reason should suffice to show you, viz., that God, the prototype of love and beneficence, can never have been inactive. However far off in the past you may imagine the beginning of His action, can you suppose Him to have been for a single moment inactive?"

22. Matter is generally defined as being "that which has extension," "that which can make an impression upon our senses," "that which possesses impenetrability." Are these definitions correct?

"From your point of view they are correct, because you can only define in accordance with what you know. But matter exists in states which are unknown to you. It may be, for instance, so ethereal and subtle as to make no impression upon your senses; and yet it is still matter, although it would not be such for you."

— What definition can you give of matter?

"Matter is the element which enchains spirit, the instrument which serves it, and upon which, at the same time, it exerts its action."

From this point of view it may be said that matter is the agent, the intermediary, through which, and upon which, spirit acts.

23. What is spirit?

"The intelligent principle of the universe."

— What is the essential nature of spirit?

"It is not possible to explain the nature of spirit in your language. For you it is not *a thing*, because it is not palpable; but for us it is *a thing.*"

24. Is spirit synonymous with intelligence?

"Intelligence is an essential attribute of spirit, but both merge in a unitary principle, so that, for you, they may be said to be the same thing."

25. Is spirit independent of matter, or is it only one of the properties of matter, as colours are a property of light, and as sound is a property of the air?

"Spirit and matter are distinct from one another; but the union of spirit and matter is necessary to give intelligent activity to matter."

— *Is this union equally necessary to the manifestation of spirit? (We refer, in this question, to the principle of intelligence, abstractly considered, without reference to the individualities designated by that term.)*

"It is necessary for you, because you are not organised for perceiving spirit apart from matter. Your senses are not formed for that order of perception."

26. *Can spirit be conceived of without matter, and matter without spirit?*

"Undoubtedly, as objects of thought."

27. *There are, then, two general elements of the universe— matter and spirit?"*

"Yes; and above them both is God, the Creator, Parent of all things. These three elements are the principle of all that exists— the universal trinity. But to the material element must be added the universal fluid which plays the part of intermediary between spirit and matter, the nature of the latter being too gross for spirit to be able to act directly upon it. Although, from another point of view, this fluid may be classed as forming part of the material element, it is, nevertheless, distinguished from that element by certain special properties of its own. If it could be classed simply and absolutely as matter, there would be no reason why spirit also should not be classed as matter. It is intermediary between spirit and matter. It is fluid, just as matter is matter, and is susceptible of being made, through its innumerable combinations with matter, under the directing action of spirit, to produce the infinite variety of things of which you know as yet but a very small portion. This universal, primitive, or elementary fluid, being the agent employed by spirit in acting upon matter, is the principle without which matter would remain for ever in a state of division, and would never acquire the properties given to it by the state of ponderability."

— *Is this fluid what we designate by the name of electricity?*

"We have said that it is susceptible of innumerable combinations. What you call the electric fluid, the magnetic fluid, etc., are modifications of the universal fluid, which, properly speaking, is only matter of a more perfect and more subtle kind, and that may be considered as having an independent existence of its own."

28. Since spirit itself is something, would it not be more correct and clearer to designate these two general elements by the terms inert matter *and* intelligent matter?

"Questions of words are of little importance for us. It is for you to formulate your definitions in such a manner as to make yourselves intelligible to one another. Your disputes almost always arise from the want of a common agreement in the use of the words you employ, owing to the incompleteness of your language in regard to all that does not strike your senses."

One fact, patent to all observers, dominates all our hypotheses. We see matter which is not intelligent; we see the action of an intelligent principle independent of matter. The origin and connection of these two things are unknown to us. Whether they have, or have not, a common source, and points of contact pre-ordained in the nature of things, whether intelligence has an independent existence of its own, or is only a property or an effect, or even whether it is (as some assume it to be) an emanation of the Divinity, are points about which we know nothing. Matter and intelligence appear to us to be distinct ; and we therefore speak of them as being two constituent elements of the universe. We see, above these, a higher intelligence which governs all things, and is distinguished from them all by essential attributes peculiar to itself; it is this Supreme Intelligence that we call God.

Properties of Matter

29. Is density an essential attribute of matter?

"Yes, of matter as understood by you, but not of matter considered as the universal fluid. The ethereal and subtle matter which forms this fluid is imponderable for you, and yet it is none the less the principle of your ponderable matter."

Density is a relative property. Beyond the sphere of attraction of the various globes of the universe, there is no such thing as "weight," just as there is neither "up" nor "down."

30. Is matter formed of one element or of several elements?

"Of one primitive element. The bodies which you regard as simple are not really elementary; they are transformations of the primitive matter."

31. Whence come the different properties of matter?

"From the modifications undergone by the elementary molecules, as the result of their union and of the action of certain conditions."

32. According to this view of the subject, savours, odours, colours, sounds, the poisonous or salutary qualities of bodies, are only the result of modifications of one and the same primitive substance?

"Yes, undoubtedly; and that only exist in virtue of the disposition of the organs destined to perceive them."

This principle is proved by the fact that the qualities of bodies are not perceived by all persons in the same manner. The same thing appears agreeable to the taste of one person, and disagreeable to that of another. What appears blue to one person appears red to another. That which is a poison for some, is wholesome for others.

33. Is the same elementary matter susceptible of undergoing all possible modifications and of acquiring all possible qualities?

"Yes; and it is this fact which is implied in the saying that *everything is in everything.*" [1]

Oxygen, hydrogen, azote, carbon, and all the other bodies which we regard as simple, are only modifications of one primitive substance. But the impossibility, in which we have hitherto found ourselves, of arriving at this primitive matter otherwise than as an intellectual deduction, causes these bodies to appear to us to be really elementary ; and we may, therefore, without impropriety, continue for the present to regard them as such.

— Does not this theory appear to bear out the opinion of those who admit only two essential properties in matter, viz., force and movement, and who regard all the other properties of matter as being merely secondary effects of these, varying according to the intensity of the force and the direction of the movement?

"That opinion is correct. But you must also add, *according to the mode of molecular arrangement*; as you see exemplified, for instance, in an opaque body, that may become transparent, and *vice versa.*"

34. Have the molecules of matter a determinate form?

"Those molecules undoubtedly have a form, but one which is not appreciable by your organs."

— Is that form constant or variable?

"Constant for the primitive elementary molecules, but variable for the secondary molecules, which are themselves only aglomerations of the primary ones; for what you term a molecule is still very far from being the elementary molecule.

Universal Space

35. Is universal space infinite or limited?

---

[1] This principle explains a phenomenon familiar to all magnetisers, viz., the imparting to any given substance—to water, for example—of very diferent qualities, such as specific flavours, or even the active qualities

"Infinite. Suppose the existence of boundaries, what would there be beyond them? This consideration confounds human reason; and nevertheless your reason itself tells you that it cannot be otherwise. It is thus with the idea of infinity, under whatever aspect you consider it. The idea of infinity cannot be comprehended in your narrow sphere."

If we imagine a limit to space, no matter how far off our thought may place this limit, our reason tells us that there must still be something beyond it ; and so on, step by step, until we arrive at the idea of infinity ; for the "something beyond," the existence of which is recognised by our thought as necessity, were it only an absolute void, would still be space.

36. Does an absolute void exist in any part of space?

"No there is no void. What appears like a void to you is occupied by matter in a state in which it escapes the action of your senses and of your instruments."

of other substances. As there is but one primitive element, and as the properties of different bodies are only modifications of this element, it follows that the substance of the most inoffensive and of the most deleterious bodies is absolutely the same. Thus water, which is formed of one equivalent of oxygen and two equivalents of hydrogen, becomes corrosive if we double the proportion of oxygen. An analogous transformation may be produced through the action of animal magnetism, directed by the human will.

CHAPTER III

CREATION

1. FORMATION OF WORLDS—2. PRODUCTION OF LIVING
BEINGS—3. PEOPLING OF THE EARTH : ADAM—4. DI-
VERSITY OF HUMAN RACES—5. PLURALITY OF WORLDS—
6. THE BIBLICAL ACCOUNT OF THE CREATION.

Formation of Worlds

The universe comprises the infinity of worlds, both of those we see and
those we do not see ; all animate and inanimate beings ; all the stars that
revolve in space, and all fluids with which space is filled.

*37. Has the universe been created, or has it existed from all
eternity, like God?*

"Assuredly the universe cannot have made itself; and if it had
existed from all eternity, like God, it could not be the work of God."

Reason tells us that the universe cannot have made itself, and that, as
it could not be the work of chance, it must be the work of God.

38. How did God create the universe?

"To borrow a well-known expression, by His will. Nothing
can give a better idea of the action of that all-powerfull will than
those grand words of Genesis, "God said, 'Let there be light,'
and there was light."

39. Can we know how worlds are formed?

"All that can be said on this subject, within the limits of your
comprehension, is this : Worlds are formed by the condensation
of the matter disseminated in space."

*40. Are comets, as is now supposed, a commencement of con-
densation of the primitive matter—worlds in course of formation?*

"Yes; but it is absurd to believe in the influence attributed
to them. I mean, the influence which is commonly attributed
to them; for all the heavenly bodies have their share of influence
in the production of certain physical phenomena."

*41. Is it possible for a completely formed world to disappear,
and for the matter of which it is composed to be again disseminated
in space?*

"Yes. God renews worlds as He renews the living beings that inhabit them."

42. *Can we know the length of time employed in the formation of worlds—of the earth, for instance?*

"This is a matter in regard to which I can tell you nothing, for it is only known to the Creator, and foolish indeed would he be who should pretend to possess such knowledge, or to number the ages of such a formation."

Production of Living Beings

43. *When did the earth begin to be peopled?*

"In the beginning all was chaos; the elements were mixed up in a state of confusion. Gradually those elements settled into their proper places, and then appeared the orders of living beings appropriate to the successive states of the globe."

44. *Whence came the living beings that appeared upon the earth?*

"The germs of these were contained in the earth itself, awaiting the favourable moment for their development. The organic principles came together on the cessation of the force which held them asunder, and those principles formed the germs of all the living beings that have peopled the earth. Those germs remained latent and inert, like the chrysalis and the seed of plants, until the arrival of the proper moment for the vivification of each species. The beings of each species then came together and multiplied."

45. *Where were the organic elements before the formation of the earth?*

"They existed, so to say, in the fluidic state, in space, in the midst of the spirits, or in other planets, awaiting the creation of the earth in order to begin a new existence on a new globe."

Chemistry shows us the molecules of inorganic bodies uniting to produce crystals of regular forms that are invariable for each species, as soon as those molecules find themselves in the conditions necessary to their combination. The slightest disturbance of those conditions suffices to prevent the union of the material elements, or, at least, to prevent the regular arrangement of the latter which constitutes the crystal. Why should not the same action take place among the organic elements? We preserve for years the seeds of plants and of animals, which are only vivified at a certain temperature and under certain conditions: grains of wheat have been seen to germinate after the lapse of centuries. The is, then, in seeds a **latent principle of vitality**, which only awaits the concourse of favourable circumstances to develop itself. May not that which takes place under our eyes every day have also taken place at the origin of the globe? Does this view of the formation of living beings brought forth out of chaos by the action of the forces of nature itself detract in any way from the

glory of God ? So far from doing this, the view of creation thus presented
to us is more consonant than any other with our sense of the vastness
of His power exerting its sway over all the worlds of infinity through the
action of universal laws. This theory, it is true, does not solve the problem
of the origin of the vital elements, but Nature has mysteries which it is
as yet impossible for us to explain.

46. *Do any living beings come into existence spontaneously
at the present day?*

"Yes; but the primal germs of these already existed in a latent
state. You are constantly witnesses of this phenomenon. Do not
the tissues of the human body and of animals contain the germs
of a multitude of parasites, that only await for their development
the occurrence of the putrid fermentation necessary to their life?
Each of you contains a slumbering world of microscopic beings in
process of creation."

47. *Was the human species among the organic elements
contained in the terrestrial globe?*

"Yes; and it made its appearance at the time appointed by the
Creator. Hence the statement that man was 'formed out of the
dust of the ground.'"

48. *Can we ascertain the epoch of the appearance of man and
of the other living beings on the earth?*

"No; all your calculations are chimerical."

49. *If the germs of the human race were among the organic
elements of the globe, why are human beings not produced
spontaneously at the present day, as they were at the time of its
origin?*

"The first beginning of things is hidden from us nevertheless,
it may be asserted that the earliest progenitors of the human race,
when once brought into existence, absorbed in themselves the
elements necessary to their formation in order to transmit those
elements according to the laws of reproduction. The same may
be said in regard to all the different species of living beings."

Peopling of the Earth — Adam

50. *Did the human race begin with one man only?*

"No; he whom you call Adam was neither the first nor the
only man who peopled the earth."

51. *Is it possible to know at what period Adam lived?*

"About the period which you assign to him; that is to say, about
4 000 years before Christ."

The man of whom, under the name of Adam, tradition has preserved the memory, was one of those who, in some one of the countries of the globe, survived one of the great cataclysms which at various epochs have changed its surface, and who became the founder of one of the races that people the earth at the present day. The laws of nature render it impossible that the amount of progress which we know to have been accomplished by the human race of our planet long before the time of Christ could have been accomplished so rapidly as must have been the case if it had only been in existence upon the globe since the period assigned as the date of Adam. The opinion most consonant with reason is that which regards the story of Adam as a myth, or as an allegory personifying the earliest ages of the world.

Diversity of Human Races

52. What is the cause of the physical and moral differences that distinguish the various races of men upon the earth?

"Climate, modes of life, and social habits. The same differences would be produced in the case of two children of the same mother, if brought up far from one another, and surrounded by different influences and conditions; for the children thus diversely brought up would present no moral resemblance to each other."

53. Did the human race come into existence on various points of the globe?

"Yes, and at various epochs; and this is one of the causes of the diversity of human races. The people of the primitive periods, being dispersed abroad in different climates, and forming alliances with those of other countries than their own, gave rise perpetually to new types of humanity."

— *Do these differences constitute distinct species?*

"Certainly not. All of them constitute but a single family. Do the differences between the varieties of the same fruit prevent their all belonging to the same species?"

54. If the human species do not all proceed from the same progenitor, should they, on that account, cease to regard one another as brothers?

"All men are brothers in virtue of their common relation to the Creator, because they are animated by the same spirit, and tend towards the same goal. The human mind is always prone to attach too literal a meaning to statements which are necessarily imperfect and incomplete."

Plurality of Worlds

55. Are all the globes that revolve in space inhabited?

"Yes; and the people of the earth are far from being, as you

suppose, the first in intelligence, goodness, and general development. There are many men having a high opinion of themselves
who even imagine that your little globe alone, of all the countless
myriads of globes around you, has the privilege of being inhabited
by reasoning beings. They fancy that God has created the universe
only for them. Insensate vanity!"

God has peopled the globes of the universe with living beings, all of
whom concur in working out the aims of His providence. To believe that
the presence of living beings is confined to the one point of the universe
inhabited by us is to cast a doubt on the wisdom of God, who has made
nothing in vain, and who must therefore have assigned to all the other globes
of the universe a destination more important than that of gratifying our
eyes with the spectacle of a starry night. Moreover, there is nothing in
the position, size, or physical constitution of the earth to warrant the supposition that it alone, of the countless myriads of globes disseminated throughout
the infinity of space, has the privilege of being inhabited.

56. *Is the physical constitution of all globes the same?*
"No; they do not at all resemble one another."

57. *The physical constitution of the various worlds not being
the same for all, does it follow that the beings who inhabit them
have different organisations?*
"Undoubtedly it does; just as, in your world, fishes are organised
for living in the water, and birds for living in the air."

58. *Are the planets furthest removed from the sun stinted in
light and heat, the sun only appearing to them of the size of one
of the fixed stars?*
"Do you suppose that there are no other sources of light and
heat than the sun? And do you count for nothing the action of
electricity, which, in certain worlds, plays a very much more important part than in your earth? Besides, how do you know that
the beings of those worlds see in the same manner as you do,
and with the aid of organs such as yours?"

The conditions of existence for the beings who inhabit the various worlds
must be supposed to be appropriate to the sphere in which they are destined
to live. If we had never seen fishes, we should be at a loss to understand
how any living beings could exist in the sea. So in regard to all the other
worlds, which doutless contain elements that are unknown to us. In our
own earth, are not the long polar nights illumined by the electrical displays
of the aurora borealis? Is it impossible that, in certain worlds, electricity
may be more abundant than in ours, and may subserve, in its general economy,
various important uses not imaginable by us? And may not those worlds
contain in themselves the sources of the heat and light required by their
inhabitants?

The Biblical Account of the Creation

59. The different nations of the earth have formed to themselves widely divergent ideas of the creation; ideas always in

harmony with their degree of scientific advancement. Reason and science concur in admitting the fantastic character of certain theories. The explanation of the subject now given through spirit-communication is confirmatory of the opinion which has long been adopted by the most enlightened exponents of modern science.

This explanation will no doubt be objected to, on the ground that it is in contradiction with the statements of the Bible; but a careful examination of those statements shows us that this contradiction is more apparent than real, and that it results from the interpretation which has been given to expressions whose meaning is allegorical rather than historical.

The question of the personality of Adam, regarded as the first man, and sole progenitor of the human race, is not the only one in regard to which the religious convictions of the world have necessarily undergone modification. The hypothesis of the rotation of the earth round the sun appeared, at one time, to be in such utter opposition to the letter of the Bible, that every species of persecution was directed against it, and against those who advocated it. Yet the earth continued to move on in its orbit in defiance of anathemas; and no one, at the present day, could contest the fact of its movement without doing violence to his own powers of reasoning.

The Bible also tells us that the world was created in six days, and fixes the epoch of this creation at about 4000 years before the Cristian era. Previously to that period the earth did not exist. At that period it was produced out of nothing. Such is the formal declaration of the sacred text; yet science, positive, inexorable, steps in with proof to the contrary. The history of the formation of the globe is written in indestructible characters in the worlds of fossils, proving beyond the possibility of denial that the six days of the creation are successive periods, each of which may have been of millions of ages. This is not a mere matter of statement or of opinion. It is a fact as incontestably certain as is the motion of the earth, and one that theology itself can no longer refuse to admit, although this admission furnishes another example of the errors into which we are led by attributing literal truth to language which is often of a figurative nature. Are we therefore to conclude that the Bible is a mere tissue of errors? No; but we must admit that men have erred in their method of interpreting it.

Geology, in its study of the archives written in the structure of the globe itself, has ascertained the order of succession in which the different species of living beings have appeared on its surface, and this order is found to be in accordance with the sequence indicated in the book of Genesis, with this difference, viz., that the earth, instead of issuing miraculously from the hand of God in the course of a few days, accomplished its formation under the impulsion of the Divine will, but according to the laws and through the action of the forces of nature, in the course of periods incalculable by us. Does God appear less great and less powerful for having accomplished the work of creation through the action of forces, and according to laws, of His own ordaining? And is the result of the creative energy less sublime for not having been accomplished instantaneously? Evidently not; and puerile indeed must be the mind that does not recognise the grandeur of the Almighty Power implied in this evolution of the worlds of the universe through the action of eternal laws. Science, so far from diminishing the glory of the Divine action, displays that action under an aspect still more sublime, and more consonant with our intuitive sense of the power and majesty of God, by showing that it has been accomplished without derogation from the laws which are the expression of the Divine will in the realm of nature.

Modern science, in accordance with the Mosaic record, proves that man was the last in the order of creation of living beings. But Moses puts the universal deluge at the year of the world 1654, while geology seems to show that the great diluvian cataclysm occurred before the appearance of man, because, up to the present time, the primitive strata contain no traces of his presence, nor of that of the animals contemporaneous with him. But this point is far from being decided. Various recent discoveries suggest the possibility of our being destined to ascertain that the antiquity of the human race is much greater than has been hitherto supposed; and should this greater antiquity become a matter of certainty, it would prove that the letter of the Bible, in regard to the date assigned by it to the creation of man, as in regard to so many other matters, can only be understood in an allegorical sense. That the geological deluge is not that of Noah is evident from the lapse of time required for the formation of the fossiliferous strata; and, if traces should eventually be discovered of the existence of the human race before the geological deluge, it would be evident either that Adam was not the first man, or that his creation dates back from a period indefinitely remote. There is no arguing against fact; and the antiquity of the human race, if proved by geological discovery, would have to be admitted, just as has been done in regard to the movement of the earth and the six days of the creation.

The existence of the human race before the geological deluge, it may be objected, is still doubtful. But the same objection cannot be urged against the following considerations:—Admitting that man first appeared upon the earth 4000 years before Christ, if the whole of the human race, with the exception of a single family, were destroyed 1650 years afterwards, it follows that the peopling of the earth dates only from the time of Noah—that is to say, only 2500 years before Christ. But when the Hebrews emigrated to Egypt in the eighteenth century before Christ, they found that country densely populated, and already in possession of an advanced civilisation. History also shows that, at the same period, India and various other countries were equally populous and flourishing, to say nothing of the chronological tables of other nations, which claim to go back to periods yet more remote. We must, therefore, suppose that, from the twenty-fourth to the eighteenth century before Christ—that is to say, in the space of 600 years—the posterity of a single individual was able to people all the immense countries which had then been discovered, not to speak of those which were then unknown, but which we have no reason to conclude were destitute of inhabitants; and we must suppose, still further, that the human race, during this brief period, was able to raise itself from the crass ignorance of the primitive savage state to the highest degree of intellectual development—suppositions utterly irreconcilable with anthropological laws.

The diversity of the various human races confirms this view of the subject. Climate and modes of life undoubtedly modify the physical characteristics of mankind, but we know the extent to which these modifications can be carried, and physiological examination conclusively proves that there are between the different races of men constitutional differences too profound to have been produced merely by differences of climate. The crossing of races produces intermediary types; it tends to efface the extremes of characteristic peculiarities; but it does not produce these peculiarities, and, therefore, creates only new varieties. But the crossing of races presupposes the existence of races distinct from each other; and how is

the existence of these to be explained if we attribute their origin
to a common stock, especially if we restrict the production of
these various races to so brief a period? How is it possible to
suppose, for example, that the descendants of Noah could have
been, in so short a time, transformed into Ethiopians? Such a
metamorphosis would be as inadmissible as that of a wolf into
a sheep, of a beetle into an elephant, of a bird into a fish. No
preconceived opinion can withstand, in the long run, the evidence
of opposing facts. But, on the contrary, all difficulty disappears
if we assume that man existed at a period anterior to that which
has hitherto been commonly assigned to his creation; that Adam
commenced, some 6000 years ago, the peopling of a country until
then uninhabited; that the deluge of Noah was a local catastrophe,
erroneously confounded with the great geological cataclysm; and,
finally, if we make due allowance for the allegorical form of
expression characteristic of the Oriental style, and common to the
sacred books of every people.

It is unwise to insist upon a literal interpretation of figurative
statements of which the inaccuracy may, at any moment, be
rendered evident by the progress of scientific discovery; but the
fundamental propositions of religion, so far from having anything
to fear from the discoveries of science, are strengthened and
ennobled by being brought into harmony with those discoveries.
And it is only when the religious sentiment shall have been en
lightened by its union with scientific truth that religious belief,
thus rendered invulnerable to the attacks of scepticism, will take
the place of scepticism in the minds and hearts of men.

CHAPTER IV

THE VITAL PRINCIPLE

1. ORGANIC AND INORGANIC BEINGS—2. LIFE AND DEATH—3. INTELLIGENCE AND INSTINCT.

Organic and Inorganic Beings

Organic beings are those which have in themselves a source of activity that produces the phenomena of life. They are born, grow, reproduce their own species, and die. They are provided with organs specially adapted to the accomplishment of the different acts of their life, to the satisfaction of their needs, and to their preservation. They include men, animals, and plants.

Inorganic beings are those which possess neither vitality nor the power of spontaneous movement, and are formed by the mere aggregation of matter; as minerals, water, air etc.

60. *Is the force which unites the elements of matter in organic and inorganic bodies the same?*

"Yes; the law of attraction is the same for all."

61. *Is there any difference between the matter of organic and inorganic bodies?*

"The matter of both classes of bodies is the same, but in organic bodies it is animalised."

62. *What is the cause of the animalisation of matter?*
"Its union with the vital principle."

63. *Does the vital principle reside in a special agent, or is it only a property of organised matter; in other words, is it an effect or a cause?*

"It is both. Life is an effect produced by the action of an agent upon matter; this agent, without matter, is not life, just as matter cannot become alive without this agent. It gives life to all beings that absorb and assimilate it."

64. *We have seen that spirit and matter are two constituent elements of the universe. Does the vital principle constitute a third element?*

"It is, undoubtedly, one of the elements necessary to the constitution of the universe; but it has its source in a special modification of the universal matter, modified to that end. For you, it is an elementary body, like oxygen or hydrogen, which, nevertheless, are not primitive elements; for all the bodies known to you, though appearing to you to be simple, are modifications of the primal fluid."

— *This statement seems to imply that vitality is not due to a distinct primitive agent, but is a special property of the universal matter, resulting from certain modifications of the latter.*

"Your conclusion is the natural consequence of what we have stated."

65. *Does the vital principle reside in any one of the bodies known to us?*

"It has its source in the universal fluid; it is what you call the magnetic fluid, or the electric fluid, animalised. It is the intermediary, the link between spirit and matter."

66. *Is the vital principle the same for all organic beings?*

"Yes; but modified according to species. It is that principle which gives them the power of originating movement and activity, and distinguishes them from inert matter; for the movement of matter is not spontaneous. Matter is moved; it does not originate movement."

67. *Is vitality a permanent attribute of the vital principle, or is vitality only developed by the play of the organs in which it is manifested?*

"It is only developed in connection with a body. Have we not said that this agent, without matter, is not life? The union of the two is necessary to the production of life."

— *Would it be correct to say that vitality is latent when the vital agent is not united with a body?*

"Yes; that is the case."

The totality of the organs of a body constitutes a sort of mechanism which receives its impulsion from the active or vital principle that resides in them. The vital principle is the motive power of organised bodies. And while the vital principle gives impulsion to the organs in which it resides, the play of those organs develops and keeps up the activity of the vital principle, somewhat as friction develops heat.

Life and Death

68. *What is the cause of the death of organic beings?*

"The exhaustion of their bodily organs."

— *Would it be correct to compare death to the cessation of movement in a machine that had got out of gear?*

"Yes; when the machine gets out of order, its action ceases. When the body falls ill, life withdraws from it."

69. Why is death caused more certainly by a lesion of the heart than by that of any other organ?

"The heart is a life-making machine. But the heart is not the only organ of which the lesion causes death; it is only one of the wheels essential to the working of the machine."

70. What becomes of the matter and the vital principle of organic beings after their death?

"The inert matter is decomposed, and serves to form other bodies; the vital principle returns to the general mass of the universal fluid."

On the death of an organic being, the elements of which its body was composed undergo new combinations that form new beings. These, in their turn, draw the principle of life and activity from the universal source ; they absorb and assimilate it, and restore it again to that source when they cease to exist.

The organs of organic beings are, so to say, impregnated with the vital fluid. This fluid gives to every part of an organised being the activity which brings its parts into union after certain lesions, and reestablishes functions that have been temporarily suspended. But when the elements essential to the play of the organism have been destroyed, or too deeply injured, the vital fluid is powerless to transmit to them the movement which constitutes life, and the being dies.

The organs of a body necessarily react, more or less powerfully, upon one another ; their reciprocity of action results from their harmony among themselves. When from any cause this harmony is destroyed, their functions cease ; just as a piece of machinery comes to a stand-still when the essential portions of its mechanism get out of order, or as a clock stops when its works are worn out by use, accidentally broken, so that the spring is no longer able to keep it going.

We have an image of life and death still more exact in the electric battery. The battery, like all natural bodies, contains electricity in a latent state ; but the electrical phenomena are only manifested when the fluid is set in motion by a special cause. When this movement is superinduced, the battery may be said to become alive ; but when the cause of the electrical activity ceases, the phenomena cease to occur, and the battery relapses into a state of inertia. Organic bodies may thus be said to be a sort of electric battery, in which the movement of the fluid produces the phenomena of life, and in which the cessation of that movement produces death.

The quantity of vital fluid present in organic beings is not the same in all ; it varies in the various species of living beings, and is not constantly the same, either in the same individual or in the individuals of the same species. There are some which may be said to be saturated with it, and others in which it exists in very small proportions. Hence certain species are endowed with a more active and more tenacious life, resulting from the superabundance of the vital fluid present in their organism.

The amount of vital fluid contained in a given organism may be exhausted, and may thus become insufficient for the maintenance of life, unless it be renewed by the absorption and assimilation of the substances in which that fluid resides.

The vital fluid may be transmitted by one individual to another individual. An organisation in which it exists more abundantly may impart it to another in which it is deficient ; and may thus, in certain cases, rekindle the vital flame when on the point of being extinguished.

Intelligence and Instinct

71. *Is intelligence an attribute of the vital principle?*

"No; for the plants live and do not think; they have only organic life. Intelligence and matter are independent of one another; for a body may live without intelligence; but intelligence can only manifest itself by means of material organs. Animalised matter can only be rendered intelligent by its union with spirit."

Intelligence is a faculty which is proper to certain classes of organic beings, and which gives to these the power to think, the will to act, the consciousness of their existence and individuality, and the means of establishing relations with the external world and providing for the needs of their special mode of existence.

We may therefore distinguish : Ist, Inanimate beings, formed of matter alone, without life or intelligence—the bodies of the mineral world ; 2d, Animated non-thinking beings, formed of matter and endowed with vitality, but without intelligence ; 3d, Animated and thinking beings, formed of matter, endowed with vitality, and possessed of an intelligent principle which gives them the faculty of thought.

72. *What is the source of intelligence?*

"We have already told you: the universal intelligence."

— *Wouldt it be correct to say that every intelligent being draws a portion of intelligence from the universal source, and assimilates it as it draws and assimilates the principle of material life?*

"Such a comparison would be far from exact, for intelligence is a faculty that is proper to each being, and constitutes its moral individuality. Besides, we have told you that there are things which man is unable to fathom; and this, for the present, is one of them."

73. *Is instinct independent of intelligence?*

"No, not precisely so, for it is a species of intelligence. Instinct is an unreasoning intelligence, by means of which the lower orders of beings provide for their wants."

74. *Is it possible to establish a line of demarcation between instinct and intelligence; that is to say, to define precisely where the one ends and the other begins?*

"No, for they often blend into one another. But the actions which belong to instinct and those which belong to intelligence are easily distinguished."

75. *Is it correct to say that the instinctive faculties diminish in proportion with the growth of the intellectual faculties?*

"No; instinct always continues to exist, but man neglects it. Instinct, as well as reason, may lead us in the right direction.

Its guidance almost always makes itself felt, and sometimes more surely than that of reason. It never goes astray."

— *Why is it that reason is not always an infallible guide?*

"It would be infallible if it were not perverted by a false education, by pride, and by selfishness. Instinct does not reason. Reason leaves freedom to choice, and gives man free-will."

Instinct is a rudimentary intelligence, differing from intelligence properly so called in this particular, viz., that its manifestations are almost always spontaneous, whereas those of intelligence are the result of combination and of deliberation.

The manifestations of instinct vary according to the differences of species and of their needs. In beings that possess self-consciousness and the perception of things external to themselves, it is allied to intelligence, that is to say, to freedom of will and of action.

BOOK SECOND—THE SPIRIT-WORLD, OR WORLD OF SPIRITS

CHAPTER I

SPIRITS

1. ORIGIN AND NATURE OF SPIRITS—2. PRIMITIVE AND NORMAL WORLD—3. FORM AND UBIQUITY OF SPIRITS—4. THE PERISPIRIT—5. DIFFERENT ORDERS OF SPIRITS—6. SPIRIT-HIERARCHY—7. PROGRESSION OF SPIRITS—8. ANGELS AND DEMONS.

Origin and Nature of Spirits

76. What definition can be given of spirits?

"Spirits may be defined as the intelligent beings of the creation. They constitute the population of the universe, in contradistinction to the forms of the material world."

NOTA. The word **spirit** is here employed to designate the individuality of extra-corporeal beings, and not the universal intelligent element.

77. Are spirits beings distinct from the Deity, or are they only emanations from or portions of the Deity, and called, for that reason, "sons" or "children" of God?

"Spirits are the work of God, just as a machine is the work of the mechanician who made it: the machine is the man's work, but it is not the man. You know that when a man has made a fine or useful thing, he calls it his 'child'—his 'creation.' It is thus with us in relation to God. We are His children in this sense, because we are His work."

78. Have spirits had a beginning, or have they existed, like God, from all eternity?

"If spirits had not had a beginning, they would be equal with God; whereas they are His creation, and subject to His will. That God has existed from all eternity is incontestable; but as to when and how He created us, we know nothing. You may say that we have had no beginning in this sense, that, God being eternal, He must have incessantly created. But as to when and how each of us was made, this, I repeat, is known to no one. It is the great mystery."

79. Since there are two general elements in the universe, viz., the intelligent element and the material element, would it be correct to say that spirits are formed from the intelligent element as inert bodies are formed from the material element?

"It is evident that such is the case. Spirits are the individualisation of the intelligent principle, as bodies are the individualisation of the material principle. It is the epoch and mode of this formation that are unknown to us."

80. Is the creation of spirits always going on, or did it only take place at the beginning of time?

"It is always going on; that is to say, God has never ceased to create."

81. Are spirits formed spontaneously, or do they proceed from one another?

"God creates them as He creates all other creatures, by His will. But we must again repeat that their origin is a mystery."

82. Is it correct to say that spirits are immaterial?

"How is it possible to define a thing in regard to which no terms of comparison exist, and which your language is incompetent to express? Can one who is born blind define light? 'Immaterial' is not the right word; 'incorporeal' would be nearer the truth, for you must understand that a spirit, being a creation, must be something real. Spirit is quintessentialised matter,[1] but matter existing in a state which has no analogue within the circle of your comprehension, and so ethereal that it could not be perceived by your senses."

We say that spirits are immaterial, because their essence differs from everything that we know under the name of "matter." A nation of blind people would have no terms for expressing light and its effects. One who is born blind imagines that the only modes of perception are hearing, smell, taste, and touch: he does not comprehend the other ideas that would be given him by the sense of sight which he lacks. So, in regard to the essence of superhuman beings, we are really blind. We can only define them by means of comparisons that are necessarily imperfect or by an effort of our imagination.

---

[1] Subsequent spirit-communications have declared the universe to consist of three elements or modes of substantiality—viz., Soul, Force, Matter ; and, while asserting that the two former are **non-material substances**, restrict the term "matter" to the element from which bodies are formed.—TRANS.

*83. Is there an end to the duration of spirits? We can under-
stand that the principle from which they emanate should be
eternal; but what we desire to know is, whether their individuality
has a term, and whether, after a given lapse of time, longer or
shorter, the element from which they are formed is not disseminated, does not return to the mass from which they were
produced, as is the case with material bodies? It is difficult to
understand that what has had a beginning should not also have
an end.*

"There are many things that you do not understand, because
your intelligence is limited; but that is no reason for rejecting
them. The child does not understand all that is understood by
its father, nor does an ignorant man understand all that is understood by a learned one. We tell you that the existence of spirits
has no end; that is all we can say on the subject at present."

Primitive and Normal World

84. Do spirits constitute a world apart from that which we see?
"Yes; the world of spirits or incorporeal intelligences."

*85. Which of the two, the spirit-world or the corporeal world,
is the principal one in the order of the universe?*
"The spirit-world. It is pre-existent to, and survives, everything else."

*86. Might the corporeal world never have existed, or cease
to exist, without changing the essentiality of the spirit-world?*
"Yes; they are independent of each other, and yet their correlation is incessant, for they react incessantly upon each other."

*87. Do spirits occupy a determinate and circumscribed region
in space?*
"Spirits are everywhere; the infinitudes of space are peopled
with them in infinite numbers. Unperceived by you, they are
incessantly beside you, observing and acting upon you; for spirits
are one of the powers of Nature, and are the instruments employed
by God for the accomplishment of His providential designs. But
all spirits do not go everywhere; there are regions of which the
entrance is interdicted to those who are less advanced."

Form and Ubiquity of Spirits

*88. Have souls a determinate, circumscribed, and unvarying
form?*

"Not for eyes such as yours; but, for us, they have a form, though one only to be vaguely imagined by you as a flame, a gleam, or an ethereal spark."

— *Is this flame or spark of any colour?*

"If you could see it, it would appear to you to vary from a dull grey to the brilliancy of the ruby, according to the degree of the spirit's purity."

Genii are usually represented with a flame or a star above their foreheads—a sort of allegorical allusion to the essential nature of spirits. The flame or star is placed upon the head because the head is the seat of intelligence.

89. Do spirits employ any time in transporting themselves through space?

"Yes; but their motion is as rapid as that of thought."

— *Is not thought the movement of the soul itself, a transportation of the soul itself to the place or the object thought of by it?*

"Wherever the thought is, there the soul is, since it is the soul that thinks. Thought is an attribute."

90. When a spirit travels from one place to another, is he conscious of the distance he traverses and of the extent of space through which he passes; or is he suddenly transported to the place to which he wishes to go?

"A spirit can travel in either way. He can, if he will, take cognisance of the distance he passes through, or he can rid himself entirely of the sense of distance. This depends on the spirit's will, and also on his degree of purity."

91. Does matter constitute an obstacle to the movement of a spirit?

"No; spirits pass through everything; the air, the earth, water, fire even, are equally accessible to them."

92. Have spirits the gift of ubiquity? In other words, can a spirit divide itself, or exist at several points of space at the same time?

"There can be no division of any given spirit; but every spirit is a centre which radiates in all directions, and it is thus that a spirit may appear to be in several places at once. The sun is only one body, yet it radiates in all directions, and sends out its rays to great distances; but it is not divided."

— *Have all spirits the same power of radiation?*

"There is a great difference between them in this respect: it depends on the degree of their purity."

Each spirit is an indivisible unity, but each spirit has the power of extending his thought on all sides without thereby dividing himself. It is only in this sense that the gift of ubiquity attributed to spirits is to be understood. It is thus that a spark sends out its brightness far and wide, and may be perceived from every point of the horizon. It is thus, also, that a man, without changing his place, and without dividing himself, may transmit orders, signals, etc., to many distant points in many different directions.

Perispirit

93. *Is the spirit, properly so called, without a covering, or is it, as some declare, surrounded by a substance of some kind?*

"The spirit is enveloped in a substance which would appear to you as mere vapour, but which, nevertheless, appears very gross to us, thought it is sufficiently vaporous to allow the spirit to float in the atmosphere, and to transport himself through space at pleasure."

As the germ of a fruit is surrounded by the **perisperm,** so the spirit, properly so called, is surrounded by an envelope which, by analogy, may be designated as the **perispirit.**

94. *Whence does the spirit draw its semi-material envelope?*

"From the universal fluid of each globe. For this reason the perispirit is not the same in all globes. In passing from one globe to another, the spirit changes its envelope as you change a garment."

— *When spirits who inhabit worlds of a higher degree than ours come among us, are they obliged to take on a grosser order of perispirit?*

"Yes; they are obliged to clothe themselves with your matter in order to be able to enter your world."

95. *Does the semi-material envelope of the spirit assume determinate forms, and can it become perceptible for us?*

"Yes; it can assume any form that the spirit may choose to give to it. It is thus that a spirit is able sometimes to make himself visible to you, whether in dreams or in your waking state, and can take a form that may be visible, and even palpable, for your senses."

Different Orders of Spirits

96. *Are all spirits equal, or does there exist among them a hierarchy of ranks?*

"They are of different degrees according to the degree of purification to which they have attained."

Spirit — Hierarchy

97. Is there a fixed number of order or degrees of purification among spirits?

"The number of such orders is unlimited, because there is nothing like a barrier or line of demarcation between the different degrees of elevation; and, therefore, as there are no fixed or arbitrary divisions among spirits, the number of orders may be increased or diminished according to the point of view from which they are considered. Nevertheless, if we consider the general characteristics of spirits, we may reduce them to three principal orders or degrees.

"We may place in the first or highest rank those who have reached the degree of relative perfection which constitutes what may be called 'pure spirits.' We may place in the second rank those who have reached the middle of the ascensional ladder, those who have achieved the degree of purification in which aspiration after perfection has become the ruling desire. We may place in the third or lowest rank all those imperfect spirits who are still on the lower rungs of the ladder. They are characterised by ignorance, the love of evil, and all the low passions that retard their progress upwards."

98. Have spirits of the second order only the aspiration after perfection; have they also the power to achieve it?

"They have that power in degrees proportionate to the degree of purification at which they have severally arrived. Some of them are distinguished by their scientific knowledge, others by their wisdom and their kindness; but all of them have still to undergo the discipline of trial through temptation and suffering."

99. Are all spirits of the third order essentially bad?

"No. Some of them are inactive and neutral, not doing either good or evil; others, on the contrary, take pleasure in evil, and are delighted when they find an opportunity of doing wrong. Others, again, are frivolous, foolish, fantastic, mischievous rather than wicked, tricksy rather than positively malicious; amusing themselves by mystifying the human beings on whom they are able to act, and causing them various petty annoyances for their own diversion."

Spirit — Hierarchy

100. Preliminary Observations. — The classification of spirits is based upon the degree of their advancement, upon the qualities which they have acquired, and upon the imperfections from which they have still to free themselves. This classification, however, is by no means absolute. It is only in its totality that the character of each category is distinctly marked, for each category merges in the one above it by imperceptible gradations, the peculiarities of the successive categories shading off into one another at their extremities, as is the case in the various reigns of nature, in the colours of the rainbow, in the phases of a human life. Spirits may, therefore, be divided into a number of classes more or less considerable, according to the point of view from which we consider the subject. It is in this matter as in all other systems of scientific classification. The systems adopted may be more or less complete, more or less rational, more or less convenient for the understanding; but, whatever may be their form, they change nothing in regard to the facts of the science which employs them. That the answers of spirits, when questioned on this point, should vary as to the number of the categories into which they are divided is, therefore, a matter of no practical importance. Too much weight has been attributed to this apparent contradiction by those who forget that disincarnate intelligences attach no importance whatever to mere conventionalities. For them, the meaning of a statement is the only important point about it. They leave to us the question of its form, the choice of terms and of classification,—in a word, all that belongs to the making of systems.

Another thing that should never be lost sight of is the fact that there are among spirits, as well as among men, some who are very ignorant, and that we cannot be too much on our guard against a tendency to believe that all spirits know everything simply because they are spirits. The work of classification demands method, analysis, and a thorough knowledge of the subject investigated. But those who, in the spirit-world, possess only a small amount of knowledge, are as incompetent as are ignorant human beings to embrace the whole of any subject or to formulate a system. They have no idea, or but a very imperfect one, of any sort of classification. All spirits superior to themselves appear to them to be of the highest order; for they are as incapable of discriminating the various shades of knowledge, capacity, and morality by which they are distinguished, as one of our savages would be to discriminate the various characteristics of civilised men. And even those who are capable of this discrimination may vary, in their appreciation of details, according to their special point of view, especially in regard to a matter which, from its very nature, has nothing fixed or absolute about it. Linnæus, Jussieu, Tournefort, have each their special system of classification, but the nature of botany has not been changed by this diversity of system among botanists. The latter have not invented either plants or their characteristics; they have merely observed certain analogies, according to which they have formed certain groups or classes. We have proceeded in the same way. We have not invented either spirits or their characteristics. We have seen and observed them, we have judged them by their own words and acts, and we have classed them by order of similitude, basing our classification on the data furnished by themselves.

The higher spirits generally admit the existence of three principal categories, or main divisions, among the people of the other world. In the lowest of these, at the bottom of the ladder, are the imperfect spirits who are characterised by the predominance of the instincts of materiality over the moral nature, and by the propensity to evil. Those of the second degree are characterised by the predominance of the moral nature over the material instincts, and by the desire of good. They constitute the category of good spirits. The first or highest category consists of those who have reached the state of pure spirits, and have thus attained to the supreme degree of perfection imaginable by us.

This division of spirits into three well-marked categories appears to us to be perfectly rational; and, having arrived at this general classification, it only remained for us to bring out, through a sufficient number of subdivisions, the principal shades of the three great spirit-categories thus established. And this we have done, with the aid of the spirits themselves, whose friendly instructions have never failed us in the carrying out of the work upon which we have been led to enter.

With the aid of the following table it will be easy for us to determine the rank and degree of superiority or inferiority of the spirits with whom we may enter into communication, and, consequently, the degree of esteem and confidence to which they are entitled. The power of determining these points may be said to constitute the key to spiritist investigation; for it alone, by enlightening us in regard to the intellectual and moral inequalities of spirits, can explain the anomalies presented by spirit-communications. We have, however, to remark that spirits do not, in all cases, belong exclusively to such and such a class. Their

progress in knowledge and purity being only accomplished
gradually, and often, for a time, more in the one than in the
other, they may unite the characteristics of several subdivisions;
a point which is easily settled by observing their language and
their acts.

THIRD ORDER—IMPERFECT SPIRITS

101. General Characteristics.—Predominant influence of matter
over spirit. Propension to evil. Ignorance, pride, selfishness,
and all the evil passions which result from these.

They have the intuition of the existence of God, but they
have no comprehension of Him.

They are not all of them thoroughly bad; in many of them
there is more of frivolity, want of reasoning power, and love
of mischief, than of downright wickedness. Some of them do
neither good nor evil; but the very fact that they do no good
denotes their inferiority. Others, on the contrary, take pleasure
in evil, and are gratified when they find an opportunity of doing
wrong.

Among spirits of this order, a certain amount of intelligence is
often allied with malice and the love of mischief; but, whatever
may be their intellectual development, their ideas are wanting in
elevation, and their sentiments are more or less abject.

Their knowledge of the things of the spirit-world is narrow,
and the little they know about them is confused with the ideas and
prejudices of the corporeal life. They can give only false and
incomplete notions of the spirit-world; but the attentive observer
may always find in their communications, however imperfect, the
confirmation of the great truths proclaimed by spirits of the higher
orders.

Their character is revealed by their language. Every spirit
who, in his communications, betrays an evil intention, may be
ranged in the third order; consequently every evil thought suggested
to our mind comes to us from a spirit of that order.

They see the happiness enjoyed by good spirits, and this sight
causes them perpetual torment; for they experience all the agonies
produced by envy and jealousy.

They preserve the remembrance and the perception of the sufferings of corporeal life; and this impression is often more painful
than the reality. They suffer, in fact, both from the ills they
have themselves endured, and from those which they have caused

to be endured by others. And as these sufferings endure for a very long time, they believe themselves to be destined to suffer for ever. God, for their punishment, wills that they should believe this.

They may be subdivided into five principal classes:—

102. Tenth Class—Impure Spirits.—They are inclined to evil, and make it the object of all their thoughts and activities. As spirits, they give to men perfidious counsels, stir up discord and distrust, and assume every sort of mask in order the more effectually to deceive. They beset those whose character is weak enough to lead them to yield to their suggestions, and whom they thus draw aside from the path of progress, rejoicing when they are to retard their advancement by causing them to succumb under the appointed trials of the corporeal life.

Spirits of this class may be recognised by their language, for the employment of coarse or trivial expressions by spirits, as by men, is always an indication of moral, if not of intellectual, inferiority. Their communications show the baseness of their inclinations; and though they may try to impose upon us by speaking with an appearance of reason and propriety, they are unable to keep up that false appearance, and end by betraying their real quality.

Certain nations have made of them infernal deities; others designate them by the name of *demons, evil genii, evil spirits.*

The human beings in whom they are incarnated are addicted to all the vices engendered by vile and degrading passions—sensuality, cruelty, roguery, hypocrisy, cupidity, avarice. They do evil for its own sake, without any definite motive; and, from hatred to all that is good, they generally choose their victims from among honest and worthy people. They are the pests of humanity, to whatever rank of society they belong; and the varnish of a civilised education is ineffectual to cure or to hide their degrading defects.

103. Ninth Class — Frivolous Spirits. — They are ignorant, mischievous, unreasonable, and addicted to mockery. They meddle with everything, and reply to every question without paying any attention to truth. They delight in causing petty annoyances, in raising false hopes of petty joys, in misleading people by mystifications and trickery. The spirits vulgarly called hobgoblins, will-o'-the-wisps, gnomes, etc., belong to this class. They are under the orders of spirits of a higher category, who make use of them as we do of servants.

In their communications with men their language is often witty
and facetious, but shallow. They are quick to seize the oddities
and absurdities of men and things, on which they comment with
sarcastic sharpness. If they borrow distinguished names, as they
are fond of doing, it is rather for the fun of the thing than from
any intention to deceive by so doing.

104. *Eighth Class—Spirits who Pretend to more Science than
they Possess.*—Their knowledge is often considerable, but they
imagine themselves to know a good deal more than they know in
reality. Having made a certain amount of progress from various
points of view, their language has an air of gravity that may
easily give a false impression as to their capacities and enlightenment; but their ideas are generally nothing more than the reflexion
of the prejudices and false reasoning of their terrestrial life. Their
statements contain a mixture of truths and absurdities, in the
midst of which traces of presumption, pride, jealousy, and
obstinacy, from which they have not yet freed themselves, are
abundantly perceptible.

105. *Seventh Class—Neutral Spirits.*—They are not sufficiently
advanced to take an active part in doing good, nor are they bad
enough to be active in doing wrong. They incline sometimes to
the one, sometimes to the other; and do not rise above the ordinary
level of humanity, either in point of morality or of intelligence.
They are strongly attached to the things of this world, whose gross
satisfactions they regret.

106. *Sixth Class—Noisy and Boisterous Spirits.*—Spirits of
this kind do not, strictly speaking, form a distinct class in virtue
of their personal qualities; they may belong to all the classes of
the third order. They often manifest their presence by the production of phenomena perceptible by the senses, such as raps,
the movement and abnormal displacing of solid bodies, the agitation
of the air, etc. They appear to be, more than any other class of
spirits, attached to matter; they seem to be the principal agents
in determining the vicissitudes of the elements of the globe, and
to act upon the air, water, fire, and the various bodies in the entrails
of the earth. Whenever these phenomena present a character of
intention and intelligence, it is impossible to attribute them to a
mere fortuitous and physical cause. All spirits are able to produce
physical phenomena; but spirits of elevated degree usually leave
them to those of a lower order, more apt for action upon matter

than for the things of intelligence, and, when they judge it to be useful to produce physical manifestations, employ spirits of subaltern degree as their auxiliaries.

SECOND ORDER—GOOD SPIRITS

107. General Characteristics.—Predominance of spirit over matter; desire of excellence. Their qualities and their power for good are proportionate to the degree at which they have arrived. Some of them possess scientific knowledge, others have acquired wisdom and charity; the more advanced among them combine knowledge with moral excellence. Not being yet completely dematerialised, they preserve the traces of their corporeal existence, more or less strongly marked, according to their rank—traces which are seen either in their mode of expressing themselves, in their habits, or even, in some cases, in the characteristic eccentricities and hobbies still retained by them. But for these weaknesses and imperfections they would be able to pass into the category of spirits of the first order.

They have acquired the comprehension of the idea of God and of infinity, and already share the felicity of the higher spheres. They find their happiness both in the accomplishment of good and in the prevention of evil. The affection by which they are united affords them ineffable delight, troubled neither by envy, remorse, nor any other of the evil passions which make the torment of spirits of lower degree; but they have still to undergo the discipline of trial until they have completed the work of their purification.

As spirits, they infuse good and noble thoughts into the minds of men, turn them from the path of evil, protect those whose course of life renders them worthy of their aid, and neutralise by their suggestions, the influence of lower spirits on the minds of those who do not willingly yield to the evil counsels of the latter.

The human beings in whom they are incarnated are upright and benevolent; they are actuated neither by pride, selfishness, nor ambition; they feel neither hatred, rancour, envy, nor jealousy, and do good for its own sake.

To this order belong the spirits commonly designated in the popular beliefs by the names of *good genii, protecting genii, good spirits.* In periods of ignorance and superstition, men have regarded them as beneficent divinities.

They may be divided into four principal groups:—

108.   Fifth Class—Benevolent Spirits.—Their dominant quality
is kindness.   They take pleasure in rendering service to men and
in protecting them, but their knowledge is somewhat narrow.
They have progressed in morality rather than in intelligence.

109.   Fourth Class — Learned Spirits. — They are specially
distinguished by the extent of their knowledge.   They are less
interested in moral questions than in scientific investigation, for
which they have a greater aptitude; but their scientific studies are
always prosecuted with a view to practical utility, and they are
entirely free from the base passions common to spirits of the
lower degrees of advancement.

110.   Third Class—Wise Spirits.—The most elevated moral
qualities form their distinctive characteristics.   Without having
arrived at the possession of unlimited knowledge, they have reached
a development of intellectual capacity that enables them to judge
correctly of men and of things.

111.   Second Class—High Spirits.—They unite, in a very
high degree, scientific knowledge, wisdom, and goodness.   Their
language, inspired only by the purest benevolence, is always noble
and elevated, often sublime.   Their superiority renders them more
apt than any others to impart to us just and true ideas in relation
to the incorporeal world, within the limits of the knowledge permitted to mankind.   They willingly enter into communication with
those who seek for truth in simplicity and sincerity, and who are
sufficiently freed from the bonds of materiality to be capable of
understanding it; but they turn from those whose inquiries are
prompted only by curiosity, or who are drawn away from the
path of rectitude by the attractions of materiality.

When, under exceptional circumstances, they incarnate themselves in this earth, it is always for the accomplishment of a
mission of progress; and they thus show us the highest type of
perfection to which we can aspire in the present world.

FIRST ORDER—PURE SPIRITS

112.   General Characteristics.—The influence of matter null; a
superiority, both intellectual and moral, so absolute as to constitute
what, in comparison with the spirits of all the other orders, may
be termed perfection.

113. First and only Class.—They have passed up through every degree of the scale of progress, and have freed themselves from all the impurities of materiality. Having attained the sum of perfection of which created beings are susceptible, they have no longer to undergo either trials or expiations. Being no longer subject to reincarnation in perishable bodies, they enter on the life of eternity in the immediate presence of God. They are in the enjoyment of a beatitude which is unalterable, because they are no longer subject to the wants or vicissitudes of material life; but this beatitude is not *the monotonous idleness of perpetual contemplation.* They are the messengers and ministers of God, the executors of His orders in the maintenance of universal harmony. They exercise a sovereign command over all spirits inferior to themselves, aid them in accomplishing the work of their purification, and assign to each of them a mission proportioned to the progress already made by them. To assist men in their distresses, to excite them to the love of good or to the expiation of the faults which keep them back on the road to the supreme felicity, are for them congenial occupations. They are sometimes spoken of as angels, archangels, or seraphim.

They can, when they choose to do so, enter into communication with men; but presumptuous indeed would he be who should pretend to have them at his orders.

Progression of Spirits

114. Are spirits good or bad by nature, or are they the same spirits made better through their own efforts?

"The same spirits made better through their own efforts. In growing better they pass from a lower to a higher order."

115. Are some spirits created good and others created bad?

"God has created all spirits in a state of simplicity and ignorance; that is to say, without knowledge. He has given to each of them a mission, with a view to enlighten them and to make them gradually arrive at perfection through the knowledge of the truth, and thus to bring them nearer and nearer to Himself. This perfection is, for them, the condition of eternal and unalloyed happiness. Spirits acquire knowledge by passing through the trials imposed on them by God. Some of them accept these trials with submission, and arrive more quickly at the aim of their destiny: others undergo them with murmuring, and thus remain, through their own fault, at a distance from the perfection and the felicity promised to them."

— *According to this statement, it would appear that spirits, at their origin, are like children, ignorant and without experience, but acquiring, little by little, the knowledge which they lack, by passing through the different phases of human life?*

"Yes; the comparison is correct. The child, if rebellious, remains ignorant and faulty; he profits more or less according to his docility. But the life of man has a term; whereas that of spirits stretches out into infinity."

116. *Do any spirits remain for ever in the lower ranks?*

"No; all become perfect. They change in course of time, however long may be the process of amendment; for, as we have already said, a just and merciful parent cannot condemn his children to eternal banishment. Can you suppose that God, so great, so good, so just, is less kind than you are?"

117. *Does it depend on the spirits themselves to hasten their progress towards perfection?*

"Certainly; they reach the goal more or less quickly according to the strength of their desire and the degree of their submission to the will of God. Does not a docile child learn faster than one who is obstinate and idle?"

118. *Can spirits degenerate?*

"No; in proportion as they advance, they understand what has retarded their progress. When a spirit has finished with any given trial, he has learned the lesson of that trial, and never forgets it. He may remain stationary; but he never degenerates."

119. *Could God exonerate spirits from the trials which they have to undergo in order to reach the highest rank?*

"If they had been created perfect, they would not have merited the enjoyment of the benefits of that perfection. Where would be the merit without the struggle? Besides, the inequality which exists between spirits is necessary to the development of their personality; and, moreover, the mission which each spirit accomplishes at each step of his progress is an element of the providential plan for ensuring the harmony of the universe."

Since, in social life, all men may reach the highest posts, we might as well ask why the sovereign of a country does not make a general of each of his soldiers, why all subaltern functionaries are not made heads of departments, why all scholars are not schoolmasters. But there is this difference between the life of the social and the spirit worlds, viz., that the first is limited, and does not afford to every one the possibility of raising himself to the highest rank ; whereas the second is unlimited, and ensures to every one the possibility of attaining to supreme degree.

120. Do all spirits pass by the road of evil to arrive at good?
"Not by the road of evil, but by that of ignorance."

121. How is it that some spirits have followed the road of good, and others the road of evil?
"Have they not their free-will? God has not created any spirits bad; He has created them simple and ignorant, that is to say, possessing an equal aptitude for good and for evil. Those who become bad become so of their own free-will."

122. How can spirits, at their origin, when they have not yet acquired self-consciousness, possess freedom of choice between good and evil? Is there in them any principle, any tendency, which inclines them towards either road rather than towards the other?
"Free-will is developed in proportion as the spirit acquires the consciousness of himself. Freedom would not exist for the spirit if his choice were solicited by a cause independent of his will. The cause which determines his choice is not in him, but is exterior to him, in the influences to which he voluntarily yields in virtue of the freedom of his will. It is this choice that is represented under the grand figure of the fall of man and of original sin. Some spirits have yielded to temptation; others have withstood it."

— Whence come the influences that act upon him?
"From the imperfect spirits, who seek to take possession of him and to dominate him, and who are happy to see him succumb. It is this temptation that is allegorically pictured as Satan."

— Does this influence act upon a spirit only at its origin?
"It follows him through all the phases of his existence as a spirit, until he has acquired such thorough self-command that evil spirits renounce the attempt to obsess him."

123. Why has God permitted it to be possible for spirits to take the wrong road?
"The wisdom of God is shown in the freedom of choice which He leaves to every spirit, for each has thus the merit of his deeds."

124. Since there are spirits who, from the beginning, follow unswervingly the right path, and others who wander into the lowest depths of evil, there are, no doubt, many degrees of deviation etween these two extremes?

"Yes, certainly; and these degrees constitute the paths of the great majority of spirits."

125. *Will the spirits who have chosen the wrong road be able to reach the same degree of elevation as the others?*

"Yes; but *the eternities* will be longer in their case."

This expression, **"the eternities,"** must be understood as referring to the belief of spirits of inferior degree in the perpetuity their sufferings, resulting from the fact that it is not given to them to foresee the termination of those sufferings, and that this conviction of the perpetuity of the latter is renewed after every new trial to which they have succumbed.

126. *Are spirits who have reached the supreme degree after wandering into the wrong road less meritorious than the others in the sight of God?*

"God regards the wanderers who have returned to the right road with the same approval and the same affection as the others. They have been classed, for a time, as evil spirits, because they succumbed to the temptation of evil; but, before their fall, they were merely neutral in regard to good and evil, like all other spirits."

127. *Are all spirits created equal in point of intellectual capacity?*

"They are all created equal, but not knowing from whence they come; for their free-will must have its fling. They progress more or less rapidly in intelligence as in morality."

The spirits who, from the beginning, follow the right road, do not thereby attain at once to the state of perfection ; for, although they are free from evil tendencies, they have none the less to acquire the experience and the varied knowledge indispensable to their perfection. They may be compared to children who, however good their natural instincts, need to be developed and enlightened, and who cannot attain to maturity without transition. But, just as some men are good and others bad from their infancy, so some spirits are good and others bad from their beginning ; with this radical difference, however, that the child possesses instincts already formed, whereas the spirit, at his formation, is neither bad nor good, but possesses all possible tendencies, and strikes out his path, in the direction of good or evil, through the action of his own free-will.

128. *Do the beings whom we call angels, archangels, seraphim, form a special category of a nature different from that of other spirits?*

"No; the spirits who have purified themselves from all imperfection, have reached the highest degree of the scale of progress, and united in themselves all species of perfection."

The word **angel** is generally supposed to imply the idea of moral perfection ; but it is often applied, nevertheless, to all beings, good or bad, beyond the pale of humanity. We say, "a good angel," "a bad angel," "an angel of light," "the angel of darkness," etc. In those cases, it is synonymous with **spirit** or **genius.** It is employed here in its highest sense.

129. Have the angels passed up through all the degrees of progress?

"They have passed up through all those degrees, but with the difference which we have already mentioned. Some of them, accepting their mission without murmuring, have reached the goal more quickly ; others have been longer in reaching the same goal."

130. If the opinion which admits that some beings have been created perfect and superior to all others be erroneous, how is it that this opinion is to be found in the tradition of almost every people?

"Your world has not existed from all eternity. Long before it was called into being, hosts of spirits had already attained to the supreme degree, and, therefore, the people of your earth naturally supposed those perfected spirits to have always been at the same degree of elevation."

131. Are there any demons in the usual acceptation of that term?

"If demons existed, they would be the work of God; but would it be just on the part of God to have created beings condemned eternally to evil and to misery? If demons exist, it is in your low world, and in other worlds of similar degree, that they are to be found. They are the human hypocrites who represent a just God as being cruel and vindictive, and who imagine that they make themselves agreeable to Him by the abominations they commit in His name."

It is only in its modern acceptation that the word **demon** implies the idea of evil spirits, for the Greek work **daimōn,** from which it is derived, signifies **genius, intelligence,** and is applied indiscriminately to all incorporeal beings, whether good or bad.

Demons or devils,[1] according to the common acceptation of these words, are supposed to be a class of beings essentially bad. If they exist, they must necessarily be, like everything else, a creation of God ; but God, who is sovereignly just and good, cannot have created beings predestined to evil by their very nature, and condemned beforehand to eternal misery. If, on the contrary, they are not a creation of God, they must either have existed, like Him, from all eternity, or there must be several creators. The first requisite of every theory is to be consistent with itself ; but that which asserts the existence of demons, in the popular acceptation of

---

[1] The Zoroastrian term, **Dev,** is the designation of spirits under the orders of Ahriman, the genius of evil, who, with their leader, will eventually be "converted," and share the beatitude of the just.—**Zendavesta,** A. DU PERRON. Paris, 1771. Vol. i. p. 2, pp. 164, 202. etc. — TRANS.

the term, lacks this essential condition of theoretic soundness. It was natural that the religious belief of peoples who, knowing nothing of the attributes of God, were backward enough to admit the existence of maleficent deities, should also admit the existence of demons ; but, on the part of those who acknowledge the goodness of God to be His distinguishing quality, it is illogical and contradictory to suppose that He can have created beings doomed to evil, and destined to do evil for ever, for such a supposition is the negation of His goodness. The partisans of the belief in devils appeal to the words of Christ in support of their doctrine ; and it is certainly not we who would contest the autority of His teachings, which we would fain see established, not merely on the lips of men, but also in their hearts. But are those partisans quite sure of the meaning attached by Him to the word "devil"? Is it not fully admitted that the allegorical form is one of the distinctive characteristics of His utterances, and that the Gospels contain many things which are not to be taken literally? To prove that such is the case, we need only quote the following passage:—

"Immediately after the tribulation of those days the sun shall be darkened, and the moon shall not give her light, and the stars shall fall from heaven, and the powers of the heavens shall be shaken : And then shall appear the sign of the Son of Man in heaven. .... Verily I say unto you, This generation shall not pass till all these things are fulfilled" (Matt. xxiv, 29, 30, 34.) Have we not seen that the **form** of the biblical text, in reference to the creation and movement of the earth, is contradicted by the discoveries of science? May it not be the same in regard to certain figurative expressions employed by Christ in order to adapt His teachings to the time and the scene of His mission? Christ could not have made a statement knowing it to be false. If, therefore, His sayings contain statements which appear to be contrary to reason, it is evident either that we do not understand their meaning or that we have interpreted them erroneously.

Men have done in regard to devils what they have done in regard to angels. Just as they have imagined that there are beings who were created perfect from all eternity, so they have imagined that spirits of the lower degrees were beings essentially and eternally bad. The words **demon, devil**, ought, therefore, to be understood as indicating impure spirits who are often no better that the imaginary beings designated by those names, but with this difference, viz., that their state of impurity and inferiority is only transitory. They are the imperfect spirits who rebel against the discipline of trial to which they are subjected, and who, therefore, have to undergo that discipline for a longer period, but who will, nevertheless, reach the goal in time, when they shall have made up their minds to do so. The words **demon, devil,** might accordingly be employed in this sense ; but as they have come to be understood exclusively as conveying the meaning now shown to be false, their employment might lead into error by seeming to recognise the existence of beings specially created for evil.

As regards the term "Satan," it is evidently a personification of the principle of evil under an allegorical form ; for it is impossible to admit the existence of a being who fights against God as an independent and rival power, and whose sole business in life is to contravene His designs. As images and figures are necessary in order to strike the human imagination, men have pictured to themselves the beings of the incorporeal world under a material form, with attributes indicative of their good or bad qualities. It is thus that the ancients, wishing to personify the idea of time, represented it under the figure of an old man with a scythe and an hour-glass. To have personified it under the figure of a youth would have been contrary to common sense. The same may be said of the allegories of Fortune, Truth, etc. The moderns have represented the angels or pure spirits under the form of radiant beings with white wings—emblem of purity ; Satan, with horns, claws, and the attributes of bestiality—emblems of the lowest passions; and the vulgar, prone to understand such representations literally, have taken these allegorical embodiments of abstract ideas for real personalities, as they formerly did in regard to the allegorical personifications of the old mythology.

CHAPTER II

INCARNATION OF SPIRITS

1. AIM OF INCARNATION—2. THE SOUL—3. MATERIALISM.

Aim of Incarnation

132. What is the aim of the incarnation of spirits?

"It is a necessity imposed on them by God, as the means of attaining perfection. For some of them it is an expiation; for others, a mission. In order to attain perfection, *it is necessary for them to undergo all the vicissitudes of corporeal existence.* It is the experience acquired by expiation that constitutes its usefulness. Incarnation has also another aim—viz., that of fitting the spirit to perform his share in the work of creation; for which purpose he is made to assume a corporeal apparatus in harmony with the material state of each world into which he is sent, and by means of which he is enabled to accomplish the special work, in connection with that world, which has been appointed to him by the divine ordering. He is thus made to contribute his quota towards the general weal, while achieving his own advancement."

The action of corporeal beings is necessary to the carrying on of the work of the universe ; but God in His wisdom has willed that this action should furnish them with the means of progress and of advancement towards Himself. And thus, through an admirable law of His providence, all things are linked together, and solidarity is established between all the realms of nature.

133. Is incarnation necessary for the spirits who, from the beginning, have followed the right road?

"All are created simple and ignorant; they gain instruction in the struggles and tribulations of corporeal life. God, being just, could not make some of them happy, without trouble and without exertion, and consequently without merit."

— *But it so, what do spirits gain by having followed the right road, since they are not thereby exempted from the pains of corporeal life?*

"They arrive more quickly at the goal. And besides, the sufferings of life are often a consequence of the imperfection of the spirit; therefore, the fewer his imperfections, the less will be his sufferings. He who is neither envious, jealous, avaricious, nor ambitious, will not have to undergo the torments which are a consequence of those defects."

The Soul

134. What is the soul?
"An incarnate spirit."
— *What was the soul before its union with a body?*
"A spirit."
— *Souls and spirits are, then, the very same thing?*
"Yes; souls are only spirits. Before uniting itself with a body, the soul is one of the intelligent beings who people the invisible world, and who temporarily assume a fleshly body in order to effect their purification and enlightenment."

135. Is there in man anything else than a soul and a body?
"There is the link which unites the soul and the body."
— *What is the nature of that link?*
"It is semi-material—that is to say, of a nature intermediate between soul and body, as it must necessarily be, in order that they may be enabled to communicate with each other. It is by means of this link that the spirit acts upon matter, and that matter acts reciprocally upon the spirit."

Man is thus formed of three essential elements or parts :—
Ist. The body, or material being, analogous to the animals, and animated by the same vital principle ;
2d. The soul, or incarnated spirit, of which the body is the habitation :
3d. The intermediary principle, or **perispirit**; a semi-material substance, which constitutes the innermost envelope of the spirit, and unites the soul with the body. This triplicity is analogous to that of the fruit, which consists of the germ, the perisperm, and the rind or shell.

136. Is the soul independent of the vital principle?
"The body is only the envelope of the soul, as we have repeatedly told you."
— *Can a body exist without a soul?*
"Yes; but it is only when the body ceases to live that the soul quits it. Previous to birth, the union between the soul and the body is not complete; but, when this union is definitively established, it is only the death of the body that can sever the bonds that unite it to the soul, and thus allow the soul to withdraw

from it. Organic life may vitalise a body without a soul, but the soul cannot inhabit a body deprived of organic life."

— *What would our body be if it had no soul?*

"A mass of flesh without intelligence; anything you choose to call it, excepting *a man*."

137. *Can the same spirit incarnate itself in two different bodies at the same time?*

"No; the spirit is indivisible, and cannot simultaneously animate two different beings." (*Vide,* in *The Medium's Book*, the chapter on *Bi-corporeality and Transfiguration.*)

138. *What is to be thought of the opinion of those who regard the soul as being the principle of material life?*

"That is a question of definition; we attach but slight importance to mere words. You should begin by agreeing among yourselves as to the exact meaning of the expressions you employ."

139. *Certain spirits, and certain philosophers before them, have defined the soul as* "An animated spark that has emanated from the Great Whole"; *why this contradiction?*

"There is nothing contradictory in such a definition. Everything depends on the meaning you attribute to the words you use. Why have you not a word for each thing?"

The word **soul** is employed to express very different things. Sometimes it is used to designate the principle of life ; and in this sense it is correct to say, **figuratively,** that the soul is an animated spark that has emanated from the Great Whole. These latter words designate the universal source of the vital principle, of which each being absorbs a portion, that returns to the general mass after its death. This idea does not exclude that of a moral being, a distinct personality, independent of matter, and preserving its own individuality It is this being which, at other times, is called **the soul**, and it is in this sense that we speak of the soul as an incarnate **spirit**. In giving different definitions of **soul**, the spirits who have given them have spoken according to their various ways of applyng that word, and also according to the terrestrial ideas with which they are more or less imbued This apparent confusion results from the insufficiency of human language, which does not possess a specific word for each idea ; an insufficiency that gives rise to a vast number of misapprehensions and discussions. It is for this reason that the higher spirits tell us to begin by distinctly defining the meaning of the words we employ.[1]

140. *What is to be thought of the theory according to which the soul is subdivided into as many parts as there are muscles in the body, and thus presides over each of the bodily functions?*

"That, again, depends on the meaning attached to the word *soul*. If by *soul* is meant the vital fluid, that theory is right; if

---

[1] **Vide,** in the Introduction, the explanation of the word **soul,** sec. ii.

the word is used to express an incarnate spirit, it is wrong. We have already told you that a spirit is indivisible; it transmits movement to the bodily organs through the intermediary fluids, but it undergoes no division."

— *Nevertheless, there are spirits who have given this definition.*

"Spirits who are ignorant may mistake the effect for the cause."

The soul acts through the intermediary of the bodily organs, and those organs are animated by the vital fluid which is distributed among them, and more abundantly in those which constitute the centres or **foci** of movement for each organism. But this explanation becomes inadmissible when the term **soul** is employed to designate the spirit which inhabits the body during life and quits it at death.

141. *Is there any thruth in the opinion of those who suppose that the soul is exterior to the body and environs it?*

"The soul is not shut up in the body like a bird in a cage. It radiates in all directions, and manifests itself outside the body as a light radiates from a glass globe, or as a sound is propagated from a sonorous centre. In this sense the soul may be said to be exterior to the body, but it is not therefore to be considered as enveloping the body. The soul has two envelopes; the first, or innermost, of these, of a light and subtle nature, is what you call the *perispirit*; the other, gross, material, heavy, is the body. The soul is the centre of both these envelopes, like the germ in the stone of the fruit, as we have already said."

142. *What is to be thought of that other theory according to which the formation of the soul of the child is carried on to completion during the successive periods of the human lifetime?*

"The spirit is a unit; and is as entire in the child as in the adult. It is only the bodily organs, or instruments of the manifestations of the soul, that are gradually developed and completed in the course of a lifetime. Here, again, you mistake the effect for the cause."

143. *Why do not all spirits define the soul in the same way?*

"All spirits are not equally enlightened in regard to these matters. Some spirits are still so little advanced intellectually as to be incapable of understanding abstract ideas; they are like children in your world. Other spirits are full of false learning, and make a vain parade of words in order to impose their authority upon those who listen to them. They, also, resemble too many in your world. And besides, even spirits who are really enlightened may express themselves in terms which appear to be different, but which, at bottom, mean the same thing, especially in regard to matters which your language is incapable of expressing clearly, and which can only be spoken of to you by means of figures and comparisons that you mistake for literal statements of fact."

144. What is to be understood by the soul of the world?

"The universal principle of life and intelligence from which individualities are produced. But, very often, they who make use of these terms do not know what they mean by them. The word *soul* is so elastic that every one interprets it according to his own imaginings. Certain persons have also attributed a soul to the earth, which must be understood as indicating the assemblage of devoted spirits who direct your actions in the right direction when you listen to them, and who are, as it were, the lieutenants of God in the administration of your globe."

145. How is it that so many philosophers, both ancient and modern, have so long been discussing psychological questions without having arrived at the truth?

"Those men were precursors of the eternal truths of the true spiritist doctrine, for which they have prepared the way. They were men, and therefore subject to error, because they often mistook their own ideas for the true light; but their very errors have served the cause of truth by bringing into relief both sides of the argument. Moreover, among those errors are to be found many great truths which a comparative study of the various theories thus put forth would enable you to discover."

146. Has the soul a circumscribed and determinate seat in the body?

"No but it may be said to reside more especially in the head, in the case of men of great genius and of all who think much, and in the heart, in the case of those who feel much, and whose actions have always a humanitarian aim."

— What is to be thought of the opinion of those who place the soul in a centre of organic life?

"The spirit may be said to inhabit more especially such a part of your organism, because it is to such a part that all the sensations converge; but those who place it in what they consider to be the centre of vitality confound it with the vital fluid or principle. Nevertheless, it may be said that the soul is more especially present in the organs which serve for the manifestation of the intellectual and moral qualities."

Materialism

147. Why is it that anatomists, physiologists, and, in general, those who apply themselves to the pursuit of the natural sciences, are so apt to fall into materialism?

"The physiologist refers everything to the standard of his senses. Human pride imagines that it knows everything, and refuses to admit that there can be anything which transcends the human understanding. Science itself inspires some minds with presumption; they think that nature can have nothing hidden from them."

148. Is it not regrettable that materialism should be a consequence of studies which ought, on the contrary, to show men the superiority of the intelligence that governs the world?

"It is not true that materialism is a consequence of those studies; it is a result of the imperfection which leads men to draw a false conclusion from their studies, for men may make a bad use of the very best things. The idea of annihilation, moreover, troubles those who profess to hold it more than they will allow to be seen; and those who are the loudest in proclaiming their materialistic convictions are often more boastful than brave. The greater number of the so-called materialists are only such because they have no rational ground of belief in a future life. Show a firm anchor of rational belief in a future state to those who see only a yawning void before them, and they will grasp it with the eagerness of drowning men."

There are those who, through an aberration of the intellect, can see nothing in organised beings but the action of matter, and attribute to this action all the phenomena of existence. They have seen, in the human body, only the action of an electrical machine ; they have studied the mechanism of life only in the play of the bodily organs; they have often seen life extinguished by the rupture of a filament, and they have seen nothing but this filament. They have looked to see whether anything still remained, and as they have found nothing but matter that has become inert, as they have neither seen the soul escape from the body nor been able to take hold of it, they have concluded that everything is reducible to the properties of matter, and that death is consequently the annihilation of all thought. A melancholy conclusion, if such were really the case ; for, were it so, good and evil would be alike devoid of aim ; every man would be justified in thinking only of himself, and in subordinating every other consideration to the satisfaction of his material instincts. Thus all social ties would be broken, and the holiest affections would be destroyed for ever. Happily for mankind, these ideas are far from being general. Their area may even be said to be a narrow one, limited to the scope of individual opinions ; for nowhere have they been erected into a system of doctrine. A state of society founded on such a basis would contain within itself the seeds of its own dissolution ; and its members would tear each other to pieces like so many ferocious beasts of prey.

Man· has an intuitive belief that, for him, everything does not end with the life of his body ; he has a horror of annihilation. No matter how obstinately men may have set themselves against the idea of a future life, there are very few who, on the approach of death, do not anxiously ask themselves what is going to become of them ; for the thought of bidding an eternal adieu to life is appalling to the stoutest heart. Who, indeed could look with indifference on the prospect of an absolute and eternal separation from all that he has loved? Who, without terror, could behold, yawning beneath him, the bottomless abyss of nothingness in which all his faculties and aspirations are to be swallowed up for ever? Who could calmly say to himself, "After my death there will be nothing for me but the void of annihilation; all will be ended. A few days hence, all memory of me will have been blotted out from the remembrance of those who survive me, and the earth itself will retain no trace of my passage. Even the good that I have done will be forgotten by the ungrateful mortals whom I have benefited. And there is nothing to compensate me for all this loss, no other prospect, beyond this ruin, than that of my body devoured by worms !"

Is there not something horrible in such a picture, something that sends an icy chill through the heart? Religion teaches us that such cannot be our destiny ; and reason confirms the teachings of religion. But the vague, indefinite assurance of a future existence, which is all that is given us either by religion or by reason, cannot satisfy our natural desire for some positive proof in a matter of such paramount importance for us ; and it is just the lack of such proof, in regard to a future life, that, in so many cases, engenders doubt as to its reality.

"Admitting that we have a soul," many very naturally ask, "what is our soul? Has it a form, an appearance of any kind? Is it a limited being, or is it something undefined and impersonal? Some say that it is 'a breath of God :' others, that it is a spark: others, again, declare it to be 'part of the Great Whole, the principle of life and of intelligence.' But what do we learn from these statements? What is the good of our possessing a soul, if our soul is to be merged in immensity like a drop of water in the ocean? Is not the loss of our individuality equivalent, so far as we are concerned, to annihilation? The soul is said to be immaterial ; but that which is immaterial can have no defined proportions, and therefore can have no reality for us. Religion also teaches that we shall be happy, or unhappy, according to the good or the evil we have done ; but of what nature are the happiness or unhappiness thus promised us in another life? Is that happiness a state of beatitude in the bosom of God, an external contemplation, with no other employment than that of singing the praises of the Creator? And the flames of hell, are they a reality or a figure of speech? The Church itself attributes to them a figurative meaning ; but of what nature are the sufferings thus figuratively shadowed forth? And where is the scene of those sufferings? In short, what shall we **be**, what shall we **do**, what shall we **see**, in that other world which is said to await us all?"

No one, it is averred, has ever come back to give us an account of that world. But this statement is erroneous; and the mission of Spiritism is precisely to enlighten us in regard to the future which awaits us ; to enable us, within certain limits, to see and to touch it, not merely as a deduction of our reason, but through the evidence of facts. Thanks to the communications made to us by the people of that other world, the latter is no longer a mere presumption, a probability, which each one pictures to himself according to his own fancy, which poets embellish with fictitious and allegorical images that serve only to deceive us ; it is that other world itself, in its reality, which is now brought before us, for it is the beings of the life beyond the grave who come to us, who describe to us the situations in which they find themselves, who tell us what they are doing, who allow us to become, so to say, the spectators of the details of their new order of life, and who thus show us the inevitable fate which is reserved for each of us according to our merits or our misdeeds.

Is there anything anti-religious in such a demonstration? Assuredly not ; since it furnishes unbelievers with a ground of belief, and inspires lukewarm believers with renewed fervour and confidence.

Spiritism is thus seen to be the most powerful auxiliary of religion. And, if it be such, it must be acknowledged to exist by the permission of God, for the purpose of giving new strength to our wavering convictions, and thus of leading us back into the right road by the prospect of our future happiness.

CHAPTER III

1. THE SOUL AFTER DEATH : ITS INDIVIDUALITY :
ETERNAL LIFE—2. SEPARATION OF SOUL AND BODY—3.
TEMPORARILY CONFUSED STATE OF THE SOUL
AFTER DEATH.

The Soul After Death

149. What becomes of the soul at the moment of death?

"It becomes again a spirit; that is to say, it returns into the world of spirits, which it had quitted for a short time."

150. Does the soul, after death, preserve its individuality?

"Yes, it never loses its individuality. What would the soul be if it did not preserve it?"

— *How does the soul preserve the consciousness of its individuality, since it no longer has its material body?*

"It still has a fluid peculiar to itself, which it draws from the atmosphere of its planet, and which represents the appearance of its last incarnation—its *perispirit.*"

— *Does the soul take nothing of this life away with it?*

"Nothing but the remembrance of that life and the desire to go to a better world. This remembrance is full of sweetness or of bitterness according to the use it has made of the earthly life it has quitted. The more advanced is the degree of its purification, the more clearly does it perceive the futility of all that it has left behind it upon the earth."

151. What is to be thought of the opinion that the soul after death returns to the universal whole?

"Does not the mass of spirits, considered in its totality, constitute a whole? Does it not constitute a world? When you are in an assembly you form an integral part of that assembly, and yet you still retain your individuality."

152. What proof can we have of the individuality of the soul after death?

"Is not this proof furnished by the communications which you obtain? If you were not blind, you would see; if you were not deaf, you would hear; for you are often spoken to by a voice which reveals to you the existence of a being exterior to yourself."

Those who think that the soul returns after death into the universal whole are in error if they imagine that it loses its individuality, like a drop of water that falls into the ocean ; they are right if they mean by **the universal whole** the totality of incorporeal beings, of which each soul or spirit is an element.

If souls were blended together into a mass, they would possess only the qualities common to the totality of the mass ; there would be nothing to distinguish them from one another, and they would have no special, intellectual, or moral qualities of their own. But the communications we obtain from spirits give abundant evidence of the possession by each spirit of the consciousness of the **me,** and of a distinct will, personal to itself ; the infinite diversity of characteristcs of all kinds presented by them is at once the consequence and the evidence of their distinctive personal individuality. If, after death, there were nothing but what is called the "Great Whole," absorbing all individualities, this whole would be uniform in its characteristics ; and, in that case, all the communications received from the invisible world would be identical. But as among the denizens of that other world we meet with some who are good and some who are bad, some who are learned and some who are ignorant, some who are happy and some who are unhappy, and as they present us with every shade of character, some being frivolous and others serious, etc., it is evident that they are different individualities, perfectly distinct from one another. This individuality becomes still more evident when they are able to prove their identity by unmistakable tokens, by personal details relating to their terrestrial life, and susceptible of being verified ; and it cannot be a matter of doubt when they manifest themselves to our sight under the form of apparitions. The individuality of the soul has been taught theoretically as an article of faith ; Spiritism renders it patent, as an evident, and, so to say, a **material** fact.

153. In what sense should we understand eternal life?

"It is the life of the spirit that is eternal; that of the body is transitory and fleeting. When the body dies, the soul re-enters the eternal life."

— *Would it not be more correct to apply the term* eternal life *to the life of the purified spirits; of those who, having attained to the degree of relative perfection, have no longer to undergo the discipline of suffering?*

"The life of that degree might rather be termed eternal happiness; but this is a question of words. You may call things as you please, provided you are agreed among yourselves as to your meaning."

Separation of Soul and Body

154. Is the separation of the soul from the body a painful process?

"No; the body often suffers more during life than at the moment of death, when the soul is usually unconscious of what is occurring to the body. The sensations experienced at the moment of death are often *a source of enjoyment for the spirit*, who recognises them as putting an end to the term of his exile."

In cases of natural death, where dissolution occurs as a consequence of the exhaustion of the bodily organs through age, man passes out of life without perceiving that he is doing so. It is like the flame of a lamp that goes out for want of aliment.

155. *How is the separation of soul and body effected?*

"The bonds which retained the soul being broken, it disengages itself from the body."

— *Is this separation effected instantaneously, and by means of an abrupt transition? Is there any distinctly marked line of demarcation between life and death?*

"No; the soul disengages itself gradually. It does not escape at once from the body, like a bird whose cage is suddenly opened. The two states touch and run into each other; and the spirit extricates himself, little by little, from his fleshly bonds, which are *loosed, but not broken*."

During life, a spirit is held to the body by his semi-material envelope, or **perispirit.** Death is the destruction of the body only, but not of this second envelope, which separates itself from the body when the play of organic life ceases in the latter. Observation shows us that the separation of the **perispirit** from the body is not suddenly completed at the moment of death, but is only effected gradually, and more or less slowly in different individuals. In some cases it is effected so quickly that the **perispirit** is entirely separated from the body within a few hours of the death of the latter ; but, in other cases, and especially in the case of those whose life has been grossly **material and sensual,** this deliverance is much less rapid, and sometimes takes days, weeks, and even months, for its accomplishment. This delay does not imply the slightest persistence of vitality in the body, nor any possibility of its return to life, but is simply the result of a certain affinity between the body and the spirit ; which affinity is always more or less tenacious in proportion to the preponderance of materiality in the affections of the spirit during his earthly life. It is, in fact, only rational to suppose that the more closely a spirit has identified himself with matter, the greater will be his difficulty in separating himself from his material body ; while, on the contrary, intellectual and moral activity, and habitual elevation of thought, effect a commencement of this separation even during the life of the body, and therefore, when death occurs, the separation is almost instantaneous. The study of a great number of individuals after their death has shown that affinity which, in some cases, continues to exist between the soul and the body is sometimes extremely painful ; for it causes the spirit to perceive all the horror of the decomposition of the latter. This experience is exceptional, and peculiar to certain kinds of life and to certain kinds of death. It sometimes occurs in the case of those who have committed suicide.

156. *Can the definitive separation of the soul and body take place before the complete cessation of organic life?*

"It sometimes happens that the soul has quitted the body before the last agony comes on, so that the latter is only the closing act of merely organic life. The dying man has no longer any conssciousness of himself, and nevertheless there still remains in him a faint breathing of vitality. The body is a machine that is kept in movement by the heart. It continues to live as long as the heart causes the blood to circulate in the veins, and has no need of the soul to do that."

157. *Does the soul sometimes, at the moment of death, experience an aspiration or an ecstasy that gives it a foreglimpse of the world into which it is about to return?*

"The soul often feels the loosening of the bonds that attach it to the body, *and does its utmost to hasten and complete the work of separation.* Already partially freed from matter, it beholds the future unrolled before it, and enjoys, in anticipation, the spirit-state upon which it is about to re-enter."

158. *Do the transformations of the caterpillar—which, first of all, crawls upon the ground, and then shuts itself up in its chrysalis in seeming death, to be reborn therefrom into a new and brilliant existence—give us anything like a true idea of the relation between our terrestrial life, the tomb, and our new existence beyond the latter?*

"An idea on a very small scale. The image is good; but, nevertheless, it would not do to accept it literally, as you so often do in regard to such images."

159. *What sensation is experienced by the soul at the moment when it recovers its consciousness in the world of spirits?*

"That depends on circumstances. He who has done evil from the love of evil is overwhelmed with shame for his wrong-doing. With the righteous it is very different. His soul seems to be eased of a heavy load, for it does not dread the most searching glance."

160. *Does the spirit find himself at once in company with those whom he knew upon the earth, and who died before him?*

"Yes; and more or less promptly according to the degree of his affection for them and of theirs for him. They often come to meet him on his return to the spirit-world, and *help to free him from the bonds of matter.* Others whom he formerly knew, but whom he had lost sight of during his sojourn on the earth, also come to meet him. He sees those who are in erraticity, and he goes to visit those who are still incarnated."

161. *In cases of violent or accidental death, when the organs have not been weakened by age or by sickness, does the separation of the soul take place simultaneously with the cessation of organic life?*

"It does so usually; and, at any rate, the interval between them, in all such cases, is very brief."

162. *After decapitation, for instance, does a man retain consciousness for a longer or shorter time?*

"He frequently does so for a few minutes, until the organic life of the body is completely extinct; but, on the other hand, the fear of death often causes a man to lose consciousness before the moment of execution."

The question here proposed refers simply to the consciousness which the victim may have of himself as a man, through the intermediary of his bodily organs, and not as a spirit. If he have not lost this consciousness before execution, he may retain it for a few moments afterwards ; but this persistence of consciousness can only be of very short duration, and must necessarily cease with the cessation of the organic life of the brain. The cessation of the human consciousness, however, by no means implies the complete separation of the **perispirit** from the body. On the contrary, in all cases in which death has resulted from violence, and not from a gradual extinction of the vital forces, the bonds which unite the body to the perispirit are more tenacious, and the separation is effected more slowly.

Temporarily — Confused State of the Soul After Death

163. *Does the soul, on quitting the body, find itself at once in possession of its self-consciousness?*

"Not at once. It is for a time in a state of confusion which obscures all its perceptions."

164. *Do all spirits experience, in the same degree and for the same length of time, the confusion which follows the separation of the soul from the body?*

"No; this depends entirely on their degree of elevation. He who has already accomplished a certain amount of purification recovers his consciousness almost immediately, because he had already freed himself from the thraldom of materiality during his bodily life; whereas the carnally minded man, he whose conscience is not clear, retains the impression of matter for a much longer time."

165. *Does a knowledge of Spiritism exercise any influence on the duration of this state of confusion?*

"It exercises a very considerable influence on that duration, because it enables the spirit to understand beforehand the new situation in which it is about to find itself; but the practice of rectitude during the earthly life, and a clear conscience, are the conditions which conduce most powerfully to shorten it."

At the moment of death, everything appears confused. The soul takes some time to recover its self-consciousness, for it is as though stunned, and in a state similar to that of a man waking out of a deep sleep, and trying to understand his own situation. It gradually regains clearness of thought and the memory of the past in proportion to the weakening of the influence of the material envelope from which it has just freed itself, and the clearing away of the sort of fog that obscured its consciousness.

The duration of the state of confusion that follows death varies greatly in different cases. It may be only of a few hours, and it may be, of several months, or even years. Those with whom it lasts the least are they who, during the earthly life, have identified themselves most closely with their future state, because they are soonest able to understand their new situation. This state of confusion assumes special aspects according to characterial peculiarities, and also according to different modes of death. In all cases of violent or sudden death, by suicide, by capital punisment, accident, apoplexy, etc., the spirit is surprised, astounded, and does not believe himself to be dead. He obstinately persists in asserting the contrary ; and, nevertheless, he sees the body he has quitted as something apart from himself ; he knows that body to be his own, and he cannot make out how it should be separated from him. He goes about among the persons with whom he is united by the ties of affection, speaks to them, and cannot conceive why they do not hear him. This sort of illusion lasts until the entire separation of the **perispirit** from the earthly body, for it is only when this is accomplished that the spirit begins to understand his situation, and becomes aware that he no longer forms part of the world of human beings. Death having come upon him by surprise, the spirit is stunned by the suddenness of the change that has taken place in him. For him, death is still synonymous with destruction, annihilation ; and as he thinks, sees, hears, it seems to him that he cannot be dead. And this illusion is still further strengthened by his seeing himself with a body similar in form to the one he has quitted ; for he does not at first perceive its ethereal nature, but supposes it to be solid and compact like the other ; and when his attention has been called to this point, he is astonished at finding that it is not palpable. This phenomenon is analogous to that which occurs in the case of somnambulists, who, when thrown for the first time into the magnetic sleep, cannot believe that they are not awake. Sleep, according to their idea of it, is synonymous with suspension of the perceptive faculties ; and as they think freely, and see, they appear to themselves not to be asleep. Some spirits present this peculiarity, even in cases where death has not supervened unexpectedly ; but it more frequently occurs in the case of those who, although they may have been ill, had no expectation of death. The curious spectacle is then presented of a spirit attending his own funeral as though it were that of someone else, and speaking of it as of something which in no way concerns him, until the moment when at length he comprehends the true state of the case.

In the mental confusion which follows death, there is nothing painful for him who has lived an upright life. He is calm, and his perceptions are those of a peaceful awaking out of sleep. But for him whose conscience is not clean, it is full of anxiety and anguish that become more and more poignant in proportion as he recovers consciousness.

In cases of collective death, in which many persons have perished together in the same catastrophe, it has been observed that they do not always see one another immediately afterwards. In the state of confusion which follows death, each spirit goes his own way, or concerns himself only with those in whom he takes an interest.

CHAPTER IV.

PLURALITY OF EXISTENCES.

Reincarnation.

166. How can the soul that has not attained to perfection during the corporeal life complete the work of its purification?

"By undergoing the trial of a new existence."

— How does the soul accomplish this new existence? Is it through its transformation as a spirit?

"The soul, in purifying itself, undoubtedly undergoes a transformation; but, in order to effect this transformation, it needs the trial of corporeal life."

— The soul has then, many corporeal existences?

"Yes; we all have many such existences. Those who maintain the contrary wish to keep you in the same ignorance in which they are themselves."

— It would seem to result from this statement that the soul, after having quitted one body, takes another one; in other words, that it reincarnates itself in a new body. Is it thus that this statement is to be understood?

"Evidently so."

167. What is the aim of reincarnation?

"Expiation; progressive improvement of mankind. Without this aim, where would be its justice?"

168. Is the number of corporeal existences limited, or does a spirit go on reincarnating himself for ever?

"In each new existence, a spirit takes a step forwards in the path of progress; when he has stripped himself of all his impurities, he has no further need of the trials of corporeal life."

169. Is the number of incarnations the same for all spirits?

"No; he who advances quickly spares himself many trials. Nevertheless, these successive incarnations are always very numerous, for progress is almost infinite."

170. What does the spirit become after its last incarnation?

"It enters upon the state of perfect happiness, as a purified spirit."

Justice of Reincarnation.

171. What foundation is there for the doctrine of reincarnation?

"The justice of God, and revelation; for, as we have already remarked, an affectionate father always leaves a door of repentance open for his erring children. Does not reason itself tell you that it would be unjust to inflict an eternal privation of happiness on those who have not had the opportunity of improving themselves? Are not all men God's children? It is only among selfish human beings that injustice, implacable hatred, and irremissible punishments are to be found."

All spirits tend towards perfection, and are furnished by God with the means of advancement through the trials of corporeal life; but the divine justice compels them to accomplish, in new existences, that which they have not been able to do, or to complete, in a previous trial.

It would not be consistent with the justice or with the goodness of God to sentence to eternal suffering those who may have encountered obstacles to their improvement independent of their will, and resulting from the very nature of the conditions in which they found themselves placed. If the fate of mankind were irrevocably fixed after death, God would not have weighed the actions of all in the same scales, and would not have treated them with impartiality.

The doctrine of reincarnation—that is to say, the doctrine which proclaims that men have many successive existences—is the only one which answers to the idea we form to ourselves of the justice of God in regard to those who are placed, by circumstances over which they have no control, in conditions unfavourable to their moral advancement ; the only one which can explain the future, and furnish us with a sound basis for our hopes, because it offers us the means of redeeming our errors through new trials. This doctrine is indicated by the teachings of reason, as well as by those of our spirit-instructors.

He who is conscious of his own inferiority derives a consoling hope from the doctrine of reincarnation. If he believes in the justice of God, he cannot hope to be placed, at once and for all eternity, on a level with those who have made a better use of life than he has done ; but the knowledge that this inferiority will not exclude him for ever from the supreme felicity, and that he will be able to conquer this felicity through new efforts, revives his courage and sustains his energy. Who does not regret, at the end of his career, that the experience he has acquired should have come too late to allow of his turning it to useful account? This tardily acquired experience will not be lost for him ; he will profit by it in a new corporeal life.

Incarnation in Different Worlds

172. Do we accomplish all our different corporeal existences upon this earth?

"Not all of them, for those existences take place in many different worlds. The world in which you now are is neither the first nor the last of these, but is one of those that are the most material, and the furthest removed from perfection."

173. Does the soul, at each new corporeal existence, pass from one world to another, or can it accomplish several existences on the same globe?

"It may live many times on the same globe, if it be not sufficiently advanced to pass into a higher one."

— *We may, then, re-appear several times upon the earth?*

"Certainly."

— *Can we come back to it after having lived in other worlds?*

"Assuredly you can; you may already have lived elsewhere as upon the earth."

174. Is it necessary to live again upon this earth?

"No; but if you do not advance, you may go into a world no better than this one, or even worse."

175. Is there any advantage in coming back to inhabit this earth?

"No special advantage, unless it be the fulfilment of a mission; in that case the spirit advances, whether incarnated in this earth or elsewhere."

— *Would it not be happier to remain as a spirit?*

"No, no! for we should remain stationary; and we want to advance towards God."

176. Can spirits come to this world, for the first time, after having been incarnated in other worlds?

"Yes; just as you may go into other ones. *All the worlds of the universe are united by the bonds of solidarity*; that which is not accomplished in one of them is accomplished in another."

— *Some of those who are now upon this earth are here, then, for the first time?*

"Many of them are so; and at various degrees of advancement."

— *Is there any sign by which we can know the spirits who are here for the first time?*

"Such knowledge would not be of the slightest use to you."

177. *In order to arrive at the perfection and the supreme felicity which are the final aim of mankind, is it necessary for a spirit to pass through all the worlds that exist in the universe?*

"No; for there are a great number of worlds of the same degree, in which a spirit would learn nothing new."

— *How, then, are we to explain the plurality of his existences upon the same globe?*

"He may find himself, each time he comes back, in very different situations, which afford him the opportunity of acquiring new experience."

178. *Can spirits live corporeally in a world relatively inferior to the one in which they have already lived?*

"Yes; when they have to fulfil a mission in aid of progress; and in that case they joyfully accept the tribulations of such an existence, because these will furnish them with the means of advancement."

— *May this not occur also as an expiation? and may not rebellious spirits be sent by God into worlds of lower degree?*

"Spirits may remain stationary, but they never retrograde; those who are rebellious are punished by not advancing, and by having to recommence their misused existences under the conditions suited to their nature."

— *Who are they that are compelled to recommence the same existence?*

"They who fail in the fulfilment of their mission, or in the endurance of the trial appointed to them."

179. *Have all the human beings who inhabit any given world arrived at the same degree of perfection?*

"No; it is in the other worlds as upon the earth; there are some who are more advanced, and others who are less so."

180. *In passing from this world into another one, does a spirit retain the intelligence which he possessed in this one?*

"Undoubtedly he does; intelligence is never lost. But he may not have the same means of manifesting it for that depends both on his degree of advancement and on the quality of the body he will take." (Vide, *Influence of Organism.*)

181. *Have the human beings who inhabit the other worlds bodies like ours?*

"They undoubtedly have bodies, because it is necessary for the spirit to be clothed with matter in order to act upon matter; but this envelope is more or less material according to the degree of purity at which each spirit has arrived, and it is these gradations of purity that decide the different worlds through which we have to pass; for in our Father's house are many mansions, and therefore many degrees among those mansions. There are some who know this, and possess the consciousness of this fact, while upon the earth; and there are others who have no such intuition."

182. Can we obtain any exact knowledge of the physical and moral state of the different worlds?

"We, spirits, can only reply according to the degree at which you have arrived; that is to say, that we must not reveal these things to all, because some are not in the state which would enable them to understand such revelations, *and would be confused by them.*"

In proportion as a spirit becomes purified, the body with which he clothes himself also approaches more nearly to the spirit-nature. The matter of which his body is composed is less dense ; he no longer crawls heavily on the surface of the ground ; his bodily needs are less gross ; and the various living beings in those higher worlds are no longer obliged to destroy one another in order to feed themselves. A spirit incarnated in those worlds enjoys a greater degree of freedon, and possesses, in regard to objects at a distance, orders of perception of a nature unknown to us ; he sees with his eyes what we see only in thought.

The purification of spirits determines the moral excellence of the corporeal beings in whom they are incarnated. The animal passions become weaker, and selfishness gives place to the sentiment of fraternity.

Thus, in worlds of higher degree than our earth, wars are unknown, because no one thinks of doing harm to his fellow-beings, and there is consequently no motive for hatred or discord. The foresight of their future, which is intuitive in the people of those worlds, and the sense of security resulting from a conscience void of remorse, cause them to look forward to death without fear, as being simply a process of transformation, the approach of which they perceive without the sightest uneasiness.

The duration of a lifetime, in the different worlds, appears to be proportionate to the degree of moral and physical superiority of each world ; and this is perfectly consonant with reason. The less material is the body, the less subject is it to the vicissitudes which disorganise it ; the purer the spirit, the less subject is it to the passions which undermine and destroy it. This correspondence between moral and physical conditions is a proof of the beneficence of providential law, even in worlds of low degree ; as the duration of the suffering which is the characteristic of life in those worlds is thus rendered proportionally shorter.

183. In passing from one world to another, does the spirit pass through a new infancy?

"Infancy is, in all worlds, a necessary transition; but it is not, in all of them, so stupid as it in yours."

184. Has a spirit the choice of the new world which he is to inhabit?

"Not always; but he can make his demand, and it may be granted, but only if he have deserved it; for the various worlds are only accessible to spirits according to the degree of their elevation."

— *If a spirit make no such demand, what is it that decides as to the world in which he will be reincarnated?*

"The degree of his elevation."

185. *Is the physical and moral state of the living beings of each globe always the same?*

"No; worlds, like the beings that live in them, are subject to the law of progress. All have begun, like yours, by being in a state of inferiority; and the earth will undergo a transformation similar to that which has been accomplished by the others. It will become a terrestrial paradise, when the men by whom it is inhabited have become good."

The races which now people the earth will gradually disappear, and will be succeeded by others more and more perfect. Those transformed races will succeed the races now upon the earth, as these have succeeded earlier races, still more gross than the present ones.

186. *Are there worlds in which the spirit, ceasing to inhabit a material body, has no longer any other envelope than the* perispirit?

"Yes, and this envelope itself becomes so etherealised that, for you, it is as though it did not exist. This is the state of the fully purified spirits."

— *It would seem, from this statement, that there is no clearly marked line of demarcation between the state of the latter incarnations and that of pure spirit?*

"No such demarcation exists. The difference between them growing gradually less and less, they blend into one another as the darkness of night melts into the dawn."

187. *Is the substance of the* perispirit *the same in all globes?*

"No; it is more or less ethereal. On passing from one world to another, a spirit clothes himself with the matter proper to each, changing his envelope with the rapidity of lightning."

188. *Do the pure spirits inhabit special worlds, or are they in universal space without being attached to any particular globe?*

"The pure spirits inhabit certain worlds, but they are not confined to them as men are confined to the earth; they possess, in a higher degree than any others, the power of instantaneous locomotion, which is equivalent to ubiquity."

According to the statements of spirits, the earth, as regards the physical and moral qualities of its inhabitants, is one of the least advanced of all the globes of our solar system. Mars is stated to be at a point even lower than that of the earth, and Jupiter to be greatly superior to the earth in every respect. The sun is not a world inhabited by corporeal beings, but is a place of meeting for the spirits of a higher order who, from thence, send out the radiations of their thought towards the other worlds of our solar system, which they govern through the instrumentality of spirits of a less elevated degree, to whom they transmit their action by the intermediary of the universal fluid. As regards its physical constitution, the sun would appear to be a focus of electricity ; and all the other suns seem to be identical with ours in nature and function.

The size of planets, and their distance from the sun, have no necessary relation with their degree of advancement ; for Venus is said to be more advanced than the earth, and Saturn is declared to be less advanced than Jupiter.

The souls of many persons well known on this earth are said to be reincarnated in Jupiter, one of the worlds nearest to perfection ; and much surprise has been felt on hearing it stated that persons who, when here, were not supposed to merit such a favour, should have been admitted into so advanced a globe. But there is nothing in this fact that need surprise us, if we consider, first, that certain spirits who have inhabited this planet may have been sent hither in fulfilment of a mission which, to our eyes, did not seem to place them in the foremost rank ; secondly, that they may have had, between their lives here and in Jupiter, intermediary existences in which they have advanced ; and thirdly, that there are innumerable degrees of development in that world as in this one, and that there may be as much difference between these degrees as there is, amongst us, between the savage and the civilised man. It no more follows that a spirit is on a level with the most advanced beings of Jupiter because he inhabits that planet than it follows that an ignoramus is on a level with a philosopher because he inhabits the same town.

The conditions of longevity, also, are as various in other worlds as they are on our earth ; and no comparison can be established between the ages of those who inhabit them. A person who had died some years previously, on being evoked, stated that he had been incarnated for six months in a world the name of which is unknown to us. Being questioned as to his age in that world, he replied, "That is a point which I am unable to decide ; because, in the first place, we do not count time in the same way as you do, and, in the next place, our mode of existence is not the same as yours. Our development is much more rapid in this world ; for, although it is only six of your months since I came here, I may say that, as regards intelligence, I am about what one usually is at the age of thirty in your earth."

A great number of similar replies have been given by other spirits ; and these statements contain nothing improbable. Do we not see upon our earth a host of animals that acquire their normal development in the course of a few months? Why should not men do the same in other spheres? And it is to be remarked, moreover, that the degree of development acquired by a man at the age of thirty upon the earth may be only a sort of infancy in comparison with what he is destined to arrive at in worlds of higher degree. Short-sighted indeed are they who look upon our present selves as being in all respects the normal type of creation ; and to suppose that there can be no other modes of existence than our present one, is, in sooth, a strange narrowing of our idea of the possibilities of the divine action.

Progressive Transmigrations

189. Does the spirit enjoy the plenitude of his faculties from the beginning of his formation?

"No ; for the spirit, like the man, has his infancy. Spirits at their origin have only an instinctive existence, and have scarcely any consciousness of themselves or of their acts; it is only little by little that their intelligence is developed."

190. What is the state of the soul at its first incarnation?

"A state analogous to that of infancy, considered in its relation to a human life. Its intelligence is only beginning to unfold itself; it may be said to be *essaying to live.*"

191. Are the souls of our savages souls in a state of infancy?

"Of *relative* infancy; but they are souls that have already accomplished a certain amount of development, for they have passions."

— *Passions, then, are a sign of development?*

"Of development, yes, but not of perfection. They are a sign of activity, and of the consciousness of the *me*; while, on the contrary, in the primitive state of the soul, intelligence and vitality exist only as germs."

The life of a spirit in his totality goes through successive phases similar to those of a corporeal lifetime. He passes gradually from the embryonic state to that of infancy, and arrives, through a succession of periods, at the adult state, which is that of his perfection, with this difference, however, that it is not subject either to decrepitude or to decline, like the corporeal life ; that the life of a spirit, though it has had a beginning, will have no end ; that he takes what appears from our point of view to be an immense length of time in passing from the state of spirit-infancy to the attainment of his complete development ; and that he accomplishes this progression, not in one and the same sphere, but by passing through different worlds. The life of a spirit is thus composed of a series of corporeal existences, each of which affords him an opportunity of progress ; as each of his corporeal existences is composed of a series of days, in each of wich he acquires a new increment of experience and of knowledge. But just as in a human lifetime there are days which bear no fruit, so in the life of a spirit there are corporeal existences which are barren of profitable result, because he has failed to make a right use of them.

192. Is it possible for us, by leading a perfect life in our present existence, to overleap all the intervening steps of the ascent, and thus to arrive at the state of pure spirits, without passing through the intermediate degrees?

"No; for what a man imagines to be perfect is very far from perfection; there are qualities which are entirely unknown to him, and which he could not now be made to comprehend. He may be as perfect as it is possible for his terrestrial nature to be; but he will still be very far from the true and absolute perfection. It is just as with the child, who, however precocious he may be, must necessarily pass through youth to reach adult life; or as the sick man, who must pass through convalescence before arriving at the complete recovery of his health. And besides, a spirit must

advance in knowledge as well as in morality; if he have advanced
in only one of these directions, he will have to advance equally in
the other, in order to reach the top of the ladder of perfection.
But it is none the less certain that the more a man advances in
his present life the shorter and the less painful will be the trials
he will have to undergo in his subsequent existences."

— *Can a man, at least, insure for himself, after his present life,
a future existence less full of bitterness than this one?*

"Yes, undoubtedly, he can abridge the length and the difficulties
of the road. *It is only he who does not care to advance that
remains always at the same point.*"

*193. Can a man in his new existences descend to a lower point
than that which he has already reached?*

"As regards his *social position*, yes; but not as regards his degree
of progress as a spirit."

*194. Can the soul of a good man, in a new incarnation, animate
the body of a scoundrel?*

"No; because a spirit cannot degenerate."

— *Can the soul of a bad man become the soul of a good man?*

"Yes, if he have repented; and, in that case, his new incarnation
is the reward of his efforts at amendment."

The line of march of all spirits is always progressive, never retrograde.
They raise themselves gradually in the hierarchy of existence ; they never
descend from the rank at which they have once arrived. In the course
of their different corporeal existences they may descend in rank as **men,**
but not as spirits. Thus the soul of one who has been at the pinnacle of
earthly power may, in a subsequent incarnation, animate the humblest
day-labourer, and **vice versa** ; for the elevation of ranks among men is
often in the inverse ratio of that of the moral sentiments. Herod was a
king, and Jesus, a carpenter.

*195. Might not the certainty of being able to improve one's
self in a future existence lead some persons to persist in evil
courses, through knowing that they will always be able to amend
at some later period?*

"He who could make such a calculation would have no real
belief in anything; and such an one would not be any more
restrained by the idea of incurring eternal punishment, because his
reason would reject that idea, which leads to every sort of un-
belief. An imperfect spirit, it is true, might reason in that way
during his corporeal life; but when he is freed from his material
body, he thinks very differently; for he soon perceives that he
has made a great mistake in his calculations, *and this perception*

causes him to carry an opposite sentiment into his next incarnation. It is thus that progress is accomplished; and it is thus also that you have upon the earth some men who are farther advanced than others, because some possess experience that the others have not yet acquired, but that will be gradually acquired by them. It depends upon each spirit to hasten his own advancement or to retard it indefinitely."

The man who has an unsatisfactory position desires to change it as soon as possible. He who is convinced that the tribulations of the present life are the consequences of his own imperfections will seek to insure for himself a new existence of a less painful character ; and this conviction will draw him away from the wrong road much more effectually than the threat of eternal flames, which he does not believe in.

196. *As spirits can only be ameliorated by undergoing the tribulations of corporeal existence, it would seem to follow that the material life is a sort of* sieve *or* strainer, *by which the beings of the spirit-world are obliged to pass in order to arrive at perfection?*

"Yes; that is the case. They improve themselves under the trials of corporeal life by avoiding evil, and by practising what is good. But it is only through many successive incarnations or purifications that they succeed, after a lapse of time which is longer or shorter *according to the amount of effort put forth by them,* in reaching the goal towards which they tend."

— *Is it the body that influences the spirit for its amelioration, or is it the spirit that influences the body?*

"Your spirit is everything; your body is a garment that rots, and nothing more."

A material image of the various degrees of purification of the soul is furnished by the juice of the grape. It contains the liquid called spirit or alcohol, but weakened by the presence of various foreign elements which change its nature, so that it is only brought to a state of absolute purity after several distillations, at each of which it is cleared of some portion of its impurity. The still represents the corporeal body into which the spirit enters for its purification ; the foreign elements represent the imperfections from which the **perispirit** is gradually freed, in proportion as the spirit approaches the state of relative perfection.

Fate of Children After Death

197. *Is the spirit of a child who dies in infancy as advanced as that of an adult?*

"He is sometimes much more so; for he may previously have lived longer and acquired more experience, especially if he be a spirit who has already made considerable progress."

— The spirit of a child may, then, be more advanced than that of his father?

"That is very frequently the case. Do you not often see examples of this superiority in your world?"

198. In the case of a child who has died in infancy, and without having been able to do evil, does his spirit belong to the higher degrees of the spirit-hierarchy?

"If he have done no evil, he has also done nothing good; and God does not exonerate him from the trials which he has to undergo. If such a spirit belongs to a high degree, it is not because he was a child, but because he had achieved that degree of advancement as the result of his previous existences."

199. Why is it that life is so often cut short in childhood?

"The duration of the life of a child may be, for the spirit thus incarnated, the complement of an existence interrupted before its appointed term; and his death is often *a trial or an expiation for his parents.*"

— What becomes of the spirit of a child who dies in infancy?

"He recommences a new existence."

If man had but a single existence, and if, after this existence, his future state were fixed for all eternity, by what standard of merit could eternal felicity be adjudged to that half of the human race which dies in childhood, and by what would it be exonerated from the conditions of progress, often so painful, imposed on the other half? Such an ordering could not be reconciled with the justice of God. Through the reincarnation of spirits the most absolute justice is equally meted out to all. The possibilities of the future are open to all, without exception, and without favour to any. Those who are the last to arrive have only themselves to blame for the delay. Each man must merit happiness by his own right action, as he has to bear the consequences of his own wrong-doing.

It is, moreover, most irrational to consider childhood as a normal state of innocence. Do we not see children endowed with the vilest instincts at an age at which even the most vicious surroundings cannot have begun to exercise any influence upon them? Do we not see many who seem to bring with them at birth cunning, falseness, perfidy, and even the instincts of thieving and murder, and this in spite of the good examples by which they are surrounded? Human law absolves them from their misdeeds, because it regards them as having acted without discernment ; and it is right in doing so, for they really act instinctively rather than from deliberate intent. But whence proceed the instinctual differences observable in children of the same age, brought up amidst the same conditions, and subjected to the same influences? Whence comes this precocious perversity. if not from the inferiority of the spirit himself, since education has had nothing to do with producing it? Those who are vicious are so because their spirit has made less progress ; and, that being the case, each will have to suffer the consequences of his inferiority, not on account of his wrong-doing as a child, but as the result of his evil courses in his former existences. And thus the action of providential law is the same for each, and the justice of God reaches equally to all.

Sex in Spirits

200. Have spirits sex?

"Not as you understand sex; for sex, in that sense, depends on the corporeal organisation. Love and sympathy exist among them, but founded on similarity of sentiments."

201. Can a spirit, who has animated the body of a man, animate the body of a woman in a new existence, and vice versâ?

"Yes; the same spirits animate men and women."

202. Does a spirit, when existing in the spirit-world, prefer to be incarnated as a man or as a woman?

"That is a point in regard to which a spirit is indifferent, and which is always decided in view of the trials which he has to undergo in his new corporeal life."

Spirits incarnate themselves as men or as women, because they are of no sex ; and, as it is necessary for them to develop themselves in every direction, both sexes, as well as every variety of social position, furnish them with special trials and duties, and with the opportunity of acquiring experience. A spirit who had always incarnated itself as a man would be only known by men, and **vice versâ.**

Relationship — Filiation

203. Do parents transmit to their children a part of their soul, or do they only give them the animal life to which another soul afterwards adds the moral life?

"The animal life only is given by the parents, for the soul is indivisible. A stupid father may have clever children, and *vice versâ.*"

204. As we have had many existences, do our relationships extend beyond our present existence?

"It cannot be otherwise. The succession of their corporeal existences establishes among spirits a variety of relationships which date back from their former existences; and these relationships are often the cause of the sympathies or antipathies which you sometimes feel towards persons whom you seem to meet for the first time."

205. The doctrine of reincarnation appears, to some minds, to destroy family ties, by carrying them back to periods anterior to our present existence.

"It extends those ties, but it does not destroy them; on the contrary, the conviction that the relationships of the present life are based upon anterior affections renders the ties between members of the same family less precarious. It makes the duties of fraternity even more imperative, because in your neighbour, or in your servant, may be incarnated some spirit who has formerly been united to you by the closest ties of consanguinity or of affection."

— *It nevertheless diminishes the importance which many persons attach to their ancestry, since we may have had for our father a spirit who has belonged to a different race, or who has lived in a different social position.*

"That is true; but this importance is usually founded on pride: for what most people honour in their ancestors is title, rank, and fortune. Many a one, who would blush to have an honest shoemaker for his grandfather, boasts of his descent from some debauchee of noble birth. But, no matter what men may say or do, they will not prevent things from going on according to the divine ordering; for God has not regulated the laws of nature to meet the demands of human vanity."

206. If there be no filiation among the spirits successively incarnated as the descendants of the same family, does it follow that it is absurd to honour the memory of one's ancestors?

"Assuredly not; for one ought to rejoice in belonging to a family in which elevated spirits have been incarnated. Although spirits do not proceed from one another, their affection for those who are related to them by family-ties is none the less real; for they are often led to incarnate themselves in such and such a family by pre-existing causes of sympathy, and by the influence of attractions due to relationships contracted in anterior lives. But you may be very sure that the spirits of your ancestors are in no way gratified by the honours you pay to their memory from a sentiment of pride. Their merits, however great they may have been, can only add to your deserts by stimulating your efforts to follow the good examples they may have given you; and it is only through this emulation of their good qualities that your remembrance can become for them not only agreeable but useful also."

Physical and Moral Likeness

207. Parents often transmit physical resemblance to their children; do they also transmit to them moral resemblance?

"No; because they have different souls or spirits. The body proceeds from the body, but the spirit does not proceed from any

other spirit. Between the descendants of the same race there is
no other relationship than that of consanguinity."

— *What is the cause of the moral resemblance that sometimes
exists between parents and children?*

"The attractive influence of moral sympathy, which orings
together spirits who are animated by similar sentiments and
tendencies."

*208. Are the spirits of the parents without influence upon the
spirit of their child after its birth?*

"They exercise, on the contrary, a very great influence upon it.
As we have already told you, spirits are made to conduce to one
another's progress. To the spirits of the parents is confided
the mission of developing those of their children by the training
they give to them; it is a task which is appointed to them, *and
which they cannot without guilt fail to fulfil.*"

*209. How is it that good and virtuous parents often give birth
to children of perverse and evil nature? In other words, how is
it that the good qualities of the parents do not always attract to
them, through sympathy, a good spirit to animate their child?*

"A wicked spirit may ask to be allowed to have virtuous parents,
in the hope that their counsels may help him to amend his ways;
and God often confides such an one to the care of virtuous persons,
in order that he may be benefited by their affection and care."

*210. Can parents, by their intentions and their prayers, attract
a good spirit into the body of their child, instead of an inferior
spirit?*

"No; but they can improve the spirit of the child whom they
have brought into the world, and is confided to them for that
purpose. It is their duty to do this; but bad children are often sent
as a trial for the improvement of the parents also."

*211. What is the cause of the similarity of character so often
existing among brothers, especially between twins?*

"The sympathy of two spirits who are attracted by the similarity
of their sentiments, *and who are happy to be together.*"

*212. In children whose bodies are joined together, and who
have some of their organs in common, are there two spirits,—that
is to say, two souls?*

"Yes; but their resemblance to one another often makes them
seem to you as though there were but one."

213. Since spirits incarnate themselves in twins from sympathy, whence comes the aversion that is sometimes felt by twins for one another?

"It is not a rule that only sympathetic spirits are incarnated as twins. Bad spirits may have been brought into this relation by their desire to struggle against each other on the stage of corporeal life."

214. In what way should we interpret the stories of children fighting in their mother's womb?

"As a figurative representation of their hatred to one another, which, to indicate its inveteracy, is made to date from before their birth. You rarely make sufficient allowance for the figurative and poetic element in certain statements."

215. What is the cause of the distinctive character which we observe in each people?

"Spirits constitute different families, formed by the similarity of their tendencies, which are more or less purified according to their elevation. Each people is a great family formed by the assembling together of sympathetic spirits. The tendency of the members of these families to unite together is the source of the resemblance which constitutes the distinctive character of each people. Do you suppose that good and benevolent spirits would seek to incarnate themselves among a rude and brutal people? No; spirits sympathise with masses of men as they sympathise with individuals. They go to the region of the earth with which they are most in harmony."

216. Does a spirit, in his new existence, retain any traces of the moral character of his former existences?

"Yes, he may do so; but, as he improves, he changes. His social position, also, may be greatly changed in his successive lives. If, having been a master in one existence, he becomes a slave in another, his tastes will be altogether different, and it would be difficult for you to recognise him. A spirit being the same in his various incarnations, there may be certain analogies between the manifestations of character in his successive lives; but these manifestations will, nevertheless, be modified by the change of conditions and habits incident to each of his new corporeal existences, until, through the ameliorations thus gradually effected, his character has been completely changed, he who was proud and cruel becoming humble and humane through repentance and effort."

217. Does a man, in his different incarnations, retain any traces of the physical character of his preceding existences?

"The body is destroyed, and the new one has no connection with the old one. Nevertheless, the spirit is reflected in the body; and although the body is only matter, yet, being modelled on the capacities of the spirit, the latter impresses upon it a certain character that is more particularly visible in the face, and especially in the eyes, which have been truly declared to be the mirror of the soul—that is to say, that the face reflects the soul more especially than does the rest of the body. And this is so true that a very ugly face may please when it forms part of the envelope of a good, wise, and humane spirit; while, on the other hand, very handsome faces may cause you no pleasurable emotion, or may even excite a movement of repulsion. It might seem, at first sight, that only well-made bodies could be the envelopes of good spirits, and yet you see every day virtuous and superior men with deformed bodies. Without there being any very marked resemblance between them, the similarity of tastes and tendencies may, therefore, give what is commonly called a *family-likeness* to the corporeal bodies successively assumed by the same spirit."

The body with which the soul is clothed in a new incarnation not having any **necessary** connection with the one which it has quitted (since it may belong to quite another race), it would be absurd to infer a succession of existences from a resemblance which may be only fortuitous ; but, nevertheless, the qualities of the spirit often modify the organs which serve for their manifestations, and impress upon the countenance, and even on the general manner, a distinctive stamp. It is thus that an expression of nobility and dignity may be found under the humblest exterior, while the fine clothes of the grandee are often unable to hide the baseness and ignominy of their wearer. Some persons, who have risen from the lowest position, adopt without effort the habits and manners of the higher ranks, and seem to have **returned to** their native element ; while others, notwithstanding their advantages of birth and education, always seem to be out of their proper place in refined society. How can these facts be explained unless as a reflex of what the spirit has been in his former existences?

Innate Ideas

218. Does a spirit retain, when incarnated, any trace of the perceptions he has had, and the knowledge he had acquired, in its former existences?

"There remains with him a vague remembrance, which gives him what you call innate ideas."

— *Then the theory of innate ideas is not a chimera?*

"No; the knowledge acquired in each existence is not lost. A spirit, when freed from matter, always remembers what he has learned. He may, during incarnation, forget partially and for a time, but the latent intuition which he preserves of all that he has once known aids him in advancing. Were it not for this intuition of past acquisitions, he would always have to begin his education over again. A spirit, at each new existence, takes his departure from the point at which he had arrived at the close of his preceding existence."

219. *If that be the case, there must be a very close connection between two successive existences?*

"That connection is not always so close as you might suppose it to be; for the conditions of the two existences are often very different, and, in the interval between them, the spirit may have made considerable progress."—(216)

220. *What is the origin of the extraordinary faculties of those individuals who, without any preparatory study, appear to possess intuitively certain branches of knowledge, such as languages, arithmetic, etc.?*

"The vague remembrance of their past; the result of progress previously made by the soul, but of which it has no present consciousness. From what else could those intuitions be derived? The body changes, but the spirit does not change, although he changes his garment."

221. *In changing our body, can we lose certain intellectual faculties, as, for instance, the taste for an art?*

"Yes, if you have sullied that faculty, or made a bad use of it. Moreover, an intellectual faculty may be made to slumber during an entire existence, because the spirit wishes to exercise another faculty having no connection with the one which, in that case, remains latent, but will come again into play in a later existence."

222. *Is it to a retrospective remembrance that are due the instinctive sentiment of the existence of God, and the presentiment of a future life, which appear to be natural to man, even in the savage state?*

"Yes, to a remembrance which man has preserved of what he knew as a spirit before he was incarnated; but pride often stifles this sentiment."

— *Is it to this same remembrance that are due certain beliefs analogous to spiritist doctrine, which are found among every people?*

"That doctrine is as old as the world, and is, therefore, to be found everywhere; a ubiquity which proves it to be true. The incarnate spirit, preserving the intuition of his state as a spirit, possesses an instinctive consciousness of the invisible world; but this intuition is often perverted by prejudices, and debased by the admixture of superstitions resulting from ignorance."

CHAPTER V

PLURALITY OF EXISTENCES

223. "The dogma of reincarnation," it is sometimes objected, "is not new; it is a resuscitation of the doctrine of Pythagoras." We have never said that spiritist doctrine was of modern invention; on the contrary, as the inter-communication of spirits with men occurs in virtue of natural law, it must have existed from the beginning of time, and we have always endeavoured to prove that traces of this inter-communication are to be found in the earliest annals of antiquity. Pythagoras, as is well known, was not the author of the system of metempsychosis; he borrowed it from the philosophers of Hindoostan and of Egypt, by whom it had been held from time immemorial. The idea of the transmigration of soul was, therefore, in the earliest ages of the world, a general belief, equally admitted by the common people and by the most eminent thinkers of that period.

By what road did this idea come to them? Did it reach them through revelation or through intuition?

In regard to this point we know nothing; but it may be safely assumed that no idea could thus have traversed the successive ages of the worlds, and have commanded the assent of the highest intellects of the human race, if it had not been based on some solid ground of truth and reason. The antiquity of this doctrine should therefore be considered as an argument in its favour, rather than as an objection. But, at the same time, it must not be forgotten that there is, between the antique doctrine of metempsychosis and the modern doctrine of reincarnation, this capital difference, viz., that the spirits who inculcate the latter reject absolutely the idea that the human soul can pass into an animal, and *vice versâ*.

The spirits, therefore, who now proclaim the dogma of the plurality of our corporeal existences reassert a doctrine which had its birth in the earliest ages of the world, and which has maintained its footing to the present day in the convictions of many minds; but they present this dogma under an aspect which is more rational, more conformable with the natural law of progress, and more in harmony with the wisdom of the Creator, through the stripping away of accessories added to it by superstition. A circumstance worthy of notice is the fact that it is not in this book alone that the doctrine in question has been inculcated by them of late years; for, even before its publication, numerous communications of a similar nature had already been obtained in various countries, and their number has since been greatly increased.

It may here be asked, why it is that the statements of all spirits are not in unison in regard to this subject? To this question we shall recur elsewhere.

Let us, for the present, examine the matter from another point of view, entirely irrespective of any assumed declarations of spirits in regard to it. Let us put the latter entirely aside for the moment; let us suppose them to have made no statement whatever in regard to it; let us even suppose the very existence of spirits not to have been surmised. Placing ouselves a moment on neutral ground, and admitting, as equally possible, the hypotheses of the *plurality* and of the *unity* of corporeal existences, let us see which of these hypotheses is most in harmony with the dictates of reason and with the requirements of our own interest.

There are persons who reject the idea of reincarnation simply because they do not like it, declaring that their present existence has been quite enough for them, and that they have no wish to recommence a similar one. Of such persons we would merely inquire whether they suppose that God has consulted their wishes and opinions in regulating the universe? Either the law of reincarnation exists, or it does not exist. If it exists, no matter how displeasing it may be to them, they will be compelled to submit to it; for God will not ask their permission to enforce it. It is as though a sick man should say, "I have suffered enough today; I do not chose to suffer-to-morrow." No matter what may be his unwillingness to suffer, he will nevertheless be obliged to go on suffering, not only on the morrow, but day after day, until he is cured. In like manner, if it be their destiny to live again corporeally, they will thus live again, they will be reincarnated. In vain will they rebel against necessity, like a child refusing to go to school, or a condemned criminal refusing to go to prison. They will be compelled to submit to their fate, no matter how unwilling they may be to do so. Such objections are too puerile to deserve a more serious examination. Let us say, however, for the consolation of those who urge them, that the spiritist doctrine of reincarnation is by no means so terrible as they imagine it to be; that the conditions of their next existence depend on themselves, and will be happy or unhappy according to the deeds done by them in this present life; and *that they may even, by their action in this life, raise themselves above the danger of falling again into the mire of expiation.*

We take it for granted that those whom we are addressing believe in some sort of future after death, and that they do not look forward either to annihilation or to a drowning of their soul in a universal whole, without individuality, like so many drops of rain in the ocean; which comes to much the same thing. But, if you believe in a future state of existence, you probably do not suppose that it will be the same for all; for, in that case, where would be the utility of doing right? Why should men place any restraint upon themselves? Why should they not satisfy all their passions, all their desires, even at the expense of the rest of the world, if the result is to be the same in all cases? On the contrary, you no doubt believe that our future will be more or less happy according to what we have done in our present life; and you have doubtless the desire to be as happy as possible in the future to which you look forward, since it will be for all eternity! Do you, perchance, consider yourself to be one of the most excellent of those who have ever existed upon the earth, and therefore entitled to supreme felicity? No. You admit, then, that there are some who are better than you, and who have consequently a right to a higher place, although you do not deserve to be classed among the reprobate. Place yourself, then, in thought, for a moment, in the medium condition which, according to your own admission, will properly be yours, and suppose that some one comes to you and says, "You suffer; you are not so happy as you might be; and meanwhile you see others in the enjoyment of unmixed happiness. Would you like to exchange your position for theirs?" "Undoubtedly, I should," you reply; "what must I do to bring about such a result?" "Something very simple; you have only to begin again what you have done badly, and try to do it better." Would you hesitate to accept the offer, even at the cost of several existences of trial?

Let us take another illustration, still more prosaic. Suppose that someone comes to a man who, though not in a state of absolute destitution, has to endure many privations through the smallness of his means, and says to him, "Here is an immense fortune, of which you may have the enjoyment, on condition that you work hard during one minute." The laziest of men, in response to such an offer, would say, without hesitation, "I am ready to work for one minute, for two minutes, for an hour, for a whole day if necessary! What is a day's labour in comparison with the certainty of ease and plenty for all the rest of my life?"

But what is the duration of a corporeal life in comparison with eternity? Less than a minute; less than a moment.

We sometimes hear people bring forward the following argument:—"God, who is sovereignly good, cannot impose upon man the hard necessity of recommencing a series of sorrows and tribulations." But would there be more kindness in condemning a man to perpetual suffering for a few moments of error than in giving him the means of repairing his faults?

"Two manufacturers had each a workman who might hope to become some day the partner of his employer. But it happened that both workmen made so very bad a use of their day that they merited dismissal. One of the manufacturers drove away his unfaithful workman, despite his supplications; and this workman, being unable to obtain any other employment, died of want. The other said to his workman—'You have wasted a day; you owe me compensation for the loss you have thus caused me. You have done your work badly; you owe me reparation for it. I give you leave to begin it over again. Try to do well, and I will keep you in my employ, and you may still aspire to the superior position which I had promised you.'"

Need we ask which of the manufacturers has shown himself to be the most humane? And would God, who is clemency itself, be more inexorable than a just and compassionate man? The idea that our fate is decided forever by a few years of trial, and notwithstanding the fact that it was not in our power to attain to perfection while we remained upon the earth, fills the mind with anguish; while the contrary idea is eminently consoling, for it leaves us hope. Thus, without pronouncing for or against the plurality of existences, without admitting either hypothesis in preference to the other, we assert that, if the matter were left to our own choice, there is no one who would prefer incurring a sentence against which there should be no appeal. A philosopher has said that "if God did not exist, it would be necessary to invent Him for the happiness of the human race;" the same might be said in regard to the plurality of existences. But, as we have already remarked, God does not ask our permission in the establishment of providential ordering; He does not consult our preferences in the matter. Either the law of reincarnation exists, or it does not exist; let us see on which side is the balance of probabilities, considering the matter from another point of view, but still leaving out of sight all idea of any statements that have been made by spirits in regard to it, and examining the question merely as matter of philosophic inquiry.

If the law of reincarnation do not exist, we can have but one corporeal existence; and if our present corporeal life be our only one, the soul of each individual must have been created at the same time as his body; unless, indeed, we assume the anteriority of the soul, in which case we should have to inquire what was the state of the soul before its union with the body, and whether this state did not constitute an existence of some kind or other. There is no middle ground. Either the soul existed before its union with the body, or it did not. If it existed, what was its condition? Was it possessed of self-consciousness? If not, its state must have been nearly equivalent to non-existence. If possessed of individuality, it must have been either progressive or stationary; in either case, what was its degree of advancement on uniting itself to the body? If, on the contrary, it be assumed, according to the general belief, that the soul is born into existence at the same time as the body—or that, previous to the birth of the body, it possesses only negative faculties—we have to propose the following questions:—

1. Why do souls manifest so great a diversity of aptitudes independently of the ideas acquired by education?

2. Whence comes the extra-normal aptitude for certain arts and sciences displayed by many children while still very young, although others remain in a state of inferiority, or of mediocrity, all their life?

3. Whence do some individuals derive the innate or intuitive ideas that are lacking in others?

4. Whence do some children derive the precocious instincts of vice or of virtue, the innate sentiments of dignity or of baseness,

which often contrast so strikingly with the situation into which they are born?

5. Why is it that some men, independently of education, are more advanced than others?

6. Why is it that among the races which people the globe some are savage and others civilised? If you took a Hottentot baby from its mother's breast, and brought it up in our most renowned schools, could you succeed in making of it a Laplace or a Newton? What is the philosophy or the theosophy that can solve these problems? Either the souls of men are equal at their birth, or they are unequal. If they are equal, why these inequalities of aptitude? Will it be said that these inequalities depend on the corporeal organisation of each child? But such a doctrine would be the most monstrous and the most immoral of hypotheses; for, in that case, man would be a mere machine, the sport of matter; he would not be responsible for his actions, but would have the right to throw all the blame of his wrong-doing on the imperfections of his physical frame. If, on the other hand, souls are created unequal, God must have created them so; but, in that case, why is this innate superiority accorded to some and denied to others? And would such partiality be consistent with the justice of God, and the equal love He bears to all His creatures?

Admit, on the contrary, a succession of existences, and every-thing is explained. Men bring with them, at their birth in flesh, the amount of intuition they have previously acquired. They are more or less advanced, according to the number of existences they have previously accomplished, according as they are nearer to or farther from the common starting-point; exactly as, in a company made up of individuals of different ages, each will possess a degree of development proportionate to the number of years he has already lived; the succession of years being, to the life of the body, what the succession of existences is to the life of the soul. Bring together in the same place, at the same time, a thousand individuals of all ages, from the new-born babe to the patriarch of eighty. Suppose that a veil is thrown over their past, and that you, in your ignorance of that past, imagine them all to have been born on the same day. You would naturally wonder how it is that some are big and others little; that some are wrinkled and others fresh; that some are learned and others ignorant; but if the cloud which hid their past were dispersed, and you discovered that some had lived longer than others, all these differences would be explained. God, in His justice, could not create souls more or less perfect. But granting the plurality of our corporeal exist-ences, there is nothing in the differences of quality that we see around us in any way inconsistent with the most rigorous equity; for what we see around us is then perceived to have its roots, not in the present, but in the past.

Is this argument based on any pre-conceived system or gratuitous supposition? No. We start from a fact that is patent and in-contestable—viz., the inequality of natural aptitudes and of intellectual and moral development; and we find this fact to be inexplicable by any of the theories in vogue, while the explanation of this fact afforded by another theory is at once simple, natural, and rational. Is it reasonable to prefer a theory which does not explain this fact to one which does?

In regard to the sixth question, it will doubtless be replied that the Hottentot is of an inferior race; in which case we beg to inquire whether a Hottentot is or is not a man? If he be not a man, why try to make him a Christian? If he be a man, why has God refused to him and to his race the privileges accorded to the Caucasian race? Spiritist philosophy is too broad to admit the existence of different species of men; it recognises only men whose spiritual part is more or less backward, but who are all capable of the same progress. Is not this view of the human race more conformable with the justice of God?

We have considering the soul in regard to its past and its present; if we consider it in regard to the future, we are met by difficulties which the theories in vogue are equally unable to explain:—

1. If our future destiny is to be decided solely by our present existence, what will be in the future the respective positions of the savage and of the civilised man? Will they be on the same level, or will there be a difference in the sum of their eternal felicity?

2. Will the man who has laboured diligently all his life to advance his moral and intellectual improvement be placed in the same rank with the man who, not through his own fault, but because he has had neither the time nor the opportunity for advancing, has remained at a lower point of moral and intellectual improvement?

3. Can the man who has done wrong because the means of enlightenment have been denied to him be justly punished for wrong-doing which has not been the result of his own choice?

4. We endeavour to enlighten, moralise, and civilise mankind; but, for one whom we are able to enlighten, there are millions who die every year without the light having reached them. What is to be the fate of these millions? Are they to be treated as reprobates? and, if they are not to be so treated, how have they deserved to be placed in the same category with those who have become enlightened and moralised?

5. What is to be the fate of children who die before they have been able to do either good or evil? If they are to be received among the supremely happy, why should this favour be granted to them without their having done anything to deserve it? And in virtue of what privilege are they exempted from undergoing the tribulations of the earthly life?

Which of the doctrines hitherto propounded can solve these problems? But, if we admit the fact of our consecutive existences, all these problems are solved in conformity with the divine justice. What we are not able to do in one existence we do in another. None are exempted from the action of the law of progress; every one is rewarded progressively, according to his deserts, but no one is excluded from the eventual attainment of the highest felicity, no matter what may be the obstacles he has to encounter on the road.

The questions growing out of the subject we are considering might be multiplied indefinitely, for the psychologic and moral problems which can only find their solution in the plurality of existences are innumerable. In the present considerations we have restricted our inquiry to those which are most general in their nature. "But," it may still be urged by some objetors, "whatever may be the arguments in its favour, the doctrine of reincarnation is not admitted by the Church; its acceptance would therefore be the overthrow of religion."

It is not our intention to treat of the question, in this place, under the special aspect suggested by the foregoing objection; it is sufficient for our present purpose to have shown the eminently moral and rational character of the doctrine we are considering. But it may be confidently asserted, that a doctrine which is both moral and rational cannot be antagonistic to a religion which proclaims the Divine Being to be the most perfect goodness and the highest reason. What, we may ask in our turn, would have become of the Church if, in opposition to the convictions of mankind and the testimony of science, it had persisted in rejecting over-whelming evidence, and had cast out from its bosom all who did not believe in the movement of the sun or in the six days of creation? What would be the credit or authority possessed among enlightened nations by a religious system that should inculcate manifest errors as articles of belief? Whenever any matter of evidence has been established, the Church has wisely sided with the evidence. If it be proved that the facts of human life are irreconcilable, on any other supposition, with a belief in the justice of God—if various points of the Christian dogma can only be explained with the aid of this doctrine, the Church will be compelled to admit its truth, and to acknowledge that the apparent antagonism between them is only apparent. We shall show, elsewhere, that religion has no more to fear from the acceptance of this doctrine than from the discovery of the motion of the earth and of the periods of geologic formation, which, at first sight, appear to contradict the statements of the Bible. Moreover, the principle of reincarnation is implied in many passages of Holy Writ, and is explicitly formulated in the Gospels:—

"When they came down from the mountain (after the transfiguration), Jesus gave this commandment, and said to them—'Speak to no one of what you have just seen, until the Son of Man shall have been resuscitated from among the dead.' His disciples thereupon began to question Him, and inquired, 'Why, then, do the Scribes say that Elias must first come?' But Jesus replied to them, 'It is true that Elias must come, and that he will re-establish all things. But I declare to you that Elias has already come, and they did not know him, but have made him suffer as they listed. It is thus that they will put to death the Son of Man.' Then His disciples understood that He spoke to them of John the Baptist." (St Matthew, chap. xvii.)

Since John the Baptist is declared by Christ to have been Elias, it follows that the spirit or soul of Elias must have been reincarnated in the body of John the Baptist.

But whatever may be our opinion in regard to reincarnation, whether we accept it or whether we reject it, it is certain that we shall have to undergo it, if it really exists, notwithstanding any belief of ours to the contrary. The point which we here desire to establish is this, viz., that the teaching of the spirits who proclaim it is eminently Christian, that it is founded on the doctrines of the immortality of the soul, of future rewards and punishments, of the justice of God, of human free-will, and the moral code of Christ; and that, therefore, it cannot be anti-religious.

We have argued the matter, as we remarked above, without reference to statements made by spirits; such statements being, for many minds, without authority. If we, and so many others, have adopted the hypothesis of the plurality of existences, we have done so not merely because it has been proclaimed by spirits, but because it has appeared to us to be eminently rational, and because it solves problems that are insoluble by the opposite hypothesis. Had it been suggested to us by a mere mortal, we should, therefore, have adopted it with equal confidence, renouncing, with equal promptitude, our preconceived opinions on the subject; for when an opinion has been shown to be erroneous, even self-love has more to lose than to gain by persisting in holding it. In like manner, we should have rejected the doctrine of reincarnation, even though proclaimed by spirits, if it had appeared to us to be contrary to reason, as, indeed, we have rejected many other ideas which spirits have sought to inculcate, for we know, by experience, that we can no more give a blind acceptance to ideas put forth by spirits than we can to those put forth by men.

The principal merit of the doctrine of reincarnation is, then, to our minds, that it is supremely rational. But it has also in its favour the confirmation of facts—facts positive and, so to say, material, which are apparent to all who study the question with . patience and perseverance, and in presence of which all doubt as to the reality of the law in question is impossible. When the appreciation of these facts shall have become popularised, like those which have revealed to us the formation and rotation of the earth, they who now oppose this doctrine will be compelled to renounce their opposition.

To sum up:—We assert the doctrine of the plurality of existences is the only one which explains what, without this doctrine, is inexplicable; that it is at once eminently consolatory and strictly conformable with the most rigorous justice; and that it is the anchor of safety which God in His mercy has provided for mankind.

The words of Jesus Himself are explicit as to the truth of this last assertion; for we read in the 3d chapter of the Gospel accord-

ing to St John that Jesus, replying to Nicodemus, thus expressed
Himself :—

"Verily, verily, I tell thee that, *if a man be not born again,* he
cannot see the kingdom of God." And when Nicodemus inquires,
"How can a man be born when he is old? Can he enter again
into his mother's womb and be born a second time?" Jesus
replies, "Except a man be born of water and of the spirit, he cannot
enter the kingdom of God. What is born of the flesh is flesh, and
what is born of the spirit is spirit. Be not amazed at what I have
told thee; *you must be born again."* (Vide *Resurrection of the
Body,* No. 1010.)

Wandering Spirits

223. Is the soul reincarnated immediately after its separation from the body?

"Sometimes immediately, but more often after intervals of longer or shorter duration. In the higher worlds, reincarnation is almost always immediate. Corporeal matter in those worlds being less gross than in the worlds of lower advancement, a spirit, while incarnated in them, retains the use of nearly all his spirit-faculties, his normal condition being that of your somnambulists in their lucid state."

224. What becomes of the soul in the intervals between its successive incarnations?

"It becomes an errant or wandering spirit, aspiring after a new destiny. Its state is one of waiting and expectancy."

— *How long may these intervals last?*

"From a few hours to thousands of ages. Strictly speaking, there are no fixed limits to the period of erraticity or wandering, which may be prolonged for a very considerable time, but which, however, is never perpetual. A spirit is always enabled, sooner or later, to commence a new existence which serves to effect the purification of its preceding existences."

— *Does the duration of the state of erraticity depend on the will of the spirit, or may it be imposed as an expiation?*

"It is a consequence of the spirit's free-will. Spirits act with full discernment; but, in some cases, the prolongation of this state is a punishment inflicted by God, while in others, it has been granted to them at their own request, to enable them to pursue studies which they can prosecute more effectually in the disincarnate state."

225. Is erraticity necessarily a sign of inferiority on the part of spirits?

"No, for there are errant spirits of every degree. Incarnation is a transitional state, as we have already told you. In their normal state, spirits are disengaged from matter."

226. Would it be correct to say that all spirits who are not incarnated are errant?

"Yes, as regards those who are to be reincarnated; but the pure spirits who have attained to perfection are not errant; their state is definitive."

In virtue of their special qualities, spirits are of different orders or degrees of advancement, through which they pass successively as they become purified. As regards their state, they may be—1. **Incarnated,** that is to say, united to a material body ; 2. **Errant** or **wandering,** that is to say disengaged from the material body and awaiting a new incarnation for purposes of improvement; 3. **Pure spirits,** that is to say, perfected, and having no further need of incarnation.

227. In what way do wandering spirits obtain instruction? It can hardly be in the same way as men.

"They study their past, and seek out the means of raising themselves to a higher degree. Possessed of vision, they observe all that is going on in the regions through which they pass. They listen to the discourse of enlightened men, and to the counsels of spirits more advanced than themselves, and they thus acquire new ideas."

228. Do spirits retain any human passion?

"Elevated spirits, on quitting their bodily envelope, leave behind them the evil passions of humanity, and retain only the love of goodness. But inferior spirits retain their earthly imperfections. Were it not for this retention, they would be of the highest order."

229. How is it that spirits, on quitting the earth, do not leave behind them all their evil passions, since they are then able to perceive the disastrous consequences of those passions?

"You have among you persons who are, for instance, excessively jealous; do you imagine that they lose this defect at once on quitting your world? There remains with spirits, after their departure from the earthly life, and especially with those who have had strongly marked passions, a sort of atmosphere by which they are enveloped, and which keeps up all their former evil qualities; for spirits are not entirely freed from the influence of materiality. It is only occasionally that they obtain glimpses of the truth, showing them, as it were, the true parth which they ought to follow."

230. *Do spirits progress in the state of erraticity?*

"They may make a great advance in that state, in proportion to their efforts and desires after improvement, but it is in the corporeal life that they put in practice the new ideas they have thus acquired."

231. *Are wandering spirits happy or unhappy?*

"More or less so according to their deserts. They suffer from the passions of which they have retained the principle, or they are happy in proportion as they are more or less dematerialised. In the state of erraticity, a spirit perceives what he needs in order to become happier, and he is thus stimulated to seek out the means of attaining what he lacks. But he is not always permitted to reincarnate himself when he desires to do so, and the prolongation of erraticity then becomes a punishment."

232. *Can spirits in the state of erraticity enter all the other worlds?*

"That depends on their degree of advancement. When a spirit has quitted the body, he is not necessarily disengaged entirely from matter, and he still belongs to the world in which he has lived, or to a world of the same degree, unless he has raised himself during his earthly life to a world of higher degree; and this progressive elevation should be the constant aim of every spirit, for without it he would never attain to perfection. A spirit, however, may enter worlds of higher degree; but, in that case, he finds himself to be a stranger in them. He can only obtain, as it were, a glimpse of them; but such glimpses often serve to quicken his desire to improve and to advance, that he may become worthy of the felicity which is enjoyed in them, and may thus be enabled to inhabit them in course of time."

233. *Do spirits who are already purified ever come into worlds of lower degree?*

"They come into them very frequently in order to help them forward. Unless they did so, those worlds would be left to themselves, without guides to direct them."

Transitional Worlds

234. Are there, as has been stated, worlds which serve as stations and resting-places for errant spirits?

"Yes; there are worlds which are specially adapted for the reception of wandering beings, worlds which they may temporalily inhabit; a sort of camping-ground in which they may bivouac for a time, and repose after a too lengthened erraticity—a state which is always somewhat wearisome. Those worlds constitute intermediary stations between the worlds of other orders, and are graduated according to the nature of the spirits who are to come into them, and who will find in them the conditions of a rest more or less enjoyable."

— Can the spirits who occupy these worlds quit them at pleasure?

"Yes, they can leave them for any other region to which they may have to go. They are like birds of passage alighting on an island in order to rest and recover strength for reaching their destination."

235. Do spirits progress during their sojourns in the transitional worlds?

"Certainly; those who thus come together do so with a view to their instruction, and in order more readily to obtain permission to enter a higher region. and thus to advance their progress towards the perfection which is their aim."

236. Are the transitional worlds of a special nature, and destined to be for ever the sojourn of wandering spirits?

"No; their position in the hierarchy of worlds is only temporary."

— Are they, at the same time, inhabited by corporeal beings?

"No; their surface is sterile. Those who inhabit them have no corporeal wants."

— Is this sterility permanent, and does it result from anything special in their nature?

"No; their sterility is only transitional."

— Such worlds are, then, void of everything like the beauties of nature?

"The inexhaustible richness of creation is manifested by beauties of immensity that are no less admirable than the terrestrial harmonies which you call the beauties of nature."

— Since the state of those worlds is only transitory, will the state of our earth, at some future time, be of that character?

"Such has already been its state."

— *At what epoch?*

"During its formation."

Nothing in nature is useless ; everything has its purpose, its destination. There is no void ; every portion of immensity is inhabited. Life is everywhere. Thus, during the long series of ages which preceded man's appearance upon the earth, during the vast periods of transition attested by the superposition of the geologic strata, before even the earliest formation of organised beings, upon that formless mass, in that arid chaos in which the elements existed in a state of fusion, there was no absence of life. Beings who had neither human wants nor human sensations found therein a welcome refuge. The will of God had ordained that the earth, even in that embryonic state, should be useful. Who, then, would venture to say that, of the innumerable orbs which circulate in immensity, one only, and one of the smallest of them all, lost in the crowd, has the exclusive privilege of being inhabited? What, in that case, would be the use of the others? Would God have created them merely to regale our eyes? Such a supposition, of which the absurdity is incompatible with the wisdom that appears in all His works, becomes still more evidently inadmissible when we reflect on the myriads of heavenly bodies which we are unable to perceive. On the other hand, no one can deny the grandeur and sublimity of the idea that worlds in course of formation, and which are still unfitted for the habitation of material life, are, nevertheless, peopled with living beings appropriate to its condition—an idea which may possibly contain the solution of more than one problem as yet obscure.

Perceptions, Sensations, and Suffering of Spirits

237. Does the soul, when it has returned into the world of spirits, still possess the perceptions it possessed in the earthly life?

"Yes; and others which it did not possess in that life, because its body acted as a veil which obscured them. Intelligence is an attribute of spirit; but it is manifested more freely when not hindered by the trammels of flesh."

238. Are the perceptions and knowledge of spirits unlimited? In a word, do they know everything?

"The nearer they approach to perfection, the more they know. Spirits of the higher orders possess a wide range of knowledge; those of the lower orders are more or less ignorant in regard to everything."

239. Do spirits comprehend the first principle of things?

"That depends on their degree of elevation and of purity: inferior spirits know no more than men."

240. Do spirits perceive duration as we do?

"No; and this is why you do not always understand us when you seek to fix dates and epochs."

The life of spirits is exterior to the idea of time as perceived by us. The idea of duration may be said to be annihilated for them ; ages, which seem so long to us, appear to them only as so many instants lapsing into eternity, just as the inequalities of the earth's surface are effaced and disappear beneath the gaze of the aeronaut as he mounts into space.

241. Do spirits take a truer and more precise view of the present than we do?

"Their view, in comparison with yours, is pretty much what eyesight is in comparison with blindness. They see what you do not see; they judge, therefore, otherwise than you do. But we must remind you that this depends on their degree of elevation."

242. How do spirits acquire the knowledge of the past, and is this knowledge without limits for them?

"The past, when we turn our attention to it, is perceived by us as though it were present, exactly as is the case with you, when you call to mind something which may have struck you in the course of your present exile; with this difference, however, that, as our view is no longer obscured by the material veil which covers your intelligence, we remember things that are at present effaced from your memory. But spirits do not know everything; for example, their creation."

243. Do spirits foresee the future?

"That, again, depends on their degree of advancement. Very often, they foresee it only partially; but, even when they foresee it more clearly, *they are not always permitted to reveal it.* When they foresee it, it appears to them to be present. A spirit sees the future more clearly in proportion as he approaches God. After death, the soul sees and embraces at a glance *all its past emigrations,* but it cannot see what God has in store for it. This foreknowledge is only possessed by the soul that has attained to entire union with God, after a long succession of existences."

-- Do spirits, arrived at absolute perfection, possess the complete knowledge of the future?

"'Complete' is not the word; for God alone is the sovereign master, and none can attain to equality with Him."

244. Do spirits see God?

"Only spirits of the highest order see and understand Him; spirits of lower order feel and divine Him."

— When a spirit of lower degree says that such and such a thing is permitted to him or forbidden by God, how does he know that such ordering is really by Him?

"He does not see God, but he feels His sovereignty; and when anything is not to be done or said, he feels a sort of intuition, an invisible warning, which commands him to abstain. Are not you yourselves sometimes conscious of a secret impression, enjoining on you to do or not to do, as the case may be? It is the same thing with us, but in a higher degree; for you can easily understand that, the essence of spirits being more supple than yours, they are better able to receive the divine monitions."

— *Are the divine commands transmitted to each spirit directly by God, or through the intermediary of other spirits?*

"Those commands do not come direct from God; in order to communicate directly with God, a spirit must have made himself worthy of such communication. God transmits His orders through spirits of higher degrees of wisdom and purity."

245. Is spirit-sight circumscribed, as is the sight of corporeal beings?

"No; it resides in them."

246. Do spirits require light in order to see?

"They see of themselves, and have no need of any exterior light. There is, for them, no other darkness than that in which they may be made to find themselves as expiation."

247. Do spirits need to travel in order to see two different points? Can they, for instance, see the two hemispheres of the globe at the same time?

"As spirits transport themselves from point to point with the rapidity of thought, they may be said to see everywhere at the same time. A spirit's thought may radiate at the same moment on many different points; but this faculty depends on his purity. The more impure the spirit, the narrower is his range of sight. It is only the higher spirits who can take in a whole at a single glance."

The faculty of vision, among spirits, is a property inherent in their nature, and which resides in their whole being, as light resides in every part of a luminous body. It is a sort of universal lucidity, which extends to everything, which embraces at once time, space, and things, and in relation to which, darkness or material obstacles have no existence. And a moment's reflection shows us that this must necessarily be the case. In the human being, sight being produced by the play of an organ acted upon by light, it follows that, without light, man finds himself in darkness ; but the faculty of vision being an attribute of the spirit himself, independently of any exterior agent, spirit-sight is independent of light. (Vide **Ubiquity**, N.º 92, p. 91.)

248. Do spirits see things as distintly as we do?

"More distinctly, for their sight penetrates what yours cannot penetrate: nothing obscures it."

249. Do spirits perceive sounds?

"Yes; they perceive sounds that your obtuse senses cannot perceive."

— *Does the faculty of hearing reside in the whole of a spirit's being, like the faculty of sight?*

"All the perceptive faculties of a spirit are attributes of his nature, and form part of his being. When he is clothed with a material body, his perceptions reach him only through the channel of his bodily organs; but the perceptions of a spirit, when restored to the state of freedom, are no longer localised."

250. The perceptive faculties being attributes of a spirit's nature, is it possible for him to withdraw himself from their action?

"A spirit only sees and hears what he chooses to see and hear. This statement, however, is to be taken in a general sense, and mainly as regards spirits of the higher orders; for imperfect spirits are compelled to see and hear, and often against their will, whatever may be useful for their amelioration."

251. Are spirits affected by music?

"Do you mean the music of your earth? What is it in comparison with the music of the celestial spheres, of that harmony of which nothing in your earth can give you any idea? The one is to the other as is the howl of the savage to the most lovely melody. Spirits of low degree, however, may take pleasure in hearing your music, because they are not yet able to appreciate anything more sublime. Music has inexhaustible charms for spirits, owing to the great development of their sensitive qualities; I mean, celestial music, than which the spiritual imagination can conceive of nothing more exquisitely sweet and beautiful."

252. Are spirits sensible of the beauties of nature?

"The beauties of nature are so different in the different globes, that spirits are far from knowing them all. They are sensible of them in proportion to their aptitude for appreciating and comprehending them; but, for spirits of a high degree of advancement, there are beauties of general harmony in which beauties of detail are, so to say, lost sight of."

253. Do spirits experience our physical needs and sufferings?

"They *know* them, because they have undergone them; but they do not, like you, experience them materially: they are spirits."

254. Do spirits experience fatigue and the need of rest?

"They cannot feel fatigue as you understand it, and consequently they have no need of your corporeal rest, because they have no organs whose strength requires to be restored. But a spirit may be said to take rest, inasmuch as he is not constantly in a state of activity. He does not act materially; his action is altogether intellectual, and his resting is altogether moral; that is to say, that there are moments when his thought becomes less active, and is no longer directed to any special object, and this constitutes for him a state which is really one of repose, but a kind of repose which cannot be likened to that of the body. The sort of fatigue which may be felt by spirits is proportionate to their inferiority; for, the higher their degree of elevation, the less is their need of rest."

255. When a spirit says that he suffers, what is the nature of the suffering he feels?

"Mental anguish, which causes him tortures far more painful than any physical sufferings."

256. How is it, then, that spirits sometimes complain of suffering from cold or heat?

"Such sensations on their part are caused by the remembrance of sufferings endured by them in the earthly life, and are sometimes as painful as though they were real; but complaints of that nature are often only figures by which, for lack of any better means of description, they endeavour to express the situation in which they find themselves. When they remember their earthly body, they experience the same sort of impression which makes you feel for a few moments, when you have taken off a cloak, as though you had it still upon your shoulders."

Theoretic Explanation of the Nature of Sensation in Spirits

257. The body is the instrument of pain, of which, if not the primary cause, it is, at least, the immediate cause. The soul possesses the faculty of perceiving the pain thus caused; the perception of pain is, therefore, the effect of this action of the soul. The remembrance of pain retained by a spirit may be very painful,

but cannot exercise any physical action. The tissues of the soul cannot be disorganised either by cold or heat; the soul can neither freeze nor burn. But do we not constantly see that the remembrance or the aprehension of physical pain may produce all the effect of reality, and may even occasion death? We know that recently-amputated patients often complain of felling pain in the limb they have lost: yet it is evident that the amputated limb cannot really be the seat, nor even the point of departure, of the pain feel, which is due solely to the action of the brain, that has retained and reproduces the impression of the pain formerly experienced by them. It may therefore be inferred that the suffering felt by spirits after death is of a similar nature. A careful study of the perispirit, which plays so important a part in all spirit-phenomena, the indications afforded by apparitions, whether vaporous or tangible, the state of the spirit at the moment of death, the striking pictures presented by the victims of suicide and of capital punishment, by the spirits of those who have been absorbed in carnal enjoyments, and a great variety of other facts, haye thrown new light on this question, and have given rise to the explanations of which we offer the following summary:—

The perispirit is the link which unites the spirit with the material body. It is drawn from the surrounding atmosphere, from the universal fluid; it participates at once in the nature of electricity, of the magnetic fluid, and of inert matter. It may be said to be the quintessence of matter; it is the principle of organic life, but it is not that of intellectual life, the principle of which is in the spirit. It is also the agent of all the sensations of the outer life. Those sensations are localised in the earthly body by the organs which serve as their channels. When the body is destroyed, those sensations become general. This explains why a spirit never says that he suffers in his head or in his feet. But we must take care not to confound the sensations of the perispirit, rendered independent by the death of the body, with the sensations experienced through the body; for the latter can only be understood as offering a means of comparison with the former, but not as being analogous to them. When freed from the body, a spirit may suffer, but this suffering is not the suffering of the body. And yet it is not a suffering exclusively moral, like remorse, for example, for he complains of feeling cold or hot, although he suffers no more in summer than in winter, and we have seen spirits pass through flames without feeling any painful effect therefrom, temperature making no impression upon them. The pain which they feel is therefore not a physical pain in the proper sense of that term; it is a vague feeling perceived in himself by a spirit, and which he himself is not always able to account for, precisely because his pain is not localised, and is not produced by any exterior agents: it is a remembrance rather than a reality, but a remembrance as painful as though it were a reality. Nevertheless, spirit-suffering is sometimes more than a remembrance, as we shall see.

Observation has shown us that the perispirit, at death, disengages itself more or less slowly from the body. During the first few moments which follow dissolution, a spirit does not clearly understand his own situation. He does not think himself dead, for he feels himself living. He sees his body beside him, he knows that it is his, and he does not understand that he is separated from it; and this state of indecision continues as long as there remains the slightest connection between the body and the perispirit. One who had committed suicide said to us, "No, I am not dead," and added, *"and yet I feel the worms that are devouring my body."* Now, most assuredly, the worms were not devouring his perispirit, still less could they be devouring the spirit himself. But, as the separation between the body and the perispirit was not complete, a sort of moral repercussion transmitted to the latter the sensation of what was taking place in the former. Repercussion is perhaps hardly the word to be employed in this case, as it may seem to imply an effect too nearly akin to materiality; it was rather the sight of what was going on in the decaying body, to which he was still attached by his perispirit, that produced in him an illusion which he mistook for reality. Thus, in his case, it was not a remembrance, for he had not, during his earthly life, been devoured by worms. It was the feeling of something which was actually taking place. We see, by the examination of the case here alluded to, the deductions that may be drawn from an attentive observation of facts. During life, the body receives external impressions and transmits them to the spirit through the intermediary of the perispirit, which constitutes, probably, what is called the nervous fluid. The body, when dead, no longer feels anything, because there is in it no longer either spirit or perispirit. The perispirit, when disengaged from the body, still experiences sensation; but, as sensation no longer reaches it through a limited channel, its sensation is general. Now, as the perispirit is, in reality, only an agent for the transmission of sensations to the spirit, by whom alone they are perceived, it follows that the perispirit, if it could exist without a spirit, would no more be able to feel any sensation than is the body when it is dead; and it also follows that the spirit, if it had no perispirit, would be inacessible to any painful sensation, as is the case with spirits who are completely purified. We know that, in proportion as the spirit progresses, the essence of its perispirit becomes more and more etherealised; whence it follows that the influence of matter diminishes in proportion to the advancement of the spirit, that is to say, in proportion as his perispirit becomes less and less gross.

But, it may be urged, it is through the perispirit that agreeable sensations are transmitted to the spirit, as well as disagreeable ones; therefore, if the purified spirit be inaccessible to the latter, he must also be to the former. Yes, undoubtedly so, as far as regards those which proceed solely from the influence of the matter which is known to us. The sound of our instruments, the perfume of our flowers, produce no impression upon spirits of the highest orders; and yet they experience sensations of the most vivid character, of a charm indescribable for us, and of which it is impossible for us to form any idea, because we are, in regard to that order of sensations, in the same position as that in which men, born blind, are in regard to light. We know that they exist; but our knowledge is inadequate to explain their nature or the mode in which they are produced. We know that spirits possess perception, sensation, hearing, sight, and that these faculties are attributes of their whole being, and not, as in men, of a part of their being.

But we seek in vain to understand by what intermediary these faculties act; of this we know nothing. Spirits themselves can give us no explanation of the matter, because our language can no more be made to express ideas which are beyond the range of our comprehension than the language of savages can be made to furnish terms for expressing our arts, our sciences, or our philosophic doctrines.

In saying that spirits are inaccessible to the impressions of earthly matter, we must be understood as speaking of spirits of very high order, to whose etherealised envelope there is nothing analogous in our lower sphere. It is different with spirits whose perispirit is of denser quality, for they perceive our sounds and our odours, though no longer through special parts of their personality, as they did during life. The molecular vibrations may be said to be felt by them throughout their whole being, reaching thus their *common sensorium*, which is the spirit himself, although in a different manner, and causing, perhaps, a different impression, which may produce a modification of the resulting perception. They hear the sound of our voice, and yet are able to understand us, without the help of speech, by the mere transmission of thought; and this penetration is the more easy for them in proportion as they are more dematerialised. Their sight is independent of our light. The faculty of vision is an essential attribute of the soul, for whom darkness has no existence; but it is more extended, more penetrating, in those whose purification is more advanced. The soul or spirit, therefore, possesses in itself the faculty of all perceptions; during our corporeal life these are deadened by the grossness of our physical organs, but, in the extra-corporeal life, they become more and more vivid as our semi-material envelope becomes more and more etherealised.

This envelope is drawn from the atmosphere in which the spirit finds himself for the time being, and varies according to the nature of the different worlds. In passing from one world to another, spirits change their envelope as we change a garment when we pass from summer to winter, or from the pole to the equator. The most elevated spirits, when they come to visit us, assume a terrestrial perispirit, which they retain during their stay among us, and their perceptions are therefore produced, while they are thus clothed upon, in the same way as those of the lower spirits, of whom this grosser order of perispirit is the appropriate envelope; but all spirits, whether high or low, only hear and feel what they choose to hear and to feel.[1] Without possessing organs of sensation, spirits are able to render their perceptions active, or to prevent their action : there is but one thing which they are compelled to hear, and that is the counsels of their guides. The sight of spirits is always active, but they are able, nevertheless, to render themselves invisible to one another, according to the rank they occupy; those of a higher rank having the power of hiding themselves from those who are below them, although a spirit of lower rank cannot hide himself from those who are above him. In the first moments after death, the sight of a spirit is always dim and confused; it becomes cleared as he becomes freed from the body, acquiring not only the same clearness which it possessed during life, but also the power of penetrating bodies which are opaque for us. As for the extension of a spirit's vision through space,

---

[1] **Vide,** for the exception to this general law, the cases mentioned in No. 250.

and into the future and the past, *that* depends entirely on his degree of purity and of consequent elevation.

"This theory," it will be said, "is anything but encouraging. We had thought that, once freed from our gross bodily envelope, the instrument of all our sufferings, we should suffer no more; and now you tell us that we shall still suffer in the other life, although not in the same way as we do here. But suffering is none the less painful, whatever its nature; and this prospect is by no means an agreeable one." Alas, yes! We may still have to suffer, to suffer much, and for a long time; but we may also have no more to suffer, even from the very moment of quitting the corporeal life.

The sufferings of our present existence are sometimes independent of ourselves; but they are often the consequences of our own volition. If we trace our sufferings back to their source, we see that the greater number of them are due to causes which we might have avoided. How many ills, how many infirmities, does man owe to his excesses, his ambition—in a word, to the indulgence of his various passions! He who should live soberly in all respects, who should never run into excesses of any kind, who should be always simple in his tastes, modest in his desires, would escape a large proportion of the tribulations of human life. It is the same with regard to spirit-life, the sufferings of which are always the consequence of the manner in which a spirit has lived upon the earth. In that life undoubtedly he will no longer suffer from gout or rheumatism; but his wrong-doing down here will cause him to experience other sufferings no less painful. We have seen that those sufferings are the result of the links which exist between a spirit and matter; that the more completely he is freed from the influence of matter—in other words, the more dematerialised he is—the fewer are the painful sensations experienced by him. It depends, therefore, on each of us to free ourselves from the influence of matter by our action in this present life. Man possesses free-will, and, consequently, the power of electing to do or not to do. Let him conquer his animal passions; let him rid himself of hatred, envy, jealousy, pride; let him throw off the yoke of selfishness; let him purify his soul by cultivating noble sentiments; let him do good; let him attach to the things of this world only the degree of importance which they deserve,—and he will, even under his present corporeal envelope, have effected his purification, and achieved his deliverance from the influence of matter, which will cease for him on his quitting that envelope. For such a one the remembrance of physical sufferings endured by him in the life he has quitted has nothing painful, and produces no disagreeable impression, because they affected his body only, and left no trace in his soul. He is happy to be relieved from them; and the calmness of a good conscience exempts him from all moral suffering.

We have questioned many thousands of spirits having belonged to every class of society; we have studied them at every period of their, spirit-life, from the instant of their quitting the body. We have followed them step by step in that life beyond the grave, with a view to ascertaining the changes that should take place in their ideas and sensations; and this examination—in which it has not always been the most commonplace spirits that have furnished us the least valuable subjects of study—has invariably shown us, on the one hand, that the sufferings of spirits are the direct result of the misconduct of which they have to undergo the consequences, and, on the other hand, that their new existence is the source of ineffable happiness for those who have followed the right road. From which it follows that those who suffer do so because they have so willed it, and have only themselves to thank for their suffering, in the other world, as in this one.

Choice of Trials

258. In the state of erraticity, and before taking on a new corporeal existence, does a spirit foresee the things which will happen to him in that new existence?

"He chooses for himself the kind of trials which he will undergo,. and it is in this freedom of choice that his freewill consists."

— *It is not God, then, who imposes upon him the tribulations of life as a chastisement?*

"Nothing comes to pass without the permission of God, for it is He who has established all the laws that rule the universe. You would have to inquire why He has made such and such a law, instead of taking some other way. In giving to a spirit the liberty of choice, He leaves to him the entire responsibility of his acts and of their consequences. There is nothing to bar his future; the right road is open to him as freely as the wrong road. But if he succumbs, there still remains to him the consoling fact that all is not over with him, and that God in His goodness allows him to recommence the task which he has done badly. You must, moreover, always distinguish between what is the work of God's will and what is the work of man's will. If a danger threatens you, it is not you who have created this danger, but God; but you have voluntarily elected to expose yourself to this danger, because you have seen in so doing a means of advancement, and God has permitted you to do so."

259. If the spirit has the choice of the kind of trials which he will undergo, does it follow that all the tribulations we experience in the earthly life have been foreseen and chosen by us?

"It would not be correct to say that such has been the case with all of them; for you cannot be said to have chosen and foreseen all the things which happen to you in this life, and all their details. You have chosen the *kind* of trial to which you are subjected; the details of this trial are a consequence of the general situation which you have chosen, and are often the result of your own actions.

"If, for instance, a spirit has chosen to be born among malefactors, he knew to what *kind* of temptations he was exposing himself, but not each one of the actions which he would accomplish; those actions are the effect of his volition, of his free-will. A spirit knows that, in choosing such and such a road, he will have such and such a kind of struggle to undergo; he knows, therefore, the nature of the vicissitudes which he will encounter, but he does not know whether these will present themselves under one form or under another. The details of events spring from circumstances and the force of things. It is only the leading events of his new life, those which will exercise a determining effect on his destiny, that are foreseen by him. If you enter upon a road full of ruts, you know that you must walk very warily, because you run a risk of stumbling; but you do not know the exact place where you will stumble, and it may be that, if you are sufficiently on your guard, you will not stumble at all. If, when you are passing along a street, a tile falls upon your head, you must not suppose that 'it was written,' as the common saying is."

260. How can a spirit choose to be born among those who are leading a bad life?

"It is necessary for him to be sent into the conditions which will furnish the elements of the trial he has demanded. To this end, there must be a correspondence between the imperfection of which he desires to freen himself, and the social surroundings into which he is born. For example, if he have to struggle against the instinct of brigandage, it is necessary for him to be thrown among brigands."

— *If, then, there were no evil livers upon the earth, spirits could not find in it the conditions necessary to certain kinds of trial?*

"Would there be any reason for complaining, if such were the case? The case you suppose is that of the worlds of higher order, to which evil has no access, and which are therefore inhabited only by good spirits. Try to bring about such a state of things as soon as possible in your earth."

261. *Is it necessary for the spirit, in the course of the trials to which he has to submit in order to arrive at perfection, to undergo every sort of temptation? Must he encounter all the circumstances that can excite in him pride, jealousy, avarice, sensuality, etc.?*

"Certainly not, since there are, as you know, many spirits who take from the beginning a road which spares them the necessity of undergoing many of those trials; but he who suffers himself to be drawn into the wrong road, exposes himself to all the dangers of that road. A spirit, for instance, may ask for riches, and his demand may be granted; and, in that case, he will become, according to his character, avaricious or prodigal, selfish or generous, and will make a noble use of his wealth, or waste it on vanity or sensuality; but this does not imply that he will be compelled to run the gauntlet of all the evil tendencies that may be fostered by the possession of riches."

262. *As a spirit, at its origin, is simple, ignorant, and without experience, how can he make an intelligent choice of an existence, and how can he be responsible for such a choice?*

"God supplies what is lacking through his inexperience, by tracing out for him the road which he has to follow, as you do for the infant in its cradle; but he allows him, little by little, to become the master of his choice, in proportion as his free-will becomes developed; and it is then that he often loses his way and takes the wrong road, if he do not listen to the advice of the good spirits, who endeavour to instruct him; it is this which may be called the fall of man."

— *When a spirit is in possession of his free-will, does the choice of his corporeal existence always depend solely on his own*

*volition, or is this existence sometimes imposed on him by God
as an expiation?*

"God can afford to wait; He never hurries the work of expiation.
Nevertheless, God does sometimes impose an existence upon a
spirit, when the latter, through his ignorance or his obstinacy, is
incapable of perceiving what would be to his advantage, and
when He sees that this existence may subserve his purification and
advancement, while furnishing him also with the conditions of
expiation."

263. Do spirits make their choice immediately after death?

"No; many of them believe their sufferings to be eternal: you
have already been told that this is a chastisement."

*264. What is it that decides a spirit's choice of the trials which
he determines to undergo?*

"He chooses those which may serve to expiate faults, and at
the same time help him to advance more quickly. In view of these
ends, some may impose upon themselves a life of poverty privations,
in order to exercise themselves in bearing them with courage;
others may wish to test their powers of resistance by the temptations of fortune and of power, much more dangerous, because of
the bad use that may be made of them, and the evil passions that
may be developed by them; others, again, may desire to strengthen
their good resolutions by having to struggle against the influence
of vicious surroundings."

*265. If some spirits elect to expose themselves to the contact
of vice as a trial of their virtue, may it not be that others make a
similar choice from a desire to live amidst surroundings in unison
with their depraved tastes, and in which they may give free course
to their sensual tendencies?*

"Such instances undoubtedly occur; but only among those whose
moral sense is still but imperfectly developed. *In such cases, the
needed trial occurs spontaneously, and they are subjected to it for
a longer time.* Sooner or later, they will understand that indulgence of the animal instincts leads to disastrous consequences,
which they will undergo during a period so long that it will seem
to them to be eternal; and God sometimes leaves them in this
state until they have comprehended the gravity of their fault, and
demand, of their own accord, to be allowed to repair it by undergoing trials of a profitable nature."

266. Does it not seem natural to make choice of such trials as are least painful?

"From your point of view, it would seem to be so, but not from that of the spirit; when he is freed from materiality, his illusions cease, and he thinks differently".

Man, while upon the earth, and subjected to the influence of carnal ideas, sees only the painful aspect of the trials he is called upon to undergo ; and it therefore appears to him to be natural to choose the trials that are allied to material enjoyments. But when he has returned to spirit-life, he compares those gross and fugitive enjoyments with the unchangeable felicity of which he obtains occasional glimpses, and judges that such felicity will be cheaply purchased by a little temporary suffering. A spirit may therefore, make choice of the hardest trial, and consequently of the most painful existence, in the hope of thereby attaining more rapidly to a happier state, just as a sick man often chooses the most unpalatable medicine in the hope of obtaining a more rapid cure. He who aspires to immortalise his name by the discovery of an unknown country does not seek a flowery road. He takes the road which will bring him most surely to the aim he has in view, and he is not deterred from following it even by the dangers it may offer. On the contrary, he braves those dangers for the sake of the glory he will win if he succeeds.

The doctrine of our freedom in the choice of our successive existences and of the trials which we have to undergo ceases to appear strange when we consider that spirits, being freed from matter, judge of things differently from men. They perceive the ends which these trials are intended to work out—ends far more important for them than the fugitive enjoyments of earth. After each existence, they see the steps they have already accomplished, and comprehend what they still lack for the attainment of the purity which alone enable them to reach the goal ; and they willingly submit to the vicissitudes of corporeal life, demanding of their own accord to be allowed to undergo those which will aid them to advance most rapidly. There is, therefore, nothing surprising in a spirit making choice of a hard or painful life. He knows that he cannot, in his present state of imperfection, enjoy the perfect hapiness to which he aspires ; but he obtains glimpses of that happiness, and he seeks to effect his own improvement, as the sole means to its attainment.

Do we not, every day, witness examples of a similar choice? What is the action of the man who labours, without cessation or repose, to amass the property which will enable him eventually to live in comfort, but the discharge of a task which he has voluntarily assumed as the means of insuring for himself a more prosperous future? The soldier who offers himself for the accomplishment of a perilous mission, the traveller who braves dangers no less formidable in the interest of science or of his own fortune, are examples of the voluntary incurring of hardships for the sake of the honour or profit that will result from their successful endurance. What will not men undergo for gain or for glory? Is not every sort of competitive examination a trial to which men voluntarily submit in the hope of obtaining advancement in the career they have chosen? He who would gain a high position in science, art, industry, is obliged to pass through all the lower degrees which lead up to it, and which constitute so many trials. Human life is thus seen to be modelled on spirit-life, presenting the same vicissitudes on a smaller scale. And as in the earthly life we often make choice of the hardest conditions as means to the attainment of the highest ends, why should not a disincarnate spirit, who sees farther than he saw when incarnated in an earthly body, and for whom the bodily life is only a fugitive incident, make choice of a laborious or painful existence, if it may lead him ou towards an eternal felicity? Those who say that, since spirits have the power choosing their existences, they will demand to be princes and millionaires, are like the purblind, who only see what they touch, or like greedy children, who, when asked what occupation they would prefer to follow, reply that they would like to be pastry-cooks or confectioners.

It is with a spirit as with a traveller, who, in the depths of a valley obscured by fog, sees neither the length nor the extremities of his road. When he has reached the top of the hill, and the fog has cleared away, his view takes in both the road along which he has come and that by which he has still to go. He sees the point which he has to reach, and the obstacles he has to overcome in reaching it, and he is thus able to take his measures for successfully accomplishing his journey. A spirit, while incarnated, is like the traveller at the foot of the hill ; when freed from terrestrial trammels, he is like the traveller who has reached the top of the hill. The aim of the traveller is to obtain rest after fatigue ; the aim of the spirit is to attain to perfect happiness after tribulations and trials. Spirits say that, in the state of erraticity, they seek, study, observe, in order to make their choice wisely. Have we not examples of analogous action in corporeal life? Do we not often spend years in deciding on the career upon which, at length, we freely fix our choice, because we consider it to be the one in which we are most likely to succeed? If, after all, we fail in the one we have chosen, we seek out another ; and each career thus embraced by us constitutes a phase, a period, of our life. Is not each day employed by us in deciding what we shall do on the morrow? And what, for a spirit, are his different corporeal existences, but so many phases, periods, days, in comparison with his spirit life, which, as we know, is his normal life, the corporeal life being only a transitional passage?

267. *Can a spirit make his choice while in the corporeal state?*

"His desire may exercise a certain amount of influence, according to the quality of his intention; but, when he returns to spirit-life, he often judges things very differently. It is only as a spirit that he makes his choice; but he may, nevertheless, make it during the material life, for a spirit, even while incarnated, has occasional moments in which he is independent of the matter he inhabits."

— *Many persons desire earthly greatness and riches, but not assuredly, either as expiation or as trial.*

"Undoubtedly; in such cases it is their material instinct which desires greatness in order to enjoy its satisfactions. The spirit could only desire it in order to understand its vicissitudes."

268. *Until a spirit has reached the state of perfect purity, has he constantly to undergo trials?*

"Yes; but not such as you understand by that term. By the term *trials*, you understand only material tribulations. But when a spirit has reached a certain degree of purification, although he is not yet perfect, he has no more tribulations of that kind to undergo. He has, nevertheless, to perform cretain duties which advance his own improvement, but there is nothing painful in these, as, for example, the duty of aiding others to work out their own improvement."

269. *Is it possible for a spirit to make a mistake as to the efficacy of the trial he chooses?*

"He may choose one which exceeds his strength, and, in that case, he will succumb; or he may choose one from which he will reap no profit whatever, as, for instance, if he seeks to lead an idle and useless life. But, in such cases, he perceives, on returning to the spirit-world, that he has gained nothing, and he then demands to make up for lost time."

270. What is the cause of the vocations of some persons, and their spontaneous desire to follow one career rather than another?

"It seems to me that you yourselves might answer this question. Is not the existence of such vocations a necessary consequence of what we have told you concerning the choice of trials, and of the progress accomplished in a preceding existence?"

271. As a spirit in the wandering state studies the various conditions of corporeal life that will aid him to progress, how can he suppose that he will do so by being born, for example, among cannibals?

"Those who are born among cannibals are not advanced spirits, but spirits who are still at the cannibal degree, or, it may be, who are even lower than cannibals."

We know that our anthropophagi are not at the lowest degree of the scale, and that there are worlds in which are found degrees of brutishness and ferocity that have no analogues in our earth. The spirits of those worlds are, therefore, lower than the lowest of our world, and to come among our savages is, for them, a step in advance, as it would be for our cannibals to exercise, in a civilised community, some profession obliging them to shed blood. If they take no higher aim, it is because their moral backwardness does not allow of their comprehending any higher degree of progress. A spirit can only advance gradually ; he cannot clear at a single bound the distance which separates barbarism from civilisation. And in this impossibility we see one of the causes that necessitate reincarnation, which is thus seen to be really a consequence of the justice of God ; for what would become of the millions of human beings who die every day in the lowest depths of degradation, if they had no means of arriving at higher states? And why should God have refused to them the favours granted to other men?

272. Can spirits, coming from a world of lower degree than the earth, or from the lowest of our human races, such as our cannibals, for instance, be born among our civilised peoples?

"Yes, such spirits sometimes come into your world, through trying to reach a degree too far above them; but they are out of their proper place among you, because they bring with them instincts and habits that clash with the convictions and habits of the society into which they have strayed."

Such beings present us with the melancholy spectacle of ferocity in the midst of civilisation. For them, to return among cannibals is not a going down, but only a resuming of their proper place ; and they may even gain by so doing.

273. Might a man belonging to a civilised race be reincarnated, as an expiation, in a savage race?

"Yes; but that would depend on the kind of expiation he had incurred. A master who had been cruel to his slaves might become a slave in his turn, and undergo the torments he had inflicted on others. He who has wielded authority may, in a new existence, be obliged to obey those who formerly bent to his will. Such an existence may be imposed upon him as an expiation if he have abused his power. But a good spirit may also choose an influential existence among the people of some lower race, in order to hasten their advancement; in that case, such a reincarnation is a mission."

Relationships Beyond the Grave

274. Do the different degrees which exist in the advancement of spirits establish among the latter a hierarchy of powers? Are there, among spirits, subordination and authority?

"Yes; the authority of spirits over one another, in virtue of their relative superiority, is very great, and gives to the higher ones a moral ascendancy over the lower ones which is absolutely irresistible."

— *Can spirits of lower degree withdraw themselves from the authority of those who are higher than themselves?*

"I have said that the authority which comes of superiority is *irresistible.*"

275. Do the power and consideration which a man may have enjoyed in the earthly life give him supremacy in the spirit-world?

"No; for in that world the humble are exalted and the proud abased. Read the Psalms."

— *In what sense should we understand exalting and abasing?*

"Do you not know that spirits are of different orders, according to their degree of merit? Therefore, he who has held the highest rank upon the earth may find himself in the lowest rank in the world of spirits, while his servitor may be in the highest. Is not this clear to you? Has not Jesus said that 'Whosoever exalteth himself shall be abased, and whosoever humbleth himself shall be exalted?'"

276. When one who has been great upon the earth finds himself occupying an inferior place in the spirit-world, does he feel humiliated by this change of position?

"Often exceedingly so; especially if he have been haughty and jealous."

277. *When a soldier, after a battle, meets his general in the spirit-world, does he still acknowledge him as his superior?*

"Titles are nothing; intrinsic superiority is everything."

278. *Do spirits of different orders mix together in the other life?*

"Yes, and no; that is to say, they see each other, but they are none the less removed. They shun or approach one another according to the antipathies or sympathies of their sentiments, just as is the case among yourselves. *The spirit-life is a whole world of varied conditions and relationships, of which the earthly life is only the obscured reflex.* Those of the same rank are drawn together by a sort of affinity, and form groups or families of spirits united by sympathy and a common aim—the good, by the desire to do what is good, and the bad, by the desire to do evil, by the shame of their wrong-doing, and by the wish to find themselves among those whom they resemble."

The spirit-world is like a great city, in which men of all ranks and conditions see and meet one another without mixing together ; in which various social circles are formed by similarity of tastes ; in which vice and virtue elbow each other without speaking to one another.

279. *Are all spirits reciprocally accessible to one another?*

"The good go everywhere, as it is necessary that they should do, in order to bring their influence to bear upon the evil-minded. But the regions inhabited by them are inaccessible to inferior spirits, so that the latter cannot trouble those happy abodes by the introduction of evil passions."

280. *What is the nature of the relations between good and bad spirits?*

"The good ones endeavour to combat the evil tendencies of the others, *in order to aid them to raise themselves to a higher degree*; this intercourse, is, for the former, a mission."

281. *Why do inferior spirits take pleasure in inducing us to do wrong?*

"From jealousy. Not having earned a place among the good, their desire is to prevent, as far as in them lies, other spirits, as yet inexperienced, from attaining to the happiness from which they are excluded. They desire to make others suffer what they suffer themselves. Do you not see the working of the same desire among yourselves?"

282. How do spirits hold communication with one another?

"They see and comprehend one another. Speech is material; it is a reflex of spirit. The universal fluid establishes a constant communication between them; it is the vehicle by which thought is transmitted, as the air, in your world, is the vehicle of sound. This fluid constitutes a sort of universal telegraph, which unites all worlds, and enables spirits to correspond from one world to another."

283. Can spirits hide their thoughts from each other? Can they hide themselves from one another?

"No; with them everything is open, and especially so with those who have attained to perfection. They may withdraw from one another, but they are always visible to each other. This, however, is not an absolute rule, for the higher spirits are perfectly able to render themselves invisible to the lower ones, when they consider it to be useful to do so."

284. How can spirits, who have no longer a body, establish their individuality, and cause it to be distinguishable from that of the other spiritual beings by whom they are surrounded?

"Their individuality is established by their perispirit, which makes of each spirit a separate personality, distinct from all others, as the body does among men."

285. Do spirits recognise one another as having lived together upon the earth? Does the son recognise his father, the friend, his friend?

"Yes; and from generation to generation."

— *How do those who have known each other on the earth recognise one another in the world of spirits?*

"We see our past life, and read therein as in a book; on seeing the past of our friends and our enemies, we see their passage from life to death."

286. Does the soul see, immediately on quitting its mortal remains, the relations and friends who have returned before it into the world of spirits?

"Immediately is not always the right word; for, as we have said, the soul requires some time to resume its self-consciousness, and to shake off the veil of materiality."

287. How is the soul received on its return to the spirit-world?

"That of the righteous, as a dearly-beloved brother, whose return has been long waited for; that of the wicked, with contempt."

288. What sentiment is experienced by impure spirits at the sight of another bad spirit, on his arrival among them?

"Such spirits are gratified at seeing others who resemble them, and who, like them, are deprived of the highest happiness; just as a band of scoundrels, upon the earth, are gratified at meeting with another scoundrel like themselves."

289. Do our relatives and friends sometimes come to meet us when we are leaving the earth?

"Yes, they come to meet the soul of those they love; they felicitate it as one who has returned from a journey if it have escaped the dangers of the road, *and they aid it in freeing itself from the bonds of the flesh.* To be met thus by those they have loved is a favour granted to the souls of the upright; while the soul of the wicked is punished by being left alone, or is only surrounded by spirits like itself."

290. Are relatives and friends always reunited after death?

"That depends on their elevation, and on the road they have to follow for their advancement. If one of them is further advanced, and progresses more rapidly than the other, they cannot remain together: they may see one another occasionally, but they can only be definitively reunited when he who was behind is able to keep pace with him who was before, or when both of them shall have reached the state of perfection. Moreover, the privation of the sight of relatives and friends is sometimes inflicted on a spirit as a punishment."

Sympathies and Antipathies of Spirits — Eternal Halves

291. Have spirits special personal affections among themselves, besides the general sympathy resulting from similarity?

"Yes, just as among men; but the link between spirits is stronger when the body is absent, because it is no longer exposed to the vicissitudes of the passions."

292. Do spirits experience hatreds among themselves?

"Hatreds only exist among impure spirits. It is they who sow hatreds and dissensions among men."

293. Do those who have been enemies on earth always retain their resentment against one another in the spirit-world?

"No; for they often see that their hatred was stupid, and perceive the puerility of the object by which it was excited. It is only imperfect spirits who retain the animosities of the earthly life, of which they rid themselves in proportion as they become purified. Spirits whose anger, as men, has been caused by some merely material interest, forget their dissension as soon as they are dematerialised. The cause of their dissension no longer existing, they may, if there be no antipathy between them, see each other again with pleasure."

Just as two schoolboys, when they have reached the age of reason, perceive the folly of their boyish quarrels, and no longer keep up a grudge against each other on account of them.

294. Is the remembrance of wrongs they may have done one another, as men, an obstacle to sympathy between two spirits?

"Yes, it tends to keep them apart."

295. What is the sentiment, after death, of those whom we have wronged?

"If they are good, they forgive you as soon as you repent; if they are bad, they may retain resentment against you, and may even pursue you with their anger in another existence. This may be permitted by God as a chastisement."

296. Are the individual affections of spirits susceptible of change?

No; for they cannot be mistaken in one another. The mask under which hypocrites hide themselves on earth has no existence in the world of spirits, and their affections, when they are pure, are therefore unchangeable. The love which unites them is a source of supreme felicity."

297. Does the affection which two spirits have felt for each other upon the earth always continue in the spirit-world?

"Yes, undoubtedly, if that affection were founded on sympathy; but, if physical causes have had more share in it than sympathy, it ceases with those causes. Affections are more solid and lasting among spirits than among men, because they are not subordinated to the caprices of material interests and self-love."

298. Is it true that the souls of those who will eventually be united in affection are predestined to this union from their beginning, and that each of us has thus, in some part of the universe, his other half, to whom he will some day be necessarily reunited?

"No, there is no such thing as any special and fated union between any two souls. Union exists between all spirits, but in different degrees, according to the rank they occupy,—that is to say, according to the degree of perfection they have acquired; and the greater their perfection, the more united they are. It is discord that produces all the ills of human life. The complete and perfect happiness at which all spirits eventually arrive is the result of concord."

299. In what way should we understand the term other half, sometimes employed by spirits to designate other spirits for whom they have special sympathy?

"The expression is incorrect. If one spirit were the half of another spirit, he would, if separated from that other, be incomplete."

300. When two perfectly sympathetic spirits are reunited in the other world, are they thus reunited for all eternity, or can they separate from each other and unite themselves with other spirits?

"All spirits are united among themselves. I speak of those who have reached the state of perfection. In the spheres below that state, when a spirit passes from a lower sphere to a higher one, he does not always feel the same sympathy for those whom he has quitted."

301. When two spirits are completely sympathetic, are they the complement of each other, or is that sympathy the result of their perfect identity of character?

"The sympathy which attracts one spirit to another is the result of the perfect concordance of their tendencies and instincts. If one of them were necessary to complete the other, he would lose his individuality."

302. Does similarity of thoughts and of sentiments suffice to constitute the kind of identity which is necessary to the production of perfect sympathy, or is uniformity of acquired knowledge also required for its production?

"Perfect sympathy between two spirits results from equality in the degree of their elevation."

303. May spirits, who are not now sympathetic, become so in the future?

Yes, all will be sympathetic in course of time. Thus, of two spirits who were once together, one may have advanced more rapidly than the other; but the other, though now in a lower sphere, will by and by have advanced sufficiently to be able to enter the higher sphere in which the former is now residing. And their reunion will take place all the sooner if the one who was most advanced should fail in the trials he has still to undergo, and so should remain for a time just where he now is, without making any further progress."

— *May two spirits, who are now sympathetic, cease to be so?*

"Certainly, if one of them is wanting in energy, and lags behind, while the other is advancing."

The hypothesis of twin-souls is merely a figurative representation of the union of two sympathetic spirits, and must not be understood literally. The spirits who have made use of this expression are certainly not of high order; and, therefore, as their range of thought is necessarily narrow, they have sought to convey their meaning by using the terms they were accustomed to employ in their earthly life. The idea that two souls were created for each other, and that, after having been separated for a longer or shorter period, they will necessarily be eventually reunited for all eternity, is, therefore, to be entirely rejected.

Remembrance of Corporeal Existence

304. Does spirit remember his corporeal existence?

"Yes; having lived many times as a human being, he remembers what he has been, and often smiles pityingly at the follies of his past."

As a man, who has reached the age of reason, smiles at the follies of his youth and the sillinesses of his childhood.

305. Does the remembrance of his corporeal existence present itself to a spirit, complete, and spontaneously, immediately after his death?

"No; it comes back to him little by little, in proportion as he fixes his attention upon it, as objects gradually become visible out of a fog."

306. Does a spirit remember the details of all the events of his life? Does he take in the whole of his life at a single retrospective glance?

"He remembers the things of his life more or less distinctly and in detail, according to the influence they have exercised on his state as a spirit; but you can easily understand that there are many things in his life to which he attaches no importance, and which he does not even seek to remember."

— *Could he remember them if he wished to do so?*

"He has the power of recalling the most minute details of every incident of his life, and even of his thoughts; but when no useful purpose would be served by exerting this power, he does not exert it."

307. *In what way does his past life present itself to a spirit's memory? Is it through an effort of his imagination, or is it like a picture displayed before his eyes?*

"It comes back to him in both ways. All the actions which he has an interest in remembering appear to him as though they were present; the others are seen by him more or less vaguely in his thought, or are entirely forgotten. The more dematerialised he is, the less importance does he attach to material things. It has often happened to you, on evoking some wandering spirit who has just left the earth, to find that he remembers neither the names of persons whom he liked, nor details which to you appear to be important. He cares but little about them, and they have faded from his memory. But you always find that he perfectly remembers the main facts of his life which have conduced to his intellectual and moral progress."

308. *Does a spirit remember all the existences which have preceded the one he has just quitted?*

"His entire past is spread out before him like the stages already accomplished by a traveller, but, as we have told you, he does not remember all his past actions with absolute precision; he remembers them more or less clearly in proportion to the influence they have had upon his present state. As to his earliest existences, those which may be regarded as constituting the period of spirit-infancy, they are lost in vagueness, and disappear in the night of oblivion."

309. *How does a spirit regard the body he has just quitted?*

"As an uncomfortable garment *that hampered him,* and that he is delighted to be rid of."

— *What feeling is produced in him by seeing the decomposition of his body?*

"Almost always that of indifference; as something about which
he no longer cares."

*310. After a time, does a spirit recognise the mortal remains,
or other objects, that once belonged to him?*

"Sometimes he does so; but this depends on the more or less
elevated point of view from which he regards terrestrial things."

*311. Is a spirit's attention attracted to the material relics of
himself by the respect entertained for those objects by his survivors,
and does he see this respect with pleasure?*

"A spirit is always gratified at being held in kindly remembrance
by those he has left. The objects thus preserved in remembrance
of him serve to recall him to the memory of those by whom they
are preserved; but it is the action of their thought which attracts
him, and not those objects."

*312. Do spirits retain the remembrance of the sufferings
endured by them in their last corporeal existence?*

"They frequently do so; and this remembrance makes them
realise all the more vividly the worth of the felicity they enjoy
as spirits."

*313. Does he who has been happy down here regret his
terrestrial enjoyments on quitting the earth?*

"Only spirits of inferior degree can regret material satisfactions
in harmony with impurity of nature, and which are expiated by
suffering. For spirits of higher degrees of elevation, the happiness
of eternity is immeasurably preferable to the ephemeral pleasures
of the earthly life."

As the adult despises wath constituted the delights of is infance.

*314. When a man, who has commenced a series of important
labours in view of some useful end, has seen these labours interrupted by death, does he, in the other world, feel regret at
having had to leave them unfinished?*

"No, because he sees that others are destined to complete them.
On the contrary, he endeavours to act upon the minds of other
human beings, so as to lead them to carry on what he had begun.
His aim while upon the earth was to be useful to the human race:
his aim is the same in the spirit-world."

*315. When a man has left behind him works of art or of
literature, does he preserve for them in the other life the interest
he took in them while living upon the earth?*

"He judges them from another point of view, according to his elevation, and he often blames what he formerly admired."

316. *Does a spirit still take an interest in the labours which are going on upon the earth, in the progress of the arts and sciences?*

"That depends on his degree of elevation, and on the mission he may have to fulfil. What appears magnificent to you often appears a very small matter to spirits; if they take an interest in it, it is only as a man of learning takes an interest in the work of a school-boy. They examine whatever indicates the elevation of incarnated spirits and mark the degree of their progress."

317. *Do spirits, after death, retain any preference for their native country?*

"For spirits of elevated degree, their country is the universe; in regard to the earth, their only preference is for the place in which there is the greatest number of persons with whom they are in sympathy."

The situation of spirits, and their way of looking at things, are infinitely varied, according to their various degrees of moral and intellectual development. Spirits of a high order generally make but short sojourns upon the earth ; all that goes on here is so paltry in comparison with the grandeurs of infinity, the matters to which men attribute most importance appear to them so puerile, that the things of this earth have very little interest for them, unless they have been sent to it for the purpose of quickning the progress of its people. Spirits of lower degree visit our earth more frequently, but they judge its affairs from a higher point of view than that of their corporeal life. The common ruck of spirits may be said to be sedentary among us ; they constitute the great mass of the ambient population of the invisible world. They retain very much the same ideas, tastes, and tendencies which they had while clothed with their corporeal envelope, and mix themselves up with our gatherings, our occupation, our amusements in all of which they take a part more or less active according to their character. Being no longer able to satisfy their material passions, they take delight in witnessing the excesses of those who abandon themselves to their indulgence, to which they excite them by every means in their power. Among their number are some who are better disposed, and who see and observe in order to acquire knowledge and to advance.

318. *Do spirits modify their ideas in the other life?*

"Very considerably. A spirit's ideas undergo very great modifications in proportion as he becomes dematerialised. He may sometimes retain the same ideas for a long period, but little by little the influence of matter diminishes, and he sees more clearly. It is then that he seeks for the means of advancing."

319. *As spirits had already lived in the other world before being incarnated, why do they feel astonished on reentering that world?*

"This feeling is only momentary, and results from the confusion that follows their waking; they soon recover their knowledge of themselves, as the memory of the past comes back to them, and the impression of the terrestrial life becomes effaced." (*Vide* *163 et seq.*)

Commemoration of the Dead — Funerals

320.   Are spirits affected by the remembrance of those whom they have loved on earth?

"Very much more so than you are apt to suppose. If they are happy, this remembrance adds to their happiness; if they are unhappy, it affords them consolation."

321.   Are spirits specially attracted towards their friends upon the earth by the return of the day which, in some countries, is consecrated to the memory of those who have quitted this life? Do they make it a point to meet those who, on that day, go to pray beside the graves where their mortal remains are interred?

"Spirits answer to the call of affectionate remembrance on that day as they do on any other day."

— *Do they, on that day, go specially to the burial-place of their corporeal body?*

"They go to the cemeteries in greater numbers on that day, because called thither by the thoughts of a greater number of persons, but each spirit goes solely for his own friends, and not for the crowd of those who care nothing about him."

— *In what form do they come to these places, and what would be their appearance if they could render themselves visible to us?*

"The form and appearance by which they were known during their lifetime."

322.   Do the spirits of those who are forgotten, and whose graves no one visits, go to the cemeteries notwithstanding this neglect?   Do they feel regret at seeing that no one remembers them?

"What is the earth to them? They are only linked to it by the heart. If, upon the earth, no affection is felt for a spirit, there is nothing that can attach him to it; he has the whole universe before him."

323.   Does a visit made to his grave give more pleasure to a spirit than a prayer offered for him by friends in their own home?

"A visit made to his grave is a way of showing to a spirit that he is not forgotten; it is a sign. As I have told you, it is the prayer that sanctifies the action of the memory; the place where it is offered is of little importance, if it come from the heart."

324. When statues or other monuments are erected to persons who have quitted this life, are the spirits of those persons present at their inauguration; and do they witness such ceremonies with pleasure?

"Spirits often attend on such occasions, when able to do so; but they attach less importance to the honours paid to them than to the remembrance in which they are held."

325. What makes some persons desire to be buried in one place rather than in another? Do they go thither more willingly after their death? And is it a sign of inferiority on the part of a spirit that he should attribute importance to a matter so purely material?

"That desire is prompted by a spirit's affection for certain places, and is a sign of moral inferiority. To an elevated spirit, what is one spot of earth more than another? Does he not know that his soul will be reunited with those he loves, even though their bones are separated?

— *Is it futile to bring together the mortal remains of all the members of a family in the same burial-place?*

"Such reunion is of little importance to spirits; but it is useful to men, whose remembrance of those who have gone before them is thus strengthened and rendered more serious."

326. When the soul has returned into spirit-life, is it gratified by the honours paid to its mortal remains?

"When a spirit has reached a certain degree of advancement, he is purified from terrestrial vanities, for he comprehends their futility. But there are many spirits who, in the early period of their return to the other life, take great pleasure in the honours paid to their memory, or are much disturbed at finding themselves forgotten; for they still retain some of the false ideas they held during their earthly life."

327. Do spirits ever attend their own funeral?

"Spirits very often do so; but, in many cases, without understanding what is going on, being still in the state of confusion that usually follows death."

— *Do they feel flattered by the presence of a large concourse of persons at their funeral?*

"More or less so, according to the sentiment which has brought them together."

328. Is a spirit ever present at the meetings of his heirs?

"Almost always. Providence has so ordained it for the spirit's own instruction, and for the chastisement of selfishness. The deceased is thus enabled to judge of the worth of the protestations of affection and devotion addressed to him during his life; and his disappointment on witnessing the rapacity of those who dispute the property he has left is often very great. But the punishment of greedy heirs will come in due time."

329. Is the respect which mankind, in all ages and among all peoples, has always instinctively shown to the dead, to be attributed to an intuitive belief in a future state of existence?

"The one is the natural consequence of the other; were it not for that belief, such respect would have neither object nor meaning."

Preludes to Return

*330. Do spirits foresee the epoch of their next return to
corporeal life?*

"They have the presentiment of that return, as a blind man feels
the heat of the fire he is approaching.They know that they will be
reincarnated, as you know that you will die; but without knowing
when the change will occur."—(166.)

— *Reincarnation, then, is a necessity of spirit-life, as death is
a necessity of corporeal life?*

"Certainly."

*331. Do all spirits occupy themselves beforehand with their
approaching incarnation?*

"There are some who never give it a thought, and who even
know nothing about it; that depends on their greater or less
degree of advancement. In some cases, the uncertainty in which
they are left in regard to their future is a punishment."

*332. Can a spirit hasten or retard the moment of his rein-
carnation?*

"He may hasten it by the action of a strong desire; he may
also put it off if he shrink from the trial awaiting him (for the
cowardly and the indifferent are to be found among spirits as
among men), but he cannot do so with impunity. He suffers from
such delay, as the sick man suffers who shrinks from employing
the remedy which alone can cure him."

333. If a spirit found himself tolerably happy in an average condition among errant spirits, could he prolong that state inde-finitely?

"No, not indefinitely. The necessity of advancing is one which is felt by every spirit, sooner or later. All spirits have to ascend; it is their destiny."

334. Is the union of a given soul with a given body predestined beforehand, or is the choice of a body only made at the last moment?

"The spirit who is to animate a given body is always designated beforehand. Each spirit, on choosing the trial he elects to undergo, demands to be reincarnated; and God, who sees and knows all things, has foreseen and foreknown that such and such a soul would be united to such and such a body."

335. Is the spirit allowed to choose the body into which he will enter, or does he only choose the kind of life which is to serve for his trial?

"He may choose a body also, for the imperfections of a given body are so many trials that will aid his advancement, if he succeeds in vanquishing the obstacles thus placed in his way. This choice does not always depend on himself, but he may ask to be allowed to make it."

— *Could a spirit refuse, at the last moment, to enter into the body that had been chosen by him?*

"If he refused, he would suffer much more than one who had not attempted to undergo a new trial."

336. Could it happen that a child about to be born should find no spirit willing to incarnate himself in it?

"God provides for all contingences. Every child who is pre-destined to be born *viable,* is also predestined to have a soul. Nothing is ever created without design."

337. Is the union of a given soul with a given body ever imposed by God?

"It is sometimes imposed, as well as the different trials to be undergone by a spirit, and especially when the latter is still too backward to be able to choose wisely for himself. A spirit may be constrained, as an expiation, to unite himself with the body of a child that, by the circumstances of its birth, and the position it will have in the world, will become for him an instrument of chastisement."

338. If several spirits demanded to incarnate themselves in a body about to be born, in what way would the decision be made between them?

"In such a case, it is God who judges as to which spirit is best fitted to fulfil the destiny appointed for the child; but, as I have already told you, the spirit is designated before the instant in which he is to unite himself with the body."

339. Is the moment of incarnation accompanied by a confusion similar to that which follows the spirit's separation from the body?

"Yes, but much greater and especially much longer. At death, the spirit is emancipated from the state of slavery; at birth, he re-enters it."

340. Does the moment in which he is to reincarnate himself appear to a spirit as a solemn one? Does he accomplish that act as something serious and important for him?

"He is like a traveller who embarks on a perilous voyage, and who does not know whether he may not find his death in the waves among which he is venturing."

Just as the death of the body is a sort of re-birth for the spirit, so reincarnation is for him a sort of death, or rather of exile and claustration. He quits the world of spirits for the corporeal world just as a man quits the corporeal world for the world of spirits. A spirit knows that he will be reincarnated, just as a man knows that he will die; but, like the latter, he only becomes aware of the change at the moment when it occurs. It is at this moment that the confusion produced by the change takes possession of him, as is the case with a man in the act of dying; and this confusion lasts until his new existence is fully established. The commencement of reincarnation is, for the spirit, a sort of dying.

341. Is a spirit's uncertainty, in regard to the successful issue of the trials he is about to undergo in his new life, a cause of anxiety to him before his incarnation?

"Yes, of very great anxiety, since those trials will retard or hasten his advancement, according as he shall have borne them ill or well."

342. Is a spirit accompanied, at the moment of his reincarnation, by spirit-friends who come to be present at his departure from the spirit-world, as they come to receive him when he returns to it?

"That depends on the sphere which the spirit inhabits. If he belongs to a sphere in which affection reigns, spirits who love him remain with him to the last moment, encourage him, and often even follow him in his new life."

343. Is it the spirit-friends who thus follow us in our earthly life that we sometimes see in our dreams manifesting affection for us, but whose features are unknown to us?

"Yes, in very many cases; they come to visit you as you visit a prisoner in his cell."

Union of Soul and Body

344. At what moment is the soul united to the body?

"The union begins at the moment of conception, but is only complete at the moment of birth. From the moment of conception, the spirit designated to inhabit a given body is united to that body by a fluidic link, which becomes closer and closer up to the instant of birth; the cry then uttered by the infant announces that he is numbered among the living."

345. Is the union between the spirit and the body definitive from the moment of conception? Could the spirit, during this first period of that union, renounce inhabiting the body designed for him?

"The union between them is definitive in this sense——namely, that no other spirit could replace the one who has been designated for that body. But, as the links which hold them together are at first very weak, they are easily broken, and may be severed by the will of a spirit who draws back from the trial he had chosen. But, in that case, the child does not live."

346. What becomes of a spirit, if the body he has chosen happens to die before birth?

"He chooses another body."

— *What can be the use of premature deaths?*

"Such deaths are most frequently caused by the imperfections of matter."

347. What benefit can a spirit derive from his incarnation in a body which dies a few days after birth?

"In such a case, the new being's consciousness of his existence is so slightly developed that his death is of little importance. As we have told you, such deaths are often intended mainly as a trial for the parents."

348. Does a spirit know beforehand that the body he chooses has no chance of living?

"He sometimes knows it; but if he chooses it on this account. it is because he shrinks from the trial he foresees."

349. When, from any cause, a spirit has failed to accomplish a proposed incarnation, is another existence provided for him immediately?

"Not always immediately. The spirit requires time to make a new choice, unless his instantaneous reincarnation had been previously decided upon."

350. When a spirit is definitively united to an infant body, and it is thus too late for him to refuse this union, does he sometimes regret the choice he has made?

"If you mean to ask whether, as a man, he may complain of the life he has to undergo, and whether he may not wish it were otherwise, I answer, Yes; but if you mean to ask whether he regrets the choice he has made, I answer, No, for he does not remember that he has made it. A spirit, when once incarnated. cannot regret a choice which he is not conscious of having made; but he may find the burden he has assumed too heavy, and, if he believes it to be beyond his strength, he may have recourse to suicide."

351. Does a spirit, in the interval between conception and birth, enjoy the use of all his faculties?

"He does so more or less according to the various periods of gestation; for he is not yet incarnated in his new body, but only attached to it. From the instant of conception confusion begins to take possession of the spirit, who is thus made aware that the moment has come for him to enter upon a new existence; and this confusion becomes more and more dense until the period of birth. In the interval between these two terms, his state is nearly that of an incarnated spirit during the sleep of the body. In proportions as the moment of birth approaches, his ideas become effaced, together with his remembrance of the past, of which. when once he has entered upon corporeal life, he is no longer conscious. But this remembrance comes back to him little by little when he has returned to the spirit-world."

352. Does the spirit, at the moment of birth, recover the plenitude of his faculties?

"No; they are gradually developed with the growth of his organs. The corporeal life is for him a new existence; he has to learn the use of his bodily instruments. His ideas come back to him little by little, as in the case of a man who, waking out of slumber, should find himself in a different situation from that in which he was before he fell asleep."

353. The union of the spirit and the body not being completely and definitively consummated until birth has taken place, can the fœtus be considered as having a soul?

"The spirit who is to animate it exists, as it were, outside of it; strictly speaking, therefore, it has no soul, since the incarnation of the latter is only in course of being effected; but it is linked to the soul which it is to have."

354. What is the nature of intra-uterine life?

"That of the plant which vegetates. The fœtus, however, lives with vegetable and animal life, to which the union of a soul with the child-body at birth adds spiritual life."

355. Are there, as is indicated by science, children so consti-tuted that they cannot live, and if so, for what purpose are they produced?

"That often happens. Such births are permitted as a trial, either for the parents or for the spirit appointed to animate it."

356. Are there, among still-born children, some who were never intended for the incarnation of a spirit?

"Yes, there are some who never had a spirit assigned to them, for whom nothing was to be done. In such a case, it is simply as a trial for the parents that the child arrives."

— *Can a being of this nature come to its term?*

"Yes, sometimes; but it does not live."

— *Every child that survives its birth has, then, necessarily a spirit incarnated in it?*

"What would it be if such were not the case? It would not be a human being."

357. What are, for a spirit, the consequences of abortion?

"It is an existence that is null, and must be commenced over again."

358. Is artificial abortion a crime, no matter at what period of gestation it may be produced?

"Every transgression of the law of God is a crime. The mother, or any other, who takes the life of an unborn child, is necessarily criminal; for, by so doing, a soul is prevented from undergoing the trial of which the body thus destroyed was to have been the instrument."

359. In cases in which the life of the mother would be endangered by the birth of the child, is it a crime to sacrifice the child in order to save the mother?

"It is better to sacrifice the being whose existence is not yet complete than the being whose existence is complete."

360. Is it rational to treat the fœtus with the same respect as the body of a child that has lived?

"In the one, as in the other, you should recognise the will and the handiwork of God, and these are always to be respected."

Moral and Intellectual Faculties

361. Whence has man his moral qualities, good or bad?

"They are those of the spirit who is incarnated in him. The purer is that spirit, the more decidedly is the man inclined to goodness."

— *It would seem, then, that a good man is the incarnation of a good spirit, and a vicious man that of a bad spirit?*

"Yes; but you should rather say 'of an imperfect spirit,' otherwise it might be supposed that there are spirits who will always remain bad, what you call devils."

362. What is the character of the individuals in whom light and foolish spirits are incarnated?

"They are hare-brained, prankish, and sometimes mischievous."

363. Have spirits any passions that do not belong to humanity?

"No; if they had, they would communicate them to you."

364. Is it one and the same spirit that gives a man both his moral and his intellectual qualities?

"Certainly it is the same. A man has not two spirits in him."

365. How comes it that some men, who are very intelligent, which shows that they have in them a spirit of considerable advancement, are also extremely vicious?

"It is because the spirit incarnated in a man is not sufficiently purified, and the man yelds to the influence of other spirits still worse than himself. The upward progress of a spirit is accomplished by slow degrees; but this progress does not take place simultaneously in all directions. At one period of his career he may advance in knowledge, at another in morality."

366. What is to be thought of the opinion according to which a man's various intellectual and moral faculties are the product of so many different spirits incarnated in him, and each possessing a special aptitude?

"The absurdity of such an opinion becomes evident on a moment's reflection. Each spirit is destined to possess all possible aptitudes; but, in order to progress, he must possess one sole and unitary will. If a man were an amalgam of different spirits, this unitary will would not exist, and he would possess no individuality, because, at his death, all the spirits would fly off in different directions, like birds escaped from a cage. Men often complain of not comprehending certain things, and yet how ingenious they are in multiplying difficulties, while they have within reach the simplest and most natural of explanations! Such an opinion is but another instance of the way in which men so often take the effect for the cause. It does for man what the pagans did for God. They believed in the existence of as many gods as there are phenomena in the universe; but, even among them, the more sensible ones only saw in those phenomena a variety of effects having for their cause one and the same God."

The physical and moral worlds offer us, in regard to this subject, numerous points of comparison. While the attention of mankind was confined to the appearance of natural phenomena, they believed in the existence of many kinds of matter. In the present day, it is seen that all those phenomena, however varied, may very probably be merely the result of modifications of a single elementary matter. The various faculties of a human being are manifestations of one and the same cause, which is the soul or spirit incarnated in him, and not of several souls ; just as the different sounds of an organ are the product of one and the same air, and not of as many sorts of air as there are sounds. According to the theory in question, when a man acquires or loses aptitudes or tendencies, such modifications would be the result of the coming or going of a corresponding number of the spirits conjoined with him, which would make of him a multiple being without individuality, and, consequently, without responsibility. This theory, moreover, is disproved by the numerous manifestations of spirits which conclusively demonstrate their personality and their identity.

Influence of Organism

367. Does a spirit, in uniting itself with a body, identify itself with matter?

"Matter is only the envelope of the spirit, as clothing is the envelope of the body. A spirit, in uniting himself with a body, retains the attributes of his spiritual nature."

368. *Does a spirit exercise his faculties in full freedom after his union with a body?*

"The exercise of faculties depends on the organs which serve them for instruments. Their exercise is weakened by the grossness of matter."

— *It would appear, then, that the material envelope is an obstacle to the free manifestation of a spirit's faculties, as the opacity of ground glass is an obstacle to the free emission of light?*

"Yes, an obstacle which is excedingly opaque."

The action exercised upon a spirit by the gross matter of his body may also be compared to that of muddy water, impeding the movements of the objects plunged into it.

369. *Is the free exercise of a spirit's faculties subordinated, during his incarnation, to the development of his corporeal organs?*

"Those organs are the soul's instruments for the manifestation of its faculties; that manifestation is, therefore, necessarily subordinated to the degree of development and perfection of those organs, as the perfection of a piece of manual work depends on the goodness of the tool employed."

370. *May we, from the influence of the corporeal organs, infer a connection between the development of the cerebral organs and that of the moral and intellectual faculties?*

"Do not confound effect and cause. A spirit always possesses the faculties that belong to him; but you must remember that it is not the organs that give the faculties, but the faculties that incite to the development of the organs."

— *According to this view of the subject, the diversity of aptitudes in each man depends solely on the state of his spirit?*

"To say that it does so 'solely,' would not be altogether correct. The qualities of the incarnated spirit are, undoubtedly, the determining principle of those aptitudes; but allowance must be made for the influence of matter, which hinders every man, more or less, in the exercise of the faculties inherent in his soul."

A spirit, in incarnating himself, brings with him certain characterical predispositions ; therefore, if we admit the existence, for each of these, of a special organ in the brain, the development of the cerebral organs is seen to be an effect, and not a cause. If his faculties were a result of his bodily organs, man would be a mere machine, without free-will, and would not be responsible for his actions. Moreover, if such were the case, we should be forced to admit that the greatest geniuses—men of science, poets, artists—are only such because a lucky chance has given them certain special organs ; whence it would follow, still further, that, but for the chance-acquisition of those organs, they would not have been geniuses, and that the stupidest of men might have been a Newton, a Virgil, or a Raphael, if he had been provided with certain organs ; a supposition still more flagrantly absurd, if we attempt to apply it to the explanation of the moral qualities. For, according to this system, Saint Vincent de Paul, had he been gifted by nature with such and such an organ, might have been a scoundrel ; and the greatest scoundrel alive, had he only been gifted with an organ of an opposite nature, might have been a Saint Vincent de Paul. If, on the contrary, we admit that our special organs, supposing such to exist, are an effect and not a cause, that they are developed by the exercise of the faculties to which they correspond, as muscles are developed by movement, we arrive at a theory which is certainly not irrational. Let us employ an illustration equally conclusive and commonplace. By certain physiognomic signs we recognise a man who is addicted to drink. Is it those signs that make him a drunkard, or is it his drunkenness that produces those signs? It may be safely asserted that our organs are a consequence of our faculties.

Idiocy — Madness

371. Is there any foundation for the common belief that the souls of idiots are of a nature inferior to those of others?

"No; they have a human soul, which is often more intelligent than you suppose, and which suffers acutely from the insufficiency of its means of communication, as the dumb man suffers from his inability to speak."

372. What is the aim of Providence in creating beings so ill-treated by nature as idiots?

"Idiots are incarnations of spirits who are undergoing punishment, and who suffer from the constraint they experience, and from their inability to manifest themselves by means of organs which are undeveloped, or out of order."

— Then it is not correct to say that organs are without influence upon faculties?

"We have never said that organs are without influence. They have very great influence on the manifestation of faculties, but they do not give faculties; there is just the difference. A skilful player will not make good music with a bad instrument, but that will not prevent his being a good player."

It is necessary to distinguish between the normal state and the pathologic state. In the normal state, the moral strength of an incarnated spirit enables him to triumph over the obstacles which are placed in his way by matter ; but there are cases in which matter opposes a resistance so powerful that the manifestations of the spirit incarnated in it are hindered or changed from what he intended, as in idiocy and madness. These cases are pathologic ; and as the soul, in such states, is not in the enjoyment of its full liberty, human law itself exempts such persons from the responsibility of their actions.

373. What merit can there be in the existence of beings who, like idiots, can do neither good nor evil, and therefore cannot progress?

"Such an existence is imposed as an expiation of the abuse which a spirit has made of certain faculties; it constitutes a pause in his career."

— *The body of an idiot may, then, contain a spirit that has animated a man of genius in a preceding existence?*

"Yes; genius sometimes becomes a scourge when it is abused."

Intellectual superiority is not always accompanied by an equal degree of moral superiority, and the greatest geniuses may have much to expiate. For this reason, they often have to undergo an existence inferior to the one they have previously accomplished, which is a cause of suffering for them ; the hindrances to the manifestation of his faculties thus imposed upon a spirit being like chains that fetter the movements of a vigorous man. The idiot may be said to be lame in the brain, as the halt is lame in the legs, and the blind, in the eyes.

374. Is the idiot, in the spirit-state, conscious of his mental condition?

"Yes; very often. He comprehends that the chains which hinder his action are a trial and an expiation."

375. When a man is mad, what is the state of his spirit?

"A spirit, in the state of freedom, receives his impressions directly, and exerts his action directly upon matter; but when incarnated, he is in an altogether different condition, and compelled to act only through the instrumentality of special organs. If some or all of those organs are injured, his actions or his impressions, as far as those organs are concerned, are interrupted. If he loses his eyes, he becomes blind; if he loses his hearing, he becomes deaf; and so on. Suppose that the organ which presides over the manifestations of intelligence and of will is partially or entirely weakened or modified in its action, and you will easily understand that the spirit, having at his service only organs that are incomplete or diverted from their proper action, must experience a functional perturbation of which he is perfectly conscious, but is not able to arrest the course."

— *It is then always the body, and not the spirit, that is disorganised?*

"Yes; but you must not forget that, just as a spirit acts upon matter, matter, to a certain extent, reacts upon him; and that he may therefore find himself, for the time being, subjected to the influence of the false impressions consequent on the vitiated state of his organs of perception and of action. And it may happen, when this mental aberration has continued for a long time, that the repetition of the same perverted action may exercise upon a spirit an influence from which he is only delivered after his complete separation from all material impressions."

376. How is it that madness sometimes leads to suicide?

"In such cases, the spirit suffers from the constraint which he feels, and from his inability to manifest himself freely; and he therefore seeks death as a means of breaking his chains."

377. Does the spirit of a madman continue to feel, after death, the derangement from which he suffered in his corporeal life?

"He may continue to feel it for some time after death, until he is completely freed from matter; just as a man, on waking, continues to feel, for some little time, the confusion in which he has been plunged by sleep."

378. How can brain-disease act upon a spirit after his death?

"It is an effect of remembrance, which weighs like a burden upon the spirit; and as he was not aware of all that took place during his madness, he always needs a certain amount of time for recovering the hang of his ideas. It is for this reason that the continuance of his uneasiness after death is always proportioned to the longer or shorter continuance of the corporeal insanity from which he has previously suffered. A spirit, when freed from the body, still feels, for a longer or shorter time, the impression of the links that united him with it."

Infancy

379. Is the spirit who animates the body of a child as developed as that of an adult?

"He may be more so, if, before reincarnating himself, he bad progressed farther; it is only the imperfection of his organs that prevents him from manifesting himself. He acts according to the state of the instrument by which alone, when incarnated, he can manifest himself."

380. During the infancy of his body, and without reference to the obstacle opposed to his free manifestation by the imperfection of his organs, does a spirit think as a child, or as an adult?

"While he remains a child, it is evident that his organs of thought, not being developed, cannot give him all the intuition of an adult; his range of intellect is therefore only narrow, until increasing age has ripened his reason. The confusion which accompanies incarnation does not cease, all at once, at the moment of birth; it its only dissipated gradually with the development of the bodily organs."

The observation of a fact of human life furnishes us with a confirmation of the preceding reply—viz., that the dreams of childhood have not the character of those of adult age. Their object is almost always childish; a characteristic indication of the nature of a spirit's thoughts during the infancy of his organs.

381. At the death of a child, does its spirit at once regain his former vigour?

"He should do so, since he is freed from his fleshly envelope; but, in point of fact, he only regains his former lucidity when the separation is complete—that is to say, when there is no longer any connection between the spirit and the body."

382. Does the incarnated spirit suffer, during the state of childhood, from the constraint imposed on him by the imperfections of his organs?

"No; that state is a necessity. It is a part of the ordination of nature, and of the providential plan. *It constitutes a time of repose for the spirit.*"

383. What is the use, for a spirit, of passing through the state of infancy?

"The aim of incarnation is the improvement of the spirit subjected to it; and a spirit is more accessible during childhood to the impressions he receives, and which may conduce to his advancement—the end to which all those who are entrusted with his education should contribute."

384. Why is it that the infant's first utterances are those of weeping?

"It is in order to excite the mother's interest on his behalf, and to ensure to him the care he needs. Can you not understand that if a child, before he is able to speak, uttered only cries of joy, those around him would trouble themselves very little about his wants? In all these arrangements admire the wisdom of Providence."

385. Whence comes the change which occurs in the character of the young on the approach of manhood: is it the spirit that becomes modified?

"The spirit, regaining possession of himself, shows himself such as he was before his incarnation.

"You know not the secrets hidden under the seeming innocence of children. You know neither what they are, nor what they have been, nor what they will be; and nevertheless you love and cherish them as though they were a part of yourselves, and to such a degree, that the love of a mother for her children is reputed to be the greatest love that one being can have for another. Whence comes the sweet affection, the tender benevolence, that even strangers feel for a child? Do you know its origin? No; but I will now explain it to you.

"Children are beings sent by God into new existences, and, in order that they may not be able to reproach Him with having been unduly severe to them, He gives them all the external appearances of innocence; even in the case of a child of the worst possible nature, its misdeeds are covered by its unconsciousness of the quality of its acts. This apparent innocence does not constitute for children any real superiority over what they previously were; it is merely the image of what they ought to be, and, if they are not such, it will be on themselves alone that the punishment will fall.

"But it is not merely for themselves that God has given to children this appearance of innocence; it is given to them also, and especially, in view of their parents, whose love is so necessary to them in their weakness: for this love would be greatly diminished by the sight of a harsh or cross-grained nature, whereas, believing their children to be good and gentle, they give them all their affection, and surround them with the most minute and delicate care. But, when children no longer need this protection, this assistance, which has been given them during fifteen or twenty years, their real character and individuality reappears in all its nudity. He who is really good remains good; but, even then, his character reveals many traits and shades that were hidden during his earlier years.

"You see that God's ways are always for the best; and that, for the pure in heart, they are easily explicable.

"Get it well into your minds that the spirit of the child who is born among you may have come from a world in which he has acquired habits totally different from yours; how would it be possible for this new being, coming among you with passions, inclinations, tastes, entirely opposed to yours, to accommodate

himself to your world, if he came among you in any other way
than in that which has been ordained by God—that is to say, by
passing through the sieve of infancy? It is through this sifting
process of infancy that all the thoughts, all the characteristics, all
the varieties of beings engendered by the crowd of worlds in
which creatures pursue the work of growth, are eventually mingled.
And you, also, on dying, find yourselves in a sort of infancy, and
in the midst of a new family of brothers; and in your new non-
terrestrial existence you are ignorant of the habits, manners,
relations of a world which is new to you, and you find it
difficult to express yourselves in a language which you are not
accustomed to employ, a language more living than is your thought
to-day. (319.)

"Childhood possesses yet another utility. Spirits only enter into
corporeal life in order to effect their improvement, their self-
amelioration. The weakness of corporeal youth tends to render
them more pliable, more amenable to the counsels of those whose
experience should aid their progress. It is thus that evil tendencies
are repressed, and faulty characters are gradually reformed; and
this repression and reformation constitute the duty confided by
God to those who assume the parental relation, a sacred mission
of which parents will have to render a solemn account to Him.

"You see, therefore, that childhood is not only useful, necessary,
indispensable, but that it is, moreover, the natural result of the laws
which God has established, and which govern the universe."

Terrestrial Sympathies and Antipathies

*386. Could two beings, who have already known and loved each
other, meet again and recognise one another, in another corporeal
existence?*

"They could not recognise one another; but they might be
attracted to each other. The attraction resulting from the ties
of a former existence is often the cause of the most intimate
affectional unions of a subsequent existence. It often happens
in your world that two persons are drawn together by circumstances
which appear to be merely fortuitous, but which are really due
to the attraction exercised upon one another by two spirits *who are
unconsciously seeking each other amidst the crowds by whom they
are surrounded.*"

— *Would it not be more agreeable for them to recognise each
other?*

"Not always; the remembrance of past existences would be attended with greater disadvantages than you suppose. After death they would recognise one another, and would then remember the periods they had passed together." (392.)

387. *Is sympathy always the result of anterior acquaintanceship?*

"No; two spirits who are in harmony naturally seek one another, without their having been previously acquainted with each other as men."

388. *May it not be that the meetings which sometimes take place between two persons, and which are attributed to chance, are really due to the action of some sort of sympathetic relationship?*

"There are, among thinking beings, orders of relationship with which you are not yet acquainted. Magnetism is the pilot of the science that will enable you to understand them at a future period."

389. *What is the cause of the instinctive repulsion sometimes excited in us by persons whom we see for the first time?*

"The latent antipathy of two spirits who divine each other's nature, and recognise one another, without the need of speaking together."

390. *Is instinctive antipathy always the sign of an evil nature on the part of one or both of the parties who feel it?*

"Two spirits are not necessarily evil because they are not sympathetic; for antipathy may spring from a want of similarity in their way of thinking. But in proportion as they ascend, these shades of difference are effaced, and their antipathy disappears."

391. *Does the antipathy of two persons take its first beginning on the part of the better or the worse one of the two?*

"It may begin simultaneously on the part of both; but, in such a case, its causes and effects are different. A bad spirit feels antipathy against whoever is able to judge and to unmask him. On seeing such a person for the first time, he knows that he will be disapproved by him; his repulsion changes into hatred or jealousy, and inspires him with the desire of doing harm to the object of his antipathy. A good spirit feels repulsion for a bad one, because he knows that he will not be understood by him, and that they do not share the same sentiments; but, strong in his own superiority, he feels neither hatred nor jealousy towards him, and contents himself with avoiding and pitying him."

Forgetfulness of the Past

392. Why does the incarnated spirit lose the remembrance of his past?

"Man cannot, and may not, know everything; God, in His wisdom, has so ordained. Without the veil which hides certain things from his view, man would be dazzled, like one who passes suddenly from darkness to light. *Through the forgetfulness of his past a man is more fully himself.*"

393. How can a man be responsible for deeds, and atone for faults, of which he has no remembrance? How can he profit by the experience acquired in existences which he has forgotten? We could understand that the tribulations of life might be a lesson for him if he remembered the wrong-doing which has brought them upon him; but if he forgets his former existences, each new existence is, for him, as though it were his first, and thus the work is always to be begun over again. How is this to be reconciled with the justice of God?

"With each new existence a spirit becomes more intelligent, and better able to distinguish between good and evil. Where would be his freedom if he remembered all his past? When a spirit re-enters his primitive life (the spirit-life), his whole past unrolls itself before him. He sees the faults which he has committed, and which are the cause of his suffering, and he also sees what would have prevented him from committing them; he comprehends the justice of the situation which is assigned to him, and he then seeks out the new existence that may serve to repair the mistakes of the one which has just passed away. He demands new trials analogous to those in which he has failed, or which he considers likely to aid his advancement; and he demands of the spirits who are his superiors to aid him in the new task he is about to undertake, for he knows that the spirit who will be appointed as his guide in that new existence will endeavour to make him cure himself of his faults by giving him a sort of intuition of those he has committed in the past. This intuition is the evil thought, the criminal desire, which often come to you, and which you instinctively resist, attributing your resistance to the principles you have received from your parents, while it is due in reality to the voice of your conscience; and that voice is the reminiscence of your past, warning you not to fall again into the faults you have already committed. He who, having entered upon a new existence, undergoes its trials

with fortitude, and resists its temptations to wrong-doing, rises
in the hierarchy of spirits, and takes a higher place when he returns
into the normal life."

If we have not an **exact remembrance,** during our corporeal life, of what
we have been, and of the good or evil we have done, in our preceding
existences, we have **the intuition** of our past, of which we have a reminiscence in the instinctive tendencies that our conscience, which is the desire
we have conceived to avoid commiting our past faults in the future, warns us
to resist.

*394. In worlds more advanced than ours, where the human
race is not a prey to our physical wants and infirmities, do men
understand that they are better off than we are? Happiness is
usually relative; it is felt to be such by comparison with a state
that is less happy. As some of those worlds, though better than
ours, have not reached perfection, the men by whom they are
inhabited must have their own troubles and annoyances. Among
us, the rich man, although he has not to endure the physical
privations that torture the poor, is none the less a prey to tribulations of other kinds that embitter his life. What I ask is,
whether the inhabitants of those worlds do not consider themselves
to be just as unhappy, according to their standard of happiness,
as we consider ourselves to be according to ours; and whether they
do not, like us, complain of their fate, not having the remembrance
of an inferior existence to serve them as a standard of comparison?*

"To this question two different answers must be given. There
are some worlds among those of which you speak the inhabitants
of which have a very clear and exact remembrance of their past
existences, and therefore can and do appreciate the happiness which
God permits them to enjoy. But there are others, of which the
inhabitants, though placed, as you say, in better conditions than
yours, are, nevertheless, subject to great annoyances, and even to
much unhappiness, and who do not appreciate the more favourable
conditions of their life, because they have no remembrance of a
state still more unhappy. But if they do not rightly appreciate
those conditions as men, they appreciate them more justly on their
return to the spirit-world."

Is there not, in the forgetfulness of our past existences, and especially
when they have been painful, a striking proof of the wisdom and beneficence of Providential arrangements? It is only in worlds of higher advancement, and when the remembrance of our painful existences in the past
is nothing more to us than the. shadowy remembrance of an unpleasant
dream, that those existences are allowed to present themselves to our memory. Would not the painfulness of present suffering, in worlds of low
degree, be greatly aggravated by the remembrance of all the miseries
we may have had to undergo in the past? These considerations should
lead us to conclude that whatever has been appointed by God is for the

best, and that it is not our province to find fault with His works, nor to decide upon the way in which He ought to have regulated the universe.

The remembrance of our former personality would be attended, in our present existence, with many very serious disadvantages. In some cases, it would cause us cruel humiliation ; in others, it might incite us to pride and vanity ; in all cases, it would be a hindrance to the action of our free-will. God gives us for our amelioration just what is necessary and sufficient to that end, viz., the voice of our conscience and our instinctive tendencies. He keeps from us what would be for us a source of injury. Moreover, if we retained the remembrance of our own former personalities and doings, we should also remember those of other people ; a kind of knowledge that would necessarily exercise a disastrous influence upon our social relations. Not always having reason to be proud of our past, it is evidently better for us that a veil should be thrown over it. And these considerations are in perfect accordance with the statements of spirits in regard to the existence of higher worlds than ours. In those worlds, in which moral excellence reigns, there is nothing painful in the remembrance of the past, and therefore the inhabitants of those happier worlds remember their preceding existence as we remember to-day what we did yesterday. As to the sojourns they may have made in worlds of lower degree, it is no more to them, as we have already said, than the remembrance of a disagreeable dream.

395. Can we obtain any revelations respecting our former existences?

"Not in all cases. There are, however, many who know who they have been and what they have done. If it were permitted to them to speak openly, they would make curious revelations about the past."

396. Some persons believe themselves to have a vague remembrance of an unknown past, which comes before them like the fugitive image of a dream that one vainly endeavours to recall. Is this belief only an illusion?

"It is sometimes real, but it is often an illusion to be guarded against; for it may be merely the effect of an excited imagination."

397. In corporeal existences of a more elevated nature than ours, is the reminiscence of our anterior existences more exact?

"Yes; in proportion as the body is less material, the spirit incarnated in it remembers them more clearly. The remembrance of the past is always clearer in those who inhabit worlds of a higher order."

398. A man's instinctive tendencies being a reflex of his past, does it follow that, by studying those tendencies, he can ascertain what are the faults he has formerly committed?

"Undoubtedly he can do so up to a certain point; but he would also have to take account of the improvement which may have been effected in his spirit, and of the resolutions taken by him in the state of erraticity. His present existence may be very much better than his preceding one."

— *Might it be worse?—that is to say, might a man commit, in a subsequent existence, faults which he had not committed in the preceding one?*

"That depends on his advancement. If he were unable to resist temptation, he might be drawn into new faults as a consequence of the situation chosen by him; but such faults must be considered as indicating a state which is stationary rather than retrograde, for a spirit may advance or remain stationary, but he never goes back."

399. *The vicissitudes of corporeal life being at once an expiation of the faults of the past and lessons for the future, can we, from the nature of those vicissitudes, infer the character of our preceding existence?*

"You can do so very frequently, since the nature of the punishment incurred always corresponds to that of the fault committed. Nevertheless, it would not do to consider this as being an absolute rule. The instintive tendencies furnish a more certain indication; for the trials undergone by a spirit are as much for the future as for the past."

When a spirit has reached the end of the term assigned by Providence to his errant life, he chooses for himself the trials which he determines to undergo in order to hasten his progress—that is to say, the kind of existence which he believes will be most likely to furnish him with the means of advancing ; and the trials of this new existence always correspond to the faults which he has to expiate. If he triumphs in this new struggle, he rises in grade; if he succumbs, he has to try again.

A spirit always possesses free-will. It is in virtue of this free-will that he chooses, when in the spirit-state, the trials he elects to undergo in the corporeal life, and that he deliberates, when in the incarnate state whether he will do, or not do, and chooses between good and evil. To deny a man's free-will would be to reduce him to a machine.

When a spirit has re-entered corporeal life, he experiences a temporary forgetfulness of his former existences, as though these were hidden from him by a veil. Sometimes, however, he preserves a vague consciousness of them, and they may, under certain circumstances, be revealed to him ; but this only occurs as a result of the decision of higher spirits, who make that revelation spontaneously for some useful end, and never for the gratification of idle curiosity.

A spirit's future existences cannot, in any case, be revealed to him during the corporeal life, because they will depend on the manner in which he accomplishes his present existence, and on his own ulterior choice.

Temporary forgetfulness of the faults he has committed is no obstacle to a spirit's improvement ; for if he have not a precise remembrance of them, the knowledge he had of them in the state of erraticity, and the desire he then conceived to repair them, guide him intuitively, and inspire him with the intention of resisting the evil tendency. This intention is the voice of his conscience, and is seconded by the spirits who assist him, if he gives heed to the suggestions with which they inspire him.

Although a man does not know exactly what may have been his acts in his former existences, he always knows the kind of faults of which he has been guilty, and what has been his ruling characteristic. He has only to study himself, and he will know what he has been, not by what he is, but by his tendencies.

The vicissitudes of corporeal life are both an expiation of faults in the past, and trials designed to render us better for the future. They purify and elevate, provided we bear them resignedly and unrepiningly.

The nature of the vicissitudes and trials that we have to undergo may also enlighten us in regard to what we have been and what we have done, just as we infer the crimes of which a convict has been guilty from the penalty inflicted on him by the law. Thus, he who has sinned through pride will be punished by the humiliations of an inferior position ; the self-indulgent and avaricious, by poverty ; the hard-hearted, by the severities he will undergo ; the tyrant, by slavery ; a bad son, by the ingratitude of his children ; the idle, by subjection to hard and incessant labour; and so on.

CHAPTER VIII

EMANCIPATION OF THE SOUL

1. SLEEP AND DREAMS—2. VISITS BETWEEN THE SPIRITS OF LIVING PERSONS—3. TRANSMISSION OF THOUGHT—4. LETHARGY, CATALEPSY : APPARENT DEATH—5. SOMNAMBULISM—6. TRANCE—7. SECOND-SIGHT—8. THEORY OF SOMNAMBULISM, TRANCE, AND SECOND-SIGHT.

Sleep and Dreams

400. Does the incarnated spirit reside willingly in his corporeal envelope?

"You might as well ask whether a prisoner willingly remains locked up in prison. The incarnated spirit aspires incessantly after his deliverance; and the grosser his envelope, the more desirous is he to be rid of it."

401. Does the soul take rest, like the body, during sleep?

"No; a spirit is never inactive. The bonds which unite him to the body are relaxed during sleep; and as the body does not then need his presence, he travels through space, *and enters into more direct relation with other spirits.*"

402. How can we ascertain the fact of a spirit's liberty during sleep?

"By dreams. Be very sure that, when his body is asleep, a spirit enjoys the use of faculties of which he is unconscious while his body is awake. He remembers the past, and sometimes foresees the future: he acquires more power, and is able to enter into communication with other spirits, *either in this world or in some other.*

"You often say, 'I have had a strange dream, a frightful dream, without any likeness to reality' You are mistaken in thinking it to be so; for it is often a reminiscence of places and things which you have seen in the past, or a foresight of those which you will see in another existence, or in this one at some future time. The body being torpid, the spirit tries to break his chain, and seeks, in the past or in the future, for the means of doing so.

"Poor human beings! how little do you know of the commonest phenomena of your life! You fancy yourselves to be very learned, and you are puzzled by the most ordinary things. To questions that any child might ask, 'What do we do when we are asleep?' 'What are dreams?' you are incapable of replying.

"Sleep effects a partial freeing of the soul from the body. When you sleep, your spirit is, for the time being, in the state in which you will be after your death. The spirits who at death are promptly freed from matter are those who, during their life, have had what may be called *intelligent sleep*. Such persons, when they sleep, regain the society of other spirits superior to themselves. They go about with them, conversing with them, and gaining instruction from them; they even work, in the spirit-world, at undertakings which, on dying, they find already begun or completed. From this you see how little death should be dreaded, since, according to the saying of St. Paul, you 'die daily.'

"What we have just stated refers to spirits of an elevated degree of advancement. As for those of the common mass of men, who, after their death, remain for long hours in the state of confusion and uncertainty of which you have been told by such, they go, during sleep, into worlds of lower rank than the earth, to which they are drawn back by old affections, or by the attraction of pleasures still baser than those to which they are addicted in your world; visits in which they gather ideas still viler, more ignoble, and more mischievous than those which they had professed during their waking hours. And that which engenders sympathy in the earthly life is nothing else than the fact that you feel yourselves, on waking, affectionately attracted towards those with whom you have passed eight or nine hours of happiness or pleasure. On the other hand, the explanation of the invincible antipathies you sometimes feel for certain persons is also to be found in the intuitive knowledge you have thus acquired of the fact that those persons have another conscience than yours, because you know them without having previously seen them with your bodily eyes. It is this same fact, moreover, that explains the indifference of some people for others; they do not care to make new friends, because they know that they have others by whom they are loved and cherished. In a word, sleep has more influence than you think upon your life.

"Through the effects of sleep, incarnated spirits are always in connection with the spirit-world; and it is in consideration of this fact that spirits of a higher order consent, without much repugnance, to incarnate themselves among you. God has willed that, during their contact with vice, they may go forth and fortify themselves afresh at the source of rectitude, in order that they, who have come into your world to instruct others, may not fall into evil themselves. Sleep is the gate opened for them by God, that they may pass through it to their friends in the spirit-world; it is their recreation after labour, while awaiting the great deliverance, the final liberation, that will restore them to their true place.

"Dreams are the remembrance of what your spirit has seen during sleep; but you must remark that you do not always dream, because you do not always remember what you have seen, or all that you have seen. Your dreams do not always reflect the action of your soul in its full development; for they are often only the reflex of the confusion that accompanies your departure or your return, mingled with the vague remembrance of what you have done, or of what has occupied your thoughts, in your waking state. In what other way can you explain the absurd dreams which are dreamed by the wisest as by the silliest of mankind? Bad spirits, also, make use of dreams to torment weak and timid souls.

"You will see, ere long, the development of another kind of dream, a kind which is as ancient as the one you know, but one of which you are ignorant. The dream we allude to is that of Jeanne Darc,[1] of Jacob, of the Jewish prophets, and of certain Hindoo ascetics—a dream which is the remembrance of the soul's experiences while entirely freed from the body, the remembrance of the second life, of which I spoke just now.

"You should carefully endeavour to distinguish these two kinds of dreams among those which you are able to recall: unless you do this, you will be in danger of falling into contradictions and errors that would be prejudicial to your belief."

Dreams are a product of the emancipation of the soul, rendered more active by the suspension of the active life of relation, and enjoying a sort of indefinite clairvoyance which extends to places at a great distance from us, or that we have never seen, or even to other worlds. To this state of emancipation is also due the remembrance which retraces to our memory the events that have occurred in our present existence or in preceding existences ; the strangeness of the images of what has taken place in worlds unknown to us, mixed up with the things of the present world, producing the confused and whimsical medleys that seem to be equally devoid of connection and of meaning.

The incoherence of dreams is still farther explained by the gaps resulting from the incompleteness of our remembrance of what has appeared to us in our nightly visions—an incompleteness similar to that of a narrative from which whole sentences, or parts of sentences, have been omitted by

1 Joan of Arc.

chance, and whose remaining fragments, having been thrown together
again at random, have lost all intelligible meaning.

403.   Why do we not always remember our dreams?

"What you call sleep is only the repose of the body, for the
spirit is always in motion.   During sleep he recovers a portion of
his liberty, and enters into communication with those who are dear
to him, either in this world, or in other worlds; but as the matter
of the body is heavy and gross, it is difficult for him to retain,
on waking, the impressions he has received during sleep, because
those impressions were not received by him through the bodily
organs."

404.   What is to be thought of the signification attributed to dreams?

"Dreams are not really indications in the sense attributed to
them by fortune-tellers; for it is absurd to believe that a certain
kind of dream announces the happening of a certain kind of
event.   But they, are indications in this sense—viz., that they
present images which are real for the spirit, though they may have
nothing to do with what takes place in his present corporeal life.
Dreams are also, in many cases, as we have said, a remembrance;
they may also be sometimes a presentiment of the future, if
permitted by God, or the sight of something which is taking place
at the time in some other place to which the soul has transported
itself.   Have you not many instances proving that persons may
appear to their relatives and friends in dreams, and give them
notice of what is happening to them?   What are apparitions, if
not the soul or spirit of persons who come to communicate with
you?   When you acquire the certainty that what you saw has
really taken place, is it not a proof that it was no freak of your
imagination, especially if what you saw were something which you
had not thought of when you were awake?"

405.   We often see in dreams things which appear to be presentiments, but which do not come to pass,—how is this?

"Those things may take place in the experience of the spirit,
though not in that of the body; that is to say, that the spirit sees
what he wishes to see *because he goes to find it.*   You must not
forget that, during sleep, the spirit is always more or less under
the influence of matter; that, consequently, he is never completely
free from terrestrial ideas, and that the objects of his waking
thoughts may therefore give to his dreams the appearance of what

he desires or of what he fears, thus producing what may be properly termed an effect of the imagination. When the mind is much busied with any idea, it is apt to connect everything it sees with that idea."

406. When, in a dream, we see persons who are well known to us doing things which they are not in any way thinking of, is it not a mere effect of the imagination?

"Of which they are not thinking? How do you know that it is so? Their spirit may come to visit yours, as yours may go to visit theirs; and you do not always know, in your waking state, what they may be thinking of. And besides, you often, in your dreams, apply to persons whom you know, and according to your own desires, reminiscences of what took place, or is taking place, in other existences."

407. Is it necessary to the emancipation of the soul that the sleep of the body should be complete?

"No; the spirit recovers his liberty as soon as the senses become torpid. He takes advantage, in order to emancipate himself, of every moment of respite left him by the body. As soon as there occurs any prostration of the vital forces, the spirit disengages himself from the body, and the feebler the body, the freer is the spirit."

It is for this reason that dozing, or a mere dulling of the senses, often presents the same images as dreaming.

408. We sometimes seem to hear within ourselves words distinctly pronounced, but having no connection with what we are thinking of,—what is the cause of this?

"Yes, you often hear words, and even whole sentences, especially when your senses begin to grow torpid. It is sometimes the faint echo of the utterance of a spirit who wishes to communicate with you."

409. Often, when only half-asleep, and with our eyes closed, we see distinct images, figures of which we perceive the minutest details,—is this an effect of vision or of imagination?

"The body being torpid, the spirit tries to break his chain. He goes away and sees; if the sleep were deeper, the vision would be a dream."

410. We sometimes, when asleep, or half-asleep, have ideas which seem to us to be excellent, but which, despite all the efforts we make to recall them, are effaced from our memory on waking,—whence come these ideas?

"They are the result of the freedom of the spirit, who emancipates himself from the body, and enjoys the use of other faculties during this moment of liberty; and they are often counsels given you by other spirits."

— *What is the use of such ideas and counsels, since we lose the remembrance of them, and cannot profit by them?*

"Those ideas often belong rather to the world of spirits than to the corporeal world; but, in general, though the body may forget them, the spirit remembers them, and the idea recurs to him at the proper time, in his waking state, as though it were an inspiration of the moment."

411. Does the incarnated spirit, when he is freed from matter and acting as a spirit, know the epoch of his death?

"He often has the presentiment of it. He sometimes has a very clear foreknowledge of it; and it is this which gives him the intuition of it in his waking state. It is this, also, which enables some persons to foresee the time of their death with perfect exactness."

412. Can the activity of the spirit, during the repose or the sleep of the body, cause fatigue to the latter?

"Yes, for the spirit is attached to the body, as the captive-balloon is fastened to the post; and, just as the post is shaken by the movements of the balloon, so the activity of the spirit reacts upon the body, and may cause it to feel fatigued."

Visits Between the Spirits of Living Persons

413. The emancipation of the soul during sleep would seem to indicate that we live simultaneously two lives; the life of the body, which is that of exterior relation, and the life of the soul, which is that of occult relation,—is this so?

"During the emancipation of the soul, the life of the latter takes precedence of the life of the body; this, however, does not, strictly speaking, constitute two lives, but rather two phases of one and the same life, for a man does not live a double life."

414. Can two persons, who are acquainted with each other, visit one another in sleep?

"Yes; and many others, who, in their waking state, do not know that they are acquainted, meet and converse together. You may, without suspecting it, have friends in another country. The fact of going, during sleep, to visit friends, relatives, acquaintances, persons who can be of use to you, is extremely frequent; and you yourselves accomplish these visits almost every night."

415. What can be the use of these nocturnal meetings, since we do not remember them?

"The intuition of them generally remains with you in your waking state, and is often the origin of ideas which afterwards occur to you, as it were, spontaneously, without your being able to account for them, but which are really those you had obtained in the spirit-intercourse carried on by you during your sleep."

416. Can a man ensure the making of spirit-visits by the exertion of his will? Can he do so, for example, by saying to himself, on going to sleep, "I will to-night meet such and such a person in spirit, and speak with him about such and such a thing"?

"This is what takes place. The man falls asleep, and his spirit wakens to the other life; but his spirit is often very far from following out the plan which had been resolved upon by the man, for the life of the man excites but little interest in a spirit when he is emancipated from matter. This statement, however, only applies to men who have already reached a certain degree of elevation. The others pass their spirit-existence very differently. They give free rein to their passions, or remain inactive. It may happen, therefore, according to the aim of the proposed action, that a spirit may go to see the parties he had, as a man, proposed to visit; but it does not follow that, because he has willed to do so in his waking state, he will necessarily do so in his state of freedom."

417. Can a number of incarnate spirits, during sleep, meet together, and form assemblies?

"Undoubtedly they can. The ties of friendship, old or new, often bring together spirits who are happy to be in each other's company."

By the term **old** must be understood the ties of friendship contracted in anterior existences. We bring back with us, on waking, an intuition of the ideas which we have derived from these occult meetings, but of the source of which we are ignorant.

418. If a person believed one of his friends to be dead who is not dead, could he meet him as a spirit, and thus learn that he is living? Could he, in such a case, preserve the intuition of this fact on waking?

"He could, certainly, as a spirit, see his friend, and know what is his situation; and if the belief in the death of that friend had not been imposed on him as an expiation, he might retain an impression of his existence, as, in the contrary case, he might retain that of his death."

Occult Transmission of Thought

419. Whence comes it that the same idea—that of a discovery, for instance—so often suggests itself at the same time to several persons, although they may be at a distance from one another?

"We have already said that, during sleep, spirits communicate with one another; well, when his body awakes, a spirit remembers what he has learned, and the man thinks he has invented it. Thus several persons may find out the same thing at the same time. When you say that an idea is 'in the air,' you employ a figure of speech that is much nearer the truth than suppose. Every one helps unconsciously to propagate it."

In this way our spirit often reveals to other spirits, without our being aware of it, that which formed the object of our meditations before we went to sleep.

420. Can spirits communicate between themselves when the body is awake?

"A spirit is not enclosed in his body as in a box, but radiates around it in every direction. He can, therefore, hold communication with other spirits even in the waking state, although he does so with more difficulty."

421. How comes it that two persons, perfectly awake, often have the same thought at the same moment?

"It is because two spirits, who are in sympathy, may communicate their thought to each other even when the body is not asleep."

There is, between spirits, a communication of thoughts which sometimes enables two persons to see and understand one another without having any need of human speech. They may be said to speak the language of spirits.

Lethargy, Catalepsy, Apparent Death

422. In lethargy and catalepsy, the patients generally see and hear what takes place around them, but are unable to manifest their impressions. Is it through the eyes and ears of the body that these impressions are received?

"No; they are received by the spirit. The spirit is conscious, but cannot express himself."

— *Why can he not express himself?*

"The state of his body prevents his doing so; and this peculiar state of his bodily organs proves that man consists of something more than a body, since the body no longer works, and yet the spirits acts."

423. Can a spirit, in a state of lethargy, separate himself entirely from his body, so as to give to the latter all the outward appearances of death, and afterwards come back and inhabit it?

"In lethargy, the body is not dead, for it still accomplishes some of its functions. Its vitality is latent, as in the chrysalis but is not annihilated; and a spirit is united to his body as long as it remains alive. When once the links which keep them together are broken by the death and disaggregation of the bodily organs, the separation is complete, and the spirit never again comes back to his body. When one who is apparently dead comes to life again, it is because the process of death was not entirely consummated."

424. Is it possible, by means of timely help, to renew the ties which were ready to break, and to give back life to a person who, but for this help, would have definitively ceased to live?

"Yes, undoubtedly; and you have proofs of this every day. Mesmerism often exercises, in such cases, a powerful restorative action, because it gives to the body the vital fluid which it lacks, and which is necessary to keep up the play of the organs."

Lethargy and catalepsy proceed from the same cause, viz., the temporary loss of sensibility and power of motion, from some as yet unexplained physiological condition. They differ in this respect, viz., that, in lethargy, the suppression of the vital force is general, and gives to the body all the appearances of death, whereas, in catalepsy, that suppression is localised, and may affect a more or less extensive portion of the body, while leaving the intelligence free to manifest itself ; a fact which does not allow it to be confounded with death. Lethargy is always natural ; catalepsy is sometimes spontaneous, but it may be produced and dissipated artificially by mesmeric action.

Somnambulism

425. Is there any connection between natural somnambulism and dreaming?

"In somnambulism the independence of the soul is more complete, and its functions are more developed, than in dreaming, and it has perceptions that it has not in dreaming, which is an imperfect somnambulism.

"In somnambulism, the spirit is entirely freed from the action of matter; the material organs, being in a sort of catalepsy, are no longer receptive of *external* impressions.

"This state most frequently occurs during sleep, because the spirit is then able to absent itself from the body which is given up to the repose that is indispensable to matter. When somnambulism occurs, it is because the spirit of the sleeper, intent upon doing something or other that requires the aid of his body, makes use of it in a manner analogous to that in which spirits make use of a table, or other material object, in producing the phenomena of physical manifestations, or of a human hand, in giving written communications. In the dreams of which a man is conscious, his organs, including those of memory, are beginning to awaken; and, as they only receive and transmit to the spirit imperfectly the impressions made on them by exterior objects or action, the spirit, who is then in a state of repose, only perceives these impressions through confused and often disconnected sensations, which, in many cases, are still further confused by being mingled with vague remembrances of his present life and anterior existences. It is easy, therefore, to understand why somnambulists do not remember their visions, and why the greater number of the dreams you remember have no rational meaning. I say *the greater number*, for it sometimes happens that dreams are the consequence of a precise remembrance of events that have occurred in one of your former lives, or even a sort of intuition of the future."

426. *Is there any connection between what is called mesmeric somnambulism and natural somnambulism?*

"They are the same thing; the only difference between them being that one of them is artificially produced."

427. *What is the nature of the agent called the magnetic or mesmeric fluid?*

"It is the vital fluid, animalised electricity; a modification of the universal fluid."

428. *What is the nature of somnambulic clairvoyance?*

"We have told you that it is *soul-sight*."

429. *How can the somnambulist see through opaque bodies?*

"It is only to your gross organs that bodies are opaque. Have we not told you that matter is not an obstacle for a spirit, since he passes freely through it? A somnambulist often tells you that he sees through his forehead, his knee, etc., because you, being plunged in matter, do not understand that he can see without the help of organs. He himself, influenced by your ideas, believes that he needs those organs; but, if you left him to himself, he would understand that he sees through every part of his body, or rather, that he sees independently of his body."

430. *Since the clairvoyance of the somnambulist is that of his soul or of his spirit, why does he not see everything, and why does he so often make mistakes?*

"In the first place, spirits of low degree do not see and comprehend everything, for, as you know, they still share your errors and your prejudices; and, in the next place, as long as they remain more or less attached to matter, they have not the use of all their spirit-faculties. God has given the faculty of clairvoyance to man for a serious and useful purpose, and not to inform him of what it is not permitted to him to know; and this is why somnambulists do not know everything."

431 *What is the source of the somnambulist's innate ideas, and how can he speak correctly of things of which he is ignorant in his waking state, and which are even above his intellectual capacity?*

"A somnambulist may possess more knowledge than you give him credit for; but this knowledge is latent in his waking state, because his envelope is too imperfect for him to be able to remember all he knows as a spirit. But, in point of fact, what is he? Like all of us, he is a spirit who has been incarnated in matter for the accomplishment of his mission, and his going into the somnambulic state rouses him from the lethargy of incarnation. We have repeatedly told you that we re-live many times. It is this changing of our existences that causes him to lose sight, in a new connection with matter, of what he may have know in a preceding one. On entering into the state which you call *a crisis*, he recalls what he has formerly known, but not always with completeness. He knows, but he cannot tell whence he deri·es his knowledge, nor in what way he possesses it. The crisis over, his reminiscences fade from his consciousness, and he re-enters the obscurity of corporeal life."

Experience shows us that somnambulists also receive communications from other spirits, who tell them what they are to say, and supply what is lacking on their part. This supplementing of their insufficiency is often and especially witnessed in medical consultations ; the spirit of the clairvoyant seeing the malady, and another spirit indicating the remedy required. This double action is often patent to bystanders, and is also frequently revealed by such expressions on the part of the somnambulist as, "I am told to say," or, "I am forbidden to say," etc. In the latter case, it is always dangerous to persist in the effort to obtain a revelation refused by the clairvoyant, because, by doing so, we open the door to frivolous and unscrupulous spirits, who prate about everything without any regard to veracity.

432. How do you explain the power of seeing at a distance possessed by some somnambulists?

"Does not the soul transport itself to a distance during sleep? It does the same thing in somnambulism."

433. Does the greater or less degree of somnambulic clairvoyance depend on the physical organisation of the body, or on the nature of the spirit incarnated in it?

"On both; but there are physical qualities that allow the spirit to liberate himself more or less easily from matter."

434. Are the faculties enjoyed by the somnambulist the same as those possessed by the spirit after death?

"They are the same, but only up to a certain point; for you have to take into account the influence of the matter to which he is still attached."

435. Can somnambulists see other spirits?

"That depends on the nature and degree of their faculties. The greater number of them see other spirits perfectly well, but they do not always recognise them at once as being such, and thus mistake them for corporeal beings; a mistake that is often made by somnambulists, and especially by those among them who know nothing of Spiritism. Not understanding anything of the essence of spirits, they are astonished at seeing them in human form, and suppose them to be living persons."

The same effect is produced at the moment of death in the consciousness of those who suppose themselves to be still living. Nothing about them appears to them to be changed. The spirits around them seem to have bodies like ours, and they take the appearance of their own body to be that of a real body of flesh.

436. When a somnambulist sees objects at a distance, does he see them with his body or with his soul?

"Why should you ask such a question, since it is the soul that sees, and not the body?"

437. Since it is the soul that transports itself to a distance, how is it that the somnambulist feels in his body the sensation of

*the heat or the cold of the place where his soul is, and which is
sometimes very far from the place where his body is?*

"His soul has not entirely quitted his body, to which it is still
attached by the link which unites them together; it is this link that
is the conductor of sensation. When two persons in two different
cities correspond with each other by electricity, it is the electricity
that constitutes the link between their thoughts, and enables them
to communicate with one another as though they were close
together."

*438. Is the state of the somnambulist influenced after death by
the use he has made of his faculty?*

"Very considerably; as is done by the good or bad use of all
the faculties that God has given to man."

Trance

*439. What difference is there between trance and som-
nambulism?*

"Trance is a more refined somnambulism. The soul, when in
trance, is still more independent."

*440. Does the soul of the ecstatic really enter into higher
worlds?*

"Yes; he sees them, and perceives the happiness of those who
are in them; but there are worlds that are inaccessible to spirits who
are not sufficiently purified."

*441. When a person in trance expresses the desire to quit the
earth, does he speak sincerely, and is he not retained by the instinct
of self-preservation?*

"That depends on the degree of the spirit's purification. If he
sees that his future situation will be better than his present one,
he makes an effort to break the links that bind him to the earth."

*442. If the ecstatic were left to himself, might his soul defin-
itively quit his body?*

"Yes, he might die; and it is therefore necessary to call him
back by everything that may attach him to the lower life, and
especially by making him see that, if he breaks the chain which
keeps him here, he will have taken the most effectual means of
preventing his staying in the world in which he perceives that he
would be happy."

443. *The ecstatic sometimes professes to see things which are evidently the product of an imagination impressed with earthly beliefs and prejudices. What he sees, therefore, is not always real?*

"What he sees is real for him; but, as his spirit is always under the influence of terrestrial ideas, he may see it in his own way, or, to speak more correctly, he may express it in a language accommodated to his prejudices, or to the ideas in which he has been brought up, or to your own, in order the better to make himself understood. It is in this way that he is most apt to err."

444. *What degree of confidence should be accorded to the revelations of persons in a state of trance?*

"The ecstatic may very frequently be mistaken, especially when he seeks to penetrate what must remain a mystery for man; for he then abandons himself to his own ideas, or becomes the sport of deceiving spirits, *who take advantage of his enthusiasm to dazzle him with false appearances.*"

445. *What inductions are to be drawn from the phenomena of somnambulism and of trance? May they not be considered as a sort of initiation into the future life?*

"It would be more correct to say that, in those states, the somnambulist may obtain glimpses of his past and future lives. Let man study those phenomena; he will find in them the solution of more than one mystery which his unassisted reason seeks in vain to penetrate."

446. *Could the phenomena of somnambulism and trance be made to accord with theoretic materialism?*

"He who should study them honestly, and without preconceived ideas, could not be either a materialist or an atheist."

Second-Sight.

447. *Is there any connection between the phenomena of what is designated as* second-sight *and those of dreaming and somnambulism?*

"They are all the same thing. What you call *second-sight* is also a state in which the spirit is partially free, although the body is not asleep. Second-sight is soul-sight."

448. *Is the faculty of second-sight a permanent one?*

"The faculty of second-sight is permanent, but its exercise is not. In worlds less material than yours, spirits free themselves from matter more easily, and enter into communication with one another simply by thought, without, however, excluding the use of articulate speech. In those worlds, second-sight is, for the greater part of their inhabitants, a permanent faculty. Their normal state may be compared to that of lucid somnambulism among you; and it is for this reason that they manifest themselves to you more easily than those who are incarnated in bodies of a grosser nature."

449. *Does second-sight occur spontaneously, or through an exertion of the will of those who possess that faculty?*

"It generally occurs spontaneously; but the will, nevertheless, often plays an important part in producing this phenomenon. Take, for example, the persons who are called fortune-tellers—and some of whom really have that power—and you will find that the action of their will helps them to this second-sight, and to what you call vision."

450. *Is second-sight susceptible of being developed by exercise?*

"Yes; effort always leads to progress, and the veil which covers things becomes more transparent."

— *Is this faculty a result of physical organisation?*

"Organisation has undoubtedly a great deal to do with it; there are organisations with which it is incompatible."

451. *How is it that second-sight appears to be hereditary in certain families?*

"This proceeds from similarity of organisation, which is transmitted, like other physical qualities; and also from the development of the faculty through a sort of education, which, also, is transmitted from one generation to another."

452. *Is it true that circumstances develop second-sight?*

"Illness, the approach of danger, any great commotion, may develop it. The body is sometimes in a state which allows of the spirit's seeing what cannot be seen with the fleshly eye."

Times of crisis and of calamity, powerful emotions, all the causes, in short, which excite the moral nature, may develop second-sight. It would seem as though Providence gave us, when in the presence of danger, the means of escaping it. All sects and all parties subjected to persecution have offered numerous instances of this fact.

453. *Are the persons who are gifted with second-sight always conscious of their faculty?*

"Not always; it appears to them to be altogether natural, and many of them suppose that, if everybody observed their own impressions, they would find themselves to be possessed of the same power."

454. May we attribute to a sort of second-sight the perspicacity of those persons who, without being remarkably gifted in other ways, possess an unusually clear judgment in relation to the things of everyday life?

"Such clearness of judgment is always due to a freer radiation of the soul, enabling the man to see more correctly than those whose perceptions are more densely veiled by matter."

— Can this lucidity of judgment, in some cases, give the fore-knowledge of future events?

"Yes, it may give presentiments; for there are many degrees in this faculty, and the same person may possess all those degrees, as he may possess only some of them."

Explanation of Somnambulism, Trance, and Second-Sight.

455.   The phenomena of natural somnambulism occur spontaneously and independently of any known external cause; but, in persons endowed with a special organisation, they may be produced artificially through the action of the mesmeric agent. The only difference between the state designated as mesmeric somnambulism, and natural somnambulism is, that the one is artificially produced, while the other is spontaneous.

Natural somnambulism is a notorious fact, the reality of which few now dispute, notwithstanding the marvellous character of the phenomena it presents. Why, then, should mesmeric somnambulism be regarded as more extraordinary or incredible, simply because it is produced artificially, like so many other things? It has been abused by charlatans, some persons will reply; but that fact only affords an additional reason for not leaving it in their hands. When science shall have taken possession of it; charlatanism will have much less credit with the masses; but, meanwhile, as somnambulism, both natural and artificial, is a fact, and as a fact cannot be argued down, it is making its way, despite the ill-will of its adversaries, and obtaining a footing even in the temple of science, which it is entering by a multitude of side-doors, instead of entering by the principal one. Its right to be there will, ere long, be fully recognised.

For the spiritist, somnambulism is more than a physical phenomenon; it is a light thrown on the subject of psychology; it is a state in which we can study the soul, because in it the soul shows itself, so to say, without covering. Now, one of the phenomena which characterise the soul is clear-seeing independently of the ordinary visual organs. Those who contest this fact do so on the ground that the somnambulist does not see at all times, and at the will of the experimentalist, as with the eyes. Need we be astonished if, the means employed being different, the results are not the same? Is it reasonable to demand identical effects in cases in which the instruments employed are not the same? The soul has its properties just as has the eye; and the former must be judged of by themselves, and not by analogy with the latter.

The cause of the clairvoyance of the mesmeric and of the natural somnambulist is identically the same: *it is an attribute of the soul*, a faculty inherent in every part of the incorporeal being which is in us, and has no other limits than those assigned to the soul itself. The somnambulist sees wherever his soul can transport itself, at no matter what distance.

In sight at distance, the somnambulist does not see from the point at which his body is, and as though through a telescope. The things he sees are present with him, as though he were at the place where they exist, because his soul is there in reality; and it is for this reason that his body is, as it were, annihilated, and seems to be deprived of sensation, until the moment when the soul comes back and retakes possession of it. This partial separation of the soul and the body is an abnormal state, which may last for a longer or shorter time, but not indefinitely; it is the cause of the fatigue felt by the body after a certain lapse of time, especially when the soul during that partial separation, busies itself with some active pursuit. The fact that soul-sight or espirit-sight is not circumscribed, and has no definite seat, explains why somnambulists are unable to assign to it any special organ or focus. They see, because they see, without knowing why or how; their sight, as spirit-sight, having no special focus. *If they refer their perception to their body*, this focus seems to them to be in the organic centres in which the vital activity is greatest, especially in the brain, in the epigastric region, or in whatever organ appears to them to be the point at which the bond between the spirit and the body is *most tenacious*.

The scope of somnambulistic lucidity is not unlimited. A spirit, even when completely free, only possesses the faculties and the knowledge appertaining to the degree of advancement at which he has arrived, a limitation which becomes still further narrowed when he is united with matter, and thus subjected to its influence. This is the reason why somnambulistic clairvoyance is neither universal nor infallible; and its infallibility is all the less to be counted on when it is turned aside from the aim which has been assigned to it by nature, and made a mere matter of curiosity and experimentation.

In the state of comparative freedom in which the somnambulist finds himself, he enters more easily into communication with other spirits, incarnate or disincarnate; and this communication is established through the contact of the fluids which compose their perispirits, and serve, like the electric wire, for the transmission of thought. The somnambulist, therefore, has no need of articulate speech as a vehicle of thought, which he feels and divines; a mode of perception that renders him eminently accessible to, and impressionable by, the influences of the moral atmosphere in which he finds himself. For the same reason, a numerous concourse of spectators, and especially of those who are attracted by a more or less malevolent curiosity, is essentially unfavourable to the manifestation of his peculiar faculties, which close up, so to say, at the contact of hostile influences, and only unfold freely in intimacy, and under the influence of sympathetic surroundings. *The presence of those who are malevolent or antipathetic produces upon him the effect of the contact of the hand upon a sensitive plant.*

The somnambulist sees, at the same time, his own spirit and his body; they are, so to say, two beings which represent to him his double existence, spiritual and corporeal, and which, nevertheless, are blended into one by the ties which united them together. The somnambulist does not always comprehend this *duality*, which often leads him to speak of himself as though he were speaking of another person; in such cases, the corporeal being sometimes speaking to the spiritual being, and the spiritual being sometimes speaking to the corporeal being.

The spirit acquires an increase of knowledge and experience in each of his corporeal existences. He loses sight of part of these gains during his reincarnation in matter, which is too gross to allow of his remembering them in their entirety; *but he remembers them as a spirit.* It is thus that some somnambulists give evidence of possessing knowledge beyond their present degree of instruction, and even of their apparent intellectual capacity. The intellectual and scientific inferiority of a somnambulist in his waking state, therefore, proves nothing against his possession of the knowledge he may display in his lucid state. According to the circumstances of the moment and the aim proposed, he may draw this knowledge from the stores of his own experience, from his clairvoyant perception of things actually occurring, or from the counsels which he receives from other spirits; but, in proportion as his own spirit is more or less advanced, he will make his statements more or less correctly.

In the phenomena of somnambulism, whether natural or mesmeric, Providence furnishes us with undeniable proof of the existence and independence of the soul, by causing us to witness the sublime spectacle of its emancipation from the fetters of the body, and thus enabling us to read our future destiny as in an open book. When a somnambulist describes what is taking place at a distance, it is equally evident that he sees what he describes, and that he does not see it with his bodily eyes. He sees himself at that distant point, and he feels himself to be transported thither. Something of himself, therefore, is really present at that distant point; and that *something*, not being his body, can only be his soul or his spirit.

While man, in search of the causes of his moral being, loses himself in abstract and unintelligible metaphysical subtleties, God places daily before his eyes, and within reach of his hand, the simplest and most certain means for the study of experimental psychology.

Trance is the state in which the soul's independence of the body is made most clearly visible, and, so to say, palpable, to the senses of the observer.

In dreaming and somnambulism, the soul wanders among terrestrial worlds; in trance, it penetrates into a sphere of existence of another order, into that of the etherealised spirits with whom it enters into communication, without, however, being able to overstep certain limits which it could not pass without entirely breaking the links that attach it to the body. Surrounded by novel splendours, enraptured by harmonies unknown to earth, penetrated by bliss that defies description, the soul enjoys a foretaste of celestial beatitude, and may be said *to have placed one foot on the threshold of eternity.*

In the state of trance, the annihilation of corporeal ties is almost complete. The body no longer possesses anything more than organic life; and we feel that the soul is only held thereto by a single thread, which any further effort on its part would break for ever.

In this state, all earthly thoughts disappear, and give place to the purified perception that is the very essence of our immaterial being. Entirely absorbed in this sublime contemplation, the ecstatic regards the earthly life as being merely a momentary halt upon our eternal way; the successes and misfortunes of this lower world, its gross joys and sorrows, appear to him only as the futile incidents of a journey of which he is delighted to foresee the end.

It is with ecstatics as with somnambulists; their lucidity may be more or less perfect, and their spirit, according as it is more or less elevated, is also more or less apt to apprehend the truth of things. In their abnormal state, there is sometimes more of nervous excitement than of true lucidity; or, to speak more correctly, their nervous excitement impairs their lucidity, and, for this reason, their revelations are often a mixture of truths and errors, of sublime ideas and absurd or even ridiculous fancies. Inferior spirits often take advantage of this nervous excitement (which is always a source of weakness to those who are unable to control it), in order to subjugate the ecstatic; and to this end they assume to his eyes the *appearances* which confirm him in the ideas and prejudices of his waking state. This subjugation of clairvoyants by the presentation of false appearances is the "rock ahead" of this order of revealment. But all of them are not equally subject to this dangerous misleading; and it is for us to weigh their statements coolly and carefully, and to judge their revelations by the light of science and of reason.

The emancipation of the soul occurs sometimes in the waking state, and gives, to those who are endowed with the faculty designated by the name of *second-sight*, the power of seeing, hearing, and feeling, *beyond the limits of the bodily senses*. They perceive things at a distance, at all points to which their soul extends its action; they see them, so to say, athwart their ordinary sight, and as though in a sort of mirage.

At the moment when the phenomenon of second-sight occurs, the physical state of the seer is visibly modified. His glance becomes vague; he looks before him without seeing; his physiognomy reflects an abnormal state of the nervous system. It is evident that his organs of sight have nothing to do with his present perceptions; for his vision continues, even when his eyes are shut.

The faculty of second-sight appears to those who are endowed with it to be as natural as ordinary sight. It seems to them to be an attribute of their being; and they are not aware of its exceptional character. They generally forget this fugitive lucidity, the remembrance of which, becoming more and more vague, disappears at length from their memory like a dream.

The power of second-sight varies from a confused sensation to a clear and distinct perception of things present or distant. In its rudimentary state, it gives to some persons tact, perspicacity, a sort of sureness, in their decisions and actions, that may be styled *the rectitude of the moral glance*. At a higher degree of development, it awakens presentiments; still further developed, it shows to the seer events that have already happened, or that are about to happen.

Natural and artificial somnambulism, trance, and second-sight are only varieties or modifications of the action of one and the same cause. Like dreams, they are a branch of natural phenomena, and have therefore existed in every age. History shows us that they have been known, and even abused, from the remotest antiquity; and they furnish the explanation of innumerable facts which superstitious prejudices have led men to regard as supernatural.

CHAPTER IX

Penetration of Our Thoughts By Spirits

456. Do spirits see everything that we do?

"They *can* do so if they choose, since they are incessantly around
you. But, practically, each spirit sees only those things to which
he directs his attention; for he pays no heed to those which do
not interest him."

457. Can spirits see our most secret thoughts?

"They often see what you would fain hide from yourselves;
neither acts nor thoughts can be hidden from them."

— *It would appear, then, to be more easy to hide a thing from
a person while living than to hide it from that same person after
his death?*

"Certainly; and when you fancy yourselves to be hidden from
every eye, you have often a crowd of spirits around you, and
watching you."

*458. What is thought of us by the spirits who are about us,
and observing us?*

"That depends on the quality of the spirits themselves. Frivolous spirits enjoy the little annoyances they cause you, and laugh
at your fits of impatience. Graver spirits pity your imperfections,
and endeavour to aid you to cure yourselves of them."

Occult Influence of Spirits on Our Thoughts and Actions.

459.   Do spirits influence our thoughts and our actions?

"Their influence upon them is greater than you suppose, for it is very often they who direct both."

460.   Have we some thoughts that originate with ourselves, and others that are suggested to us?

"Your soul is a spirit who thinks. You must have observed that many thoughts, and frequently very opposite ones, come into your mind reference to the same subject, and at the same time. In such cases, some of them are your own, and some are ours. This is the cause of your uncertainties, because you have thus in your mind two ideas that are opposed to each other."

461.   How can we distinguish between the thoughts which are our own and those which are suggested to us?

"When a thought is suggested, it is like a voice speaking to you. Your own thoughts are generally those which first occur to you. In point of fact, this distinction is not of much practical importance for you, and it is often better for you not to be able to make it. Man's action is thus left in greater freedom. If he decides for the right road, he does so more spontaneously; if he takes the wrong one, he is more distinctly responsible for his mistake."

462.   Do men of intelligence and genius always draw their ideas from their own minds?

"Their ideas sometimes come from their own spirit; but they are often suggested to them by other spirits who judge them to be capable of understanding them, and worthy of transmitting them. When they do not find the required ideas in themselves, they make an unconscious appeal for inspiration; a sort of evocation that they make without being aware of what they are doing."

If it were useful for us to be able to distinguish clearly between our own thoughts and those which are suggested to us, God would have given us the means of doing so, as he has given us that of distinguishing between day and night. When a matter has been left by Providence in a state of vagueness, it has been left so because it is better for us.

463.   It is sometimes said that our first thought is always the best,—is this true?

"It may be good or bad according to the nature of the incarnated spirit. It is always well to listen to good inspirations."

464.   How can we ascertain whether a suggested thought comes from a good spirit or from an evil one?

"Study its quality. Good spirits give only good counsels. It is for you to distinguish between the good and the bad."

465. *To what end do imperfect spirits incite us to evil?*

"To make you suffer as they do themselves."

— *Does that lessen their own sufferings?*

"No; but they do so from jealousy of those who are happier than themselves."

— *What kind of sufferings do they wish to make us undergo?*

"Those which result from being of an inferior order, and far removed from God."

466. *Why does God permit spirits to incite us to evil?*

"Imperfect spirits are used by Providence as instruments for trying men's faith and constancy in well-doing. You, being a spirit, must advance in the knowledge of the infinite. It is for this end that you are made to pass through the trials of evil in order to attain to goodness. Our mission is to lead you into the right road. When you are acted upon by evil influences, it is because you attract evil spirits to you by your evil desires, for evil spirits always come to aid you in doing the evil you desire to do; they can only help you to do wrong when you give way to evil desires. If you are inclined to commit murder, you will have about you a swarm of spirits who will keep this inclination alive in you; but you will also have others about you who will try to influence you for good, which restores the balance, and leaves you of your decision."

It is thus that God leaves to our conscience the choice of the road we decide to follow, and the liberty of yielding to one or other of the opposing influences that act upon us.

467. *Can we free ourselves from the influence of the spirits who incite us to evil?*

"Yes; for they only attach themselves to those who attract them by the evil nature of their thoughts and desires."

468. *Do spirits, whose influence is repelled by our will, renounce their temptations?*

"What else can they do? . When they see that they cannot accomplish their aim, they give up the attempt; but they continue to watch for a favourable moment, as the cat watches for the mouse."

469. By what means can we neutralise the influence of evil spirits?

"By doing only what is right, and putting all your trust in God, you repel the influence of inferior spirits, and prevent them from obtaining power over you. Take care not to listen to the suggestions of spirits who inspire you with evil thoughts, stir up discord among you, and excite in you evil passions. Distrust especially those who flatter your pride, for, in so doing, they attack you on your weakest side. This is why Jesus makes you say in the Lord's Prayer, 'Let us not succumb to temptation, but deliver us from evil.'"

470. Have the spirits who seek to lead us into evil, and who thus put our firmness in rectitude to the proof, received a mission to do this; and, is so, are they responsible for the accomplishment of such a mission?

"No spirit ever receives a mission to do evil; when he does it, he does it of his own will, and, therefore, undergoes the consequences of his wrong-doing. God may let him take his evil way, in order to try you; but He does not command him to do so, and it is for you to repel him."

471. When we feel a sensation of vague anxiety, of undefinable uneasiness, or of interior satisfaction, without any assignable cause, do these sensations proceed simply from our physical state?

"They are almost always an effect of the communications which you unconsciously receive from the spirits about you, or which you have received from them during your sleep."

472. When spirits wish to excite us to evil, do they merely take advantage of the circumstances in which we find ourselves, or can they themselves bring about the circumstances which may favour their designs?

"They take advantage of the occurence of any favourable circumstances, but they also often bring them about, by urging you on, without your being aware of it, towards the object of your unwise desire. Thus, for instance, a man picks up a roll of bank-notes by the wayside. You must not imagine that spirits have brought this money to this particular spot, but they may have suggested to the man the idea of going that way; and, when he has found the money, they may suggest to him the idea of taking possession of it, while others suggest to him the idea of restoring it to its rightful owner. It is thus in all other temptations."

Possession.

473. Can a spirit temporarily assume the envelope of a living person—that is to say, can he introduce himself into an animate body, and act in the room and place of the spirit incarnated in it?

"A spirit does not enter into a body as you enter into a house. He assimilates himself to an incarnate spirit who has the same defects and the same qualities as himself, in order that they may act conjointly; but it is always the incarnate spirit who acts at his pleasure on the matter with which he is clothed. No other spirit can substitute himself in the place of the spirit who is incarnated in a given body, for a spirit is indissolubly united with his body until the arrival of the hour that has been appointed by Providence for the termination of his material existence."

474. If there be no such thing as "possession", in the ordinary sense of that term—that is to say, cohabitation of two spirits in the same body—is it possible for one soul to find itself dominated, subjugated, obsessed by another soul to such a point as that its will is, so to say, paralysed?

"Yes; and it is this domination which really constitutes what you call *possession*. But you must understand that this domination is never established without the participation of the spirit who is subjected to it, *either through his weakness*[1] or his free-will. Men have often mistaken for cases of possession what were really cases of epilepsy or madness, demanding the help of the physician rather than of the exorciser."

The word **possession,** in its common acceptation, presupposes the existence of demons—that is to say, of a category of beings of a nature essentially evil, and the cohabitation of one of those beings with the soul of a man in the body of the latter. Since there are no such beings as demons **in the sense just defined,** and since two spirits cannot inhabit simultaneously the same body, there is no such thing as "possession" in the sense commonly attributed to that word. The word **possessed** should only be understood as expressing the state of absolute subjection to which a soul in flesh may be reduced by the imperfect spirits under whose domination it has fallen.

475. Can a soul, of its own motion, drive away the evil spirits by whom it is thus obsessed, and free itself from their domination?

---

[1] The "weakness" which sometimes brings a human being under the power of spirit-tormentors, despite the strenuous resistance of his will, is always the punitive and expiatory result of his own wrong-doing, either in his present earthly life or in a former one.—TRANS.

"You can always shake off a yoke if you are firmly resolved to do so."

476. *Might not the fascination exercised by the evil spirit be so complete that the person subjugated should be unaware of it; and, in such a case, might not a third person be able to put an end to the subjection? And what course should be taken by the latter to that end?*

"The will-power of an upright man may be useful by attracting the co-operation of good spirits in the work of deliverance; for the more upright a man is, the more power he possesses, both over imperfect spirits to drive them away, and over good ones to draw them nearer. Nevertheless, even the best of men would be powerless in such a case, unless the subjugated person lent himself to the efforts made on his behalf, for there are persons who take delight in a state of dependance which panders to their depraved tastes and desires. In no case can one who is impure in heart exercise any liberating influence, for he is despised by the good spirits, and the bad ones stand in no awe of him."

477. *Have formulas of exorcism any power over bad spirits?*

"No; when bad spirits see any one seriously endeavouring to act upon them by such means, they laugh at him, and persist in their obsession."

478. *Persons who are well-intentioned are sometimes obsessed; what are the best means of getting rid of obsessing spirits?*

"To tire out their patience, to give no heed to their suggestions, to show them that they are losing their time. When they see that they can do nothing, they go away."

479. *Is prayer efficacious as a means of putting an end to obsession?*

"Prayer is always an efficacious means of obtaining help; but you must remember that the muttering of certain words will not suffice to obtain what you desire. God helps those who help themselves, but not those who limit their action to asking for help. It is therefore necessary for the person obsessed to do his utmost to cure himself of the defects which attract evil spirits to him."

480. *What is to be thought of the casting out of devils, spoken of in the Gospels?*

"That depends on the meaning you attach to the word *devil*. If you mean by that term a bad spirit who subjugates a human being, it is evident that, when his influence is destroyed, he will really be driven away. If you attribute a malady to the devil, you may say, when you have cured the malady, that you have driven the devil away. A statement may be true or false, according to the meaning attributed to certain words. The most weighty truths may appear absurd when you look only at the form under which they are presented, and when an allegory is taken for a fact. Get this principle well into your mind, and keep it there; for it is of universal application."

Convulsionaries.

481. *Do spirits play a part in the phenomena exhibited by the individuals designated under the name of convulsionaries?*

"Yes, a very important one, as does also the agent that you call magnetism, whether employed by human beings or by spirits; for this agent is the original source of those phenomena. But charlatanism has often exaggerated those effects, and made them a matter of speculation, which has brought them into ridicule."

— *What is generally the nature of the spirits who help to produce phenomena of this kind?*

"Of slight elevation. Do you suppose that spirits of high degree would waste their time in such a way?"

482. *How can a whole population be suddenly thrown into the abnormal state of convulsions and crises?*

"Through sympathy. Moral dispositions are sometimes exceedingly contagious. You are not so ignorant of the effects of human magnetism as not to understand this, and also the part that certain spirits would naturally take in such occurrences, through sympathy with those by whom they are produced."

Among the strange peculiarities remarked in convulsionaries, several are evidently identical with those of which somnambulism and mesmerism offer numerous examples—viz., physical insensibility, thought reading, sympathetic transmission or sensations, etc. It is therefore impossible to doubt that these crisiacs are in a sort of waking somnambulism, determined by the influence which they unwittingly exercise upon each other. They are at once mesmerisers and mesmerised, unconsciously to themselves.

483. *What is the cause of the physical insensibility sometimes remarked in convulsionaries, and sometimes, also, in other persons, when subjected to the most atrocious tortures?*

"In some cases it is simply an effect of human magnetism, which acts upon the nervous system in the same manner as do certain substances. In other cases, mental excitement deadens the sensibility of the organism, the life seeming to retire from the body in order to concentrate itself in the spirit. Have you not observed that, when the spirit is intensely occupied with any matter, the body neither feels, nor sees, nor hears?

The excitement of fanaticism and enthusiasm often offer, on the part of persons subjected to a violent death, examples of a calmness and coolness that could hardly triumph over excruciating pain unless the sensibility of the patient were neutralised by a sort of moral anesthesia. We know that, in the heat of battle, a severe wound is often received without being perceived ; whilst, under ordinary circumstances, a mere scratch is felt acutely.

Since the production of these phenomena is due, in part, to the action of physical causes, in part to that of spirits, it may be asked how it can have been possible for the civil authorities, in certain cases, to put a stop to them? The reason of this is, however, very simple. The action of spirits, in these cases, is only secondary ; they do nothing more than take advantage of a natural tendency. The public authorities did not suppress this tendency, but the cause which kept up and stimulated it, thus reducing it from a state of activity to one of latency ; and they were right in so doing, because the matter was giving rise to abuses and scandal. Such intervention, nevertheless, is powerless in cases where the action of spirits is direct and spontaneous.

Affection of Certain Spirits for Certain Persons.

484. Do spirits affectionately prefer certain persons?

"Good spirits sympathise with all men who are good, or susceptible of amelioration; inferior spirits, with men who are bad, or who may become such. The attachment, in both cases, is a consequence of the similarity of sentiment."

485. Is the affection of certain spirits for certain persons exclusively one of sentiment?

"True affection has nothing of carnality; but, when a spirit attaches himself to a living person, it is not always through affection only; for there may also be in that attachment a reminiscence of human passions."

486. Do spirits take an interest in our misfortunes and our prosperity? Those who wish us well, are they grieved by the ills we undergo during life?

"Good spirits do you all the good they can, and rejoice with you in all your joys. They mourn over your afflictions when you do not bear them with resignation, because in that case affliction produces no beneficial result, for you are like the sick man who rejects the disagreeable draught that would cure him."

487. What is the kind of ills that causes most grief to our spirit-friends? Is it our physical sufferings, or our moral imperfections?

"What grieves them most is your selfishness and your hard heartedness, for these are the root of all your troubles. They smile at the imaginary sorrows that are born of pride and ambition; they rejoice in those which will shorten your term of trial."

Our spirit-friends, knowing that corporeal life is only transitory, and that the tribulations by which it is accompanied are the means that will enable us to reach a happier state, are more grieved for us by the moral imperfections which keep us back, than by physical ills, which are only transitory.
Spirits attach as little importance to misfortunes which affect us only in our earthly ideas, as we do to the trifling sorrows of childhood. Seeing the afflictions of life to be the means of our advancement, they regard them only as the passing crisis which will restore the sick man to health. They are grieved by our sufferings, as we are grieved by those of a friend ; but, judging the events of our lives from a truer point of view, they appreciate them differently. While inferior spirits try to drive us to despair, in order to hinder our advancement, the good ones seek to inspire us with the courage that will turn our trials into a source of gain for our future.

488. Have the relatives and friends who have gone before us into the other life more sympathy for us than spirits who are strangers to us?

"Undoubtedly they have; and they often protect you as spirits, according to their power."

— *Are they sensible of the affection we preserve for them?*

"Very sensible; but they forget those who forget them.".

Guardian — Angels — Protecting, Familiar, and Sympathetic Spirits.

489. Are there spirits who attach themselves to a particular individual, in order to protect and help him?

"Yes, the *spirit-brother*; what you call the *spirit-protector,* or the *good genius.*"

490. What is to be understood by the expression, "guardian-angel"?

"A spirit-protector of high degree."

491. What is the mission of a spirit-protector?

"That of a father towards his children—to lead the object of his protection into the right road, to aid him with his counsels, to console him in his afflictions, and to sustain his courage under the trials of his earthly life."

492. Is a spirit-protector attached to an individual from his birth?

"From his birth to his death; and he often follows him after death in the spirit-life, and even in several successive corporeal existences; for these existences are but every short phases of his existence as a spirit."

493. Is the mission of a spirit-protector voluntary or obligatory?

"Your spirit-protector is obliged to watch over you, because he has accepted that task; but a spirit is allowed to choose his ward among the beings who are sympathetic to him. In some cases this office is a pleasure; in others, it is a mission or a duty."

— *In attaching himself to a person, is a spirit obliged to refrain from protecting other individuals?*

"No; but he does so less exclusively."

494. Is the spirit-protector indissolubly attached to the person confided to his guardianship?

"It often happens that spirits quit their position in order to fulfil various missions; but, in that case, an exchange of wards takes place."

495. Does a spirit-protector sometimes abandon his ward when the latter persists in neglecting his counsels?

"He withdraws from him when he sees that his counsels are useless, and that there is a stubborn determination to yield to the influence of inferior spirits; but he does not abandon him entirely, and continues to make himself heard. It is not the spirit who quits the man, but the man who closes his ears against the spirit. As soon as the man calls him back, the spirit returns to him.

"If there be a doctrine that should win over the most incredulous by its charm and its beauty, it is that of the existence of spirit-protectors, or guardian-angels. To think that you have always near you beings who are superior to you, and who are always beside you to counsel you, to sustain you, to aid you in climbing the steep ascent of self-improvement, whose friendship is truer and more devoted than the most intimate union that you can contract upon the earth—is not such an idea most consoling? Those beings are near you by the command of God. It is He who has placed them beside you. They are there for love of Him, and they fulfil towards you a noble but laborious mission. They are with you wherever you may be; in the dungeon, in solitude, in the lazar-house, even in the haunts of debauchery. Nothing ever separates you from the friend whom you cannot see, but whose gentle impulsions are felt, and whose wise monitions are heard, in the innermost recesses of your heart.

"Would that you were more fully impressed with this truth! How often would it aid you in your moments of need! How often would it save you from the snares of evil spirits! But, at the great day of account, how often will your guardian-angel have to say to you, 'Did I not urge you, and yet you would not follow my leading? Did I not show you the abyss, and yet you persisted in throwing yourself into it? Did I not cause your conscience to hear the voice of truth, and have you not followed lying counsels?' Question your guardian-angels; establish between yourselves and them the affectionate intimacy which exists between tried and loving friends. Do not think to hide anything from them, for they are the eye of God, and you cannot deceive them. Think of the future; seek to advance on the upward road: your trials will be shorter, your existences happier. Men, take courage! Cast far from you all prejudices and mental reservations; enter resolutely upon the new road that opens before you! You have guides; follow them. Your goal cannot fail you, for that goal is God Himself.

"To those who may think it impossible that spirits of high degree should bind themselves to a task so laborious and demanding so much patience on their part, we reply, that we influence your souls while at many millions of leagues from you. To us, space is nothing; and, while living in another world, our spirits preserve their connection with yours. We possess qualities of which you can form no idea; but be sure that God has not imposed upon us a task above our strength, and that He has not abandoned you upon the earth without friends and without support. Every guardian-angel has his ward, over whom he watches as a father watches over his child: he rejoices when he sees him following the right road; he mourns when his counsels are neglected.

"Do not fear to weary us with your questions. Remain, on the contrary, always in connection with us: you will thus be stronger and happier. It is this communication between each man and his familiar spirit that will eventually make all men mediums, and drive out incredulity from your world. You who have received instruction, instruct in your turn: you who are possessed of talents, raise your brethren. You know not how great a work you accomplish by so doing; it is the work of Christ, the work imposed on you by God. Why has God given you intelligence and knowledge, if not to share them with your brethren, to aid them to advance on the road that leads to eternal felicity?"

The doctrine of guardian-angels watching over their wards, notwithstanding the distance which separates different worlds, has in it nothing that should excite our surprise ; it is as natural as it is grand and sublime. Do we not see a father, upon the earth, watch over his child even though at a distance from him, and aid him by the wise counsels of his letters? Why, then, should it be deemed surprising that spirits should guide, from one world to another, those whom take under their protection, since, to them, the distance which separates worlds is less than that which, on earth, separates continents? Besides, have they not the universal fluid which binds together all the worlds of the universe, and makes them part and parcel of each other—the universal vehicle of the transmission of throught, as the air is, for us, the vehicle of the transmission of sound?

496. *If a spirit abandons his ward, and no longer does him good, can he do him harm?*

"Good spirits never do harm to any one. They leave that to those who take their place; and you then accuse fate of the misfortunes which overwhelm you, while these are, in reality, the result of your own wrong-doing."

497. *Can a spirit-protector leave his ward at the mercy of a spirit who should desire to do him harm?*

"Evil spirits unite together to neutralise the action of the good ones; but the will of the ward suffices to give back all his power to the spirit-protector. The latter may find elsewhere another person whose goodwill renders it easy to help him; in such a case, he takes advantage of the opportunity of doing good, while awaiting the return of his ward."

498. *When the spirit-protector allows his ward to wander into wrong paths, is it because he is unable to cope with the malevolent spirits who mislead him?*

"It is not because he is unable, but because he does not choose to do so; he knows that his ward will become wiser and better through the trials he will have brought upon himself. The spirit-protector assists his ward through the sage counsels he suggests to his mind, but which unhappily are not always heeded. It is only the weakness, carelessness, or pride of men that gives strength to bad spirits; their power over you comes solely from your not opposing sufficient resistance to their action."

499. *Is the spirit-protector constantly with his ward? Are there no circumstances under which, without abandoning him, he may lose sight of him?*

"There are circumstances under which the presence of the spirit-protector is not necessary to the ward."

500. *Does a time arrive when the spirit no longer needs a guardian-angel?*

"Yes; when he has reached the degree of advancement which enables him to guide himself, as a time arrives when the scholar has no longer need of a master. But this does not take place upon your earth."

501. *Why is the action of spirits upon our existence occult? and why, when they are protecting us, do they not do so ostensibly?*

"If you counted on their support, you would not act of yourselves, and your spirit would not progress. In order to advance, each man needs to acquire experience, and often at his own expense. He needs to exercise his powers; otherwise he would be like a child, who is not allowed to walk alone. The action of the spirits who desire your welfare is always regulated in such a way as to leave you your free-will; for, if you had no responsability, you would not advance on the road that is to lead you to God. Man, not seeing his supporter, puts forth his own strength; his guide, however, watches over him, and calls to him from time to time, to bid him beware of danger."

502. *When the spirit-protector succeeds in leading his ward on the right road, does he ther by gain any benefit for himself?*

"It is a meritorious work which will be counted to him either for his advancement or for his happiness. He rejoices when he sees his care crowned by success, and triumphs as a teacher triumphs in the success of his pupil."

— *Is he responsible if he does not succeed?*

"No, since he has done everything that depended on him."

503. *Does the spirit-protector feel sorrow on seeing a ward taking the wrong road? and does not such a sight disturb his own felicity?*

"He is grieved at his erros, and pities him; but this affliction has none of the anguish of terrestrial paternity, because he knows that there is a remedy for the evil, and that what is not done to-day will be done to-morrow."

504. *Can we always know the name of our guardian-angel?*

"How is it possible for you to know names which have no existence for you? Do you suppose there are no spirits but those whom you know of?"

— *But how can we invoke him if we do not know who he is?*

"Give him any name you please—that of any superior spirit for whom you feel sympathy or veneration. Your spirit-guardian will answer this appeal; for all good spirits are brothers, and assist each other."

505. *Are the spirit-guardians who take well-known names always the persons who bore those names?*

"No; but they are spirits who are in sympathy with them, and who, in many cases, come by their order. You require names; they therefore take a name that will inspire you with confidence. When you are unable to execute a commission in person, you send some one in your place, who acts in your name."

506. *When we are in the spirit-life, shall we recognise our spirit-guardian?*

"Yes; for it is often a spirit whom you knew before being incarnated."

507. *Do all spirit-guardians belong to the higher classes of spirits? Are they sometimes found among those of average advancement? Can a father, for example, become the spirit-guardian of his child?*

"He may do so; but such guardianship presupposes a certain degree of elevation, and, in addition, a power or virtue granted by God. A father who watches over his child may himself be assisted by a spirit of more elevated degree."

508. *Can all spirits who have quitted the earth under favourable conditions become the protectors of those whom they love among their survivors?*

"Their power is more or less narrowed by their position, which does not always leave them full liberty of action."

509. *Have savages, and men who are very low as regards their moral state, their spirit-guardians? and if so, are these spirits of as high an order as those of men who are more advanced?*

"Every man has a spirit who watches over him; but missions are always proportional to their object. You do not give a professor of philosohy to a child who is only learning to read. The advancement of the familiar spirit is always proportioned to that of the spirit he protects. While you yourself have a spirit of higher degree who watches over you, you may, in your turn, become the protector of a spirit who is lower than you; and the progress you help him to make will contribute to your own advancement. God does not demand of any spirit more than is consistent with his nature, and with the degree at which he has arrived."

510. When a father who watches over his child is reincarnated, does he still continue to watch over him?

"His task, in that case, becomes more difficult; but, in a moment of freedom, he asks some sympathetic spirit to assist him in accomplishing it. But spirits do not undertake missions which they cannot carry on to the end.

"A spirit, when incarnated, especially in worlds in which existence is grossly material, is too much fettered by his body to be able to devote himself entirely to another—that is to say, to give him personally all the help he needs. For this reason, those who are not sufficiently elevated to suffice for the work of guardianship are themselves assisted by spirits of higher degree, so that if, from any cause, the help of one spirit should fail, his place is supplied by another."

511. Is there, besides the spirit-guardian, an evil spirit attached to each individual for the purpose of exciting him to evil, thus of furnishing him with the opportunity of struggling between good and evil?

"It would not be correct to say 'attached.' It is very true that bad spirits endeavour to draw you out of the right road when they find an opportunity of doing so; but when one of them attaches himself to an individual, he does so of his own accord, because he hopes to be listened to. In such a case, there is a struggle between the good and the evil spirit, and the victory remains with the one to whose influence the man has voluntarily subjected himself."

512. May we have several protecting spirits?

"Every man has always about him a number of sympathetic spirits of more or less elevation, who interest themselves in him from affection, as he also has others who help him to do evil."

513. Do spirits who are sympathetic to an individual act upon him in virtue of a mission to that effect?

"In some cases they may have a temporary mission; but, in general, they are only drawn to an individual by similarity of sentiments in good or in evil."

— *It would seem, then, that sympathetic spirits may be either good or bad?*

"Yes; a man is always surrounded by spirits who are in sympathy with him, whatever may be his character."

514. Are "familiar spirits" the same as "sympathetic spirits" and "spirit-guardians"?

"There are very many shades in guardianship and in sympathy; you may give to these whatever names you please. But the 'familiar spirit' is rather the general friend of the family."

From the above explanations, and from observation of the nature of spirits who attach themselves to men, we draw the following inferences :—

The spirit-protector, good genius, or guardian-angel, is the one whose mission it is to follow each man through the course of his life, and to aid him to progress. His degree of advancement is always superior to that of his ward.

Familiar spirits attach themselves to certain persons, for a longer or shorter period, in order to be useful to them within the limits (often somewhat narrow) of their possibilities ; they are generally well-intentioned, but sometimes rather backward, and even frivolous. They busy themselves with the every-day details of human life ; and only act by order, or with the permission, of the spirit-guardians.

Sympathetic spirits are those who are drawn to us by personal affection, and by a similarity of tastes in good or in evil. The duration of their relationship with us is almost always dependent on circumstances.

An evil genius is an imperfect or wicked spirit who attaches himself to a man for the purpose of perverting him ; but he acts of his own motion, and not in virtue of a mission. His tenacity is proportionate to the more or less easy access accorded to him. A man is always free to listen to the suggestions of an evil genius, or to repel them.

515. What is to be thought of those persons who seem to attach themselves to certain individuals in order to urge them on to their injury, or to guide them on the right road?

"Some persons do, in fact, exercise over others a species of fascination which seems irresistible. When this influence is used for evil, it is to be attributed to evil spirits, who make use of evil men in order the more effectually to subjugate their victim. God may permit this in order to try you."

516. Could our good or our evil genius incarnate himself in order to accompany us more closely in our earthly life?

"That sometimes occurs; but they more frequently entrust this mission to incarnated spirits who are in sympathy with them."

517. Are there spirits who attach themselves to all the members of a family in order to watch over and aid them?

"Some spirits attach themselves to the members of a family who live together, and who are united by affection; but do not attribute pride of race to spirit-guardians."

518. Spirits being attracted to individuals by their sympathies, are they similarly attracted to companies of persons united in view of special ends?

"Spirits go by preference to the places where they meet their similars; they are more at ease among such, and more sure of being listened to. Every one attracts spirits to himself according to his tendencies, whether as an individual or as an element of a collective whole, such as a society, a city, or a nation. Societies, towns, and nations are therefore assisted by spirits of more or less elevated degree, according to the character and passions which predominate in them. Imperfect spirits withdraw from those who repel them; from which it follows that the moral excellence of *collective wholes*, like that of individuals, tends to keep away bad spirits and to attract good ones, who rouse and keep alive the sense of rectitude in the masses, as others may sow among them the worst passions."

519. Have agglomerations of individuals—such as societies, cities, nations—their special spirit-guardians?

"Yes, for those assemblages constitute collective individualities, who are pursuing a common end, and who have need of a higher direction."

520. Are the spirit-guardians of masses of men of a higher degree of advancement than those who are attached to individuals?

"Their advancement is always in proportion with the degree of advancement of masses as of individuals."

521. Can certain spirits advance the progress of the arts by protecting those who cultivate them?

"There are special spirit-protectors who assist those by whom they are invoked when they judge them to be worthy of their help; but what could they do with those who fancy themselves to be what they are not? They cannot make the blind to see, nor the deaf to hear."

The ancients converted these spirit-guardians into special deities. The Muses were nothing else than the allegoric personification of the spirit-protectors of arts and sciences, just as the spirit-protectors of the family-circle designated by the name of **lares** or of **penates.** Among the moderns, the arts, the various industries, cities, countries, have also their protecting patrons, who are no other than spirit-guardians of a higher order, but under different names.

Each man having his sympathetic spirit, it follows that, in every collective whole, the generality of sympathetic spirits corresponds to the generality of individuals ; that stranger-spirits are attracted to it by identity of thoughts : in a word, that these assemblages, as well as individuals, are more or less favourably surrounded, influenced, assisted, according to the predominant character of the thoughts of those who compose them.

Among nations, the conditions which exercise an attractive action upon spirits are the habits, manners, dominant characteristics, of their people, and, above all, their legislation, because the character of a nation is reflected in its laws. Those who uphold the reign of righteousness among themselves combat the influence of evil spirits. Wherever the laws consecrate injustice, inhumanity, good spirits are in the minority ; and the mass of bad ones who flock in, attracted by that state of things, keep the people in their false ideas, and paralyse the good influences which, being only partial, are lost in the crowd, like a solitary wheat-ear in the midst of tares. It is therefore easy, by studying the characteristics of nations, or of any assemblage of men, to form to oneself an idea of the invisible population which is mixed up with them in their thoughts and in their actions.

Presentiments.

522. Is a presentiment always a warning from the spirit-guardian?

"A presentiment is a counsel privately addressed to you by a spirit who wishes you well. The same may be said of the intuition which decides the choice of his new existence by a spirit about to reincarnate himself; the voice of instinct is of the same nature. A spirit, before incarnating himself, is aware of the principal phases of his new existence—that is to say, of the kind of trials to which he is about to subject himself. When these are of a very marked character, he preserves, in his inner consciousness, a sort of impression respecting them; and this impression, which is the voice of instinct, becoming more vivid as the critical moment draws near, becomes presentiment."

523. Presentiments and the voice of instinct are always somewhat vague; what should we do when in a state of uncertainty?

"When you are in doubt, invoke your spirit-guardian, *or implore our common Master, God, to send you one of His messengers—one of us.*"

524. Are the warnings of our spirit-guardians given solely for our moral guidance, are they also given for our guidance in regard to our personal affairs?

"They are given in reference to everything that concerns you. Your spirit-guardians endeavour to lead you to take, in regard to everything that you have to do, the best possible course; but you often close your ears to their friendly counsels, and thus get yourselves into trouble thorough ycur own fault."

Our protecting spirits aid us by their counsels, and by awakening the voice of our conscience ; but as we do not always attach sufficient importance to these hints, they give us more direct warnings through the persons about us. Let a man reflect upon the various circumstances of his life, fortunate or unfortunate, and he will see that, on many occasions, he received advice which, had he followed it, would have spared him a good deal of annoyance.

Influence of Spirits en the Events of Human Life

525. Do spirits exercise an influence over the events of our lives?

"Assuredly they do; since they give you advice."

— *Do they exercise this influence in any other way than by means of the thoughts they suggest to us; that is to say, have they any direct action on the course of earthly events?*

"Yes; but their action never oversteps the laws of nature."

We erroneously imagine that the action of spirits can only be manifested by extraordinary phenomena ; we would have spirits come to our aid by means of miracles, and we imagine them to be always armed with a sort of magic wand. Such is not the case ; all that is done through their help being accomplished by natural means, their intervention usually takes place without our being aware of it. Thus, for instance, they bring about the meeting of two persons who seem to have been brought together by chance ; they suggest to the mind of some one the idea of going in a particular direction They call your attention to some special point, if the action on your part thus led up to by their suggestion, unperceived by you, will bring about the result they seek to obtain. In this way, each man supposes himself to be obeying only his own impulse, and thus always preserves the freedom of his will.

526. *As spirits possess the power of acting upon matter, can they bring about the incidents that will ensure the accomplishment of a given event? For example, a man is destined to perish in a certain way, at a certain time. He mounts a ladder; the ladder breaks, and he is killed. Have spirits caused the ladder to break, in order to accomplish the destiny previously accepted by or imposed upon this man?*

"It is very certain that spirits have the power of acting upon matter, but for the carrying out of the laws of nature, and not for derogating from them by causing the production at a given moment of some unforeseen event, in opposition to those laws. In such a case as the one you have just supposed, the ladder breaks because it is rotten, or is not strong enough to bear the man's weight. But, as it was the destiny of this man to be killed in this way, the spirits about him will have put into his mind the idea of getting upon a ladder that will break down under his weight, and his death will thus have taken place naturally, and without any miracle having been required to bring it about."

527. *Let us take another example; one in which the ordinary conditions of matter would seem to be insufficient to account for the occurrence of a given event. A man is destined to be killed by lightning. He is overtaken by a storm, and seeks refuge under a tree; the lightning strikes the tree, and he is killed. Is it by spirits that the thunderbolt has been made to fall, and to fall upon this particular man?*

"The explanation of this case is the same as that of the former one. The lightning has fallen on the tree at this particular moment,

because it was in accordance with the laws of nature that it should
do so. The lightning was not made to fall upon the tree because
the man was under it, but the man was inspired with the idea of
taking refuge under a tree upon which the lightning was about
to fall; for the tree would have been struck all the same, whether
the man had been under it or not."

528. *An ill-intentioned person hurls against some one a projectile which passes close by him, but does not touch him. Has the
missile, in such a case, been turned aside by some friendly spirit?*

"If the individual aimed at were not destined to be struck, a
friendly spirit would have suggested to him the thought of turning
aside from the path of the missile, or would have acted on his
enemy's sight in such a way as to make him take a bad aim; for
a projectile, when once impelled on its way, necessarily follows
the line of its projection."

529. *What is to be thought of the magic bullets which figure
in certain legends, and which, by a mysterious fatality, infallibly
reach their mark?*

"They are purely imaginary. Man delights in the marvellous,
and is not contented with the marvels of nature."

— May *the spirits who direct the events of our lives be thwarted
by other spirits who desire to give to our lives a different direction?*

"What God has willed must needs take place. If delay or
hindrance occur, it can only be by His appointment."

530. *Cannot frivolous and mocking spirits give rise to the
various little difficulties that defeat our projects and upset our
calculations? In a word, are they not the authors of what may
be termed the petty troubles of human life?*

"Such spirits take pleasure in causing vexations which serve as
trials for the exercise of your patience; but they tire of this game
when they see that they do not succeed in ruffling you. But it
would neither be just nor correct to charge them with all your
disappointments, the greater number of which are caused by your
own heedlessness. When your crockery is broken, the breakage is
much more likely to have been caused by your own awkwardness
than by spirit-action."

— Do *the spirits who bring about petty vexations act from
personal animosity, or do they direct their attacks against the first
person who comes handy, without any fixed aim, and simply to
gratify their malice?*

"They act from both these motives. In some cases, they are enemies whom you have made during your present life, or in some former one, and who pursue you accordingly; in others, they act without any fixed motive."

531. In the case of those who have done us harm in the earthly life, is their malevolence extinguished when they return to the spirit-world?

"In many cases, they perceive the injustice of their action, and regret the wrong they have done you; but, in other cases, they continue to pursue you with their animosity, if God permits them to do so, as a continuation of your trial."

— *Can we put an end to this sort of persecution, and by what means?*

"You can do so, in many cases, by praying for them, because, by thus rendering them good for evil, you gradually bring them to see that they are in the wrong. And, in all cases, if you can show them, by your patience, that you are able to rise superior to their machinations, they will cease to attack you, seeing that they gain nothing by so doing."

Experience proves that imperfect spirits follow up their vengeance from one existence to another, and that we are thus made to expiate, sooner or later, the wrongs we may have done to others.

532. Are spirits able to avert misfortunes from some persons, and to bring them upon others?

"Only to a certain extent; for there are misfortunes that come upon you by the decrees of Providence. But spirits can lessen your sufferings by helping you to bear them with patience and resignation.

"Know, also, that it often depends on yourselves to avert mis fortunes, or, least, to attenuate them. God has given you intelligence in order that you may make use of it, and it is especially by so doing that you enable friendly spirits to aid you most effectually—viz., by suggesting useful ideas; for they only help those who help themselves: a truth implied in the words, 'Seek, and ye shall find; knock, and it shall be opened unto you.'

"Besides, you must remember that what appears to you to be a misfortune is not always such; for the good which it is destined to work out is often greater than the seeming evil. This fact is not always recognised by you, because you are too apt to think only of the present moment, and of your own immediate satisfaction."

533. Can spirits obtain for us the gifts of fortune, if we entreat them to do so?

"They may sometimes accede to such a request as a trial for you; but they often refuse such demands, as you refuse the inconsiderate demands of a child."

— *When such favours are granted, is it by good spirits or by bad ones?*

"By both; for the quality both of the request and of the grant depends on the intention by which they are prompted. But such acquiescence is more frequent on the part of spirits who desire to lead you astray, and who find an easy means of doing this through the material pleasures procured by wealth."

534. When obstacles seem to be placed, by a sort of fatality, in the way of our projects, is it always through the influence of spirits?

"Such obstacles are sometimes thrown in your way by spirits, but they are more often attributable to your own bad management. Position and caracter have much to do with your successes or failures. If you persist in following a path which is not your right one, you become your own evil genius, and have no need to attribute to spirit-action the disappointments that result from your own obstinacy or mistake."

535. When anything fortunate happens to us, ought we to thank our spirit-guardian for it?

"Let your thanks be first for God, without whose permission nothing takes place; and, next, for the good spirits who have been His agents."

— *What would happen if we neglected to tank them?*

"That which happens to the ungrateful."

— *Yet there are persons who neither pray nor give thanks, and who nevertheless succeed in everything they do?*

"Yes; but wait to see the end of their lives. They will pay dearly for this passing prosperity, which they have not deserved; for, the more they have received, the more they will have to answer for."

Action of Spirits in the Production of the Phenomena of Nature.

536. Are the great phenomena of nature, those which we consider as perturbations of the elements, due to fortuitous causes, or have they all a providential aim?

"There is a reason for everything; nothing takes place without the permission of God."

— *Have these phenomena always some reference to mankind?*

"They have sometimes a direct reference to man; but they have often no other object than the re-establishment of the equilibrium and harmony of the physical forces of nature."

— *We fully admit that the will of God must be the primal cause of these phenomena, as of everything else; but, as we know that spirits exercise an action upon matter, and that they are the agents of the divine will, we ask whether some among them do not exert an influence upon the elements, to rouse, calm, or direct them?*

"It is evident that they must do so; it could not be otherwise. God does not exercise a direct action upon matter; He has His devoted agents at every step of the ladder of worlds."

537, *The mythology of the ancients is entirely based on spiritist ideas, with this difference, that they regarded spirits as divinities. They represented those gods or spirits with special attributes; thus, some of them had charge of the winds, others of the lightning; others, again, presided over vegetation, etc. Is this belief entirely devoid of foundation?*

"It is so far from being devoid of foundation, that it is far below the truth."

— *May there, in the same way, be spirits inhabiting the interior of the earth and presiding over the development of geological phenomena?*

"Those spirits do not positively inhabit the earth, but they preside over and direct its developments according to their various attributions. You will some day have the explanation of all these phenomena, and you will then understand them better."

538. *Do the spirits who preside over the phenomena of nature form a special category in the spirit-world; are they beings apart, or spirits who have been incarnated like us?*

"They are spirits who will be incarnated, or who have been so."

— *Do those spirits belong to the higher or lower degrees of the spirit-hierarchy?*

"That is according as their post is more or less material or intelligent; some command, others execute; those who discharge material functions are always of an inferior order, among spirits as among men."

539. In the production of certain phenomena, of storms, for example, is it a single spirit that acts, or a mass of spirits?

"A mass of spirits; or, rather, innumerable masses of spirits."

540. Do the spirits who exert an action over the phenomena of nature act with knowledge and intention, in virtue of their free-will, or from an instinctive and unreasoning impulse?

"Some act in the one way, others in the other. To employ a comparison:—Figure to yourself the myriads of animalculæ that build up islands and archipelagoes in the midst of the sea; do you believe that there can be, in this process, no providential intention, and that this transformation of the surface of the globe is not necessary to the general harmony? Yet all this is accomplished by animals of the lowest degree, in providing for their bodily wants, and without any consciousness of their being instruments of God. In the same way, spirits of the most rudimentary degrees are useful to the general whole; while *preparing to live,* and prior to their having the full consciousness of their action and free-will, they are made to concur in the development of the various departments of nature, in the production of the phenomena of which they are the unwitting agents. They begin by executing the orders of their superiors; subsequently, when their intelligence is more developed, they command in their turn, and direct the processes of the material world; still later, again, they are able to direct the things of the moral world. It is thus that everything in nature is linked together, from the primitive atom to the archangel, who himself began at the atom; an admirable law of harmony, which your mind is, as yet, too narrow to seize in its generality."

Spirits During a Battle

541. When a battle is being fought, are there spirits who assist and support each party?

"Yes, and who stimulate their courage."

The ancients represented the gods as taking part with such and such a people. Those gods were nothing else than spirits represented under allegorical figures.

542. In every war, the right is only on one side. How can spirits take the part of the one which is in the wrong?

"You know very well that there are spirits who seek only discord and destruction; for them war is war; they care little whether it be just or unjust."

543. Can spirits influence a general in the planning of a campaign?

"Without any doubt spirits can use their influence for this object, as for all other conceptions."

544. Could hostile spirits suggest to him unwise combinations in order to ruin him?

"Yes; but has he not his free-will? If his judgment do not enable him to distinguish between a good idea and a bad one, he will have to bear the consequences of his blindness, and would do better to obey than to command."

545. May a general sometimes be guided by a sort of second-sight, an intuitive perception that shows him, beforehand, the result of his combinations?

"It is often thus with a man of genius; this kind of intuition is what is called 'inspiration,' and causes him to act with a sort of certainty. It comes to him from the spirits who direct him, and who act upon him through the faculties with which he is endowed."

546. In the tumult of battle, what becomes of the spirits of those who succumb? Do they continue to take an interest in the struggle after their death?

"Some of them do so; others withdraw from it."

In the case of those who are killed in battle, as in all other cases of violent death, a spirit, during the first few moments, is in a state of bewilderment, and as though he were stunned. He does not know that he is dead ; and seems to be taking part in the action. It is only little by little that the reality of his situation becomes apparent to him.

547. Do the spirits of those who had fought against each other while alive still regard one another as enemies after death; and are they still enraged against one another?

"A spirit, under such circumstances, is never calm. At the first moment, he may still be excited against his enemy, and even pursue him; but, when he has recovered his self-possession, he sees that his animosity has no longer any motive. But he may, nevertheless, retain some traces of it for a longer or shorter period, according to his character."

— *Does he still perceive the clang of the battle field?*

"Yes; perfectly."

548. When a spirit is coolly watching a battle, as a mere spectator, does he witness the separation of the souls and bodies of those who fall, and how does this phenomenon affect him?

"Very few deaths are altogether instantaneous. In most cases, the spirit whose body has just been mortally struck is not aware of it for the moment; it is when he begins to come to himself that his spirit can be seen moving beside his corpse. This appears so natural, that the sight of the dead body does not produce any disagreeable effect. All the life of the individual being concentrated in his spirit, the latter alone attracts the attention of the spirits about him. It is with him that they converse, to him that orders are given."

Pacts With Spirits.

549. Is there any truth in the idea that pacts can be entered into with evil spirits?

"No; there is no pact, but there is sympathy, between an evil nature and evil spirits. For example; you wish to torment your neighbour, but you know not how to set about it; and you therefore call to your help some of the inferior spirits, who, like yourself, only desire to do evil, and who, in return for the help they give you in carrying out your wicked designs, expect you to help them with theirs. But it does not follow that your neighbour will not be able to get rid of such a conspiracy by an opposing conjuration and the action of his will. He who desires to do an evil deed calls evil spirits to his assistance by that mere desire; and he is then obliged to serve them as they have served him, for they, on their side, have need of his help in the evil they desire to do. What you call a *pact* consists simply in this reciprocity of assistance in evil."

The subjection to evil spirits, in which a man sometimes finds himself, proceeds from his abandoning himself to the evil thoughts suggested by them, and not from any sort of stipulations between them and him. The idea of a **pact**, in the sense commonly attached to that word, is a figurative representation of the sympathy which exists between a bad man and malicious spirits.

550. What is the meaning of the fantastic legends of persons selling their soul to Satan in order to obtain from him certain favours?

"All fables contain a teaching and a moral; your mistake is in taking them literally. The one you refer to is an allegory that may be thus explained:—He who calls evil spirits to his aid, in order to obtain from them the gifts of fortune or any other favour, rebels against Providence. He draws back from the mission he has received, and from the trials he was to have undergone, in his earthly life; and he will reap the consequences of this rebellion in the life to come. By this we do not mean to say that his soul is condemned to misery for ever; but as, instead of detaching himself from matter, he plunges himself deeper and deeper into it, his enjoyment of earthly pleasures will only have led to his suffering in the spirit-world, until he shall have redeemed himself from the thraldom of evil by new trials, perhaps heavier and more painful than those against which he now rebels. Through his indulgence in material pleasures, he brings himself under the power of impure spirits, and thus establishes between them and him a tacit compact which leads him to his ruin, but which it is always easy for him to break with the assistance of higher spirits, if he have the firm determination to do so."

Ocult Power — Talismans — Sorceres.

551. *Can a bad man, with the aid of a bad spirit who is at his orders, cause harm to his neighbour?*

"No; God would not permit it."

552. *What is to be thought of the belief in the power of certain persons to throw a spell over others?*

"Certain persons possess a very strong magnetic power, of which they may make a bad use if their own spirit is bad, and, in that case, they may be seconded by other bad spirits; but do not attach belief to any pretended magical power, which exists only in the imagination of superstitious people, ignorant of the true laws of nature. The facts adduced to prove the existence of this pretended power are facts which are really due to the action of natural causes that have been imperfectly observed, and above all, imperfectly understood."

553. *What is the effect of the formulas and practices by the aid of which certain persons profess to be able to control the wills of spirits?*

"Their only effect is to render such persons ridiculous, if they really put faith in them; and, if they do not, they are rogues who deserve to be punished. All such formulas are mere jugglery; there is no 'sacramental word,' no cabalistic sign, no talisman, that has any power over spirits; for spirits are attracted by thought and not by anything material."

— *Have not cabalistic formulas been sometimes dictated by spirits?*

"Yes; there are spirits who give you strange signs and words, and prescribe certain acts, with the aid of which you perform what you call 'conjurations;' but you may be very sure that such spirits are making game of you, and amusing themselves with your credulity."

554. *Is it not possible that he who, rightly or wrongly, has confidence in what he calls the virtue of a talisman, may attract a spirit to him by that very confidence; for in that case it would be his thought that acts, the talisman being only a sign that helps to concentrate and direct his thought?*

"Such an action is quite possible; but the nature of the spirit thus attracted would depend on the purity of intention and the elevation of sentiment of the party attracting him; and it rarely happens that one who is simple enough to believe in the virtue of a talisman is not actuated by motives of a material rather than of a moral character. At all events, such practices imply a pettiness and weakness of mind that would naturally give access to imperfect and mocking spirits."

555. *What meaning should we attach to the qualification of sorcerer?*

"Those whom you call sorcerers are persons gifted, when they are honest, with certain exceptional faculties, like the mesmeric power or second-sight; and as such persons do things that you do not comprehend, you suppose them to be endowed with supernatural power. Have not many of your learned men passed for sorcerers in the eyes of the ignorant?"

556. *Do some persons really possess the gift of healing by merely touching the sick?*

"The mesmeric power may act to that extent when it is seconded by purity of intention and ardent desire to do good, for, in such a case, good spirits come to the aid of the mesmeriser. But you must be on your guard against the way in which facts are exaggerated when recounted by persons who, being too credulous or too enthusiastic, are disposed to discover something marvellous in the simplest and most natural occurrences. You must also be on your guard against the interested recitals of persons who work on credulity with a view to their own benefit."

Benedictions an Curses

557. Do benedictions and curses draw down good and evil on those who are the object of them?

"God does not listen to an unjust malediction, and he who utters it is guilty in His eyes. As we are subjected to two opposite influences, good and evil, a curse may have a momentary action, even upon matter; but this action can never take place unless by the will of God, and as an increase of trial for him who is its object. Besides, curses are usually bestowed on the wicked, and benedictions on the good. But neither blessing nor cursing can ever turn aside the justice of Providence, which only strikes the one who is cursed if he is wicked, and only favours the one who is blessed if he merits its protection."

CHAPTER X

OCCUPATIONS AND MISSIONS OF SPIRITS

558. Have spirits anything else to do but to work out their own personal amelioration?

"They co-operate in the production of the harmony of the universe by executing the volitions of God, whose ministers they are. Spirit-life is a continual occupation, but one that has nothing in common with the painful labour of the earthly life, because there is in it neither bodily fatigue, nor the anguish of bodily wants."

559. Do inferior and imperfect spirits also subserve any useful end in the universe?

"All have duties to fulfil. Does not the lowest mason concur in the building of an edifice as really as the architect?" (540.)

560. Has each spirit special attributes?

"We all have to inhabit all regions, and to acquire a knowledge of all things, by presiding successively over all the details of the universe. But, as is said in Ecclesiastes, 'there is a time for everything.' Thus, one spirit is accomplishing his destiny, at the present day, in your world; another will accomplish his, or has already accomplished it, at another period, upon the earth, in the water, in the air, etc."

561. Are the functions discharged by spirits, in the economy of things, permanent on the part of each spirit, or do they constitute the exclusive attributes of certain classes?

"All spirits have to ascend all the steps of the ladder in order to attain to perfection. God, who is just, has not willed to give science to some without labour, while others only acquire it through painful effort."

Thus, among men, no one arrives at the highest degree of skill in any art, without having acquired the necessary knowledge through the practice of that art in all its degrees, from the lowest upwards.

562. Spirits of the highest order having nothing more to acquire, are they in a state of absolute repose, or have they, too, occupations?

"Can you suppose that they remain idle through eternity? Eternal idleness would be eternal torture."

— *What is the nature of their occupations?*

"They receive orders directly from God, transmit them throughout the universe, and superintend their execution."

563. *Are spirits incessantly occupied?*

"Incessantly? yes, if it be understood that their thought is always active, for they live by thought. But you must not suppose that the occupations of spirits are similar to the material occupations of men; their activity is itself a delight, through the consciousness they have of being useful."

— *That is easily understood as regards good spirits; but is it the same in regard to inferior spirits?*

"Inferior spirits have occupations suitable to their nature. Would you entrust intellectual undertakings to an ignorant labourer?"

564. *Are there, among spirits, some who are idle, or who do not employ themselves in anything useful?*

"Yes; but that idleness is only temporary, and depends on the development of their intelligence. Certainly, there are among spirits, as among men, some who live only for themselves; but their idlenes weighs upon them, and, sooner or later, the desire to advance causes them to feel the need of activity, and they are glad to make themselves useful. We speak of spirits arrived at the point at which they possess self-consciousness and free-will; for, at their origin, they are like new-born children, and act more from instinct than from a determinate will."

565. *Do spirits examine our works of art, and take an interest in them?*

"They examine whatever indicates the elevation of incarnated spirits and their progress."

566. *Does a spirit who has had a special occupation upon the earth, as a painter or an architect, for example, take a special interest in the labours which have formed the object of his predilections during the earthly life?*

"Everything blends into one general aim. A good spirit interests himself in whatever enables him to assist other souls in rising towards God. Besides, a spirit who has been devoted to a given pursuit, in the existence in which you have known him, may have been devoted to some other in another existence; for, in order to be perfect, he must know everything. Thus, in virtue of his greater advancement, there may be no specialty for him—a fact to which I alluded in saying that *everything blends into one general aim.* Take note, also, that what seems sublime to you, in your backward world, would be mere child's play in worlds of greater advancement. How can you suppose that the spirits who inhabit those worlds, in which there exist arts and sciences unknown to you, could admire what, in their eyes, is only the work of a tyro?"

— *We can easily conceive that this should be the case with very advanced spirits; but our question referred to more commonplace spirits, to those who have not yet raised themselves above terrestrial ideas.*

"With them it is different; their mental outlook is narrower, and they may admire what you yourselves admire."

567. *Do spirits ever take part in our occupations and pleasures?*

"Commonplace spirits, as you call them, do so; they are incessantly about you, and take, in all you do, a part which is sometimes a very active one, according to their nature; and it is necessary that they should do so, in order to push men on in the different walks of life, and to excite or moderate their passions."

Spirits busy themselves with the things of this world in proportion to their elevation or their inferiority. The higher spirits have, undoubtedly, the power of looking into the minutest details of earthly things ; but they only do so when it will be useful to progress. Spirits of lower rank attribute to such things a degree of importance proportioned to their remembrances of the earthly life, and to the earthly ideas which are not yet extinct in their memory.

568. *When spirits are charged with a mission, do they accomplish it in the state of erraticity, or in the state of incarnation?*

"They may be charged with a mission in either state. There are wandering spirits to whom such missions furnish much occupation."

569. *What are the missions with which wandering spirits may be charged?*

"They are so varied that it would be impossible to describe them; and there are some of them that you could not comprehend. Spirits execute the volitions of God, and you are not able to penetrate all His designs."

The missions of spirits have always good for their object. Whether in the spirit-state, or as men, they are charged to help forward the progress of humanity, of peoples, or of individuals, within a range of ideas more or less extensive, more or less special, to pave the way for certain events, to superintend the accomplishment of certain things. The missions of some spirits are of narrower scope, and may be said to be personal, or even local ; as the helping of the sick, the dying, the afflicted ; to watch over those of whom they become the guides and protectors, and to guide them by their counsels or by the wholesome thoughts they suggest. It may be said that there are as many sorts of spirit-missions as there are sorts of interests to watch over, whether in the physical world or in the moral world. And each spirit advances in proportion to the fidelity with which he accomplishes his task.

570. Do spirits always comprehend the designs they are charged to execute?

"No; some of them are mere blind instruments, but others fully understand the aim they are working out."

571. Is it only elevated spirits who have missions to fulfil?

"The importance of a mission is always proportioned to the capacities and elevation of the spirit who is charged with it; but the estafette who conveys a despatch fulfils a mission, though one which is not that of the general."

572. Is a spirit's mission imposed upon him, or does it depend on his own will?

"He asks for it, and is rejoiced to obtain it."

— *May the same mission be demanded by several spirits?*

"Yes, there are often several candidates for the same mission, but they are not all accepted."

573. In what does the mission of incarnated spirits consists?

"In instructing men, and aiding their advancement; and in ameliorating their institutions by direct, material means. These missions are more or less general and important; but he who tills the ground accomplishes a mission as really as he who governs or instructs. Everything in nature is linked together; and each spirit, while purifying himself by his incarnation, concurs, under the human form, to the accomplishment of the Providential plans. Each of you has a mission, because each of you can be useful in some way or other."

574. What can be the mission of those who, in this life, are wilfully idle?

"It is true that there are human beings who live only for themselves, and who do not make themselves useful in any way. They are much to be pitied, for they will have to expiate their voluntary inutility by severe sufferings, and their chastisement often begins even in their present existence, through their weariness and disgust of life."

— *Since they had the freedom of choice, why did they choose a life which could not be of any use to them?*

"Among spirits, as among men, there are lazy ones who shrink from a life of labour. God lets them take their own way; they will learn, by and by, and to their cost, the bad effects of their uselessness, and will then eagerly demand to be allowed to make up for lost time. It may be, also, that they had chosen a more useful life; but have subsequently recoiled from the trial, and allowed themselves to be misled by the suggestions of spirits who encourage them in their inactivity."

575. *The common occupations of everyday life appear to us to be duties rather than missions, properly so called. A mission, according to the idea we attach to this word, is characterised by an importance less exclusive, and especially less personal. From this point of view, how can we ascertain that a man has really a mission upon this earth?*

"By the greatness of the results he accomplishes, and the progress he causes to be made by his fellow-men."

576. *Are those who have received an important mission pre-destined thereto before their birth, and are they aware of it?*

"Yes, in some cases; but, more often, they are not aware of it. They are only vaguely conscious of an aim in coming upon the earth; their mission reveals itself to them gradually, after their birth, through the action of circumstances. God leads them on into the road which they are to take for the accomplishment of His designs."

577. *When a man does anything useful, is it always in virtue of an anterior and predestined mission, or may he receive a mission not previously foreseen?*

"Everything a man does is not the result of a predestined mission; he is often the instrument of a spirit who makes use of him in order to procure the execution of something he considers useful. For example:—A spirit thinks it would be useful to publish a book which he would write himself if he were incarnated. He seeks out the writer who will be the fittest to comprehend and develop his idea; he suggests to him the plan of the work, and directs him in its execution. In such a case, the man did not come into the world with the mission of doing this work. It is the same in regard to various works of art or scientific discoveries. During the sleep of his body, the incarnated spirit communicates directly with the spirit in erraticity, and the two take counsel together for the carrying out of their undertaking."

578. May spirit fail in his mission through his own fault?

"Yes; if he is not of a high degree of elevation."

— *What, for him, are the consequences of such a failure?*

"He is obliged to begin his task over again; this is his punishment. And, besides, he will have to undergo the consequences of the mischiefs caused by his failure."

579. Since it is from God that each spirit receives his mission, how can God have entrusted an important mission, one of general interest, to a spirit capable of failing in its discharge?

"Does not God foresee whether His general will be victorious or vanquished? Be sure that He foresees all things, and that the carrying out of His plans, when they are important, is never confided to those who will leave their work half done. The whole difficulty lies, for you, in the foreknowledge of the future which God possesses, but which you cannot understand."

580. When a spirit has incarnated himself for the accomplishment of a mission, does he feel the same anxiety in regard to it as the spirit whose mission has been undertaken as a trial?

"No; for he has the results of experience to guide him."

581. The men who enlighten the human race by their genius have certainly a mission; but there are among them many who make mistakes, and who, along with important truths, spread abroad serious errors. In what way should we regard their mission?

"As having been falsified by themselves. They are unequal to the task they have undertaken. In judging of them, however, you must take into account the circumstances in which they have been placed. Men of genius have had to speak according to their time; and teachings which appear erroneous or puerile, in the light of a later epoch, may have been sufficient for the epoch at which they were given."

582. Can paternity be considered a mission?

"It is undeniably a mission; and also a most serious duty, the responsibilities of which will exercise a more important influence upon his future than a man is apt to suppose. God has placed the child under the tutelage of his parents, in order that they should direct his steps into the path of rectitude; and he has facilitated their task by giving to the child a frail and delicate organisation, that renders him accessible to new impressions. But there are many parents who take more pains to train the trees in their gardens, and to make them bring forth a large crop of fine fruit, than to train the character of their child. If the latter succumbs through their fault, they will bear the punishment of their unfaithfulness; and the sufferings of the child in a future life will come home to them, because they have not done their part towards helping him forward on the road to happiness."

583. *If a child goes wrong, notwithstanding the care of his parents, are they responsible?*

"No; but the more vicious the disposition of the child, and the heavier their task, the greater will be their reward if they· succeed in drawing him away from the evil road."

— *If a child becomes a good man, despite the negligence or bad example of his parents, do the latter obtain any benefit therefrom?*
"God is just."

584. *What can be the mission of the conqueror whose only aim is the satisfaction of his ambition, and who, in order to attain that end, does not shrink from inflicting the calamities he brings in his train?*

"He is generally only an instrument used by God for the accomplishment of His designs; and these calamities are sometimes a means of making a people advance more rapidly."

— *The good that may result from these passing calamities is foreign to him who has been the instrument in producing them, since he had only proposed to himself a personal aim; will he, nevertheless, profit by that result?*

"Each is rewarded according to his works, the good he has *wished* to do, and the uprightness of his intentions."

Spirits, while incarnated, have occupations inherent in the nature of their corporeal existence. In the state of erraticity, or of dematerialisation, their occupations are proportioned to their degree of advancement.

Some of them journey from world to world, acquiring instruction, and preparing for a new incarnation.

Others, more advanced, devote themselves to the cause of progress by directing the course of events, and suggesting propitious ideas ; they assist the men of genius who help forward the advancement of the human race.

Others incarnate themselves again with a mission of progress.

Others take under their care individuals, families, societies, cities, countries, and peoples, and become their guardian-angels, protecting genii, and familiar spirits.

Others, again, preside over the phenomena of nature, of which they are the immediate agents.

The great mass of spirits of lower rank busy themselves with our occupations, and take part in our amusements.

Impure and imperfect spirits await, in sufferings and anguish, the moment when it shall please God to furnish them with the means of advancing. If they do harm, it is through spite against the happiness which they are not yet able to share.

CHAPTER XI

1. MINERALS AND PLANTS—2. ANIMALS AND MEN—
3. METEMPSYCHOSIS.

Minerals and Plants.

585. WHAT *do you think of the division of the natural world into three reigns, the mineral, vegetable, and animal, to which some naturalists add a fourth class—viz., the human species; or that other division of the world into two classes—vi., the organic and the inorganic? Which of these divisions is to be preferred?*

"They are all good; as to which is best, that depends on your point of view. From the point of view of matter, there are only inorganic and organic beings; from the moral point of view, there are evidently four degrees."

These four degrees are, in fact, distinguished by well-marked characteristics, although their extremes seem to blend into each other. Inert matter, which constitutes the mineral reign, possesses only mechanical force ; plants, composed of inert matter, are endowed with vitality ; animals, composed of inert matter, and endowed with vitality, have also a sort of instinctive intelligence, limited in its scope, but giving them the consciousness of their existence and of their individuality ; man, possessing all that is found in plants and animals, is raised above all the other classes by special intelligence, without fixed limits, which gives him the consciousness of his future, the perception of extramaterial things, and the knowledge of God.

586. Are plants conscious of their existence?
"No; they do not think; they have only organic life."

587. Do plants feel sensations? Do they suffer when they are mutilated?
"Plants receive the physical impressions which act upon matter, but they have no perceptions; consequently they do not feel pain."

588. Is the force which attracts plants towards each other independent of their will?
"Yes; for they do not think. It is a mechanical force of matter that acts upon matter; they could not resist it."

589. Some plants, as, for instance, the mimosa and the dionæa, have movements which give evidence of their possessing great

*sensitiveness, and, in some cases, a sort of will, as in the case of
the latter, whose lobes seize the fly that lights on it, in order to suck
its juices, and even seem to set a snare for it, in order to kill it.
Are these plants endowed with the faculty of thought? Have they
a will, and do they form an intermediate class between the vegetable and animal natures? Are they points of transition from the
one to the other?*

"Everything in nature is transition, from the very fact that
everything is different, and that everything, nevertheless, is linked
together. Plants do not think, and have consequently no will.
The oyster that opens its shell, and all the zoophytes, do not think;
they have only a blind natural instinct."

The human organism furnishes us with examples of similar movements
that take place without any participation of the will, as in the organs of
digestion and circulation ; the pylorus closes itself at the contact of certain
substances, as though to refuse them passage. It must be the same with
the sensitive plant, the movements of which do not necessarily imply
perception, and, still less, will.

*590. Is there not, in plants, an instinct of self-preservation
which leads them to seek what may be useful to them, and to avoid
what would do them harm?*

"You may call it, if you will, a sort of instinct: that depends
on the extension you give to the word; but it is purely mechanical.
When, in chemical operations, you see two bodies unite together,
it is because they suit one another, that is to say, there is an affinity
between them; but you do not call that instinct."

*591. In worlds of higher degree, are the plants, like the other
beings, of a more perfect nature?*

"Everything in those worlds is more perfect; but the plants are
always plants, as the animals are always animals, and as the men
are always men.

Animals and Men.

*592. If we compare man with the animals in reference to intel-
ligence, it seems difficult to draw a line of demarcation between
them; for some animals are, in this respect, notoriously superior to
some men. Is it possible to establish such a line of demarcation
with any precision?*

"Your philosophers are far from being agreed upon this point.
Some of them will have it that man is an animal; others are
equally sure that the animal is a man. They are all wrong. Man
is a being apart, who sometimes sinks himself very low, or who

may raise himself very high. As regards his physical nature, man is like the animals, and less well provided for than many of them; for nature has given to them all that man is obliged *to invent with the aid of his intelligence* for his needs and his preservation. His body is subject to destruction, like that of the animals; but his spirit has a destiny that he alone can understand, because he alone is completely free. Poor human beings who debase yourselves below the brutes! do you not know how to distinguish yourselves from them? Recognise the superiority of man by his possessing the notion of the existence of God."

593. Can the animals be said to act only from instinct?

"That, again, is a mere theory. It is very true that instinct predominates in the greater number of animals; but do you not see some of them act with a determinate will? This is intelligence; but of narrow range."

It is impossible to deny that some animals give evidence of possessing, besides instinct, the power of performing compound acts which denote the will to act in a determinate direction, and according to circumstances. Consequently, there is in them a sort of intelligence, but the exercise of which is mainly concentrated on the means of satisfying their physical needs, and providing for their own preservation. There is, among them, no progress, no amelioration ; no matter what the art that we admire in their labours, what they formerly did, that they do today neither better nor worse, according to constant forms and unvarying proportions. The young bird isolated from the rest of its species none the less builds its nest on the same model, without having been taught. If some of the animals are susceptible of a certain amount of education, their intellectual development, always restricted within narrow limits, is due to the action of man upon a flexible nature, for they themselves have no power of progressing ; but that artificial development is ephemeral and purely individual, for the animal, when left again to himself, speedily returns within the limits traced out for it by nature.

594. Have animals a language?

"If you mean a language formed of words and syllables, no; but if you mean a method of communication among themselves, yes. They say much more to one another than you suppose; but their language is limited, like their ideas, to their bodily wants."

— *There are animals who have no voice; have they no language?*

"They understand one another by other means. Have men no other method of communicating with one another than by speech? And the dumb, what do you say of them? The animals, being endowed with the life of relation, have means of giving one another information, and of expressing the sensations they feel. Do you suppose that fishes have no understanding among themselves? Man has not the exclusive privilege of language; but that of the animals is instinctive and limited to the scope of their wants and ideas, while that of man is perfectible, and lends itself to all the conceptions of his intelligence."

It is evident that fishes, emigrating in masses, like the swallows that follow the guide that leads them, must have the means of giving one another information, of arriving at a common understanding, and of concerting measures of general interest. It may be that they are gifted with a sense of vision sufficiently acute to allow of their distinguishing signs made by them to one another, or the water may serve them as a vehicle for the transmission of certain vibrations. It is evident that they must have some means, whatever these may be, of comprehending one another, like all other animals that have no voice, and that nevertheless perform actions in common. Should it, then, be deemed strange that spirits are able to communicate among themselves without having recourse to articulate speech? (282.)

595. *Have animals free-will in regard to their actions?*

"They are not the mere machines you suppose them to be; but their freedom of action is limited to their wants, and cannot be compared to that of man. Being far inferior to him, they have not the same duties. Their freedom is restricted to the acts of their material life."

596. *Whence comes the aptitude of certain animals to imitate human speech, and why is this aptitude found among birds, rather, for instance, than among apes, whose conformation has so much more analogy to that of man?*

"That aptitude results from a particular conformation of the vocal organs, seconded by the instinct of imitation. The ape imitates man's gestures; some birds imitate his voice."

597. *Since the animals have an intelligence which gives them a certain degree of freedom of action, is there, in them, a principle independent of matter?*

"Yes; and that survives their body."

— *Is this principle a soul, like that of man?*

"It is a soul, if you like to call it so; *that depends on the meaning you attach to this word.* But it is inferior to that of man. There is, between the soul of the animals and that of man, as great a difference as there is between the soul of man and God."

598. *Does the soul of the animals preserve, after death, its individuality and its self-consciousness?*

"It preserves its individuality, but not the consciousness of its *me.* The life of intelligence remains latent in them."

599. *Has the soul of the beasts the choice of incarnating itself in one kind of animal rather than in another?*

"No; it does not possess free-will."

600. As the soul of the animal survives its body, is it, after death, in a state of erraticity, like that of man?

"It is in a sort of erraticity, because it is not united to a body; but it is not *an errant spirit.* The errant spirit is a being who thinks and acts of his own free-will; but the soul of the animal has not the same faculty, for it is his self-consciousness which is the principal attribute of the spirit. The soul of the animal is classed, after its death, by the spirits charged with that work, and almost immediately utilised; it has not the leisure to enter into connection with other creatures."

601. Do animals follow a law progress like men?

"Yes; and it is for this reason that, in the higher worlds in which men are further advanced, the animals are more advanced also, and possess more developed means of communication. But they are always inferior to man, and subject to him; they are, for him, intelligent servitors."

There is nothing unreasonable in this statement. Suppose that our most intelligent animals, the dog, the elephant, the horse, were furnished with a bodily conformation appropriate to manual labour, what could they not do under the direction of man?

602. Do animals progress, like man, through the action of their will, or through the force of things?

"Through the force of things; this is why there is, for them, no expiation."

603. Have the animals, in the higher worlds, a knowledge of God?

"No; man is a god for them, as spirits were formerly gods for men."

604. The animals, even the advanced ones of the higher worlds, being always inferior to man, it would seem as though God had created intellectual beings condemned to a perpetual inferiority: such an arrangement does not appear to be in accordance with the unity of design and of progress discernible in all His works.

"Everything in nature is linked together by an enchaining which your intellect cannot yet seize; and things apparently the most discrepant have points of contact at the comprehension of which man will never arrive in his actual state. He may obtain a glimmering of them through an effort of his intelligence; but it is only when that intelligence shall have acquired its full development, and shall have freed itself from the prejudices of pride and of ignorance, that he will be able to see clearly into the work of God;

until then, his narrowness of thought causes him to look at everything from a low and petty point of view. Know that God cannot
contradict Himself, and that everything in nature is harmonised
by the action of general laws that never deviate from the sublime
wisdom of the Creator."

— *Intelligence, then, is a common property, and a point of
contact, between the soul of the beast and that of man?*

"Yes, but the animals have only the intelligence of material life;
in man, intelligence gives moral life."

605. *If we consider all the points of contact that exist between
man and the animals, does it not seem as though man possessed
two souls—viz., an animal soul and a spiritual soul, and that, if
he had not the latter, he might still live, but as a brute; in other
words, that the animal is a being similar to man, minus the
spiritual soul? From which it would follow that the good and bad
instincts of man result from the predominance of one or other of
these two souls.*

"No; man has not two souls; but the body has its instincts
resulting from the sensation of its organs. There is in him only
a double nature—the animal nature and the spiritual nature. By
his body he participates in the nature of the animals and their
instincts; by his soul he participates in the nature of spirits."

— *Thus, besides his own imperfection, which he has to get rid
of, a spirit has also to struggle against the influence of matter?*

"Yes, the lower a spirit's degree of advancement, the closer
are the bonds which united him with matter. Do you not see that
it must necessarily be so? No; man has not two souls: the soul
is always *one* in a single being. The soul of the animal and that
of man are distinct from one another, so that the soul of the one
cannot animate the body created for the other. But if man have
not an animal soul, placing him, by its passions, on a level with the
animals, he has his body, which often drags him down to them;
for his body is a being that is endowed with vitality, and that has
its instincts, but unintelligent, and limited to the care of its own
preservation."

A spirit, in incarnating himself in a human body, brings to it the intellectual and moral principle that renders it superior to the animals.
The two natures in man constitute for him two distinct sources of passions ;
one set of passions springing from the instincts of his animal nature, and
the other set being due to the impurities of the spirit of which he is the
incarnation, and which are in sympathy with the grossness of the animal
appetites. A spirit, as he becomes purified, frees himself gradually from
the influence of matter. While under that influence, he approaches the

nature of the brutes ; when delivered from that influence, he raises himself towards his true destination.

606. Whence do the animals derive the intelligent principle that constitutes the particular kind of soul with which they are endowed?

"From the universal intelligent element."

— *The intelligence of man and of the animals emanates, then, from one and the same principle?*

"Undoubtedly; but, in man, it has received an elaboration which raises it above that which animates the brute."

607. You have stated that the soul of man, at its origin, is in a state analogous to that of human infancy, that its intelligence is only beginning to unfold itself, and that it is essaying to live (190) ; where does the soul accomplish this earliest phase of its career?

"In a series of existences which precede the period of development that you call humanity."

— *The soul would seem, then, to have been the intelligent principle of the inferior orders of the creation?*

"Have we not said that everything in nature is linked together and tends to unity? It is in those beings, of which you are very far from knowing all, that the intelligent principle is elaborated, is gradually individualised, *and made ready to live*, as we have said, through its subjection to a sort of preparatory process, like that of germination, on the conclusion of which that principle undergoes a transformation and becomes *spirit*. It is then that the period of humanity commences for each spirit with the sense of futurity, the power of distinguishing betweed good and evil, and the responsibility of his actions; just as, after the period of infancy comes that of childhood, then youth, adolescence, and ripened manhood. Is the greatest genius humiliated by having been a shapeless fœtus in his mother's womb? If anything ought to humiliate him, it is his lowness in the scale of being, and his powerlessness to sound the depths of the divine designs and the wisdom of the laws that regulate the harmonies of the universe. Recognise the greatness of God in this admirable harmony that establishes solidarity between everything in nature. To think that God could have made anything without a purpose, and have created intelligent beings without a future, would be to blaspheme His goodness, which extends over all His creatures."

— *Does this period of humanity commence upon our earth?*

"The earth is not the starting-point of the earliest phase of human incarnation; the human period commences, in general, in worlds still lower than yours. This, however, is not an absolute rule; and it may happen that a spirit, at his entrance upon the human phase, may be fitted to live upon the earth. Such a case, however, though possible, is unfrequent; and would be an exception to the general rule."

608. *Has a man's spirit, after death, any consciousness of the existences that have preceded his entrance upon the human period?*

"No; for it is only with this period that his life, as a spirit, has begun for him. He can scarcely recall his earliest existences as a man; just as a man no longer remembers the earliest days of his infancy, and still less the time he passed in his mother's womb. This is why spirits tell you that they do not know how they began." (78.)

609. *Does a spirit, when once he has entered upon the human period, retain any traces of what he has previously been, that is to say, of the state in which he was in what may be called the ante-human period?*

"That depends on the distance which separates the two periods, and the amount of progress accomplished. During a few generations, there may be a reflex, more or less distinct, of the primitive state, for nothing in nature takes place through an abrupt transition, and there are always links which unite the extremities of the chain of beings or of events; but those traces disappear with the development of free-will. The first steps of progress are accomplished slowly, because they are not yet seconded by the will; they are accomplished more rapidly in proportion as the spirit acquires a more perfect consciousness of himself."

610. *The spirits who have said that man is a being apart from the rest of creation are, then, mistaken?*

"No, but the question had not been developed; and besides, there are things that can only be known at their appointed time. Man is, in reality, a being apart, for he has faculties that distinguish him from all others, and he has another destiny. The human species is the one which God has chosen for the incarnation of the beings *that are capable of knowing Him.*"

Metempsychosis.

611. Is not the common origin of the intellectual principle of living beings a consecration of the doctrine of the metempsychosis?

"Two things may have the same origin, and yet not resemble one another at a later period. Who could recognise the tree, with its leaves, flowers, and fruit, in the shapeless germ contained in the seed from which it has issued? From the moment when the principle of intelligence has reached the necessary degree of development for becoming spirit, and for entering upon the human phase, it has no longer any connection with its primitive state, and is no more the soul of the beasts than the tree is the seed. In man, there is no longer anything of the animal but his body, and the passions which are the joint product of his body and of the instinct of self-preservation inherent in matter. It cannot, therefore, be said that such and such a man is the incarnation of such and such an animal; and consequently the doctrine of the metempsychosis, as commonly understood, is not true."

612. Can a spirit which has animated a human body be incarnated in an animal?

"No; for such an incarnation would be a retrogradation; and a spirit never retrogrades. The river does not flow back to is source." (118.)

613. However erroneous may be the idea attached to the doctrine of the metempsychosis, may not that doctrine be a result of an intuitive reminiscence of the different existences of man?

"That intuitive reminiscence is seen in this belief as in many others; but, like the greater part of his intuitive ideas, man has perverted it."

The doctrine of the metempsychosis would be true if by that word were understood the progression of the soul from a lower state to a higher state, in which it acquires the new development that will transform its nature ; but it is false when understood as meaning that any animal can transmigrate directly into a man, and a man into an animal, which would imply the idea of a retrogradation or of a fusion. The fact that fusion is not possible between corporeal beings of two different species is an indication of their being of degrees that are not assimilable, and that such must be the case, also, with the spirits that animate them. If the same spirit could animate them alternately, it would imply the existence, between them, of an identity that would manifest itself by the possibility of corporeal reproduction. Reincarnation, as now taught by spirits, is founded, on the contrary, upon the ascensional movement of nature and upon the progression of man in his own species, which detracts nothing from his dignity. What really degrades man is the evil use he makes of the faculties which God has given him for his advancement. And, at all events, the antiquity and universality of the doctrine of the metempsychosis, and the number of eminent men who have professed it, proves that the principle of reincarnation has its roots in nature itself ; a fact which, so far from diminishing the probability of its truth, must be regarded as constituting a weighty argument in its favour.

The starting-point of spirit is one of those questions which have reference to the origin of things, and to the secret designs of God. It is not given to man to comprehend them completely, and he can only form, in regard to them, suppositions and theoretic systems, more or less probable. Spirits themselves are far from knowing everything ; and may also have, in regard to what they do not know, individual opinions more or less in harmony with fact.

It is thus, for example, that all spirits do not think alike in reference to the relations which exist between man and the animals. According to some, spirit only arrives at the human period after having been elaborated and individualised in the different degrees of the lower beings of the creation. According to others, the spirit of man has always belonged to the human race, without passing through the ascensional degrees of the animal world. The first of these theories has the advantage of giving an aim to the future of animals, which are thus seen to form the earliest links in the chain of thinking beings ; the second theory is more consonant with the dignity of man, and may be summed up as follows :—

The different species of animals do not proceed **intellectually** from one another by road of progression. Thus the spirit of the oyster does not become successively that of the fish, the bird, the quadruped, and the quadrumane. Each species is a **fixed** type, physically and morally, each individual of which draws, from the universal source of being, the sum of the intelligent principle which is necessary to it according to the nature of its organs and the work it has to accomplish in the phenomena of nature, and which it restores to the general mass of that principle at its death. Those of worlds more advanced than ours (188) are also distinct races, that are fitted to the needs of those worlds, and to the degree of advancement of the men of whom they are the auxiliaries, but that do not proceed, spiritually, from those of the earth. It is not the same with man. It is evident that, physically, he forms a link in the chain of living beings ; but there is, morally, a solution of continuity between the animals and him ; for man **alone** possesses the soul, or spirit, the divine spark, which gives him the moral sense and the extended vision which are wanting in the animals ; and this soul, spirit, spark, is, in him, the principal being, pre-existent to, and surviving, his body, and thus preserving his individuality. What is the origin of spirit? What its starting-point? Is it formed by the individualising of the intelligent principle? This is a mystery which it would be useless to attempt to penetrate, and in regard to which, as we have said, we can do no more than build up theories. What is certain, what is indicated alike by reason and by experience, is the survival of each spirit and the persistence of his individuality after death, his faculty of progressing, the happiness or unhappiness of his next state of being, according to his advancement or his backwardness in the path of purification, and all the moral consequences which flow from this certainty. As for the mysterious kinship which exists between man and the animals, that we repeat, is God's secret, like many other matters the knowledge of which, **at this time,** is of little importance to our advancement, and upon which it would be useless to insist.

CHAPTER I

DIVINE OR NATURAL LAW

1. CHARACTERISTICS OF NATURAL LAW—2. SOURCE
AND KNOWLEDGE OF NATURAL LAW—3. GOOD AND
EVIL—4. DIVISIONS OF NATURAL LAW.

Characteristics of Natural Law

614. What is to be understood by natural law?

"The law of nature is the law of God. It is the only rule that ensures the happiness of man, for it shows him what he should or should not do, and he only suffers because he disobeys it."

615. Is the law of God eternal?

"It is eternal and unchangeable as God Himself."

616. Can God have prescribed to mankind in one age what He has forbidden in another?

"God cannot be mistaken. Men are obliged to change their laws, because they are imperfect; but the laws of God are perfect. The harmony which regulates both the material universe and the moral universe is founded on laws established by God from all eternity."

617. What are the objects embraced by the divine laws? Have they reference to anything but our moral conduct?

"All the laws of nature are divine laws, since God is the author of all things. The seeker after science studies the laws of nature in the realm of matter; the seeker after goodness studies them in the soul, and practises them."

— Is it given to man to fathom both these divisions of natural law?

"Yes; *but a single existence does not suffice for doing this."*

What, indeed, are a few years for acquiring all that is necessary to constitute a perfect being, if we consider only the distance that separates the civilised man from the savage? A human life, though prolonged to its utmost possible length, is insufficient for such a work ; much more is it so when cut short before its term, as is the case with so large a proportion of the human race.

ALLAN KARDEC

Some of the divine laws regulate the movements and relations of inert matter ; they are termed physical laws, and their study is the domain of science. Others of these laws concern man, as considered in himself and in his relations to God and to his fellow-creatures ; they are termed moral laws, and regulate the life of relation as well as the life of the soul.

618. Are the divine laws the same for all worlds?

"Reason tells you that they must be adapted to the special nature of each of those various worlds, and proportioned to the degree of advancement of the beings who inhabit them."

Knowledge of Natural Law

619. Has God given to all men the means of knowing His law?

"All may know it, but all do not understand it. Those who understand it best are they who seek after goodness. All, however, will one day understand it; for the destiny of progress must be accomplished."

The justice of the various incarnations undergone by each human being is evident when seen in the light of the principle just enunciated ; since, in each new existence, his intelligence is more developed, and he comprehends more clearly what is good and what is evil. If everything had to be accomplished by each man in a single existence, what would be the fate of the many millions of human beings who die every day in the brutishness of the savage state, or in the darkness of ignorance, without having had the possibility of obtaining enlightenment? (177, 222.)

620. Does a spirit, before his union with the body, comprehend the law of God more clearly than after his incarnation?

"He comprehends that law according to the degree of development at which he has arrived, and preserves the intuitive remembrance of it after being united with a body; but the evil instincts of man often cause him to forget it."

621. Where is the law of God inscribed?
"In the conscience."

— Since man carries the law of God in his conscience, where was the need of revealing it to him?

"He had forgotten and misunderstood it; God willed that it should be recalled to his memory."

622. Has God given to some men the mission of revealing His law?

"Yes, certainly. In every age there have been men who have received this mission; spirits of higher degree, who have incarnated themselves for the purpose of advancing human progress."

623. Have not those who have professed to instruct mankind sometimes made mistakes, and led them astray by false reasonings?

"Those who, not being inspired by God, have arrogated to themselves, through ambition, a mission which they had not received, may, undoubtedly, have led them into error; neverthe ess, as, after all, they were men of genius, great truths are often to be found, even in the midst of the errors they taught."

624. *What are the characteristics of the true prophet?*

"The true prophet is an upright man who is inspired by God. He may be recognised both by his words and by his deeds. God does not employ the mouth of a liar to teach the truth."

625. *What is the most perfect type that God has offered to man as his guide and model?*

"Jesus."

Jesus is the type of the moral perfection to which man may attain upon this earth. God offers Him to our thought as our most perfect model; and the doctrine taught by Him is the purest expression of the divine law, because He was animated by the divine spirit, and was the purest being who has ever appeared upon the earth.

If some of those who have professed to instruct man in the law of God have sometimes led him astray by the inculcation of error, it is because they have allowed themselves to be swayed by sentiments of too earthly a nature, and because they have confounded the laws which regulate the conditions of the life of the soul which regulate the life of the body. Many pretended revealers have announced as divine laws what were only human laws, devised by them for serving their own passions and obtaining dominion over their fellow-men.

626. *Have the divine or natural laws been revealed to men by Jesus only, and had men, before His time, no other knowledge than that given them by intuition?*

"Have we not told you that those laws are written everywhere? All the men who have meditated upon wisdom have therefore been able to comprehend and to teach them from the remotest times. By their teachings, imperfect though they were, they have prepared the ground for the sowing of the seed. The divine laws being written in the book of nature, it has always been possible for man to know them by searching after them. For this reason, the moral precepts they consecrate have been proclaimed, in all ages, by upright men; and, for the same reason also, the elements of the moral law are to be found among every nation above the barbarian degree, although incomplete, or debased by ignorance and superstition.

627. *Since the true laws of God have been taught by Jesus, what is the use of the teachings given by spirits? Have they anything more to teach us?*

"The teachings of Jesus were often allegoric, and conveyed in parables; because He spoke according to the time and place in which He lived. The time has now come when the truth must be made intelligible for all. It is necessary to explain and develop the divine laws, because few among you understand them, and still fewer practise them. Our mission is to strike the eyes and ears of all, in order to confound pride, and to unmask the hypocrisy of those who assume the outward appearances of virtue and of religion as a cloak for their turpitudes. We are charged to prepare the reign of good announced by Jesus; to furnish the explanations that will render it impossible for men to continue to interpret the law of God according to their passions, or to pervert the meaning of what is wholly a law of love and of kindness."

628. *Why has not the truth been always placed within reach of every one?*

"Each thing can only come in its time. Truth is like light; you must be accustomed to it gradually; otherwise it only dazzles you.

"Hitherto, God has never permitted man to receive communications so full and instructive as those which he is permitted to receive at this day. There were, undoubtedly, in ancient times, as you know, individuals who were in posession of knowledge whih they considered as sacred, and which they kept as a mystery from those whom they regarded as profane. You can well understand, from what you know of the laws which govern the phenomena of spirit-communication, that they received only a few fragmentary truths, scattered through a mass of teachings that were generally emblematic, and often erroneous. Nevertheless, there is no old philosophic system, no tradition, no religion, that men should neglect to study; for they all contain the germs of great truths, which, however they may seem to contradict each other—perverted as they are by their mixture with various worthless accessories— may be easily coordinated, with the aid of the key that Spiritism gives you to a class of facts which have hitherto seemed to be contrary to reason, but of which the reality is irrefutably demonstrated at the present day. You should therefore not fail to make those old systems a subject of study, for they are rich in lessons, and may contribute largely to your instruction."

Good and Evil

629. *What definition can be given of the moral law?*

"The moral law is the rule for acting aright, that is to say, for distinguishing practically between good and evil. It is founded on the observance of the law of God. Man acts rightly when he takes the good of all as his aim and rule of action; for he then obeys the law of God."

630. How can we distinguish between good and evil?

"Good is whatever is in conformity with the law of God; and evil is whatever deviates from it. Thus, to do right, is to conform to the law of God; to do wrong, is to infringe that law."

631. Has man of himself the means of distinguishing what is good from what is evil?

"Yes, when he believes in God, and desires to do what is right. God has given him intelligence in order that he may distinguish between them."

632. As man is subject to error, may he not be mistaken in his appreciation of good and evil, and believe himself to be doing right, when, in reality, he is doing wrong?

"Jesus has said: 'Whatsoever ye would that men should do unto you, do ye even so to them.' The whole moral law is contained in that injunction. Make it your rule of action, and you will never go wrong."

633. The rule of good and evil, what may be called the rule of reciprocity or solidarity, cannot be applied to a man's to personal conduct towards himself. Does he find, in natural law, the rule of that conduct, and a safe guide?

"When you eat too much, it hurts you. God gives you, in the discomfort thus produced, the measure of what is necessary for you. When you exceed that measure, you are punished. It is the same with everything else. Natural law traces out for each man the limit of his needs: when he oversteps that limit he is punished by the suffering thus caused. If men gave heed, in all things, to the voice which says to them 'enough!' they would avoid the greater part of the ills of which they accuse nature."

634. Why does evil exist in the nature of things? I speak of moral evil. Could not God have created the human race in more favourable conditions?

"We have already told you that spirits are created simple and ignorant (115). God leaves man free to choose his road; so much the worse for him if he takes the wrong one; his pilgrimage will be all the longer. If there were no mountains, man could not comprehend the possibility of ascending and descending; if there were no rocks, he could not understand that there are such things as hard bodies. It is necessary for the spirit to acquire experience; and, to that end, he must know both good and evil. It is for this purpose that souls are united to bodies." (119.)

635. *The different social positions create new wants which are not the same for all men. Natural law would therefore appear not to be a uniform rule?*

"Those different positions are in nature, and according to the law of progress; they do not invalidate the unity of natural law, which applies to everything."

The conditions of a man's existence vary according to times and places; hence arise for him different wants, and social positions corresponding to those wants. Since this diversity is in the order of things, it must be consonant with the law of God; and this law is none the less **one** in principle. It is for reason to distinguish between real wants and wants that are factitious or conventional.

636. *Are good and evil absolute for all men?*

"The law of God is the same for all; but evil resides especially in the desire for its commission. Good is always good, and evil is always evil, whatever a man's position may be; the difference is in the degree of his responsability."

637. *When a savage, yielding to his instinctive desire, feeds on human flesh, is he guilty in so doing?*

"I have said that the essence of evil is in the will; therefore a man is more or less guilty according to his light."

Circumstances modify the relative intensity of good and of evil. A man often commits faults that are none the less reprehensible for being the consequence of the social position in which he is placed; but his responsibility is proportioned to the means he possesses of distinguishing between right and wrong. Thus the enlightened man who commits a mere injustice is more culpable in the sight of God than the ignorant savage who abandons himself to his instincts of cannibalism.

638. *Evil seems, sometimes, to be a consequence of the force of things. Such is, for instance, in some cases, the necessity of destruction, even to the extent of taking the life of a fellow-creature. Can it be said that, in such cases, there is violation of the law of God?*

"Evil, in such cases, is none the less evil, although necessary; but this necessity disappears in proportion as the soul becomes purified by passing from one existence to another; and man is then all the more culpable when he does wrong, because he comprehends more clearly the character of his action."

639. The evil we do is often the result of the position that has been made for us by other men; where, in such a case, lies the greatest amount of culpability?

"With those who have been the cause of the wrong-doing. Thus the man who has been led into evil, by the position that his fellow-creatures have made for him, is less guilty than those who have caused him to go astray, for each has to suffer the penalty, not only of the evil he has done, but of that which he has caused another to do."

640. Is he who profits by another's wrong-doing, even though he took no part in its commission, as guilty as though he had taken part in it?

"Yes; to take advantage of a crime is to take part in it. He would, perhaps, have shrunk from committing the evil deed, but if, the deed being done, he takes advantage of it, it is equivalent to doing it, and proves that he would have done it himself, if he could, *or if he dared.*"

641. Is it as reprehensible to desire to do an evil deed as to do it?

"That is as the case may be. Voluntarily to resist the desire to do wrong, especially when there is a possibility of gratifying that desire, is virtuous; but he, who has only not done the wrong thing because the opportunity was wanting, is as guilty as though he had done it."

642. In order to be acceptable in the sight of God, and to insure our future happiness, is it sufficient not to have done evil?

"No; it is necessary for each to have done good also, to the utmost limits of his ability; for each of you will have to answer, not only for all the evil he has done, but also *for all the good which he has failed to do.*"

643. Are there persons who, through their position, have no possibility of doing good?

"There are none who cannot do some good; the selfish alone find no opportunity of so doing. The mere fact of being in relation with other human beings suffices to furnish the opportunity of doing good, and every day of your lives provides this possibility for every one who is not blinded by selfishness. For doing good is not restricted to the giving of alms, but also comprehends being useful to the full extent of your power, whenever your assistance may be needed."

644. Is it not sometimes the case that the situation in which a man finds himself placed has a good deal to do with leading him into vice and crime?

"Yes, but that situation is itself a part of the trial which has been chosen by his spirit in the state of freedom; he has elected to expose himself to its temptations, in order to acquire the merit of resistance."

645. When a man is plunged, so to say, in an atmosphere of vice, does not the impulsion to evil become, for him, almost irresistible?

"The impulsion is strong, but not irresistible, for you sometimes find great virtues in an atmosphere of vice. Those who thus remain virtuous in the midst of incitements to evil are spirits who have acquired sufficient strength to resist temptation, and who, while thus testing that strength, fulfil the mission of exercising a beneficial influence on those around them."

646. Is the meritoriousness of virtuous action measured by the conditions under which that action has been accomplished? In other words, are there different degrees of meritoriousness in doing right?

"The meritoriousness of virtuous action depends on the difficulty involved in it; there would be no merit in doing right without self-denial and effort. God counts the sharing of his morsel of bread by the poor man, as of a higher merit than the giving of his superfluity by the rich one. Jesus told you this in His parable of the widow's mite."

Division o Natural Law

647. Is the whole of the law of God contained in the rule of love of the neighbour laid down by Jesus?

"That rule certainly contains all the duties of men to one another; but it is necessary to show them its various applications, or they will continue to neglect them, as they do at the present day. Besides, natural law embraces all the circumstances of life, and the rule you have cited is only a part of it. Men need precise directions; general precepts are too vague, and leave too many doors open to human interpretations."

648. What do you think of the division of natural law into ten parts, viz., the laws of adoration, labour, reproduction, preservation, society, equality, liberty, justice, love, and charity?

"The division of the law of God into ten parts is that of Moses, and may be made to include all the circumstances of life, which is the essential point. You may therefore adopt it, without its being held to have any absolute value, any more than the various other systems of classification which depend on the aspect under which the subject is considered. The last of those parts is the most important; because the law of charity includes all the others, and it is therefore through the observance of this law that mankind advances most rapidly in spiritual life."

CHAPTER II

I. THE LAW OF ADORATION

1. AIM OF ADORATION—2. EXTERNAL ACTS OF ADORA-
TION—3. LIFE OF CONTEMPLATION—4. PRAYER—5. POL-
YTHEISM—6. SACRIFICES.

Aim of Adoration

649. In what does adoration consist?

"In the elevation of the thought towards God. Through adoration
the soul draws nearer to Him."

*650. Is adoration the result of an innate sentiment, or the
product of exterior teaching?*

"Of an innate sentiment, like the belief in the Divinity. The
consciousness of his weakness leads man to bow before the Being
who can protect him."

*651. Are there peoples entirely without the sentiment of
adoration?*

"No; for there never was a people of atheists. All feel that there
is, above them, a supreme Being."

*652. May adoration be regarded as having its source in natural
law?*

"It is included in natural law, since it is the result of a sentiment
innate in man; for which reason it is found among all peoples,
though under different forms."

External Acts of Adoration

653. Are external manifestations essential to adoration?

"True adoration is in the heart. In all your actions remember
that the Master's eyes is always upon you."

— Are external acts of worship useful?

"Yes, if they are not a vain pretence. It is always useful to
set a good example; but those who perform acts of worship merely
from affectation and for the sake of appearances, and whose

conduct belies their seeming piety, set a bad example rather than a good one, and do more harm than they imagine."

654. Does God accord a preference to those who worship Him according to any particular mode?

"God prefers those who worship Him from the heart, with sincerity, and by doing what is good and avoiding what is evil, to those who fancy they honour Him by ceremonies which do not render them any better than their neighbours.

"All men are brothers, and children of God; He calls to Him all who follow His laws, whatever may be the form under which they show their obedience.

"He who has only the externals of piety is a hypocrite; he whose worship is only a pretence, and in contradiction with his conduct, sets a bad example.

"He who professes to worship Christ, and who is proud, envious, and jealous, who is hard and unforgiving to others, or ambitious of the goods of earth, is religious with the lips only, and not with the heart. God, who sees all things, will say to him, 'He who knows the truth, and does not follow it, is a hundredfold more guilty in the evil he does than the ignorant savage, and will be treated accordingly in the day of retribution.' If a blind man runs against you as he goes by, you excuse him; but if the same thing is done by a man who sees, you complain, and with reason.

"Do not ask, then, if any form of worship be more acceptable than another; for it is as though you asked whether it is more pleasing to God to be worshipped in one tongue rather than in another. Remember that the hymns addressed to Him can reach Him only through the door of the heart."

655. Is it wrong to practise the external rites of a religion in which we do not heartily believe, when this is done out of respect for those with whom we are connected, and in order not to scandalise those who think differently from us?

"In such a case, as in many others, it is the intention that decides the quality of the act. He whose only aim, in so doing, is to show respect for the belief of others, does no wrong; he does better than the man who turns them into ridicule, for the latter sins against charity. But he who goes through with such practices simply from interested motives, or from ambition, is contemptible in the sight of God and of men. God could not take pleasure in those who only pretend to humiliate themselves before Him, in order to attract the approbation of their fellow-men."

656. *Is worship performed in common preferable to individual worship?*

"When those who sympathise in thought and feeling are assembled together, they have more power to attract good spirits to them. It is the same when they are assembled for worshipping God. But you must not therefore conclude that private worship is less acceptable; for each man can worship God in his own thought."

Life of Contemplation.

657. *Have men who give themselves up to a life of contemplation, doing nothing evil, and thinking only of God, any special merit in His eyes?*

"No, for if they do nothing evil, they do nothing good; and besides, not to do good is, in itself, evil. God wills that His children should think of Him; but He does not will that they should think only of Him, since He has given men duties to discharge upon the earth. He who consumes his life in meditation and contemplation does nothing meritorious in the sight of God, because such a life is entirely personal and useless to mankind; and God will call him to account for the good he has failed to do." (640.)

Prayer.

658. *Is prayer acceptable to God?*

"Prayer is always acceptable to God when dictated by the heart, for the intention is everything in His sight; and the prayer of the heart is preferable to one read from a book, however beautiful it may be, if read with the lips rather than with the thought. Prayer is acceptable to God when it is offered with faith, fervour, and sincerity; but do not imagine that He will listen to that of the vain, proud, or selfish man, unless it be offered as an act of sincere repentance and humility."

659. *What is the general character of prayer?*

"Prayer is an act of adoration. To pray to God is to think of Him, to draw nearer to Him, to put one's self in communication with Him. He who prays may propose to himself three things: to praise, to ask, and to thank."

660.   Does prayer make men better?

"Yes; for he who prays with fervour and confidence has more strength for withstanding the temptations of evil, and for obtaining from God the help of good spirits to assist him in so doing. Such help is never refused when asked for with sincerity."

— *How is it that persons who pray a great deal are sometimes very unamiable, jealous, envious, and harsh, wanting in benevolence and forbearance, and even extremely vicious?*

"What is needed is not to pray a great deal, but to pray aright. Such persons suppose that all the virtue of prayer is in its length, and shut their eyes to their own defects. Prayer, for them, is an occupation, a means of passing their time, but not *a study of themselves.* In such cases, it is not the remedy that is inefficaceous, but the mode in which it is employed."

661.   Is there any use in asking God to forgive us our faults?

"God discerns the good and the evil: prayer does not hid faults from His eyes. He who asks of God the forgiveness of his faults, obtains that forgiveness only through a change of conduct. Good deeds are the best prayers, for deeds are of more worth than words."

662.   Is there any use in praying for others?

"The spirit of him who prays exercises an influence through his desire to do good. By prayer, he attracts to himself good spirits who take part with him in the good he desires to do."

We possess in ourselves, through our thought and our will, a power of action that extends far beyond the limits of our corporeal sphere. To pray for others is an act of our will. If our will be ardent and sincere, it calls good spirits to the aid of the party prayed for, and thus helps him by the suggestion of good thoughts, and by giving him the strength of body and of soul which he needs. But, in his case also, the prayer of the heart is everything; that of the lips is nothing.

663.   Can we, by praying for ourselves, avert our trials, or change their nature?

"Your trials are in the hands of God, and there are some of them that must be undergone to the very end; but God always takes account of the resignation with which they are borne. Prayer calls to your help good spirits who give you strength to bear them with courage, so that they seem to you less severe. Prayer is never useless when it is sincere, because ·it gives you strength, which is, of itself, an important result. 'Heaven helps him who helps himself,' is a true saying. God could change the order of nature at the various contradictory demands of His creatures; for what appears to be a great misfortune to you, from your narrow point of view, and in relation to your ephemeral life on the earth, is often a great blessing in relation to the general order of the universe; and, besides, of·how many of the troubles of his life is man himself the author, through his shortsightedness or through his wrong doing! He is punished in that wherein he has sinned. Nevertheless, your reasonable requests are granted more often than you suppose. You think your prayer has not been heeded, because God has not worked a miracle on your behalf; while, in fact. He has really assisted you, but by means so natural that they seem to you to have been the effect of chance or of the ordinary course of things. And, more often still, He suggests to your minds the thought of what you must do in order to help yourselves out of your difficulties."

664. *Is it useful to pray for the dead, and for suffering spirits, and, if so, in what way can our prayers soften or shorten their sufferings? Have they the power to turn aside the justice of God?*

"Prayer can have no effect upon the designs of God; but the spirit for whom you pray is consoled by your prayer, because you thus give him a proof of interest, and because he who is unhappy is always comforted by the kindness which compassionates his suffering. On the other hand, by your prayer, you excite him to repentance, and to the desire of doing all that in him lies to become happy; and it is this way that you may shorten the term of his suffering, provided that he, on his side, seconds your action by that of his own will. This desire for amelioration, excited by your prayer in the mind of the suffering spirit, attracts to him spirits of higher degree, who come to enlighten him, console him, and give him hope. Jesus prayed for the sheep that have gone astray; thereby showing you that you cannot, without guilt, neglect to do the same for those who have the greatest need of your prayers."

665. *What is to be thought of the opinion which rejects the idea of praying for the dead because it is not prescribed in the gospel?*

"Christ has said, to all mankind, 'Love one another.' This injunction implies, for all men, the duty of employing every possible means of testifying their affection for each other; but without entering into any details in regard to the manner of attaining that end. If it be true that nothing can turn aside the Creator from applying, to every action of every spirit, the absolute justice of which He is the type, it is none the less true that the prayer you address to Him, on behalf of a suffering spirit for whom you feel affection or compassion, is accepted by Him as a testimony of remembrance that never fails to bring relief and consolation to the sufferer. As soon as the latter manifests the slightest sign of repentance, *but only then*, help is sent to him; but he is never allowed to remain in ignorance of the fact that a sympathising heart has exerted itself on his behalf, and is always left under the consoling impression that this friendly intercession has been of use to him. Thus your intervention necessarily induces a feeling of gratitude and affection, on his part, to the friend who has given him this proof of kindness and of pity; and the mutual affection enjoined upon all men by Christ will thereby have been developed or awakened between you and him. Both of you will thus have obeyed the law of love and union imposed on all the beings of the universe; that Divine law which will usher in the reign of unity that is the aim and end of a spirit's education."[1]

666. *May we pray to spirits?*

"You may pray to good spirits as being the messengers of God, and the executants of His will; but their power, which is always proportioned to their elevation, depends entirely on the Master of all things, without whose permission nothing takes place. For this reason, prayers addressed to them are only efficacious if accepted by God."

Polytheism.

667. *How is it that polytheism, although it is false, is never-theless one of the most ancient and wide-spread of human beliefs?*

"The conception of the unity of God could only be, in the mind of man, the result of the development of his ideas. Incapable, in his ignorance, of conceiving of an immaterial being, without a determinate form, acting upon matter, man naturally attributed to Him the attributes of corporeal nature, that is to say, a form and a face; and thenceforth everything that appeared to surpass the proportions of an ordinary human intelligence was regarded by him as a divinity. Whatever he could not understand was looked upon

---

[1] This reply was given by the spirit of M. Monod, the well-known and highly-esteemed Protestant pastor of Paris, deceased in 1856. The preceding reply (No. 664) was given by the spirit of St Louis.

by him as being the work of a supernatural power; and, from that assumption, to the belief in the existence of as many distinct powers as the various effects which he beheld but could not account for, there was but a step. But there have been, in all ages, enlightened men who have comprehended the impossibility of the world's being governed by this multitude of powers, without a supreme over-ruling direction, and who have thus been led to raise their thought to the conception of the one sole God "

668. *As phenomena attesting the action of spirits have occurred in all ages of the world, and have thus been known from the earliest times, may they not have helped to induce a belief in the plurality of gods?*

"Undoubtedly; for, as men applied the term *god* to whatever surpassed humanity, spirits were, for them, so many gods. For this reason, whenever a man distinguished himself among all others by his actions, his genius, or an occult power incomprehensible by the vulgar, he was made a god of, and was worshipped as such after his death." (603.)

The word **god**, among the Ancients, had a wide range of meaning. It did not, as in our days, represent the Master of Nature, but was a generic term applied to all beings who appeared to stand outside of the pale of ordinary humanity ; and, as the manifestations that have since been known as "spiritist" had revealed to them the existence of incorporeal beings acting as one of the elementary powers of nature, they called them **gods,** just as we call them **spirits.** It is a mere question of words ; with this difference, however, that, in their ignorance, purposely kept up by those whose interests it served, they built temples and raised altars to them, making them offerings which became highly lucrative for the persons who had charge of this mode of worship ; whereas, for us, spirits are merely creatures like ourselves, more or less advanced, and having cast off their earthly envelope. If we carefully study the various attributes of the Pagan divinities, we shall easily recognise those of the spirits of our day, at every degree of the scale of spirit-life, their physical state in worlds of higher advancement, the part taken by them in the things of the earthly life, and the various properties of the perispirit.

Christianity, in bringing its Divine light to our world, has taught us to refer our adoration to the only object to which it is due. But it could not destroy what is an element of nature ; and the belief in the existence of the incorporeal beings around us has been perpetuated under various names. Their manifestations have never ceased ; but they have been diversely interpreted, and often abused under the veil of mystery beneath which they were kept. While religion has regarded them as miracles, the incredulous have looked upon them as jugglery ; but, at the present time, thanks to a more serious study of the subject, carried on in the broad daylight of scientific investigation, the doctrine of spirit-presence and spirit-action, stripped of the superstitious fancies by which it had been obscured for ages, reveals to us' one of the sublimest and most important principles of nature.

Sacrifices.

669. The custom of offering human sacrifices dates from the remotest antiquity. How can mankind have been led to believe that such an enormity could be pleasing to God?

"In the first place, through their not having comprehended God as being the source of all goodness. Among primitive peoples, matter predominates over spirit. Their moral qualities not being yet developed, they give themselves up to the instincts of brutality. In the next place, the men of the primitive periods naturally considered that a living creature must be much more valuable in the sight of God than any merely material object; and this consideration led them to immolate, to their divinities, first animals, and afterwards men, because, according to their false ideas, they thought that the value of a sacrifice was proportioned to the importance of the victim. In your earthly life, when you wish to offer a present to any one, you select a gift, the costliness of which is proportioned to the amount of attachment or consideration that you desire to testify to the person to whom you offer it. It was natural that men who were ignorant of the nature of the Deity should do the same."

— The sacrificing of animals, then, preceded that of human beings?

"Such was undoubtedly the case."

— According to this explanation, the custom of sacrificing human beings did not originate in mere cruelty?

"No; but in a false idea as to what would be acceptable to God. Look, for instance, at the story of Abraham. In later times men have still farther debased this false idea by immolating their enemies, the objects of their own personal animosity. But God has never exacted sacrifices of any kind; those of animals, no more than those of men. He could not be honoured by the useless destruction of His own creations."

670. Have human sacrifices, when offered with a pious intention, ever been pleasing to God?

"No, never; but God always weighs the intention which dictates any act. Men, being ignorant, may have believed that they were performing a laudable deed in immolating their fellow-beings; and, in such a case, God would accept their intention, but not their deed. The human race, in working out its own amelioration, naturally came to recognise its error, and to abominate the idea of sacrifices

that ought never to have entered into enlightened minds. I say
'enlightened,' because, however dense the veil of materiality in
which they were enveloped, their free-will sufficed, even then, to
give them a glimmering perception of their origin and their destiny,
and many among them already understood, by intuition, the
wickedness they were committing, but which they none the less
accomplished for the gratification of their passions."

*671. What should be thought of the wars styled "religious?"
The sentiment that induces a nation of fanatics to exterminate the
greatest possible number of those who do not share their belief,
with a view to rendering themselves acceptable to God, would seem
to proceed from the same source as that which formerly led them
to immolate their fellow-creatures as sacrifices.*

"Such wars are stirred up by evil spirits; and the men who wage
them place themselves in direct opposition to the will of God,
which is, that each man should love his brother as himself. Since
all religions, or rather all peoples, worship the same God, whatever
the name by which they call Him, why should one of them wage
a war of extermination against another, simply because its religion
is different, or has not yet reached the degree of enlightenment
arrived at by the aggressor? Not to believe the word of Him who
was sent by God and animated by His spirit is excusable on the
part of peoples who neither saw Him nor witnessed the acts performed by Him; and, at all events, how can you hope that they will
hearken to His message of peace, when you try to force it upon
them by fire and sword? It is true that they have to be enlightened, and that it is your duty to endeavour to teach them the
doctrine of Christ; but this must be done by persuasion and
gentleness; not by violence and bloodshed. The greater number
among you do not believe in the communication we have with
certain mortals; how could you expect that strangers should believe
your assertions in regard to this fact, if your acts belied the doctrine
you profess?"

*672. Was the offering of the fruits of the earth more acceptable
in the sight of God than the sacrificing of animals?*

"It must evidently be more agreeable to God to be worshipped
by the offering of the fruits of the earth, than by that of the blood
of victims. But I have already answered your question in telling
you that God's judgment is directed to the intention, and that the

outward fact is of little importance in His sight. A prayer, sent up from the depths of the heart, is a hundredfold more agreable to God than all the offerings you could possibly make to Him. I repeat it, the intention is everything; the fact, nothing."

673. Might not these offerings be rendered more agreeable to God by consecrating them to the relief of those who lack the necessaries of life, and, in that case, might not the sacrificing of animals, accomplished in view of a useful end, be as meritorious as it is the reverse when subserving no useful end, or profiting only to those who are in need of nothing? Would there not be something truly pious in consecrating to the poor the first-fruits of all that God grants to us upon the earth?

"God always blesses those who do good; to help the poor and afflicted is the best of all ways of honouring Him. I do not mean to say that God disapproves of the ceremonies you employ in praying to Him; but a good deal of the money thus spent might be more usefully employed. God loves simplicity in all things. The man who attaches more importance to externals than to the heart is a narrowminded spirit; how, then, could it be possible for God to regard a form as of any importance in comparison with the sentiment of which it is the expression?"

CHAPTER III

II. THE LAW OF LABOUR

1. NECESSITY OF LABOUR—2. LIMIT OF LABOUR. REST

Necessity of Labour.

674. Is the necessity of labour a law of nature?

"That labour is a law of nature, and is proved by the fact that it is a necessity, and that civilisation obliges man to perform a greater amount of labour, because it increases the sum of his needs and of his enjoyments."

675. Ought we to understand by "labour" only occupations of a material nature?

"No; the spirit labours like the body. Every sort of useful occupation is a labour."

676. Why is labour imposed upon mankind?

"It is a consequence of his corporeal nature. It is an expiation, and, at the same time, a means of developing his intelligence. Without labour man would remain in the infancy of intelligence. This is why he is made to owe his food, his safety, and his well-being entirely to his labour and activity. To him who is too weak in body for the rougher kinds of work, God gives intelligence to make up for it; but the action of the intelligence is also a labour."

677. Why does nature herself provide for all the wants of the animals?

"Everything in nature labours. The animals labour as really as you do, but their work, like their intelligence, is limited to the care of their own preservation; and this is why labour, among them, does not lead to progress, while, among men, it has a double aim, viz., the preservation of the body, and the development of thought, which is also a necessity for him, and which raises him continually to a higher level. When I say that the labour of the animals is limited to the care of their preservation, I mean that this is the aim which they propose to themselves in working. But they are also, unconsciously, and while providing only for their material needs, agents that second the views of the Creator; and their labour none the less concurs to the working out of the final end of nature, although you often fail to discover its immediate result."

678. In worlds more advanced than the earth, is man subjeted to the same necessity of labour?

"The nature of the labour is always relative to that of the wants it supplies; the less material are those wants, the less material is the labour. But you must not suppose that man, in those worlds, remains inactive and useless; idleness would be a torture instead of a benefit."

679. Is he who possesses a sufficiency of worldly goods for his subsistence enfranchised from the law of labour?

"From material labour perhaps, but not from the obligation of rendering himself useful according to his means, and of developing his own intelligence and that of others, which is also a labour. If the man, to whom God has apportioned a sufficiency of means for insuring his corporeal existence, be not constrained to win his bread by the sweat of his brow, the obligation of being useful to his fellow-creatures is all the greater in his case, because the portion appointed to him gives him a greater amount of leisure for doing good."

680. Are there not men who are incapable of working at anything whatever, and whose existence is entirely useless?

"God is just; He condemns only him who is voluntarily useless; for such an one lives upon the labour of others. He wills that each should make himself useful according to his faculties. (643.)

681. Does the law of nature impose upon children the obligation of labouring for their parents?

"Certainly it does, just as it imposes on parents the duty of labouring for their children. For this reason God has given a place in nature to the sentiment of filial and paternal affection, in order that the members of a family may be led, by their mutual affection, to aid each other reciprocally—a duty which is too often lost sight of in your present state of society."

Limit of Labour. Rest.

682. Rest being a necessity after labour, is it not a law of nature?

"Undoubtedly it is. Rest serves to restore the bodily powers, and is also necessary in order to give a little more freedom to the mind, enabling it to raise itself above matter."

683. What is the limit of labour?

"The limit of strength; but God leaves man at liberty to decide this point for himself."

684. What is to be thought of those who misuse their authority by imposing too heavy a labour on their inferiors?

"They commit one of the worst of crimes. Every man exercising authority is answerable for any excess of labour imposed by him on those who are under his orders, for he thereby transgresses the law of God." (273.)

685. Has man a right to repose in old age?

"Yes; he is only obliged to labour according to his strength."

— *But what resource is there for the old man who needs to work in order to support himself, and yet is unable to do so?*

"The strong should work for the weak; where family-help is not to be had, society should supply its place. Such is the law of charity."

To say that it is necessary for a man to work is not to make a complete statement of the subject; for it is also necessary that he who has to get his bread by labour should be able to find occupation, and this is far from being always the case. Whenever the suspension of labour becomes general, it assumes the proportions of a famine. Economic science seeks a remedy for this evil in the equilibrium of production and consumption; but this equilibrium, supposing it to be attainable, will always be subject to intermittences, and during these intervals the labourer must live. There is an element of the question which has not been sufficiently considered, viz., **education,** not merely the education of the intellect, not even that of the moral nature as given by books, but that which consists **in the formation of characters and habits; for education is the totality of the habits acquired.** When we consider how great a mass of individuals are thrown each day into the torrent of population, abandoned, without principles or curb, to the impulsions of their animal instincts, can we wonder at the disastrous consequences thence resulting? When the art of education shall be rightly understood and practised, each man will bring into the sphere of daily life **habits of order and forethought** for himself and for those dependent on him, and **of respect for what is worthy of being respected;** and these habits will enable him to traverse periods of difficulty with greater ease. Disorder and improvidence are social sores that can only be cured by **education rightly understood;** the generalisation of such education is the starting-point and essential element of social well-being, the only pledge of security **for all.**

CHAPTER IV

III. LAW OF REPRODUCTION

1. POPULATION OF THE GLOBE—2. SUCCESSION AND IMPROVEMENT OF RACES—3. OBSTACLES TO REPRODUCTION—4. MARRIAGE AND CELIBACY—5. POLYGAMY.

Population of the Globe.

686. Is the reproduction of living beings a law of nature?

"Evidently it is; without reproduction the corporeal world would perish."

687. If the population of the globe goes on increasing as it has hitherto done, will it, in course of time, become too numerous?

"No; the Divine overruling always provides for, and maintains, equilibrium. God permits nothing useless. Man sees but a corner of the panorama of the universe, and is therefore unable to perceive the harmony of its various departments."

Succession and Improvement of Races.

688. There are at this moment upon the earth races of men who are evidently and rapidly diminishing. Will they eventually disappear from it?

"Yes; but it is because others will have taken their place, as your place will some day be taken by others."

689. Are the men now upon the earth a new creation, or the improved descendants of the primitive human beings?

"They are the same spirits; *come back* to improve themselves with the aid of new bodies, but who are still very far from having reached perfection. Thus the present human race, which, by its increase, tends to invade the whole earth and to replace the races that are dying out, will have its period of decrease and disappearance. It will be replaced by other and more perfect races, that will descend from the present race, as the civilised men of the present day are descended from the rough-hewn savages of the primitive periods."

690. Regarded from a purely physical point of view, are the bodies of the present race of men a special creation, or have they proceeded from the bodies of the primitive races by reproduction?

"The origin of races is hidden in the night of time; but as they all belong to the great human family, whatever may have been the primitive root of each, they have been able to form alliances with one another, and thus to produce new types."

691. What, from a physical point of view, is the distinctive and dominant characteristic of primitive races?

"The development of brute·force at the expense of intellectual power. The contrary takes place at the present day; for man now acts rather through his intelligence than through his bodily strength, and yet he accomplishes a hundred-fold more than he formerly did, because he has learned to avail himself of the forces of nature, which the animals cannot do."

692. Is the improvement of the vegetable and animal races, through the applications of science, contrary to the law of nature? Would it be more conformable with that law to leave them to follow their normal course?

"It is the duty of all beings to concur, in every way, in helping forward the general progress; and man himself is employed by God as an instrument for the accomplishment of His ends. Perfection being the aim towards which everything in nature is tending, to help forward this process of improvement is to assist in working out the Divine intentions."

— But man, in his efforts to ameliorate the races of the lower reigns, is generally moved by self-interest, and has no other aim than the increase of his personal enjoyments; does not this diminish the merit of his action?

"What matters it that his merit should be null, provided the work of progress be accomplished? It is for him to render his labour meritorious by inspiring himself with a noble motive. Besides, in effecting these ameliorations, he develops his intelligence; and it is in this way that he derives the greatest benefit from his labour."

Obstacles To Reproduction.

693. Are the human laws and customs that have been established for the purpose of placing obstacles in the way of reproduction contrary to the laws of nature?

"Whatever hinders the operations of nature is contrary to the general law."

— *But there are many species of living beings, animal and vegetable, the unlimited reproduction of which would be hurtful to other species, and would soon be destructive of the human race. Is it wrong for man to arrest their reproduction?*

"God has given to man, over all the other living beings of his globe, a power which he ought to use for the general good, but not to abuse. He may regulate reproduction according to his needs; but he ought not to hinder it unnecessarily. The intelligent action of mankind is a counterpoise established by God for restoring the equilibrium of the forces of nature; and herein, again, man is distinguished from the animals, because he does this understandingly, while the animals, that also concur in maintaining this equilibrium, do so unconsciously, through the instinct of destruction which has been given to them, and which causes them, while providing for their own preservation only, to arrest the excessive development of the animal and vegetable species on which they feed, and which would otherwise become a source of danger."

694. *What is to be thought of usages intended to arrest reproduction in the interest of sensuality?*

"They prove the predominance of the body over the soul, and show how deeply man has plunged himself in matter."

Marriage and Celibacy

695. *Is marriage, that is to say, the permanent union of two beings, contrary to the law of nature?*

"It is a progress arrived at by the human race."

696. *What would be the effect, upon human society, of the abolition of mariage?*

"A return to the life of the beasts."

The free and fortuitous union of the sexes is the state of nature. Marriage is one of the first results of progress in the constitution of human society, because it establishes fraternal solidarity, being found among every people, though under different conditions. The abolition of marriage would therefore be a return to the infancy of the human race, and would place man even below certain animals that give him the example of constant unions.

697. *Is the absolute indissolubility of marriage to be found in the law of nature, or is it only an ordination of human law?*

"It is a human law, altogether contrary to the law of nature. But men may change their laws; those of nature are alone unchangeable."

698. Is voluntary celibacy meritorious in the sight of God?

"No; those who live single from selfish motives are displeasing to God, for they fail to perform their share of social duties."

699. Is not celibacy, on the part of some persons, a sacrifice made by them for the sake of devoting themselves more entirely to the service of humanity?

"That is a very different thing; I said 'from selfish motives.' Every sort of personal sacrifice is meritorious when it is made for a good end; and the greater the sacrifice, the greater the merit."

God cannot contradict Himself, nor regard as evil what He himself has made, and therefore He cannot regard the violation of His law as meritorious. But although celibacy, in itself, is not meritorious, it may become such when the renunciation of family-joys is a sacrifice accomplished in the interests of humanity. Every sacrifice of personal interests, when made for the good of others and without any reference to self, raises him who makes it above the level of his material condition.

Polygamy

700. Is polygamy or monogamy most in conformity with the law of nature?

"Polygamy is a human institution, the abolition of which marks an era of social progress. Marriage, according to the intentions of God, should be founded on the affection of the beings who enter into it. In polygamy there is no real affection; there is only sensuality."

701. Is the almost exact numerical equality existing between the sexes an indication of the proportions according to which they ought to be united?

"Yes; for every arrangement of nature has a specific purpose."

If polygamy were in accordance with the law of nature, it ought to be possible to establish it everywhere but it would be physically impossible to do so, owing to the numerical equality of the sexes.

Polygamy must therefore be regarded as a mere custom, adapted to the present state of certain peoples, and that will gradually disappear with the progress of their social improvement.

CHAPTER V

IV. THE LAW OF PRESERVATION

1. INSTINCT OF SELF-PRESERVATION—2. MEANS OF SELF-PRESERVATION—3. ENJOYMENT OF THE FRUITS OF THE EARTH—4. NECESSARIES AND SUPERFLUITIES —5. VOLUNTARY PRIVATIONS—MORTIFICATIONS.

The Instinct of Self-Preservation.

702. Is the instinct of self-preservation a law of nature?

"Undoubtedly so. It is given to all living creatures, whatever their degree of intelligence; in some it is purely mechanical, in others it is allied to reason."

703. To what end has God given the instinct of self-preservation to all living beings?

"They are all necessary to the working out of the providential plans; and therefore God has given them the desire to live. And besides, life is a necessary condition of the improvement of beings; they feel this instinctively, without understanding it."

Means of Self-Preservation.

704. Has God, while giving to man the desire to live, always furnished him with the means of doing so?

"Yes; and if man does not always find them, it is because he does not know how to avail himself of the resources around him. God could not implant in man the love of life, without giving him the means of living; and He has accordingly endowed the earth with a capacity of production sufficient to furnish all its inhabitants with the necessaries of life. It is only that which is necessary that is useful; that which is superfluous is never useful."

705. Why does not the earth always produce enough to provide mankind with the necessaries of life?

"It is because man ungratefully neglects that excellent nursing-mother! Moreover, he often accuses nature of what is the result of his own unskilfulness or want of forethought. The earth would always produce the necessaries of life, if men could content themselves therewith. If it does not suffice for all his wants, it is because men employ, in superfluities, what should be devoted to the supply of necessaries. Look at the Arab in the desert; he always finds enough to live upon, because he does not create for himself factitious needs; but when half the products of the earth are wasted in satisfying fanciful desires, ought.man to be astonished if he afterwards runs short, and has he any reason to complain if he finds himself unprovided for when a famine occurs? I repeat it; nature is not improvident, but man does not know how to regulate his use of her gifts."

706. *By the term 'fruits of the earth,' should we understand merely the products of the soil?*

"The soil is the original source of all other productions, which are, in reality, only a transformation of the products of the soil; for that reason, by 'fruits of the earth' are to be understood everything enjoyed by man in his corporeal life."

707. *There are always persons who lack the means of existence, even in the midst of abundance. Who is to blame for this?*

"In some cases, the selfishness which too often prevents men from being just to others; in other cases, and most often, themselves. Christ has said, 'Seek, and ye shall find;' but these words do not imply that you have only to cast your eyes on the ground in order to find all that you may desire, but rather that you must seek for what you want, and not indolently, but with ardour and perseverance, and without allowing yourselves to be discouraged by obstacles that are often only a means of putting your constancy, patience, and firmness to the proof." (534.)

If civilisation multiplies our needs, it also multiplies our resources and our means of existence. But it must be admitted that, in this respect, much still remains to be done ; for civilisation will only have accomplished its task when it shall no longer be possible for any human being to lack the necessaries of life, unless through his own fault. Unfortunately, too, many persons choose a path for which nature has not fitted them, and in which they necessarily fail of success. There is room in the sunshine for every one ; but on condition that each takes his own place, and not that of another. Nature cannot justly be held responsible for the results of defective social organisation, nor for those of personal selfishness and ambition.

There would, however, be blindness in denying the progress which has already been accomplished in this direction among the nations which are most advanced. Thanks to the efforts of philanthropy and of science for the amelioration of the material condition of mankind, and notwithstanding the constant increase of the population of the globe, the effects of insufficient production are considerably attenuated, so that the most unfavourable years are far less calamitous than formerly. Hygiene, unknown to our forefathers, yet so essential a condition of public and individual health, is the object of constant and enlightened solicitude ; asylums are provided for the unfortunate and the suffering: and every new discovery of science is made to contribute its quota to the general weal. Far as we still are from having attained to the perfection of social arrangements, what is already accomplished gives the measure of what may be done with the aid of perseverance, if men are reasonable enough to seek after solid and practical improvements, instead of wasting their energies on utopian projects that put them back instead of helping them forward.

708. *Are there not social positions in which the will is powerless to obtain the means of existence, and in which the privation of the barest necessaries of life is a consequence of the force of circumstances?*

"Yes; but such a position is a trial which, however severe, the party who is subjected to it knew, in the spirit-state, that he would have to undergo. His merit will result from his submission to the will of God, if his intelligence does not furnish him with the means of freeing himself from his troubles. If death supervenes, he should meet it without a murmur, remembering that the hour of his deliverance is approaching, and that *any yielding to despair at the last moment may cause him to lose the fruit of his previous resignation.*"

709. *In critical situations men have been reduced to devour their fellow-men, as the only means of saving themselves from starvation. Have they, in so doing, committed a crime? And if so, is their crime lessened by the fact that it has been committed under the excitement of the instinct of self-preservation?*

"I have already answered this question in saying that all the trials of life should be submitted to with courage and abnegation. In the cases you refer to there is both homicide and crime against nature; a double culpability that will receive double punishment."

710. *In worlds in which the corporeal organisation of living beings is of a purer nature than in the earth, do these need food?*

"Yes; but their food is in keeping with their nature. Their aliments would not be substantial enough for your gross stomachs; and, on the other hand, those beings could not digest your heavier food."

Enjoyments of the Fruits of the Earth.

711. *Have all men a right to the usufruct of the products of the earth?*

"That right is a consequence of the necessity of living. God cannot have imposed a duty without having given the means of discharging it."

712. Why has God attached an attraction to the enjoyment of material things?

"In order, first, to excite man to the accomplishment of his mission, and next, to try him by temptation."

— *What is the aim of this temptation?*

"To develop his reason, that it may preserve him from excesses."

If man had only been urged to the using of the things of the earthly life by a conviction of their utility, his indifference to them might have compromised the harmony of the universe. God has therefore given him the pleasurable attractions that solicit him to the accomplishing of the views of Providence. But God has also willed, through this attraction, to try man by temptations that incite him to abuses against which his reason should protect him.

713. Has nature marked out the proper limits of corporeal satisfactions?

"Yes, limits that coincide with your needs and your well-being. When you overstep them, you bring on satiety, and thus punish yourselves."

714. What is to be thought of the man who seeks to enhance corporeal enjoyments by inventing artificial excesses?

"Think of him as a poor wretch who is to be pitied rather than envied, for he is very near death."

— *Do you mean to physical death, or to moral death?*

"To both."

The man who, in pursuit of corporeal satisfactions, seeks an enhancement of those satisfactions in any kind of excess, places himself below the level of the brute, for the brute goes no farther than the satisfaction of a need. He abdicates the reason given to him by God for his guidance ; and the greater his excesses, the more dominion does he give to his animal nature over his spiritual nature. The maladies and infirmities, often occasioning death, that are the consequences of excess in the satisfaction of any corporeal attraction, are also punishments for thus transgressing the law of God.

Necessaries and Superfluities.

715. How can men know the limit of what is necessary?

"Wise men know it by intuition; others learn it through experience, and to their cost."

716. Has not nature traced out the limit of our needs in the requirements of our organisation?

"Yes, but man is insatiable. Nature has indicated the limits of his needs by his organisation; but his vices have deteriorated his constitution, and created for him wants that are not real needs."

717. What is to be thought of those who monopolise the productions of the earth, in order to procure for themselves superfluities, at the expense of others who lack the necessaries of life?

"They forget the law of God, and will have to answer for the privations they have caused others to endure."

There is no absolute boundary-line between the necessary and the superfluous. Civilisation has created necessities that do not exist for the savage ; and the spirits who have dictated the foregoing precepts do not mean to assert that civilised men should live like the savage. All things are relative ; and the function of reason is to determine the part to be allotted to each. Civilisation develops the moral sense, and, at the same time, the sentiment of charity, which leads men to give to each other mutual support. Those who live at the expense of other men's privations monopolise the benefits of civilisation for their own profit ; they have only the varnish of civilisation, as others have only the mask of religion.

Voluntary Privations.

718. Does the law of self-preservation make it our duty to provide for our bodily wants?

"Yes; without physical health and strength, labour is impossible."

719. Is it blamable in a man to seek after the comforts and enjoyments of corporeal life?

"The desire of corporeal well-being is natural to man. God only prohibits excess, because excess is inimical to preservation; He has not made it a crime to seek after enjoyment, if that enjoyment be not acquired at another's expense, and if it be not of a nature to weaken either your moral or your physical strength."

720. Are voluntary privations, in view of a voluntary expiation, meritorious in the sight of God?

"Do good to others, and you will thereby acquire more merit than is to be acquired by any self-imposed privations."

— *Is any voluntary privation meritorious?*

"Yes; the self-privation of useless indulgences, because it loosens man's hold on matter, and elevates his soul. What is meritorious is resistance to the temptation that solicits to excess or to indulgence in what is useless; it is the cutting down even of your necessaries, that you may have more to give to those who are in want. If your privations are only a vain pretence, they are a mere mockery."

721. At every period in the past, and among all peoples, there have been men who have lived a life of ascetic mortification; is such a life meritorious from any point of view?

"Ask yourselves *to whom such a life is useful*, and you will have the reply to your question. If such a life is only for him who leads it, and if it prevents him from doing good to others, it is only a form of selfishness, whatever the pretext with which it is coloured. True mortification, according to the dictates of Christian charity, is to impose privation and labour upon yourselves for the good of others."

722. *Is there any foundation in reason for the abstinence from certain aliments practised among various peoples?*

"Whatever man can eat without injury to his health is permitted to him. Legislators may have prohibited certain aliments for some useful end, and, in order to give greater weight to their prohibitions, have represented them as emanating from God."

723. *Is the use of animal food by man contrary to the law of nature?*

"With your physical constitution, flesh is useful for nourishing flesh; without this kind of sustenance man's strength declines. The law of preservation makes it a duty for man to keep up his health and strength, that he may fulfil the law of labour. He should therefore feed himself according to the requirements of his organisation."

724. *Is there any merit in abstinence from any particular kind of food, animal or other, when undergone as an expiation?*

"Yes, if undergone for the sake of others; but God cannot regard as meritorious any abstinence that does not impose a real privation, and that has not a serious and useful aim. This is why we say that those whose fasting is only apparent are hypocrites." (720.)

725. *What is to be thought of the mutilation of the bodies of men or of animals?*

"What is the use of asking such a question? Ask yourselves, once for all, whether a thing is or is not useful. What is useless cannot be pleasing to God, and what is hurtful is always displeasing to Him. Be very sure that God is only pleased with the sentiments that raise the soul towards Him. It is by practising His law, and not by violating it, that you can shake off your terrestrial matter."

726. *If the sufferings of this world elevate us through the manner in which we bear them, are we elevated by those which we voluntarily create for ourselves?*

"The only sufferings that can elevate you are those which come upon you naturally, because they are inflicted by God. Voluntary sufferings count for nothing when they are not useful to others. Do you suppose that those who shorten their lives by superhuman hardships, like the bonzes, fakirs, and fanatics of various sects, advance their progress thereby? Why do they not rather labour for the good of their fellow-creatures? Let them clothe the naked; let them comfort those who mourn; let them work for the infirm; let them impose privations upon themselves for the sake of the unfortunate and the needy; and their life will be useful, and pleasing to God. When your voluntary sufferings are undergone only for yourselves, they are mere selfishness; when you suffer for others, you obey the law of charity. Such are the precepts of Christ."

727. *If we ought not to create for ourselves voluntary sufferings that are of no use to others, ought we to endeavour to ward off from ourselves those which we foresee, or with which we are threatened?*

"The instinct of self-preservation has been given to all beings to guard them against dangers and sufferings. Flagellate your spirit, and not your body; mortify your pride; stifle the selfishness that eats into the heart like a devouring worm; and you will do more for your advancement than you could do by any amount of macerations out of keeping with the age in which you are living."

CHAPTER VI

V. THE LAW OF DESTRUCTION

1. NECESSARY DESTRUCTION AND UNJUSTIFIABLE
DESTRUCTION—2. DESTRUCTIVE CALAMITIES—3. WAR—
4. MURDER—5. CRUELTY—6. DUELLING—7. CAPITAL
PUNISHMENT.

Necessary Destruction and Unjustifiable Destruction.

728.   Is destruction a law of nature?

"It is necessary that all things should be destroyed that they may be re-born and regenerated; for what you call destruction is only a transformation, the aim of which is the renewing and amelioration of living beings."

— *The instinct of destruction would seem, then, to have been given to living beings for providential purposes?*

"God's creatures are the instruments which He uses for working out His ends. Living beings destroy each other for food; thus maintaining equilibrium in reproduction, which might otherwise become excessive, and also utilising the materials of their external envelopes. But it is only this envelope that is ever destroyed, and this envelope is only the accessory, and not the essential part, of a thinking being; the essential part is the intelligent principle which is indestructible, and which is elaborated in the course of the various metamorphoses that it undergoes."

729.   If destruction be necessary for the regeneration of beings, why does nature surround them with the means of self-preservation?

"In order that their destruction may not take place before the proper time. Destruction that occurs too soon retards the development of the intelligent principle. It is for this reason that God has given to each being the desire to live and to reproduce itself."

730.   Since death is to lead us to a better life, and since it delivers us from the ills of our present existence, and is therefore to be rather desired than dreaded, why has man the instinctive horror of death which causes him to shrink from it?

"We have said that man should seek to prolong his life in order to accomplish his task. To this end God has given him the instinct of self-preservation, and this instinct sustains him under all his trials; but for it, he would too often abandon himself to discouragement. The inner voice, which tells him to repel death, tells him also that he may yet do something more for his advancement. Every danger that threatens him is a warning that bids him make a profitable use of the respite granted to him by God; but he, ungrateful, gives thanks more often to his 'star' than to his Creator."

731. Why has nature placed agents of destruction side by side with the means of preservation?

"We have already told you that it is in order to maintain equilibrium, and to serve as a counterpoise. The malady and the remedy are placed side by side."

732. Is the need of destruction the same in all worlds?

"It is proportioned to the more or less material state of each world; it ceases altogether in worlds of higher physical and moral purity. In worlds more advanced than yours, the conditions of existence are altogether different."

733. Will the necessity of destruction always exist for the human race of this earth?

"The need of destruction diminishes in man in proportion as his spirit obtains ascendancy over matter. Consequently, you see that intellectual and moral development is always accompanied by a horror of destruction."

734. Has man, in his present state, an unlimited right of destruction in regard to animals?

"That right is limited to providing for his food and his safety; no abuse can be a matter of right."

735. What is to be thought of destruction that goes beyond the limits of needs and of safety; of hunting, for instance, when it has no useful aim, and is resorted to from no other motive than the pleasure of killing?

"It is a predominance of bestiality over the spiritual nature. All destruction that goes beyond the limits of your needs is a violation of the law of God. The animals only destroy according to the measure of their necessities; but man, who has free-will, destroys unnecessarily. He will be called to account for thus abusing the freedom accorded to him; for, in so doing, he yields to evil instincts from which he ought to free himself."

736. Are those peoples especially meritorious who, in regard to the taking of animal life, carry their scrupulousness to excess?

"Their sentiment in regard to this matter, though laudable in itself, being carried to excess, becomes an abuse in its turn; and its merit, moreover, is neutralised by abuses of many other sorts. That sentiment, on their part, is the result of superstitious fear, rather than of true gentleness."

Destructive Calamities.

737. What is the aim of God in visiting mankind with destructive calamities?

"To make men advance more quickly. Have we not told you that destruction is necessary to the moral regeneration of spirits, who accomplish a new step of their purification in each new existence? In order to appreciate any process correctly, you must see its results. You judge merely from your personal point of view, and you therefore regard those inflictions as calamities, because of the temporary injury they cause you; but such upsettings are often needed in order to make you reach more quickly a better order of things, and to effect, in a few years, what you would otherwise have taken centuries to accomplish." (744.)

738. Could not God employ other methods than destructive calamities for effecting the amelioration of mankind?

"Yes; and He employs them every day, for He has given to each of you the means of progressing through the knowledge of good and evil. It is because man profits so little by those other means, that it becomes necessary to chastise his pride, and to make him feel his weakness."

— *But the good man succumbs under the action of these scourges, as does the wicked; is this just?*

"During his earthly sojourn, man measures everything by the standard of his bodily life; but, after death, he judges differently, and feels that the life of the body, as we have often told you, is a very small matter. A century in your world is but *the length of a flash in eternity*, and therefore the sufferings of what you call days, months, or years, are of no importance; let this be a lesson for your future use. Spirits are the real world, pre-existent to, and surviving, everything else; they are the children of God, and the object of all His solicitude; and bodies are only the disguises under which they make their appearances in the corporeal world. In the great calamities that decimate the human race, the sufferers are like an army that, in the course of a campaign, sees its clothing tattered, worn out, or lost. The general is more anxious about his soldiers than about their coats."

— *But the victims of those scourges are none the less victims?*

"If you considered an earthly life as it is in itself, and how small a thing it is in comparison with the life of infinity, you would attach to it much less importance. Those victims will find, in another existence, an ample compensation for their sufferings, if they have borne them without murmuring."

Whether our death be the result of a public calamity or of an ordinary cause, we are none the less compelled to go when the hour of our departure has struck; the only difference is that, in the former case, a greater number go away at the same time.

If we could raise our thoughts sufficiently high to contemplate the human race as a whole, and to take in the whole of its destiny at a glance, the scourges that now seem so terrible would appear to us only as passing storms in the destiny of the globe.

739. *Are destructive calamities useful physically, notwithstanding the temporary evils occasioned by them?*

"Yes, they sometimes change the state of a country, but the good that results from them is often one that will be felt by future generations."

740. *May not such calamities also constitute for man a moral trial, compelling him to struggle with the hardest necessities of his lot?*

"They are always trials, and, as such, they furnish him with the opportunity of exercising his intelligence, of proving his patience and his resignation to the will of God, and of displaying his sentiments of abnegation, disinterestedness, and love for his neighbour, if he be not under the dominion of selfishness."

741. *Is it in man's power to avert the scourges that now afflict him?*

"Yes, a part of them; but not as is generally supposed. Many of those scourges are the consequence of his want of foresight; and, in proportion as he acquires knowledge and experience, he becomes able to avert them, that is to say, he can prevent their occurrence when he has ascertained their cause. But, among the ills that afflict humanity, there are some. of a general nature, which are imposed by the decrees of Providence, and the effect of which is felt, more or less sensibly, by each individual.

"To these, man can oppose nothing but his resignation to the divine will, though he can, and often does, aggravate their painfulness by his negligence."

In the class of destructive calamities. resulting from natural causes, and independently of the action of man, are to be placed pestilence, famine, inundations, and atmospheric influences fatal to the productions of the earth. But has not man already found. in the applications of science, in agricultural improvements, in the rotation of crops, in the study of hygienic conditions, the means of neutralising, or at least of attenuating, many of these disasters ? Are not many countries. at the present day, preserved from terrible plagues by which they were formerly ravaged? What, then, may not man accomplish for the advancement of his material well-being, when he shall have learned to make use of all the resources of his intelligence, and when he shall have added, to the care of his personal preservation, the large charity that interests itself in the well-being of the whole human race? (707.)

War.

742. What is the cause that impels man to war?

"The predominance of the animal nature over the spiritual nature, and the desire of satisfying his passions. In the barbaric state, the various peoples know no other right than that of the strongest; and their normal condition is, therefore, that of war. As men progress, war becomes less frequent, through their avoidance of the causes which lead to it; and when it becomes inevitable, they wage it more humanely."

743. Will wars ever cease on the earth?

"Yes; when men comprehend justice, and practise the law of God; all men will then be brothers."

744. What has been the aim of Providence in making war necessary?

"Freedom and progress."

— If war is destined to bring us freedom, how does it happen that its aim and upshot are so often the subjugation of the people attacked?

"Such subjugation is only momentary, and is permitted in order to *weary* the nations of servitude, and thus to urge them forward more rapidly."

745. What is to be thought of him who stirs up war for his own profit?

"Such an one is deeply guilty, and will have to undergo *many corporal existences* in order to expiate all the murders caused by him; for he will have to answer for every man who has been killed for the satisfaction of his ambition."

Murder.

746. Is murder a crime in the sight of God?

"Yes, a great crime; for he who takes the life of his fellow-man cuts short an expiation or a mission; hence the heinousness of his offence."

747. Are all murders equally heinous?

"We have said that God is just; He judges the intention rather than the deed."

748. Does God excuse murder in cases of self-defence?

"Only absolute necessity can excuse it; but if a man can only preserve his life by taking that of his aggressor, he ought to do so."

749. Is a man answerable for the murders he commits in war?

"Not when he is compelled to fight; but he is answerable for the cruelties he commits, and he will be rewarded for his humanity."

750. Is parricide or infanticide the greater crime in the sight of God?

"They are equally great; for all crime is crime."

751. How is it that the custom of infanticide prevails among peoples of considerable intellectual advancement, and is even recognised as allowable by their laws?

"Intellectual development is not always accompanied by moral rectitude. A spirit may advance in intelligence, and yet remain wicked; for he may have lived a long time without having improved morally, and gained knowledge, without acquiring moral purification."

Cruelty.

752. Is the sentiment of cruelty connected with the instinct of destruction?

"It is the instinct of destruction in its worst form, for, though destruction is sometimes necessary, cruelty never is; it is always the result of an evil nature."

753. How comes it that cruelty is the dominant characteristic of the primitive races?

"Among the primitive races, as you call them, matter has the ascendancy over spirit. They abandon themselves to the instincts of the brute; and as they care for nothing but the life of the body, they think only of their personal preservation, and this generally renders them cruel. And besides, peoples, whose development is still imperfect, are under the influence of spirits equally imperfect, with whom they are in sympathy, until the coming among them of some other people, more advanced than themselves, destroys or weakens that influence."

754. Is cruelty a result of the absence of the moral sense?

"Say that the moral sense is not developed, but do not say that it is absent; for its principle exists in every man, and is this sense which, in course of time, renders beings kind and humane. It exists, therefore, in the savage; but in him it is latent, as the principle of the perfume is in the bud, before it opens into the flowers."

All faculties exist in man in a rudimentary or latent state; they are developed according as circumstances are more or less favourable to them. The excessive development of some of them arrests or neutralises that of others. The undue excitement of the material instincts stifles, so to say, the moral sense; as the development of the moral sense gradually weakens the merely animal-faculties.

755. How is it that, in the midst of the most advanced civilisation, we sometimes find persons as cruel as the savages?

"Just as, on a tree laden with healthy fruit, you may find some that are withered. They may be said to be savages who have nothing of civilisation about them but the coat; they are wolves who have strayed into the midst of the sheep. Spirits of low degree, and very backward, may incarnate themselves among men of greater advancement, in the hope of advancing themselves; but, if the trial be too ardous, their primitive nature gets the upper hand."

756. Will the society of the good be one day purged of evil-doers?

"The human race is progressing. Those who are under the dominion of the instinct of evil, and who are out of place among good people, will gradually disappear, as the faulty grain is separated from the good when the wheat is threshed; but they will be born again under another corporeal envelope, and, as they acquire more experience, they will arrive at a clearer understanding of good and evil. You have an example of this in the plants and animals which man has discovered the art of improving, and in which he develops new qualities. It is only after several generations that the improvement becomes complete. This is a picture of the different existences of each human being."

Duelling.

757. Can duelling be considered as coming under the head of lawful self-defence?

"No; it is murder, and an absurdity worthy of barbarians. When civilisation is more advanced and *more moral,* men will see that duelling is as ridiculous as the combats which were formerly regarded as 'the judgment of God.' "

758. Can duelling be considered as murder on the part of him who, knowing his own weakness, is pretty sure of being killed?

"In such a case it is suicide."

— And when the chances are equal, is it murder or suicide?

"It is both."

In all cases, even in those in which the chances are equal, the duellist is guilty ; in the first place, because he makes a cool and deliberate attack on the life of his fellow-man, and in the second place, because he exposes his own life uselessly, and without benefit to any one.

759. What is the real nature of what is called the point of honour *in the matter of duels?*

"Pride and vanity; two sores of humanity."

— But are there not cases in which a man's honour is really at stake, and in which a refusal to fight would be an act of cowardice?

"That depends on customs and usages; each country and each century has a different way of regarding such matters. But when men are better, and more advanced morally, they will comprehend that the true point of honour is above the reach of earthly passions, and that it is neither by killing, nor by getting themselves killed, that they can obtain reparation for a wrong."

There is more real greatness and honour in confessing our wrongdoing if we are in the wrong, or in forgiving if we are in the right ; and, in all cases, in despising insults which cannot touch those who are superior to them.

Capital Punishment.

760. Will capital punishment disappear some day from human legislation?

"Capital punishment will, most assuredly, disappear in course of time; and its suppression will mark a progress on the part of the human race. When men become more enlightened, the penalty of death will be completely abolished throughout the earth; men will

no longer require to be judged by men. I speak of a time which
is still a long way ahead of you."

The social progress already made leaves much still to be desired, but
it would be unjust towards modern society not to recognise a certain amount
of progress in the restrictions which, among the most advanced nations,
have been successively applied to capital punishment, and to the crimes for
which it is inflicted. If we compare the safeguards with which the law,
among those nations, surrounds the accused, and the humanity with which
he is treated even when found guilty, with the methods of criminal proce-
dure that obtained at a period not very remote from the present, we cannot
fail to perceive that the human race is really moving forwards on a path
of progress.

761. *The law of preservation gives man the right to preserve his
own life; does he not make use of that same right when he cuts
off a dangerous member from the social body?*

"There are other means of preserving yourselves from a
dangerous individual than killing him; and besides, you ought to
open the door of repentance for the criminal, and not to close
it against him."

762. *If the penalty of death may be banished from civilised
society, was it not a necessity in times of less advancement?*

"Necessity is not the right word. Man always thinks that a
thing is necessary when he cannot manage to find anything better.
In proportion as he becomes enlightened, he understands more
clearly what is just or unjust, and repudiates the excesses committed, in times of ignorance, in the name of justice."

763. *Is the restriction of the number of the cases in which
capital punishment is inflicted an indication of progress in civilisation?*

"Can you doubt its being so? Does not your mind revolt on
reading the recital of the human butcheries that were formerly
perpetrated in the name of justice, and often in honour of the
divinity; of the tortures inflicted on the condemned, and even
on the accused, in order to wring from him, through the excess
of his sufferings, the confession of a crime which, very often, he
had not committed? Well, if you had lived in those times, you
would have thought all this very natural; and, had you been a
judge, you would probably have done the same yourself. It is
thus that what seemed to be right at one period seems barbarous
at another. The divine laws alone are eternal; human laws change
as progress advances; and they will change again and again, until
they have been brought into harmony with the laws of God."

764. Jesus said, "He that taketh the sword shall perish by the sword." Are not these words the consecration of the principle of retaliation? and is not the penalty of death, inflicted on a murderer, an application of this principle?

"Take care! You have mistaken the meaning of these words, *as of many others.* The only righteous retaliation is the justice of God; because it is applied by Him. You are all, at every moment, undergoing this retaliation, for you are punished in that wherein you have sinned, in this life *or in another one.* He who has caused his fellow-men to suffer will be placed in a situation in which he himself will suffer what he caused them to endure. This is the true meaning of the words of Jesus; for has He not also said to you, 'Forgive your enemies,' and has He not taught you to pray that God may forgive you your trespasses as you forgive those who have trespassed against you, that is to say, *exactly in proportion* as you have forgiven? Try to take in the full meaning of those words."

765. What is to be thought of the infliction of the penalty of death in the name of God?

"It is a usurpation of God's place in the administration of justice. Those who act thus show how far they are from comprehending God, and how much they still have to expiate. Capital punishment is a crime when applied in the name of God, and those who inflict it will have to answer for it as for so many murders."

CHAPTER VII

VI. SOCIAL LAW

1. NECESSITY OF SOCIAL LIFE—2. LIFE OF ISOLATION. VOW OF SILENCE—3. FAMILY-TIES.

Necessity of Social Life.

766. Is social life founded in nature?

"Certainly; God has made man for living in society. It is not without a purpose that God has given to man the faculty of speech and the other faculties necessary to the life of relation."

767. Is absolute isolation contrary to the law of nature?

"Yes, since man instinctively seeks society, and since all men are intended to help forward the work of progress by aiding one another."

768. Does man, in seeking society, only yield to a personal feeling, or is there, in this feeling, a wider providential end?

"Man must progress; he cannot do so alone, because, as he does not possess all faculties, he needs the contact of other men. In isolation he becomes brutified and etiolated."

No man possesses the complete range of faculties. Through social union men complete one another, and thus mutually secure their wellbeing and progress. It is because they need each other's help that they have been formed for living in society, and not in isolation.

Life of Isolation.

769. We can understand that the taste for social life, as a general principle, should be founded in nature, as are all other tastes; but why should a taste for absolute isolation be regarded as blameable, if a man finds satisfaction in it?

"Such satisfaction can only be a selfish one. There are also men who find satisfaction in getting drunk; do you approve of them? A mode of life, by the adoption of which you condemn yourselves not to be useful to any one, cannot be pleasing to God."

770. What is to be thought of those who live in absolute seclusion in order to escape the pernicious contact of the world?

"The life of such persons is doubly selfish. In avoiding one evil, they fall into another, since they forget the law of love and charity."

— *But if such seclusion is undergone as an expiation, through the imposing on one's self of a painful privation, is it not meritorious?*

"The best of all expiations is to do a greater amount of good than you have done of evil."

771. *What is to be thought of those who renounce the world in order to devote themselves to the relief of the unfortunate?*

"They raise themselves by their voluntary abasement. They have the double merit of placing themselves above material enjoyments, and of doing good by fulfilling the law of labour."

— *And those who seek in retirement the tranquillity required for certain kinds of labour?*

"Those who live in retirement from such a motive are not selfish; they do not separate themselves from society, since their labours are for the general good."

772. *What is to be thought of the vow of silence prescribed by certain sects from the very earliest times?*

"You should rather ask yourselves whether speech is in nature, and why God has given it? God condemns the abuse, but not the use, of the faculties He has given. Silence, however, is useful; for, in silence you have fuller possession of yourself; your spirit is freer, and can then enter into more intimate communication with us; but a vow of silence is an absurdity. Those who regard the undergoing of such voluntary privations as acts of virtue are prompted, undoubtedly, by a good intention in submitting to them; but they make a mistake in so doing, because they do not sufficiently understand the true laws of God."

The vow of silence, like the vow of isolation, deprives man of the social relations which alone can furnish him with the opportunities of doing good, and of fulfilling the law of progress.

Family — Ties.

773. *Why is it that, among the animals, parents and children forget each other, when the latter no longer need the care of the former?*

"The life of the animals is material life, but not moral life. The tenderness of the dam for her young is prompted by the instinct of preservation in regard to the beings born of her. When these beings are able to take care of themselves, her task is done; nature asks no more of her, and she therefore abandons them in order to busy herself with those that come afterwards."

774. Some persons have inferred, from the abandonment of the young of animals by their parents, that the ties of family, among mankind, are merely a result of social customs, and not a law of nature; what is to be thought of this inference?

"Man has another destiny than of the animals; why, then, should you always be trying to assimilate him to them? There is, in man, something more than physical wants; there is the necessity of progressing. Social ties are necessary to progress; and social ties are drawn closer by family-ties. For this reason, family-ties are a law of nature. God has willed that men should learn, through them, to love one another as brothers." (205.)

775. What would be the effect upon society of the relaxation of family-ties?

"A relapse into selfishness."

CHAPTER VIII

VII. THE LAW OF PROGRESS

1. STATE OF NATURE—2. MARCH OF PROGRESS—3. DE-
GENERATE PEOPLES—4. CIVILISATION—5. PROGRESS OF
HUMAN LEGISLATION—6. INFLUENCE OF SPIRITISM
UPON PROGRESS.

State of Nature.

776. Are the state of nature and the law of nature the same thing?

"No; the state of nature is the primitive state. Civilisation is incompatible with the state of nature, while the law of nature contributes to the progress of the human race."

The "state of nature" is the infancy of the human race, and the starting point of its intellectual and moral development. Man, being perfectible, and containing in himself the germ of his amelioration, is no more destined to live for ever in the state of nature, than he is destined to live for ever in the state of infancy; the state of nature is transitory, and man outgrows it through progress and civilisation. The "law of nature," on the contrary, rules the human race throughout its entire career; and men improve in proportion as they comprehend this law more clearly, and conform their action more closely to its requirements.

777. Man, in the state of nature, having fewer wants, escapes many of the tribulations he creates for himself in a state of greater advancement. What is to be thought of the opinion of those who regard the former state as being that of the most perfect felicity obtainable upon the earth?

"Such felicity is that of the brute; but there are persons who understand no other. It is being happy after the fashion of the brutes. Children, too, are happier than grown-up people."

778. Could mankind retrograde towards the state of nature?

"No; mankind must progress unceasingly, and cannot return to the state of infancy. If men have to progress, it is because God so wills it; to suppose that they could retrograde towards the primitive condition would be to deny the law of progress."

March of Progress.

*779.   Does man contain in himself the force that impels him
onward in the path of progress, or is his progress only the product
of instruction?*

"Man is developed of himself, naturally.   But all men do not
progress at the same rate, nor in the same manner; and it is thus
that most advances are made to help forward the others, through
social contact."

780.   Does moral progress always follow intellectual progress?

"It is a consequence of the latter, but does not always follow
it *immediately*."   (192-365.)

— *How can intellectual progress lead to moral progress?*

"By making man comprehend good and evil; he can then choose
between them.   The development of free-will follows the development of the intelligence and increases the responsability of human
action."

— *How comes it, then, that the most enlightened nations are
often the most perverted?*

"Complete and integral progress is the aim of existence; but
nations, like individuals, only reach it step by step.   Until the
moral sense is developed in them, they may even employ their
intelligence in doing evil.   Moral sense and intellect are two forces
which only arrive at equilibrium in the long run."   (365-751.)

781.   Has man the power of arresting the march of progress?

"No; but he has sometimes that of hindering it."

— *What is to be thought of the men who attempt to arrest the
march of progress, and to make the human race go backwards?*

"They are wretched weaklings whom God will chastise; they
will be overthrown by the torrent they have tried to arrest."

Progress being a condition of human nature, it is not in the power of any
one to prevent it.   It is **a living force** that bad laws may hamper, but not
stifle.   When these laws become incompatible with progress, progress **breaks**
them down with all those who attempt to hold them up ; and it will continue
to do so until man has brought his laws into harmony with the divine justice
which wills the good of all, and the abolition of all laws that are made
for the strong, and against the weak.

*782.   Are there not men who honestly obstruct progress while
believing themselves to be helping it forward, because, judging the
matter from their own point of view, they often regard as
"progress" what is not really such?*

"Yes; there are persons who push their little pebbles under the
great wheel; but they will not keep it from going on."

783. Does the improvement of the human race always proceed by slow progression?

"There is the regular slow progress that inevitably results from the force of things; but, when a people does not advance quickly enough, God also prepares for it, from time to time, a physical or moral shock that hastens its transformation."

Man cannot remain perpetually in ignorance, because he must reach the goal marked out for him by Providence; he is gradually enlightened by the force of things. Moral revolutions, like social revolutions, are prepared, little by little, in the ideas of a people; they go on germinating for centuries, and at length suddenly burst forth, overthrowing the crumbling edifice of the past, which is no longer in harmony with the new wants and new aspirations of the day.

Man often perceives, in these public commotions, only the momentary disorder and confusion that affect him in his material interests; but he who raises his thoughts above his own personality admires the providential working which brings good out of evil. Such commotions are the tempest and the storm that purify the atmosphere after having disturbed it.

784. Man's perversity is very great; does he not seem to be going back instead of advancing, at least, as regards morality?

"You are mistaken. Look at the human race as a whole, and you will see that it is advancing; for it has arrived at a clearer perception of what is evil, and every day witnesses the reform of some abuse. The excess of evil is required to show you the necessity of good and of reforms."

785. What is the greatest obstacle to progress?

"Pride and selfishness. I refer to moral progress; for intellectual progress is always going on, and would even seem, at the first glance, to give redoubled activity to those vices, by developing ambition and the love of riches, which, however, in their turn, stimulate man to the researches that enlighten his mind, for it is thus that all things are linked together, in the moral world as in the physical world, and that good is brought even out of evil; but this state of things will only last for a time, and will change, as men become aware of that, beyond the circle of terrestrial enjoyments, there is a happiness infinitely greater and infinitely more lasting." (See *Selfishness*, chap. xii.)

There are two kinds of progress, that mutually aid one another, and yet do not proceed side by side—intellectual progress, and moral progress. Among civilised peoples the first is receiving, at the present day, abundant encouragement; and it has accordingly reached a degree of advancement unknown to past ages. The second is very far from having reached the same point; although, if we compare the social usages of periods separated by a few centuries, we are compelled to admit that progress has also been made in this direction. Why then should the ascensional movement stop short in the region of morality any more than of intelligence? Why should there not be as great a difference between the morality of the nineteenth and the twenty-fourth centuries as between that of the fourteenth and the nineteenth? To doubt of the continuity of moral progress would be to assume either that the human race reached the summit of perfection, which would be absurd, or that it is not morally perfectable, which is disproved by experience.

Degenerate Peoples.

786. History shows us many peoples who, after having been subjected to shocks that have overthrown their nationality, have relapsed into barbarism. What progress has there been made in such cases?

"When your house threatens to fall about your ears, you pull it down, in order to build another, stronger and more commodious; but, until the latter is built, there is trouble and confusion in your dwelling.

"Comprehend this also: you are poor and live in a hovel; you become rich, and quit the hovel to live in a palace. Then comes a poor devil, such as you formerly were, and takes possession of the hovel you have quitted; and he is a gainer by the move, for he was previously altogether without shelter. Learn from this that the spirits now incarnated in the people that you call 'degenerate' are not those who composed that people in the time of its splendour; those spirits, being of advanced degree, have gone to reside in nobler habitations, and have progressed, while others less advanced have taken their vacated places, which they too will vacate in their turn."

787. Are there not races that, by their nature, are incapable of progress?

"Yes, but they are day by day becoming annihilated *corporeally*."

— *What will be the future fate of the souls that animate those races?*

"They, like all others, will arrive at perfection by passing through other existences. God deprives no one of the general heritage."

— *The most civilised men may, then, have been savages and cannibals?*

"You, yourself, have been such, more than once, before becoming what you now are."

788. The various peoples are collective individualities, that pass, like individuals, through infancy, manhood, and decrepitude. Does not this truth, attested by history, seem to imply that the most advanced peoples of this century will have their decline and their end, like those of antiquity?

"Those peoples that only live the life of the body, those whose greatness is founded only upon physical force and territorial extension, are born, grow, and die, because the strength of a people becomes exhausted like that of a man; those whose selfish laws are opposed to the progress of enlightenment and of charity die, because light kills darkness, and charity kills selfishness. But there is for nations, as for individuals, the life of the soul; and those whose laws are in harmony with the eternal laws of the Creator will continue to live, and will be the guiding-torch of the other nations."

789. *Will progress ultimately unite all the peoples of the earth into a single nation?*

"No, not into a single nation; that is impossible, because the diversities of climate give rise to diversities of habits and of needs that constitute diverse nationalities, each of which will always need laws appropriate to is special habits and needs. But charity knows nothing of latitudes. and makes no distinction between the various shades of human colour; and when the law of God shall be everywhere the basis of human law, the law of charity will be practised between nation and nation as between man and man, and all will then live in peace and happiness, because no one will attempt to wrong his neighbour, or to live at his expense."

The human race progresses through the progress of individuals, who gradually become enlightened and improved, and who, when they constitute a majority, obtain the upper hand, and draw the rest forward. Men of genius arise from time to time and give an impulse to the work of advancement ; and men having authority, instruments of God, effect in the course of a few years what the race, left to itself, would have taken several centuries to accomplish.

The progress of nations renders still more evident the justice of reincarnation. Through the efforts of its best men, a nation is made to advance intellectually and morally ; and the nation thus advanced is happier both in this world and in the next. But during its slow passage through successive centuries, thousands of its people have died every day. What will be the fate of those who have thus fallen on the way? Does their relative inferiority deprive them of the happiness reserved for those who came later? Or will their happiness be always proportioned to that inferiority? The divine justice could not permit so palpable an injustice. Through the plurality of existences, the same degree of happiness is obtainable by all, for no one is excluded from the heritage of progress. Those who have lived in a period of barbarism, come back in a period of civilisation among the same people or among another one ; and all are thus enabled to profit by the ascensional movement of the various nations of the earth, from the benefits of which movement they are excluded by the theory which assumes that there is only a single life for each individual.

Another difficulty presented by the theory referred to may be conveniently examined in this place. According to that theory, the soul is created at the same time as the body ; so that, as some men are more advanced than others, it follows that God creates for some men souls more advanced than the souls He creates for other men. But why this favouritism? How can one man, who has lived no longer than another man, often not so long, have merited to be thus endowed with a soul of a quality superior to that of the soul which has been given to that other man?

But the theory of the unity of existence presents a still graver difficulty. A nation, in the course of a thousand years, passes from barbarism to civilisation. If all men lived a thousand years, we could understand that, in this period, they would have the time to progress ; but many die every day, at all ages, and the people of the earth are incessantly renewed, so that every day we see them appear and disappear. Thus, at the end of a thousand years, no trace remains in any country of those who were living in it a thousand years before. The nation, from the state of barbarism in which it was, has become civilised—**but what is it that has thus progressed?** Is it the people who were formerly barbarian? But they died long ago. Is it the newcomers? But if the soul is created at the same time with the body, it follows that their souls were not in existence during the period of barbarism ; and we should therefore be compelled to admit that **the efforts made to civilise a people have the power, not to work out the improvement of souls that are created imperfect, but to make God create souls of a better quality than those which He created a thousand years before.**

Let us compare this theory of progress with the one now given by spirits. The souls that come into a nation in its period of civilisation have had their infancy, like all the others, but they have **lived already,** and have brought with them the advancement resulting from progress previously made ; they come into it, attracted by a state of things with which they are in sympathy, and which is suited to their present degree of advancement, so that the effect of the efforts to civilise a people is not to cause the future creation of souls of a better quality, but to attract to that people souls that have already progressed, whether they have already lived among that people, or whether they have lived elsewhere. And the progress accomplished by each people, when thus explained, furnishes also the key to the progress of the human race in its entirety, by showing that when all the peoples of the earth shall have reached the same level of moral advancement, the earth will be the resort of good spirits only, who will live together in fraternal union, and all the bad spirits who now infest it, finding themselves out of place among the others, and repelled by them, will go away, and will seek in lower worlds the surroundings that suit them, until they have rendered themselves worthy of coming back into our transformed and happier world. The theory commonly received leads also to this other consequence, viz., that the labour of social amelioration is profitable only to present and future generations ; its result is null for the generations of the past, who made the mistake of coming into the world too soon, and who have to get on as they can, weighted as they are through the faults of their barbarian epoch. According to the doctrine now set forth by spirits, the progress accomplished by later generations is equally beneficial to the generations that preceded them, and who, re-living upon the earth under improved conditions, are thus enabled to improve themselves in the focus of civilisation. (222.)

Civilisation.

790. Is civilisation a progress, or, according to some philosophers, a decadence, of the human race?

"A progress, but incomplete. Mankind does not pass suddenly from infancy to the age of reason."

— Is it reasonable to condemn civilisation?

"You should condemn those who misuse it, rather than condemn the work of God."

791. Will civilisation be eventually purified, so that the evils caused by it will disappear?

"Yes, when man's moral nature shall be as fully developed as his intelligence. The fruit cannot come before the flower."

792. *Why does not civilisation produce at once all the good it is capable of producing?*

"Because men are not as yet either ready or disposed to obtain that good."

— *May it not be also because in creating new wants it excites new passions?*

"Yes, and because all the faculties of a spirit do not progress together; everything takes time. You cannot expect perfect fruit from a civilisation that is still incomplete." (751-780.)

793. *By what signs shall we know when a civilisation has reached its apogee?*

"You will know it by its moral development. You believe yourselves to be considerably advanced, because you have made great discoveries and wonderful inventions, because you are better lodged and better clothed than the savages; but you will only have the right to call yourselves 'civilised' when you have banished from your society the vices that dishonour it, and when you live among yourselves like brothers, practising Christian charity. Until then, you are merely *enlightened nations*, having traversed only the first phase of civilisation."

Civilisation has its degrees like everything else. An incomplete civilisation is a state of transition which engenders special evils unknown to the primitive state; but it none the less constitutes a natural and necessary progress, which brings with it the remedy for the evils it occasions. In proportion as civilisation becomes perfected, it puts an end to the ills it has engendered, and these ills disappear altogether with the advance of moral progress.

Of two nations which have reached the summit of the social scale, that one may be called the most advanced in which is found the smallest amount of selfishness, cupidity, and pride; in which the habits are more moral and intellectual than material; in which intelligence can develop itself most freely; in which there is the greatest amount of kindness, good faith, and reciprocal benevolence and generosity; in which the prejudices of caste and of birth are the least rooted, for those prejudices are incompatible with the true love of the neighbour; in which tre laws sanction no privilege, and are the same for the lowest as for the highest; in which justice is administered with the least amount of partiality; in which the weak always finds support against the strong; in which human life, beliefs, and opinions are most respected; in which there is the smallest number of the poor and the unhappy; and, finally, in which every man who is willing to work is always sure of the necessaries of life.

Progress of Human Legislation.

794. *Would the laws of nature be sufficient for the regulation of human society, without the help of human laws?*

"If the laws of nature were properly understood, and if men were willing to practise them, they would be sufficient. But society has its exigencies, and requires the co-operation of special laws."

795. *What is the cause of the instability of human laws?*

"In times of barbarism the laws were made by the strongest, who framed them to their own advantage. It has therefore become necessary to modify them, as men have acquired a clearer comprehension of justice. Human laws will become more stable in proportion as they approach the standard of true justice; that is to say, in proportion as they are made for all, and become identified with natural law."

Civilisation has created for man new wants, and these wants are relative to the social state he has made for himself. He has found it necessary to regulate by human laws the rights and duties appertaining to this state; but, influenced by his passions, he has often created rights and duties that are merely imaginary, that are contrary to natural law, and that every nation effaces from its code in proportion as it progresses. Natural law is immutable and the same for all; human law is variable and progressive; it alone could consecrate, in the infancy of human societies, the right of the strongest.

796. *Is not the severity of penal legislation a necessity in the present state of society?*

"A depraved state of society requires severe laws, but your laws, unhappily, aim rather at punishing wrong doing when done, than at drying-up the fountain-head of wrong doing. It is only education that can reform mankind; when that is done, you will no longer require laws of the same severity."

797. *How can the reform of human laws be brought about?*

"It will be brought about by the force of things, and by the influence of the men of greater advancement who lead the world onward in the path of progress. It has already reformed many abuses, and it will reform many more. Wait!"

Influence of Spiritism on Progress.

798. *Will Spiritism become the general belief, or will its acceptance remain confined to the few?*

"It will certainly become the general belief, and will mark a new era in the history of the human race, because it belongs to the natural order of things, and because the time has come for it to be ranked among the branches of human knowledge. It will nevertheless have to withstand a good many violent attacks—attacks that will be prompted rather by interest than by conviction, for you must not lose sight of the fact that there are persons whose interest is to combat this belief, some from self-conceit, others from wordly considerations; but its opponents, finding themselves in a decreasing minority, will at length be obliged to rally to the general opinion, on pain of rendering themselves ridiculous."

Ideas are only transformed in the long run, never suddenly. Erroneous ideas become weakened in the course of successive generations, and finish by disappearing, little by little, with those who professed them, and who are replaced by other individuals imbued with new ideas, as is the case in regard to political principles. Look at paganism ; there is certainly no one, in our day, who professes the religious ideas of pagan times ; and yet, for several centuries after the advent of Christianity, they left traces that could only be effaced by the complete renovation of the races who held them. It will be the same with Spiritism; it will make considerable progress, but there will remain, during two or three generations, a leaven of incredulity that only time will be able to destroy. Nevertheless, its progress will be more rapid than that of Christianity, because it is Christianity itself that opens the road for it, and furnishes its basis and support. Christianity had to destroy; Spiritism has only to build up.

799. *In what way can Spiritism contribute to progress?*

"By destroying materialism, which is one of the sores of society, and thus making men understand where their true interest lies. The future life being no longer veiled by doubt, men will understand more clearly that they can insure the happiness of their future by their action in the present life. By destroying the prejudices of sects, castes, and colours, it teaches men the large solidarity that will, one day, unite them as brothers."

800. *Is it not to be feared that Spiritism may fail to triumph over the carelessness of men and their attachment to material things?*

"To suppose that any cause could transform mankind as by enchantment would show a very superficial knowledge of human nature. Ideas are modified little by little, according to the differences of individual character, and several generations are needed for the complete effacing of old habits. The transformation of mankind can therefore only be effected in the course of time, gradually, and by the contagion of example. With each new generation, a part of the veil is melted away; Spiritism is come to dissipate it entirely. But, meantime, if it should do no more than cure a man of a single defect, it would have led him to take a step forward, and would thus have done him great good, for the taking of this first step will render all his subsequent steps easier."

801. *Why have not spirits taught, from the earliest times, what they are teaching at the present day?*

"You do not teach to children what you teach to adults, and you do not give to a new-born babe the food which he could not digest; there is a time for all things. Spirits have taught many things that men have not understood or have perverted, but that they are now capable of understanding aright. Through their teaching in the past, however incomplete, they have prepared the ground to receive the seed which is now about to fructify."

802. Since Spiritism is to mark a progress on the part of the human race, why do not spirits hasten this progress by manifestations so general and so patent as to carry conviction to the most incredulous?

"You are always wanting miracles; but God sows miracles by handfuls under your feet, and yet you still have men who deny their existence. Did Christ Himself convince His contemporaries by the prodigies He accomplished? Do you not see men, at this day, denying the most evident of facts, though occurring under their very eyes? Have you not among you some who say that they would not believe, even though they saw? No; it is not by prodigies that God wills to bring men back to the truth; He wills, in His goodness, to leave to them the merit of convincing themselves through the exercise of their reason."

CHAPTER IX

VIII. THE LAW OF EQUALITY

Natural Equality

803. Are all men equal in the sight of God?

"Yes, all tend towards the same goal; and God has made His laws for the equal good of all. You often say, 'The sun shines for all;' and, in saying this, you enunciate a truth much broader, and of more general application, than you think."

All men are subjected to the action of the same natural laws. All are born in the same state of weakness, and are subject to the same sufferings; and the body of the rich is destroyed like that of the poor. God has not given to any man any natural superiority in regard either to birth or to death; all are equal in His sight.

Inequality of Aptitudes.

804. Why has God not given the same aptitudes to all men?

"All spirits have been created equal by God; but some of them have lived more, and others less, and have consequently acquired more or less development in their past existences. The difference between them lies in their various degrees of experience, and in the training of their will, which constitutes their freedom, and in virtue of which some improve themselves more rapidly; hence the diversity of aptitudes that you see around you. This medley of aptitudes is necessary, in order that every man may concur in working out the designs of Providence, within the limits of the development of his physical and intellectual strength. What one cannot do, another does; and thus each contributes his share of usefulness to the general work. Besides, *all the worlds of the universe being united by solidarity,* it is necessary that the inhabitants of the higher worlds, most of which were created before yours, should come and dwell in it, in order to set you an example."

805. Does a spirit, in passing from a higher world to a lower one, preserve, in their integrity, the faculties he had previously acquired?

"Yes; we have already told you that a spirit who has progressed cannot again fall back. He may choose, in his spirit-state, a corporeal envelope more benumbing, or a position more precarious, than those he quits; but all this is so combined as to teach him some new lesson, and thus to aid his future progress."

The diversity of human aptitudes is thus seen to be the result, not of any diversity in the creation of men, but of the various degrees of advancement attained to by the spirits who are incarnated in them. God, then, has not created the inequality of human faculties, but He has permitted spirits of different degrees of development to be thus brought into contact with each other, in order that the more forward may aid the more backward, and also in order that all men, having need of one another's help, may arrive at the practical comprehension of the law of charity that is destined to unite them.

Social Inequalities.

806. Is the inequality of social conditions a law of nature?
"No; it is the work of man, not of God."
— Will this inequality eventually disappear?
"Nothing is eternal but the laws of God. Do you not see that it is being effaced, little by little, every day? Your present inequalities will disappear with the disappearance of pride and selfishness; the only inequality that will remain is that of desert. A day will come when the members of the great family of God will no longer regard themselves as being of blood more or less pure; they will know that it is only the spirit that is more or less pure, and that this does not depend on social position."

807. What is to be thought of those who abuse the superiority of their social position by oppressing the weak to their own profit?
"They deserve to be anathematized! Sad will be their fate; for they will be oppressed in their turn, and they will be *re-born* into an existence in which they will endure all that they have caused to be endured." (684.)

Inequality of Riches.

808. Is not the inequality of riches a result of the inequality of faculties, which gives to some persons more means of acquiring than are possessed by others?

"Yes, and no. And knavery and robbery? What do you say of them?"

— But hereditary riches are not the fruit of evil passions?

"How do you know that? Go back to their source, and you will see whether it is always pure. How do you know whether they were not, in the beginning, the fruit of a spoliation or an injustice? But, without speaking of their origin, which may have been bad, do you think that the hankering after wealth, even when most honestly acquired, the secret longings to possess it more quickly, are laudable sentiments? These are what God judges; and His judgment is often more severe than that of men."

809. If a fortune has been ill-gotten in the beginning, are those who subsequently inherit it responsible for this?

"Most certainly they are not responsible for the wrong that may have been done by others, and of which they may be altogether ignorant; but you must understand that a fortune is often sent to such and such an individual for the sole purpose of giving him the opportunity of repairing an injustice. Happy for him if he comprehends this! If he does it in the name of him who committed the injustice, the reparation will be counted to both of them; for it is often the latter who has endeavoured to bring it about."

810. We may, without infringing legality, dispose of property more or less equitably. Are we held responsible, after death, for the disposition we have made of it?

"Every seed bears its fruit; the fruit of good deeds is sweet that of others is always bitter; always—remember that."

811. Is an absolute equality of riches possible? and has it ever existed?

"No, it is not possible. The diverstiy of faculties and characters is opposed to it."

— There are men, nevertheless, who believe it to be the remedy for all the ills of society. What do you think of them?

"They are framers of systems, or moved by ambition and jealousy; they do not understand that the equality they dream of would be speedily broken up by the force of things. Combat selfishness, for that is your social pest; and do not run after chimeras."

812. If equality of riches be not possible, is it the same in regard to well-being?

"No; but well-being is relative, and every one might enjoy it if men had arrived at a good understanding among themselves. For true well-being consists in employing one's time according to one's bent, and not in work for which one has no liking; and as each has different aptitudes, no useful work would be left undone. Equilibrium exists in everything; it is man who disturbs it."

— *Is it possible to arrive at this mutual understanding?*

"Men will arrive at it when they practise the law of justice."

813. *There are men who fall into destitution and misery through their own fault; surely society is not responsible in such cases?*

"Yes; we have already said that society is often the primary cause of such failures; and besides, is it not the duty of society to watch over the moral education of all its members? Society often perverts their judgment through a bad education, instead of correcting their evil tendencies." (685.)

Trials of Riches an of Poverty

814. *Why has God given wealth and power to some, and poverty to others?*

"In order to try them in different ways. Moreover, as you know, it is the spirits themselves who have selected those trials, under which they often succumb."

815. *Which of the two kinds of trial, poverty or riches, is the most to be dreaded by man?*

"They are equally dangerous. Poverty excites murmurings against Providence; riches excite to all kinds of excesses."

816. *If the rich man has more temptations to evil, has he not also more ample means of doing good?*

"That is precisely what he does not always do. He often becomes selfish, proud, and insatiable. His wants increase with his fortune, and he never thinks he has enough, even for himself."

Worldly grandeur, and authority over our fellow-creatures, are trials as great and as slippery as misfortune; for the richer and more powerful we are, **the more obligations we have to fulfil,** and the greater are our means of doing both good and evil. God tries the poor through resignation, and the rich through the use he makes of his wealth and power.

Riches and power give birth to all the passions that attach us to matter, and keep us at a distance from spiritual perfection; this is why Jesus said that it is easier for a camel to pass through the needle's eye than for a rich man to enter into the kingdom of heaven. (266.)

Equality of Rights of Men and of Women.

817. *Are men and women equal in the sight of God, and have they the same rights?*

"Has not God given to them both the knowledge of good and evil, and the faculty of progressing?"

818. *Whence comes the moral inferiority of women in some countries?*

"From the cruel and unjust supremacy which man has usurped over her. It is a result of social institutions, and of the abusive exercise of strength over weakness. Among men but little advanced morally, might is mistaken for right."

819. *For what purpose is woman physically weaker than man?*

"In order that to her may be assigned certain special functions. Man is made for rough work, as being the stronger; woman, for gentler occupations; and both are differenced that they may aid each other in passing through the trials of a life full of bitterness."

820. *Does not woman's physical weakness make her naturally dependent on man?*

"God has given strength to the one sex in order that it may protect the other, but not to reduce it to servitude."

God has fitted the organisation of each being for the functions which it has to discharge. If God has given less physical strength to woman, He has, at the same time, endowed her with a greater amount of sensibility, in harmony with the delicacy of the maternal functions and the weakness of the beings confided to her care.

821. *Are the functions to which woman is destined by nature as important as those which are allotted to man?*

"Yes, and still more important; for it is she who gives him his first notions of life."

822. *All men being equals according to the law of God, ought they also to be such according to the law of men?*

"Such equality is the very first principle of justice. Do not unto others what you would not that others should do unto you."

— *In order to be perfectly just, ought legislation to proclaim an equality of rights between men and women?*

"Equality of rights, yes, but not of functions. Each should have a specified place. Let man busy himself with the outer side of life, and woman with its inner side; each sex according to its special aptitude. Human law, in order to be just, should proclaim the equality of rights of men and women. Every privilege accorded to either sex is contrary to justice. *The emancipation of woman follows the progress of civilisation*; her subjection is a condition of barbarism. The sexes, moreover, exist only through the physical organisation. Since spirits can assume that of either sex, there is no difference between them in this respect, and thev ought consequently to enjoy the same rights."

Equality in Death.

823. Whence comes the desire of perpetuating one's memory by means of funeral monuments?

"It is the last act of pride."

— But is not the sumptuousness of funeral monuments more frequently due to the action of relatives desirous to honour the memory of the defunct, than to the defunct himself?

"In such cases it is an act of pride on the part of relatives who desire to glorify themselves; for assuredly it is not always for the one who is dead that all these demonstrations are made, but rather to gratify their own vanity by making an impression on others, and to parade their wealth. Do you imagine that the remembrance of their loved ones is less durable in the hearts of the poor, because the latter have no flowers to lay upon their graves? Do you imagine that marble can save from oblivion the name of him who has led a useless life upon the earth?"

824. Is funeral pomp blamable under all circumstances?

"No; when displayed in honour of a noble life, it is just, and conveys a useful lessen."

The grave is the place of meeting for all men—the inevitable end of all human distinctions. It is in vain that the rich man seeks to perpetuate his memory by stately monuments; time will destroy them like his body; nature has so willed it. The remembrance of his deeds, whether good or bad, will be less perishable than his tomb; the pomp of his funeral will neither cleanse away his turpitudes nor raise him a single step on the ladder of the spirit-hierarchy. (320 **et seq.**)

CHAPTER X

IX. THE LAW OF LIBERTY

1. NATURAL LIBERTY—2. SLAVERY—3. FREEDOM OF THOUGHT—4. FREEDOM OF CONSCIENCE—5. FREE-WILL —6. FATALITY—7. FOREKNOWLEDGE—8. THEORETIC SUMMARY OF THE SPRINGS OF HUMAN ACTION.

Natural Liberty

825. Are there any positions in life in which a man may flatter himself that he enjoys absolute freedom?

"No, because all of you, the greatest as well as the least, have need of one another."

826. In what condition of life could a man enjoy absolute freedom?

"That of a hermit in a desert. *As soon as two men find themselves together, they have reciprocal rights and duties to respect, and are, therefore, no longer absolutely free."*

827. Does the duty of respecting the rights of others deprive a man of the right of belonging to himself?

"In nowise; for he holds that right from nature."

828. How can we reconcile the liberal opinions professed by some persons with the despotism they themselves sometimes exercise in their own houses, and among their subordinates?

"Their intelligence is aware of the law of nature, but this perception is counterbalanced by their pride and selfishness. When their profession of liberal principles is not hypocrisy, they know what ought to be done, but do it not."

— Will their profession of liberal principles, in the earthly life, be of any avail to such persons in the other life?

"The more clearly a principle is understood by the intellect, the more inexcusable is the neglect to put it into practice. He who is sincere, though simple, is farther advanced on the divine road than he who tries to appear what he is not."

Slavery

829. Are any men intended by nature to be the property of other men?

"The absolute subjection of any man to another man is contrary to the law of God. Slavery is an abuse of strength; it disappears with progress, gradually, as all other abuses will disappear."

The human law which sanctions slavery is a law against nature, because it assimilates man to the brute, and degrades him physically and morally.

830. When slavery is already established in the habits of a people, are those who profit by that institution to blame for conforming to a usage which appears to them to be natural?

"What is wrong is always wrong, and no amount of sophistry can change a bad deed into a good one; but the responsibility of wrong doing is always proportional to the means of comprehending it possessed by the wrong-doer. He who profits by the institution of slavery is always guilty of a violation of natural law; but in this, as in everything else, the guilt is relative. Slavery having become rooted in the habits of certain peoples, men may have taken advantage of it without seeing it to be wrong, and as something which appeared to them altogether natural; but when their reason, more developed and enlightened by the teachings of Christianity, has shown them that their slave is their equal in the sight of God, they are no longer excusable."

831. Does not the inequality of natural aptitudes place some of the human races under the sway of other races of greater intelligence?

"Yes, in order that the latter may raise them to a higher level, but not that they may brutify them still more by slavery. Men have too long regarded certain human races as working-animals furnished with arms and hands, which they have believed themselves to have the right of using and selling like beasts of burden. They fancy themselves to be of purer blood; fools, who see only matter! It is not the blood that is more or less pure, but only the spirit." (361-803.)

832. There are men who treat their slaves humanely, who let them want for nothing, and who think that freedom would expose them to greater privations; what do you say of such persons?

"I say that they have a better understanding of their own interests than those who treat them cruelly; they take the same care of their cattle and horses, in order to get a better price for them at market. They are not so guilty as those who treat them badly, but they none the less treat them as merchandise, by depriving them of the right of belonging to themselves."

Freedom of Thought.

833. Is there in man something that escapes constraint, and in regard to which he enjoys absolute liberty?

"Yes, in his thought man enjoys unlimited freedom, for thought knows no obstacles. The action of thought may be hindered, but not annihilated."

834. Is man responsible for his thoughts?

"He is responsible for them to God. God alone can take cognisance of thought, and condemns or absolves it according to His justice."

Freedom of Conscience.

835. Is freedom of conscience the natural consequence of freedom of thought?

"Conscience is an inner thought that belongs to man, like all his other thoughts."

836. Has man the right to set up barriers against freedom of conscience?

"No more than against freedom of thought, for God alone has the right to judge the conscience. If man, by his laws, regulates the relations between men and men, God, by the laws of nature, regulates the relations between men and God."

837. What is the effect of the hindrances opposed to freedom of conscience?

"To constrain men to act otherwise than as they think, and thus to make hypocrites of them. Freedom of conscience is one of the characteristics of true civilisation and of progress."

838. Is every honest belief to be respected, even when completely false?

"Every belief is worthy of respect when it is sincere, and when it leads to the practice of goodness. Blamable beliefs are those which lead to the practice of evil."

839. Is it wrong to scandalise those whose belief is not the same as our own?

"To do so is to fail in charity, and to infringe on freedom of thought."

840. Is it an infringement of the freedom of conscience to place hindrances in the way of beliefs that are of a nature to cause social disturbance?

"You can only repress action; belief is inaccessible."

The repression of the external acts of a belief, when those acts are injurious to others, is not an infringement of the freedom of conscience, for such repression leaves the belief itself entirely free.

841. Ought we, out of respect for freedom of conscience, to allow of the propagation of pernicious doctrines, or may we, without infringing upon that freedom, endeavour to bring back into the path of truth those who are led astray by false principles?

"Most certainly you not only may, but should, do so; but only by following the example of Jesus, by employing gentleness and persuasion, and not by resorting to force, which would be worse than the false belief of those whom you desire to convince. Conviction cannot be imposed by violence."

842. All doctrines claiming to be the sole expression of the truth, by what signs can we recognise the one which has the best right to call itself such?

"The truest doctrine will be the one which makes the fewest hypocrites and the greatest number of really virtuous people—that is to say, of people practising the law of charity in its greatest purity and in its widest application. It is by this sign that you may recognise a doctrine as true; for no doctrine, of which the tendency to make divisions and demarcations among the children of God, can be anything but false and pernicious."

Free — Will.

843. Has man freedom of action?

"Since he has freedom of thought, he has freedom of action. Without free-will man would be a machine."

844. Does man posses free-will from his birth?

"He possesses free-will from the moment when he possesses the will to act. In the earliest portion of a lifetime free-will is almost null; it is developed and changes its object with the development of the faculties. The child, having thoughts in harmony with the wants of his age, applies his free-will to the things which belong to that age."

845. Are not the instinctive predispositions that a man brings with him at birth an obstacle to the exercise of his free-will?

"A man's instinctive predispositions are those which belonged to his spirit before his incarnation. If he is but little advanced, they may incite him to wrong-doing, in which he will be seconded by spirits who sympathise with that wrong-doing; but no incitement is irresistible when there is a determination to resist. Remember that *to will is to be able.*" (361.)

846. Has not our organism an influence on the acts of our life, and if so, does not this influence constitute an infringement of our free-will?

"Spirits are certainly influenced by matter, which may hamper them in their manifestations. This is why, in worlds in which the body is less gross than upon the earth, the faculties act more freely; but the instrument does not give the faculty. In considering this question, you must also distinguish between moral faculties and intellectual faculties. If a man has the instinct of murder, it is assuredly his spirit that possesses this instinct, and not his organs. He who annihilates his thought, in order to occupy himself only with matter, becomes like the brute, and still worse, for he no longer endeavours to preserve himself from evil, and it is this which constitutes his culpability, because he does so of his own free-will." (See No. 367 *et seq., Influence of Organism.*)

847. Does aberration of the mental faculties deprive man of free-will?

"He whose intelligence is deranged by any cause whatever is no longer master of his thoughts, and thenceforth is no longer free. Mental aberration is often a punishment for the spirit who, in another existence, has been vain or haughty, or has made a bad use of his faculties. He may be re-born in the body of an idiot, as the despot may be re-born in the body of a slave, and the hard-hearted possessor of riches, in that of a beggar; but the spirit suffers from this constraint, of which he is fully conscious; and it is in this constraint that you see the action of matter." (371 *et seq.*)

848. Is the aberration of the mental faculties produced by drunkenness an excuse for the crimes committed in that state?

"No; for the drunkard has voluntarily deprived himself of his reason in order to satisfy his brutish passions. He thus commits, not one crime, but two."

*849.   What is the dominant faculty of man in the savage state?
Is it instinct or free-will?*

"Instinct; which, however, does not prevent his acting with
entire freedom in certain things; but, like the child he uses his
freedom for the satisfaction of his needs, and obtains its development only through the development of his intelligence. Consequently, you, who are more enlightened than the savage, are
more blamable than a savage if you do wrong."

*850.   Does not social position sometimes place obstacles in the
way of free action?*

"Society has, undoubtedly, its exigencies.   God is just, and takes
everything into account; but He will hold you responsible for any
lack of effort on your part to surmount such obstacles."

Fatality.

*851.   Is there a fatality in the events of life, in the sense com-
monly attached to that word—that is to say, are the events of life
ordained beforehand, and, if so, what becomes of free-will?*

"There is no other fatality than that which results from the
determination of each spirit, on incarnating himself, to undergo
such and such trials.   By choosing those trials he makes for himself a sort of destiny which is the natural consequence of the
situation in which he has chosen to place himself.   I speak now
of physical trials only: for, as regards moral trials and temptations,
a spirit always preserves his freedom of choice between good and
evil, and is always able to yield or to resist.   A good spirit, seeing
a man hesitate, may come to his aid, but cannot influence him to
the extent of mastering his will.   On the other hand, a bad spirit—
that is to say, a spirit of inferior advancement, may trouble or
alarm him by suggesting exaggerated apprehensions; but the will
of the incarnated spirit retains, nevertheless, its entire freedom of
choice."

*852.   There are persons who seem to be pursued by a fatality
independent of their own action.   Are not their misfortunes, in
such cases, the result of predestination?*

"They may be trials which those persons are compelled to
undergo because they have been chosen by them in the spirit-
state; but you often set down to destiny what is only the consequence of your own faults.   Try to keep a clear conscience, and
you will be consoled for the greater part of your afflictions.

The true or false view we take of the things about us causes us to succeed or to fail in our enterprises; but it seems to us more easy, and less humiliating to our self-love, to attribute our failures to fate, or to destiny, than to our mistakes. If the influence of spirits sometimes contributes to our success, it is none the less true that we can always free ourselves from their influence, by repelling the ideas they suggest when they are calculated to mislead us.

853. *They are persons who escape one danger only to fall into another; it seems as though it had been impossible for them to escape death. Is there not a fatality in such cases?*

"There is nothing fatal, in the true meaning of the word, but the time of death. When that time has come, no matter under what form death presents itself, you cannot escape it."

— *If so, whatever danger may seem to threaten us, we shall not die if our hour has not come?*

"No, you will not be allowed to die—and of this you have thousands of examples; but when your hour has come, nothing can save you. God knows beforehand the manner in which each of you will quit your present life, and this is often known also to your spirit; for it is revealed to you when you make choice of such and such existence."

854. *Does it follow, from the inevitability of the hour of death, that the precautions we take in view of apparent danger are useless?*

"No, for those precautions are suggested to you in order that you may avoid the dangers with which you are threatened. They are one of the means employed by Providence to prevent death from taking place prematurely."

855. *What is the aim of Providence in making us incur dangers that are to be without result?*

"When your life is imperilled, it is a warning which you yourself have desired, in order to turn you from evil, and to make you better. When you escape from such a peril, and while still feeling the emotion excited by the danger you had incurred, you think, more or less seriously, according to the degree in which you are influenced by the suggestions of good spirits, of amending your ways. The bad spirit returning to his former post of temptation (I say *bad*, in reference to the evil that is still in him), you flatter yourself that you will escape other dangers in the same way, and you again give free scope to your passions. By the dangers you incur, God reminds you of your weakness, and of the fragility of your existence. If you examine the cause and the nature of the peril you have escaped, you will see that in many cases its consequences would have been the punishment of some fault you have committed, or of *some duty you have neglected.* God thus warns you to look into your hearts, and to pursue the work of your self-amendment." (526-532.)

856. Does a spirit know beforehand the kind of death to which he will succumb in the earthly life?

"He knows that he has exposed himself by the life he has chosen to die in some particular manner rather than in another; but he also foresees the efforts he will have to make in order to avoid the danger, and he knows that, if God so permit, he will escape it."

857. There are men who brave the perils of the battlefield with the full persuasion that their hour is not come; is there any foundation for such confidence?

"A man often has a presentiment of his end; he may, in the same way, have a presentiment that his time for dying has not yet come. These presentiments are due to the action of his spirit-protectors, who may wish to lead him to hold himself ready to go away, or to raise his courage in moments when he has especial need of it. They may also come to him from the intuition he has of the existence he has chosen, or of the mission he has accepted, and which he knows, as a spirit, that he has to fulfil." (411-522.)

858. How is it that those who have a presentiment of their death generally dread it less than others?

"It is the man, and not spirit, who dreads death; he who has the presentiment of his death thinks of it rather as a spirit than as a man. He understands that it will be a deliverance, and awaits it calmly."

859. If death is inevitable when the time appointed for it has arrived, is it the same in regard to all the accidents that may happen to us in the course of our life?

"They are often small enough to permit of our warning you against them, and sometimes of enabling you to avoid them by the direction we give to your thoughts, for we do not like physical suffering; but all this is of little importance to the life you have chosen. The true and sole fatality consists in the hour at which you have to appear in, and disappear from, the sphere of corporeal life."

— *Are there incidents which must necessarily occur in a life, and that spirits will not avert?*

"Yes, but those incidents you, in your spirit-state, foresaw when you made your choice. But, nevertheless, you must not suppose that everything which happens to you was 'written,' as people express it. An event is often the consequence of something you have done by an act of your free-will, so that, had you not done that thing, the event would not have taken place. If you burn your finger, it is not because such an incident was preordained, for it is a trifling inconvenience resulting from your own carelessness, and a consequence of the laws of matter. It is only the great sorrows, the events of serious importance and capable of influencing your moral state, that are foreordained by God, because they will be useful to your purification and instruction."

860. *Can a man, by his will and his efforts, prevent events that were to have occurred from taking place, and* vice-versâ?

"He can do so if this seeming deviation is compatible with the life he has chosen. And, in order to do good, which should be, and is, the sole end of life, he may prevent evil, especially that which might contribute to a still greater evil."

861. *Did the man who commits a murder know, in choosing his existence, that he would become a murderer?*

"No; he knew that, by choosing a life of struggle, he incurred the *risk* of killing one of his fellow-creatures; but he did not know whether he would, or would not, do so; for there is, almost always, deliberation in the murderer's mind before committing the crime, and he who deliberates is, evidently, free to do or not to do. If a spirit knew beforehand that he would commit a murder, it would imply that he was predestinated to commit that crime. No one is ever predestinated to commit a crime; and every crime, like every other action, is always the result of determination and free-will.

"You are all too apt to confound two things essentially distinct— the events of material life, and the acts of moral life. If there is, sometimes, a sort of fatality, it is only in those events of your material life of which the cause is beyond your action, and independent of your will. As to the acts of the moral life, they always emanate from the man himself, who, consequently, has always the freedom of choice; in those acts, therefore, there is *never* fatality."

862. There are persons who never succeed in anything, and who seem to be pursued by an evil genius in all their undertakings; is there not, in such cases, something that may be called a fatality?

"It is certainly a fatality, if you like to call it so, but it results from the choice of the kind of existence made by those persons in the spirit-state, because they desired to exercise their patience and resignation by a life of disappointment. But you must not suppose that this fatality is absolute, for it is often the consequence of a man's having taken a wrong path, one that is not adapted to his intelligence and aptitudes. He who tries to cross a river without knowing how to swim stands a very good chance of drowning; and the same may be said in regard to the greater part of the events of your life. If a man undertook only the things that are in harmony with his faculties, he would almost always succeed. What causes his failure is his conceit and ambition, which draw him out of his proper path, and make him mistake for a vocation what is only a desire to satisfy those passions. He fails, and through his own fault; but, instead of blaming himself, he prefers to accuse his 'star.' One who might have been a good workman, and earned his bread honourably in that capacity, prefers to make bad poetry, and dies of starvation. There would be a place for every one, if every one put himself in his right place."

863. Do not social habits often oblige a man to follow one road rather than another, and is not his choice of occupation often controlled by the opinion of those about him? Is not the sentiment which leads us to attach a certain amount of importance to the judgment of others an obstacle to the exercise of our free-will?

"Social habits are made, not by God, but by men; if men submit to them, it is because it suits them to do so, and their submission is therefore an act of their free-will, since, if they wished to enfranchise themselves from those habits, they could do so. Why, then, do they complain? It is not social habits that they should accuse, but their pride, which makes them prefer to starve rather than to derogate from what they consider to be their dignity. Nobody thanks them for this sacrifice to · opinion, though God would take note of the sacrifice of their vanity. We do not mean to say that you should brave public opinion unnecessarily, like certain persons who possess more eccentricity than true philosophy : there is as much absurdity in causing yourself to be pointed at as an oddity, or stared at as a curious animal, as there is wisdom in descending, voluntarily and unmurmuringly, when you are unable to maintain yourself at the top of the social ladder."

864. If there are persons to whom fate is unpropitious, there are others who seem to be favoured by fortune, for they succeed in everything they undertake. To what is this to be attributed?

"In many cases, to their skilful management of their affairs; but it may also be a species of trial. People are often intoxicated by success; they put their trust in their destiny, and pay in the end for their former successes by severe reverses, which greater prudence would have enabled them to avoid."

865. How can we account for the run of luck that sometimes favours people under circumstances with which neither the will nor the intelligence have anything to do; in games of hazard, for instance?

"Certain spirits have chosen beforehand certain sorts of pleasure, the luck that favours them is a temptation. He who wins as a man often loses as a spirit; such luck is a trial for his vanity and his cupidity."

866. The fatality which seems to shape our material destinies is, then, a result of our free will?

"You, yourself, have chosen your trial; the severer it is, and the better you bear it, the higher you do raise yourself. Those who pass their lives in the selfish enjoyment of plenty and of human happiness are cowardly spirits who remain stationary. Thus the number of those who are unfortunate is much greater, in your world, than of those who are fortunate, because spirits generally make choice of the trial that will be most useful to them. They see too clearly the futility of your grandeurs and your enjoyments. Besides, the most fortunate life is always more or less agitated, more or less troubled, if only by the absence of sorrow." (525 *et seq.*)

867. Whence comes the expressions "Born under a lucky star"?

"From an old superstition that connected the stars with the destiny of each human being—a figure that some people are silly enough to take for literal truth."

Foreknowledge.

868. Can the future be revealed to man?

"As a rule, the future is hidden from him; it is only in rare and exceptional cases that God permits it to be revealed.

869. Why is the future hidden from man?

"If man knew the future, he would neglect the present, and would not act with the same freedom, because he would be swayed by the thought that, if such and such a thing is to happen, there is no need to occupy one's self about it; or else he would seek to prevent it. God has willed that it should not be thus, in order that each may concur in the accomplishment of the designs of Providence, *even of those which he would desire to thwart*; and thus you, yourselves, often prepare the way, without your knowing it, for the events that will occur in the course of your life."

870. Since it is useful that the future should be hidden, why does God sometimes permit it to be revealed?

"Because in such cases this foreknowledge, instead of hindering the accomplishment of the thing that is to be, will facilitate it, by inducing the person to whom it is revealed to act in a different way from that in which he would otherwise have acted. And, besides, it is often a trial. The prospect of an event may awaken thoughts more or less virtuous. If a man becomes aware, for instance, that he will succeed to an inheritance which he had not expected, he may be tempted by a feeling of cupidity, by elation at the prospect of adding to his earthly pleasures, by a desire for the death of him to whose fortune he will succeed, in order that he may obtain possession of it more speedily; or, on the other hand, this prospect may awaken in him only good and generous thoughts. If the prediction be not fulfilled, it is another trial, viz., that of the way in which he will bear the disappointment; but he will none the less have acquired the merit or the blame of the good or bad thoughts awakened in him by his expectation of the event predicted."

871. Since God knows everything, He knows whether a man will or will not fail in a given trial; where then is the use of this trial, since it can show God nothing that He does not already know in regard to that man?

"You might as well ask why God did not create man accomplished, perfect (119); or why man has to pass through childhood before arriving at adult age (379). The aim of trial is not to enlighten God in regard to man's deserts, for God knows exactly what they are, but to leave to man the entire responsibility of his conduct, since he is free to do or not to do. Man having free choice between good and evil, trial serves to bring him under the action of temptation, and thus to give him the merit of resistance; for God, though knowing beforehand whether he will triumph or succumb, cannot, being just, either reward or punish him otherwise than according to the deeds he has done." (258.)

The same principle is practically admitted among men. Whatever may be the qualifications of a candidate for any distinction, whatever may be our confidence of his success, no grade can be conferred on him without his having undergone the prescribed examination—that is to say, without his desert having been tested by trial, just as a judge only condemns the accused for the crime he has actually committed, and not on the presumption that he could or would commit such crime.

The more we reflect on the consequences that would result from our knowledge of the future, the more clearly do we see the wisdom of Providence in hiding it from us. The certainty of our future good fortune would render us inactive; that of coming misfortune would plunge us in discouragement ; in both cases our activities would be paralysed. For this reason, the future is only shown to man as **an end** which he is to attain through his own efforts, but without knowing the sequence of events through which he will pass in attaining it. The foreknowledge of all the incidents of his journey would deprive him of his initiative and of the use of his free-will ; he would let himself be drawn, passively, by the force of events, down the slope of circumstances, without any exercise of his faculties. When the success of a matter is certain, we no longer busy ourselves about it.

Theoretic Summary of the Springs of Human Action.

872. The question of free-will may be thus summed up: Man is not fatally led into evil; the acts he accomplishes are not written down beforehand; the crimes he commits are not the result of any decree of destiny. He may have chosen, as trial and as expiation, an existence in which, through the surroundings amidst which he is placed, or the circumstances that supervene, he will be tempted to do wrong; but he always remains free to do or not to do. Thus a spirit exercises free-will, in the spirit-life, by choosing his next existence and the *kind* of trials to which it will subject him, and, in the corporeal life, by using his power of yielding to, or resisting, the temptations to which he has voluntarily subjected himself. The duty of education is to combat the evil tendencies brought by the spirit into his new existence—a duty which it will only be able to thoroughly fulfil when it shall be based on a deeper and truer knowledge of man's moral nature. Through knowledge of the laws of this department of his nature, education will be able to modify it, as it already modifies his intelligence by instruction, and his temperament by hygiene. Each spirit, when freed from matter, and in the state of erraticity, chooses his future corporeal existences according to the degree of purification to which he has already attained ; and it is in the power of making this choice, as we have previously pointed out, that his free-will principally consists This free-will is not annulled by incarnation,

for, if the incarnated spirit yields to the influence of matter, it is
always to the very trials previously chosen by him that he succumbs,
and he is always free to invoke the assistance of God and of good
spirits to help him to surmount them.   (337.)

Without free-will there would be for man neither guilt in doing
wrong, nor merit in doing right—a principle so fully recognised
in this life, that the world always apportions its blame or its praise
of any deed to the *intention*—that is to say, to the *will* of the doer;
and *will* is but another term for *freedom*.   Man, therefore, could
not seek an excuse for his misdeeds in his organisation, without
abdicating his reason and his condition as a human being, and
assimilating himself to the condition of the brute.   If he could
do so in regard to what is wrong, he would have to do the same
in regard to what is wrong, he would have to do the same in
regard to what is right; but, whenever a man does what is right,
he takes good care to claim the merit of his action, and never
thinks of attributing that merit to his organs, which proves that
he instinctively refuses to renounce, at the bidding of certain
theory-builders, the most glorious privilege of his species, viz.,
freedom of thought.

Fatality, as commonly understood, supposes an anterior and
irrevocable ordaining of all the events of human life, whatever
their degree of importance.   If such were the order of things,
man would be a machine, without a will of his own.   Of what
use would his intelligence be to him, seeing that he would be
invariably overruled in all his acts by the power of destiny?   Such
pre-ordination, if it took place, would be the destruction of all
moral freedom; there would be no such thing as human responsibility, and consequently neither good nor evil, neither virtues
nor crimes.   God, being sovereignly just, could not chastise His
creatures for faults which they had not the option of not committing, nor could He reward them for virtues which would constitute for them no merit.   It would be, moreover, the negation of
the law of progress; for, if man were thus dependent on fate,
he would make no attempt to ameliorate his position, since his
action would be both unnecessary and unavailing.

On the other hand, fatality is not a mere empty word; it really
exists in regard to the position occupied by each man upon the
earth and the part which he plays in it, *as a consequence of the
kind of existence previously made choice of by his spirit, as trial,
expiation, or mission*, **for**, in virtue of that choice, he is necessarily

subjected to the vicissitudes of the existence he has chosen, and to all the tendencies, good or bad, inherent in it; but fatality ceases at this point, for it depends on his will to yield, or not to yield, to those tendencies. *The details of events are subordinated to the circumstances to which man himself gives rise by his action,* and in regard to which he may be influenced by the good or bad thoughts suggested to him by spirits. (459.)

There is a fatality, then, in the *events* which occur independently of our action, *because they are the consequence of the choice of our existence made by our spirit in the other life;* but there can be no fatality in the *results of those events,* because we are often able to modify their results by our own prudence. *There is no fatality in regard to the acts of our moral life.*

It is only in regard to his death that man is placed under the law of an absolute and inexorable fatality; for he can neither evade the decree which has fixed the term of his existence, nor avoid the kind of death which is destined to interrupt its course.[1]

According to the common belief, man derives all his instincts from himself; they proceed either from his physical organisation, for which he is not responsible, or from his own nature, which would furnish him with an equally valid excuse for his imperfections, as, if such were the case, he might justly plead that it is through no option of his own that he has been made what he is.

The doctrine of Spiritism is evidently more moral. It admits the plenitude of man's free-will, and, in telling him that, when he does wrong, he yields to an evil suggestion made by another spirit, it leaves him the entire responsibility of his wrong-doing, because it recognises his power of resisting that suggestion, which it is evidently more easy for him to do than it would be to fight against his own nature. Thus, according to spiritist doctrine, no temptation is irresistible. A man can always close his mental ear against the occult voice which addresses itself to his inner consciousness, just as he can close it against a human voice. He can always withdraw himself from the suggestions that would tempt him to evil, by exerting his will against the tempter; asking of God, at the same time, to give him the necessary strength, and calling on good spirits to help him in vanquishing the temptation.

This view of the exciting cause of human action is the natural consequence of the totality of the teaching now being given from

---

[1] In relation to suicide and its consequences, **vide** 957, and following commentaries.

the spirit-world. It is not only sublime in point of morality; it is also eminently fitted to enhance man's self-respect. For it shows him that he is as free to shake off the yoke of an oppressor, as he is to close his house against unwelcome intrusion; that he is not a machine, set in motion by an impulsion independent of his will; that he is a reasoning being, with the power of listening to, weighing, and choosing freely between, two opposing counsels. Let us add that, while thus counselled, man is not deprived of the initiative of his action; what he does, he does of his own motion, because he is still a spirit, though incarnated in a corporeal envelope, and still preserves, as a man, the good and bad qualities he possessed as a spirit.

The faults we commit have their original source, therefore, in the imperfection of our own spirit, which has not yet acquired the moral excellence it will acquire in course of time, but which, nevertheless, is in full possession of its free-will. Corporeal life is permitted to us for the purpose of purging our spirit of its imperfections through the trials to which we are thus subjected; and it is precisely those imperfections that weaken us and render us accessible to the suggestions of other imperfect spirits, who take advantage of our weakness in trying to make us fail in the fulfilment of the task we have imposed upon ourselves. If we issue victorious from the struggle, our spirit attains a higher grade; if we fail, our spirit remains as it was, no better and no worse, but with the unsuccessful attempt to be made over again: a repetition of the same trial that may retard our advancement for a very long period. But, in proportion as we effect our improvement, our weakness diminishes, and we give less and less handle to those who would tempt us to evil; and as our moral strength constantly increases, bad spirits cease at length to act upon us.

The totality of spirits, good and bad, constitute by their incarnation the human race; and as our earth is one of the most backward worlds, more bad spirits than good ones are incarnated in it, and a general perversity is visible among mankind. Let us, then, do our utmost not to have to come back to it, but to merit admission into a world of higher degree; one of those happier worlds in which goodness reigns supreme, and in which we shall remember our sojourn in this lower world only as a period of exile.

CHAPTER XI

X. THE LAW OF JUSTICE, OF LOVE, AND OF CHARITY

1. NATURAL RIGHTS AND JUSTICE—2. RIGHT OF PROPERTY ; ROBBERY—3. CHARITY ; LOVE OF THE NEIGHBOUR—4. MATERNAL AND FILIAL AFFECTION.

Natural Rights and Justice.

873. Is the sentiment of justice natural, or the result of acquired ideas?

"It is so natural that your feeling spontaneously revolts at the idea of an injustice. Moral progress undoubtedly develops this sentiment, but it does not create it. God has placed it in the heart of man, and for this reason you often find, among simple and primitive people, notions of justice more exact than those of others who are possessed of a larger amount of knowledge."

874. If justice be a law of nature, how is it that men understand it so differently, and that the same thing appears just to one, and unjust to anoher?

"It is because your passions often mingle with this sentiment and debase it, as they do with the greater part of the natural sentiments, causing you to see things from a false point of view."

875. How should justice be defined?

"Justice consists in respect for the rights of others."

— *What determines those rights?*

"Two things: human law and natural law. Men having made laws in harmony with their character and habits, those laws have established rights that have varied with the progress of enlightenment. Your laws, at this day, though still far from perfect, no longer consecrate what were considered as rights in the Middle Ages ; those rights, which appear to you monstrous, appeared just and natural at that epoch. The rights established by men are not, therefore, always conformable with justice ; moreover, they only regulate certain social relations, while in private life there are an immense number of acts that are submitted only to the tribunal of conscience."

876. Independently of the right established by human law, what is the basis of justice according to natural law?

"Christ has told you: *'Do unto others whatsoever you would that others should do unto you.'* God has placed in the heart of man, as the true rule of all justice, the desire which each of you feels to see his own rights respected. When uncertain as to what he should do in regard to his fellow-creature in any given conjuncture, let each man ask himself what he would wish to have done to himself under the same circumstances; God could not give him a safer guide than his own conscience."

The true criterion of justice is, in fact, to desire for others what one would desire for one's self; not merely to desire for one's self what one would desire for others, which is not precisely the same thing. As it is not natural to desire harm for one's self, we are sure, in taking our personal desires as the type of our conduct towards our neighbours, never to desire anything but good for them. In all ages and in all beliefs, man has always sought to enforce his personal rights; **the sublime peculiarity of the Christian religion is its taking of personal right as the basis of the right of the neighbour.**

877. Does the necessity of living in society impose any special obligations on mankind?

"Yes, and the first of these is to respect the rights of others; he who respects those rights will always be just. In your world, where so many neglect to practise the law of justice, you have recourse to reprisals, and this causes trouble and confusion in human society. Social life gives rights and imposes corresponding duties."

878. It is possible for a man to be under an illusion as to the extent of his rights; what is there that can show him their true limit?

"The limit of the right which he would recognise on the part of his neighbour towards himself under similar circumstances, and *vice-versâ.*"

— *But if each attributes to himself the rights of his fellow-creatures, what becomes of subordination to superiors? Would not such a principle be anarchical and destructive of all power?*

"Natural rights are the same for all men, from the smallest to the greatest; God has not fashioned some men from a finer clay than others, and all are equals in His sight. Natural rights are eternal; the rights which man has established perish with his institutions. But each man feels distinctly his strength or his weakness, and will always be conscious of a sort of deference towards him whose wisdom or virtue entitles him to respect. It is important to mention this, in order that those who think themselves superior may know what are the duties that will give them a right to deference. There will be no insubordination when authority shall be attributed only to superior wisdom."

879. What would be the character of the man who should practise justice in all its purity?

"He would be truly righteous, after the example of Jesus; for he would practise the love of the neighbour and charity, without which there can be no real justice."

Right of Property — Robbery.

880. Which is the first of all the natural rights of man?

"The right to live, and therefore no one has the right to take the life of his fellow-creature, or to do anything that may compromise his personal existence."

881. Does the right to live give to man the right to amass the means of living, in order that he may repose when no longer able to work?

"Yes; but he should do this in concert with his family, like the bee, by honest labour, and not by amassing in solitary selfishness. Certain animals, even, set man an example of this kind of foresight."

882. Has man the right to defend what he has amassed by his labours?

"Has not God said, 'Thou shalt not steal?' and did not Jesus say: 'Render unto Cæsar the things that are Cæsar's?'"

What a man has amassed by honest labour is a legitimate property that he has a right to defend ; for possession of the property which is the fruit of labour is a natural right as sacred as the right to labour or to live.

883. Is the desire to posses natural to man?

"Yes; but when it is simply for himself, and for his personal satisfaction, it is selfishness."

— *But is not the desire to possess a legitimate one, since he who has enough to live upon is not a burden to others?*

"Some men are insatiable and accumulate without benefit to any one, merely to satisfy their passions. Do you suppose that this can be pleasing to God? He, on the contrary, who amasses through his labour, in order to have the means of assisting his fellow-creatures, practises the law of love and of charity, and his labour receives the blessing of God."

884. *What is the characteristic of legitimate property?*

"No property is legitimate unless acquired without injury to others." (808.)

The law of love and of justice, forbidding us to do to others what we would not that others should do to us, implicitly condemns every means of acquiring which would be contrary to that law.

885. *Is the right of property unlimited?*

"Everything that has been legitimately acquired is undoubtedly a property; but, as we have said, human legislation, being imperfect, frequently sets up conventional rights opposed to natural justice. For this reason, men reform their laws in proportion as progress is accomplished, and as they obtain a better notion of justice. What appears right in one century appears barbarous in another." (795).

Charity and Love of the Neighbour.

886. *What is the true meaning of the word* charity *as employed by Jesus?*

"Benevolence for every one, indulgence for the imperfections of others, forgiveness of injuries."

Love and charity are the complement of the law of justice; for, to love our neighbour is to do him all the good in our power, all that we should wish to have done to ourselves.

Charity, according to Jesus, is not restricted to alms-giving, but embraces all our relations with our fellow-men whether our inferiors, our equals, or our superiors. It prescribes indulgence on our part, because we need the same ourselves; it forbids us to humiliate the unfortunate, as is too often done. How many, who are ready to lavish respect and attentions on the rich, appear to think it not worth their while to be civil to the poor; and yet, the more pitiable the situation of the latter, the more scrupulously should we refrain from adding humiliation to misfortune. He who is really kind endeavours to raise his inferior in his own estimation, by diminishing the distance between them.

887. *Jesus has also said:* Love your enemies. *But would it not be contrary to our natural tendencies to love our enemies, and does not unfriendliness proceed from a want of sympathy between spirits?*

"It would certainly be impossible for a man to feel tender and ardent affection for his enemies; and Jesus did not intend to prescribe anything of the kind. To 'love your enemies' means to forgive them, and to return good for evil. By so doing, you become their superior; by vengeance, you place yourselves beneath them."

888. *What is to be thought of alms-giving?*

"To be reduced to beg degrades a man morally as well as physically; it brutifies him. In a state of society based on the law of God and justice, provision would be made for assisting *the weak* without humiliating. them; the means of living would be insured to all who are unable to work, so as not to leave their life at the mercy of chance and of individual good-will."

— *Do you blame alms-giving?*

"No; it is not the giving of alms that is reprehensible, but the way in which it is too often done. He who comprehends charity as inculcated by Jesus seeks out the needy, without waiting for the latter to hold out his hand."

"True charity is always gentle as well as benevolent, for it consists as much in the manner of doing a kindness as in the deed itself. A service, if delicately rendered, has a double value; but if rendered with haughtiness, though want may compel its acceptance, the recipient's heart is not touched by it.

"Remember, also, that ostentation destroys, in the sight of God, the merit of beneficence. Jesus has said: 'Let not your left hand know what your right hand doeth;' teaching you, by this injunction, not to tarnish charity by pride and vanity."

"You must distinguish between alms-giving, properly so-called, and beneficence. The most necessitous is not always he who begs by the wayside. Many, who are really poor, are restrained from begging by the dread of humiliation, and suffer silently and in secret: he who is really humane seeks out this hidden misery, and relieves it without ostentation.

" 'Love one another;' such is the divine law by which God governs all the worlds of the universe. Love is the law of attraction for living and organised beings; attraction is the law of love for inorganic matter."

"Never lose sight of the fact, that every spirit, whatever his degree of advancement, or his situation in reincarnation or in erraticity, is *always* placed between a superior who guides and improves him, and an inferior towards whom he has the same duties to fulfil. Be therefore charitable; not merely by the cold bestowal of a coin on the mendicant who ventures to beg it of you, but by seeking out the poverty that hides itself from view. Be indulgent for the defects of those about you; instead of despising the ignorant and the vicious, instruct them, and make them better; be gentle and benevolent to your inferiors; be the same for the humblest creatures of the lower reigns; and you will have obeyed the law of God."

SAINT VINCENT DE PAUL

889.   Are there not men who are reduced to beggary through their own fault?

"Undoubtedly there are; but if a sound moral education had taught them to practise the law of God, they would not have fallen into the excesses which have caused their ruin. It is mainly through the generalisation of such education that the improvement of your globe will be ultimately accomplished."   (707.)

Maternal and Filial Affection.

890.   Is maternal affection a virtue, or is it an instinctive feeling common to men and to animals?

"It is both. Nature has endowed the mother with the love of her offspring in order to ensure their preservation. Among the animals, maternal affection is limited to the supply of their material needs; it ceases when this care is no longer needed. In the human race, it lasts throughout life, and assumes a character of unselfish devotion that raises it to the rank of a virtue; it even survives death, and follows the career of the child from beyond the grave. You see, therefore, that there is in this affection, as it exists in man, something more than as it exists among the animals."   (205-385.)

891.   Since maternal affection is a natural sentiment, why is it that mothers often hate their children, and even, in some cases, before their birth?

"The absence of maternal affection is sometimes a trial chosen by the spirit of the child, or an expiation for him if he have been a bad father, a bad mother, or a bad son, in some previous existence. In all cases, a bad mother can only be the incarnation of a bad spirit, who seeks to throw obstacles in the path of the child, in order to make him succumb in the trial he has chosen. But such a violation of the laws of nature will not remain unpunished, and the spirit of the child will be rewarded for surmounting the obstacles thus thrown in his way."

892.   When parents have children who cause them sorrow, are they not excusable for not feeling for them the same tenderness they would have felt had their conduct been different?

"No; for the training of their children is a task that has been confided to them, and their mission is to make every possible effort to bring them back into the right road. (582, 583). Besides, the sorrows of parents are often the consequence of the bad habits they have allowed their children to contract from the cradle; a reaping of the evil harvest of which they themselves have sown the seeds."

CHAPTER XII

1. VIRTUES AND VICES—2. THE PASSIONS—3. SELFISH-
NESS—4. CHARACTERISTICS OF THE VIRTUOUS MAN.—
SELF-KNOWLEDGE.

Virtues and Vices.

893. Which is the most meritorious of all the virtues?

"All virtues are meritorious, for all of them are signs of progress
on the upward road. There is virtue in every act of voluntary
resistance to the seductive influence of evil tendencies; but the
sublimity of virtue consists in the sacrifice of self-interest to the
good of others. The highest of all virtues is that which takes the
form of the widest and most disinterested kindness."

*894. There are persons who do good from a spontaneous
impulse, without having to overcome any opposite feeling; is there
as much merit in their action as in that of others who, in doing
good, have to struggle with their own nature, and to surmount
an opposing impulse?*

"Those who have no longer to struggle against selfishness are
those who have already accomplished a certain amount of progress.
They have struggled and triumphed in the past, and their
generosity, therefore, no longer costs them any effort. To do good
seems to them to be perfectly natural, because they have acquired
the habit of kindness. They should be honoured as veterans, who
have won their grades on the field of battle.

"As you are still far from perfection, such persons strike you
with astonishment, because their action contrasts so strongly with
that of the rest of mankind, and you admire it in proportion to its
rarity; but you must know that what is the exception in your
world is the rule in worlds of more advanced degree. In those
worlds goodness is everywhere spontaneous, because they are
inhabited only by good spirits, among whom even an evil intention
would be considered as an exceptional monstrosity. It is this

general prevalence of goodness that constitutes the happiness of those worlds; it will be the same in your earth when the human race shall have been transformed, and shall rightly comprehend and practise the law of charity."

895. *Besides the defects and vices in regard to which no one can be mistaken, what is the most characteristic sign of imperfection?*

"Selfishness. Virtuous appearances are too often like gilding upon copper, that cannot stand the application of the touchstone. A man may possess good qualities which make him pass in the eyes of the world for virtuous, but those qualities, though proving him to have made a certain amount of progress, may not be capable of standing trial, and the slightest disturbance of his self-love may suffice to show his real character. Absolute disinterestedness is indeed so rare a thing in your earth, that you may well regard it with wonder, as something phenomenal.

"Attachment to material things is a sign of inferiority, because the more a man cares for the things of this world, the less does he understand his destiny; his disinterestedness, on the contrary, proves that he has arrived at a wider and clearer view of the future."

896. *There are persons who are generous, but without discernment, and who lavish their money without doing any real good, from the want of a reasonable plan for its employment; is there any merit in their action?*

"Such persons have the merit of disinterestedness, but they have not that of the good they might do. If disinterestedness be a virtue, thoughtless prodigality is always, to say the least of it, a want of judgment. Fortune is no more given to some persons to be thrown away than to others to be locked up in a safe; it is a deposit of which they will have to render an account, for they will have to answer for all the good they might have done, but failed to do, for all the tears they might have dried with the money they have wasted on those who had no need of it."

897. *Is he to blame who does good, not with a view to obtaining any reward upon the earth, but in the hope that he will be rewarded for it in the other life, and that his situation there will be the better for having done it? and will such a calculation act unfavourably on his advancement?*

"You should do good from charity—that is to say, disinterestedly.

— *But it is very natural that we should desire to advance, in order to emerge from so painful a state as our present life; spirits themselves tell us that we should practise rectitude in order to attain this end. Is it wrong, then, to hope that, through doing good, we may be better off than we are upon the earth?*

"Certainly not; but he who does good spontaneously, without even thinking of its results for himself, and simply for the sake of pleasing God and relieving his suffering neighbour, has already reached a higher degree of advancement, and is nearer to the summit of happiness, than his brother who, more selfish, does good from calculation, instead of being impelled to it solely by the sentiment of charity already naturalised in his heart."   (894.)

— *Should not a distinction be made between the good we do to our neighbour and the care we give to correcting our own defects? We can understand that there is but little merit in doing good with the idea that it will be counted to us in the other life; but is it also a sign of inferiority to amend ourselves, to conquer our passions, to correct whatever is faulty in our disposition, in the hope of bringing ourselves nearer to spirits of higher degree, and of raising ourselves to a higher position in the spirit-world?*

"No, no; by 'doing good' we merely meant being charitable. He who calculates, in every charitable deed he does, how much interest it will pay him, in the present life or in the next one, acts selfishly; but there is no selfishness in working out one's own improvement in the hope of bringing one's self nearer to God, which should be the aim of every effort."

898. The corporeal life being only a temporary sojourn in a lower state of existence, and our future life being therefore what we should mainly care for, is there any use in trying to acquire scientific knowledge that only bears upon the objects and wants of corporeal life?

"Undoubtedly there is, for such knowledge enables you to benefit your brethren; and besides, your spirit, if it have already progressed in intelligence, will ascend more rapidly in the other life, and will learn in an hour what it would take you years to learn upon the earth. No kind of knowledge is useless; all knowledge contributes more or less to your advancement, because the perfected spirit must know everything, and because progress has to be made in every direction, so that all acquired ideas help forward his development."

899. Of two men, equally rich, and both of whom employ their wealth solely for their personal satisfaction, but one of whom was born in opulence and has never known want, while the other owes his fortune to his labour, which is the more culpable?

"He who has known what it is to want, for he has felt the suffering which he does not relieve."

900. Can he who constantly accumulates, without doing good to any one, find an excuse in the fact that he will thus leave a larger fortune to his heirs?

"Such an excuse would only be a compromise with a bad conscience."

901. Of two miserly men, one denies himself the necessaries of life, and dies of want in the midst of his treasure; the other is stingy in regard to others, but is lavish in his outlay for himself, and, while he recoils from making the smallest sacrifice to render a service to his neighbour, or to subserve a noble cause, is regardless of expense in the gratification of his tastes or passions. If a kindness is asked of him, he is always short of funds; but, for the satisfying of any fancy of his own, he has always plenty of money. Which of them is the more guilty of the two, and which of them will be the worse off in the spirit-world?

"He who spends on his own enjoyment, for he is more selfish than miserly. The other is already undergoing a part of his punishment."

902. Is it wrong to desire riches as a means of doing good?

"Such a desire is laudable when it is pure; but is it always quite disinterested, and does it, never cover any secret thought of self? Is not the first person to whom one wishes to do good too often one's self?"

903. Is it wrong to study other people's defects?

"To do so merely for the sake of criticising or divulging them is very wrong, for it is a want of charity. To do so with a view to your own benefit, through your consequent avoidance of those defects in your own person, may sometimes be useful; but you must not forget that indulgence for the faults of others is one of the elements of charity. Before reproaching others with their imperfections, you should see whether others might not reproach you with the same defects. The only way to profit by such a critical examination of your neighbour's faults is by endeavouring to acquire the opposite virtues. Is he miserly? Be generous. Is he proud? Be humble and modest. Is he harsh? Be gentle. Is he shabby and petty? Be great in all you do. In a word, act in such a way as that it may not be said of you, in the words of Jesus, that you 'see the mote in your brother's eye, but do not see the beam in your own eye.'"

904. *Is it wrong to probe the sores of society for the purpose of rendering them evident?*

"That depends on the motive from which it is done. If a writer's only object be to create a scandal, it is a procuring of a personal satisfaction for himself by the presentation of pictures that are corrupting rather than instructive. The mind necessarily perceives the evils of society, but the observer who takes pleasure in portraying evil for its own sake will be punished for doing so."

— *How can we judge, in such a case, of the purity of intention and the sincerity of an author?*

"It is not always necessary to do so. If he writes good things, profit by them; if bad ones, it is a question of conscience that concerns himself. But if he desires to prove his sincerity, he must do so by the excellence of his own example."

905. *There are books that are very fine, full of moral teachings from which, though they have aided the progress of the human race, their authors have not derived much moral profit. Will the good those authors have done by their writings be counted to them as spirits?*

"The principles of morality, without a corresponding practice, are the seed without the sowing. Of what use is the seed, if you do not make it fructify and feed you? Such men are all the more guilty, because they possess the intelligence which enables them to comprehend. By not practising the virtues they recommend to others, they fail to secure the harvest they might have reaped for themselves."

906. *Is it wrong for him who does good to be conscious of the goodness of his deed, and to acknowledge that goodness to himself?*

"Since a man is conscious of the evil he does, he must also be conscious of the good he accomplishes; it is only by this testimony of his conscience that he can know whether he has done ill or well. It is by weighing all his actions in the scales of God's law, and especially of the law of justice, love, and charity, that he can decide whether they are good or bad, and can thus approve or disapprove of them. It cannot, therefore, be wrong in him to recognise the fact that he has triumphed over his evil tendencies, and to rejoice in having done so, provided he does not make this recognition a subject of vanity, for, in that case, he would be giving way to a tendency as reprehensible as any of those over which he has triumphet." (919.)

The Passions.

907. As our passions have their roots in nature, are they evil in themselves?

"No; it is only their excess that is evil, for excess implies a perversion of the will. But the principle of all his passions has been given to man for his good, and they may all spur him on to the accomplishment of great things. It is only their abuse that does harm."

908. How can we define the limit at which the passions cease to be good or bad?

"The passions are like a horse that is useful when under control, but dangerous when it obtains the mastery. A passion becomes pernicious the moment when you cease to govern it, and when it causes an injury to yourselves or to others."

The passions are levers that increase man's powers tenfold, and aid him in the accomplishment of the designs of Providence ; but if, instead of ruling them, he allows himself to be ruled by them, he falls into every sort of excess, and the same force which, held well in hand, would have been useful to him, falls upon and crushes him.

All the passions have their source in a natural sentiment or a natural want. They are therefore not evil in themselves, since they constitute one of the providentially-appointed conditions of our existence. What is usually meant by "passion" is the exaggeration of a need or a sentiment.

But this exaggeration is the excessive action of a motive-power, and not the power itself ; it is this excessive action which becomes an evil, and leads to evil consequences of every kind.

Every passion that brings man nearer to the nature of the animals takes him further from the spiritual nature.

Every sentiment that raises man above the nature of the animals is evidence of the predominance of his spiritual nature over his animal nature and brings him nearer to perfection.

909. Would a man's own efforts always suffice to enable him to vanquish his evil tendencies?

"Yes, very slight ones are often all that is needed; it is the *will* that is wanting. Alas! how few of you make any serious efforts to vanquish those tendencies!"

910. Can a man obtain efficacious help from spirits in over-coming his passions?

"If he addresses a sincere prayer for such help to God and to his good Genius, good spirits will certainly come to his aid, for it is their mission to do so." (459.)

911. Is not the action of the passions sometimes so violent that the will is powerless to withstand them?

"There are many who say '*I will,*' but whose *willing* is only on their lips, and who are not sorry that what they declare themselves to *will* does not take place. When a man is unable to vanquish his passions, it is because, through the backwardness of his spirit. he takes pleasure in yielding to them. He who controls his passions comprehends his spiritual nature; he knows that every victory over then is a triumph of his spirit over matter."

912. What is the most efficacious means of combating the predominance of the corporeal nature?

"The practice of abnegation."

Selfishness.

913. Which, among the vices, may be regarded as the root of the others?

"Selfishness, as we have repeatedly told you; for it is from selfishness that everything evil proceeds. Study all the vices, and you will see that selfishness is at the bottom of them all. Combat them as you will, you will never succeed in extirpating them until. attacking the evil in its root, you have destroyed the selfishness which is their cause. Let all your efforts tend to this end; for selfishness is the veritable social gangrene. Whoever would make, even in his earthly life, some approach towards moral excellence, must root out every selfish feeling from his heart, for selfishness is incompatible with justice, love, and charity; it neutralises every good quality."

914. Selfishness having its root in the sentiment of personal interest, it would seem that, to extirpate it entirely from the human heart, must be a very difficult matter. Is it possible to do so?

"In proportion as men become enlightened in regard to spiritual things, they attach less value to material things; and as they emancipate themselves from the thraldom of matter, they reform the human institutions by which selfishment is fostered and excited. Such should be the aim of education."

915. Selfishness being inherent in the human race, will it not always constitute an obstacle to the reign of perfect goodness upon the earth?

"It is certain that selfishness is your greatest evil; but it belongs to the inferiority of the spirits incarnated upon the earth, and not to the human race as such, and consequently, those spirits, in purifying themselves by successive incarnations, get rid of their selfishness as they do of their other impurities. Have you, upon the earth, none who have divested themselves of selfishness, and who practise charity? There are more of such than you think, but they are little known, for virtue does not seek to display itself in the glare of popularity. If there is one such among you, why should there not be ten? if there are ten, why should there not be a thousand? and so on."

916. Selfishness, so far from diminishing, increases with the civilisation that seems to strenghthen and intensify it; how can the effect be destroyed by the cause?

"The greater the development of an evil, the more hideous is it seen to be. It was necessary for selfishness to do a vast amount of harm, in order that you might see the necessity of extirpating it. When men shall have divested themselves of selfishness, they will live like brothers, doing each other no harm, but mutually aiding each other from a sentiment of *solidarity*. The strong will then be the support, and not the oppressor, of the weak; and none will lack the necessaries of life, because the law of justice will be obeyed by all. It is of this reign of justice that spirits are now charged to prepare the advent."

917. By what means can selfishness be destroyed?

"Of all human imperfections, the most difficult to root out is selfishness, because it is connected with the influence of matter, from which man, *still too near his origin*, has not yet been able to enfranchise himself, and which his laws, his social organisation, his education, all tend to maintain. Selfishness will be gradually weakened as your moral life obtains predominance over your material life, through the knowledge which Spiritism gives you of the *reality* of your future state, stripped of allegoric fables. Spiritism, when it comes to be rightly understood, and identified with the beliefs and habits of the human race, will transform all your customs, usages, and social relations. Selfishness is based on the importance you attribute to your own personality; Spiritism, on the contrary, when rightly understood, causes you to look at everything from a point of view so elevated that the sentiment of personality is lost, so to say, in the contemplation of immensity. In destroying the sentiment of self-importance, by showing its real nature, Spiritism necessarily combats selfishness.

"Man is often rendered selfish by his experience of the selfishness of others, which makes him feel the need of defending himself against them. Seeing that others think of themselves and not of him, he is led to think of himself rather than of others. But let the principle of charity and fraternity become the basis of social institutions, of the *legal* relations between nation and nation and between man and man, and each individual will think less of his own personal interests, because he will see that these have been thought of by others; he will experience the moralising influence of example and of contact. Amidst the present overflow of selfishness, much virtue is needed to enable a man to sacrifice his own interests for the sake of others, who often feel but little gratitude for such abnegation; but it is above all to those who possess this virtue that the Kingdom of Heaven is opened, and the happiness of the elect assured; while, at the day of judgment, whoever has thought only of himself will be set aside, and left to suffer from his lonelines." (785.) (FÉNÉLON.)

Laudable efforts are made to help forward the progress of the human race; the generous sentiments are encouraged, stimulated, honoured, more than has been the case at any former epoch, and yet the devouring worm of selfishness is still the pest and torment of society. It is a social disease that affects every one, and of which every one is more or less the victim; it should therefore be combated as we combat any other epidemic. To this end we must proceed as does the physician, and begin by tracing the malady to its source. We should seek out, in every department of the social fabric, from the relationships of the family to those of nations, from the cottage to the palace, all the causes, all the influences, patent or secret, that maintain and develop selfishness. The causes of the malady being discovered, the remedy will spontaneously present itself, and through the efforts of all, directed to a common end, the virus will gradually be extirpated. The cure may be slow, for the causes of the malady are many, but it is not impossible. It can only be effected, however, by going to the root of the evil, that is to say, by generalising education ; not the education which merely advances men in knowledge, but that which improves them morally. Education, rightly understood, is the key of moral progress. When the art of training the moral nature shall be understood as is the art of training the intellect, it will be possible to straighten a crooked nature as we straighten a crooked sapling. But this art demands much tact, much experience, and profound observation; it is a great mistake to suppose that the possession of scientific knowledge suffices to enable the teacher to exercise it with success. Whoever observes the life of a child, whether rich or poor, and notes all the pernicious influences that act upon its weakness from the moment of its birth, the ignorance and negligence of those who have charge of it, and the mischievous tendency of many of the means employed with a view to moralise it, will not wonder that the world should be so full if crooked sticks. But let the same skill and care be given to the training of the moral nature as to that of the intellect, and it will be seen that, even should some natures prove refractory, the greater number only need to be suitably cultivated in order to yield good fruit. (872.)

Man desires to be happy, and this desire, implanted in him by nature, prompts him to labour unceasingly to improve his condition upon the earth, and to seek out causes of the evils that afflict him, in order to remove them. When he thoughly comprehends that selfishness is one of those causes, that it engenders the pride, ambition, cupidity, envy, hatred, jealousy, by which he is continually annoyed, that it brings trouble into all the social relations, provokes dissensions, destroys confidence, converts friends into foes, and obliges each individual to remain constantly on the defensive against his neighbour, he will see that this vice is incompatible, not only with his own felicity, but even with his own security ; and the more he has suffered from it, the more keenly will he feel the necessity of fighting against it, as he fights against pestilence, dangerous animals, and every other source of disaster, for he will be compelled to do so in view of his own interest. (784.)

Selfishness is the source of all the vices, as charity is the source of all the virtues. To destroy the one, to develop the other, should be the aim of all who desire to insure their own happiness, in the present life, as in the future.

Characteristics of the Virtuous Man.

918. By what signs can we recognise a man as having accomplished the progress that will raise him in the spirit-hierarchy?

"The elevation of an incarnated spirit is proved by the conformity of all the acts of his corporeal life with the law of God, and by his comprehension of spiritual life."

The truly virtuous man is he who practises the law of justice, love, and charity, in its greatest purity. If he interrogates his conscience in regard to the acts accomplished by him, he will ask himself whether he has done nothing wrong, whether he has done **all the good in his power,** whether no one has cause to complain of him, and whether he has done to others all that he would wish others to do to him. Being filled with the sentiment of charity and kindness for all, he does good for its own sake, without hope of reward, and sacrifices his own interest to justice.

He is kind, benevolent, humane, for all, because he sees a brother in every man, whatever his race or his belief.

If God has given him power and riches, he considers them as A TRUST confided to him for the general good ; he is not vain of them, for he knows that God, who has given them to him, can take them from him.

If the constitution of society has made other men dependent on him, he treats them with kindness and benevolence, as being his equals in the sight of God; he uses his authority to raise them morally, and not to crush them by his pride.

He is indulgent for the weaknesses of others, knowing that he too needs indulgence, and remembering the words of Christ, **"Let him that is without sin cast the first stone."**

He is not vindictive, but remembers only benefits ; following the example of Jesus, he forgives all offences, for he knows that **he will only obtain forgiveness in proportion as he has forgiven.**

He respects the rights of others, as established by the law of nature, as scrupulously as he desires those rights to be respected in his own case.

Self — Knowledge.

919. What is the most efficacious method of ensuring one's own moral improvement in the present life, and resisting the attraction of evil?

"One of the sages of antiquity has told you: 'Know thyself.'"

— We fully admit the wisdom of the maxim; but this self-knowledge is just what it is most difficult to acquire. By what means can we acquire it?

"Do what I myself used to do during my life upon the earth. At the close of each day I examined my conscience, reviewed all that I had done, and asked myself whether I had not failed in some duty, whether some one might not have reason to complain of me. It was in this way that I succeeded in obtaining a knowledge of myself, and in ascertaining what there was in me that needed reforming. He who, every evening, should thus recall all the actions of the day, asking himself whether he has done ill or well, and praying God and his guardian angel to enlighten him would acquire great strength for self-improvement, for, believe me, God would assist him. Ask yourself these questions; inquire of yourself what you have done, and what was your aim in such and such a manner; whether you have done anything that you would blame in another; whether you have done anything that you would be ashamed to avow. Ask yourself also this question :—'If it pleased God to call me back, at this moment, into the other life, should I, on returning into the world of spirits, in which nothing is hidden, have to dread the sight of any one?' Examine what you may have done, first, against God; next, against your neighbour; and lastly, against yourself. The answers to these questions will either give repose to your conscience, or show you some moral malady of which you will have to cure yourself.

"Self-knowledge is, therefore, the key to individual improvement; but, you will ask, 'How is one to judge one's self? Is not each man subject to the illusions of self-love, which diminish his faults in his own eyes and find excuses for them? The miser thinks himself to be merely practising economy and foresight; the proud man thinks his pride to be only dignity.' This is true, but you have a means of ascertainment that cannot deceive you. When you are in doubt as to the quality of any one of your actions, ask yourself what would be your judgment in regard to it if it were done by another? If you would blame it in another, it cannot be less blamable when done by you, for God's justice has neither two weights nor two measures. Endeavour also to learn what is thought of it by others; and do not overlook the opinion of your enemies, for they have no interest in disguising the truth, and God often places them beside you as a mirror, to warn you more frankly than would be done by a friend. Let him, then, who is firmly resolved on self-improvement, examine his conscience in order to root out his evil tendencies, as he roots out the weeds from his garden; let him, every night, cast up his moral accounts for the day, as the tradesman counts up his profit and loss; he may be sure that the, former will be a more profitable operation than the latter. He who, after this footing up of his day's doings, can say that the balance of the account is in his favour, may sleep in peace, and fearlessly await the moment of his awaking in the other life.

"Let the questions you address to us be clear and precise, and do not hesitate to multiply them; you may well devote a few minutes to the securing of a happiness that will last for ever. Do you not labour every day with a view to insuring repose for your old age? Is not this repose the object of your desires, the aim that prompts your endurance of the fatigues and privations of the moment? But what comparison is there between a few days of rest, impaired by the infirmities of the body, and the endless rest that awaits the virtuous? And is not this latter worth the making of a few efforts? I know that many will say, 'The present is certain, and the future uncertain;' but this is precisely the error we are charged to remove from your minds, by showing you your future in such a way as to leave no doubt in your minds concerning it. This is why, having begun by producing phenomena calculated to arrest your attention through their appeal to your senses, we now give you the moral teachings that each of you is charged to spread abroad in his turn. It is to this end that we have dictated *The Spirit's Book*."

SAINT AUGUSTINE

FOURTH BOOK—HOPES AND CONSOLATIONS

CHAPTER I

EARTHLY JOYS AND SORROWS

1. HAPPINESS AND UNHAPPINESS—2. LOSS OF THOSE WE
DEATH—6. WEARINESS OF LIFE ; SUICIDE.
AFFECTIONS—4. ANTIPATHETIC UNIONS—5. FEAR OF
LOVE—3. DISAPPOINTMENTS ; INGRATITUDE ; BLIGHTED

Happiness and Unhappiness.

*920. Is it possible for man to enjoy perfect happiness upon
the earth?*

"No; for corporeal life has been appointed to him either as a
trial or an expiation; but it depends upon himself to lighten the
evils of his lot, and to render it as happy as life can be upon
the earth."

*921. We can conceive that man will be happy upon the earth
when the human race shall have been transformed; but, meanwhile, is it possible for each man to ensure for himself a moderate
amount of happiness?*

"Man is more often the artisan of his own unhappiness. If he
obeyed the law of God, he would not only spare himself much
sorrow, but would also procure for himself all the felicity that is
compatible with the grossness of earthly existence."

He who is perfectly sure that the future life is a reality regards his
corporeal life as being merely a traveller's momentary halt in a wayside
inn. and easily consoles himself for the passing annoyances of a journey
which is bringing him to a new and happier position, that will be all the
more satisfactory in proportion to the completeness of the preparations he
has made for entering upon it.

We are punished, even in the present life, for our infraction of the
laws of corporeal existence, by the sufferings which are the result of that
infraction and of our own excesses. If we trace what we call our earthly
ills back to their origin, we shall find them to be, for the most part, the
result of a first deviation from the straight road. This deviation caused us
to enter upon a wrong path, and each subsequent step brought us more
and more deeply into trouble.

*922. Earthly happiness is relative to the position of each person;
what suffices for the happiness of one would be misfortune for*

another. Is there, nevertheless, a common standard of happiness for all men?

"As regards material existence, it is the possession of the necessaries of life; as regards moral existence, it is a good conscience and the belief in a future state."

923. Does not that which ı a superfluity for one become a necessary of life for another and vice versâ, according to differences of position?

"Yes, according to your material ideas, your prejudices, your ambition, and all your absurd notions that you will gradually get rid of as you come to understand the truth of things. Undoubtedly, he who, having possessed an income of thousands, becomes reduced to as many hundreds, looks upon himself as being very unfortunate, because he can no longer cut so great a figure in the world, maintain what he calls his rank, keep horses, carriages, and lackeys, and gratify all his tastes and passions. He appears to himself to lack the very necessaries of life; but is he really so much to be pitied while, beside him, so many others are dying of cold and hunger, and have not even where to lay their head? He who is wise compares himself with what is below him, never with what is above him, unless it be to raise his soul towards the Infinite." (715.)

924. There are misfortunes which come upon men independently of their own conduct, and that befall even the most upright. Is there no way of preserving one's self from them?

"Such misfortunes must be borne with resignation and *without murmuring*, if you would progress; but you may always derive consolation from the hope of a happier future, provided you do what is needed to obtain it."

925. Why does God so often bestow the gifts of fortune on men who do not appear to have deserved such a favour?

"Wealth appears to be a favour to those who see only the present, but you must remember that fortune is often a more dangerous trial than poverty." (814 *et seq.*)

926. Does not civilisation, by creating new wants, become the source of new afflictions?

"The ills of your world are proportional to the *factitious* wants that you create for yourselves. He who is able to set bounds to his desires, and to see without envy what is above him, spares himself many of the disappointments of the earthly life. The richest of men is he who has the fewest needs.

"You envy the enjoyments of those who appear to you to be the favourites of fortune, but do you know what is in store for so many of them? If they use their wealth only for themselves, they are selfish, and, in that case, a terrible reverse awaits them. Instead of envying, you should pity them. God sometimes permits the wicked to prosper, but his prosperity is not to be envied, for he will pay for it with weeping and gnashing of teeth. If a righteous man undergoes misfortune, it is a trial from which, being bravely borne, he will reap a rich reward. Remember the words of Jesus: 'Blessed are they that mourn, for they shall be comforted.'"

927. Superfluities are certainly not indispensable to happiness, but it is otherwise in regard to the necessaries of life. Is it not, then, really a misfortune to be deprived of these?

"A man is really unfortunate only when deprived of what is necessary to life and to bodily health. If this privation be the result of his own misconduct, he has only himself to blame for it; if it be the fault of others, a heavy responsibility will rest with those who have caused it."

928. By our special aptitudes, God evidently shows to each of us our special vocation. Are not many of the ills of life attributable to our not following that vocation?

"Yes. It often happens that parents, through pride or avarice, force their children from the path traced out for them by nature; but they will be held responsible for the results of this misdirection."

— You would then approve of the son of some high personage making himself a cobbler, for instance, if he were endowed with a natural aptitude for cobbling?

"You must not go off into absurdities and exaggerations. Civilisation has its necessities. Why should the son of a man occupying a high position make himself a cobbler, if able to do something more important? Such an one might always make himself useful, according to the measure of his faculties, without running counter to common sense. For instance, if he were not fitted to make a good lawyer, he might be a good engineer, a mechanician, etc."

The placing of people in positions for which they are naturally unfit is assuredly one of the most frequent causes of failure and disappointment.

Want of aptitude for the career on which one has entered is an inexhaustible source of reverses; and as he who has thus failed in one career is often prevented by pride from seeking a resource in some humbler avocation, he is often tempted to commit suicide in order to escape what he regards as a humiliation: whereas, **if a sound moral education had raised him above the stupid prejudices of pride, he would have been at no loss to obtain the means of subsistence.**

929. *There are persons who, being utterly without resources, though surrounded by abundance, have no other prospect than starvation. What course should they take under such circumstances? Ought they to allow themselves to die of hunger?*

"No one should ever admit into his mind the idea of allowing himself to die of hunger; a man could always find the means of obtaining food if pride did not interpose itself between want and work. It has often been said that 'No work is dishonourable it honestly done;' but this is one of the aphorisms that each man is more prompt to apply to his neighbour than to himself."

930. *It is evident that, were it not for the social prejudices by which we allow ourselves to be swayed, a man would always be able to find some sort of work that would enable him to gain a living, even though he thus took a humbler position; but among those who have no such prejudices, or who put them aside, are there not some who are really unable to provide for their wants, through illness, or through other circumstances independent of their will?*

"In a society organised according to the law of Christ, no one would die of hunger."

Were society organised with wisdom and forethought, no one could lack the necessaries of life unless through his own fault; but a man's faults themselves are often the result of the circumstances in which he finds himself placed. When men shall have advanced sufficiently to practise the law of God, they will not only be better intrinsically and as individuals, but will organise their social relations on a basis of justice and charity. (793.)

931. *Why is it that, in our world, the classes that suffer are so much more numerous than those that are prosperous?*

"None of you are perfectly happy, and what the world regards as prosperity often hides the most poignant sorrows. Suffering is everywhere. However, by way of replying to the thought which prompted your question, I answer, that what you call *the suffering classes* are the most numerous, because the earth is a place of expiation. When mankind shall have made it the sojourn of goodness and of good spirits, there will be no more unhappiness in the earth, which will then be a terrestrial paradise for all its inhabitants."

932. How is it that, in this world, the wicked so often have power over the good?

"That is a consequence of the weakness of the good. The wicked are intriguing and audacious, thè good are often timid. When the latter shall be determined to have the upper hand they will have it."

933. Men are often the artisans of their own worldly sufferings; are they also the artisans of their moral sufferings?

"Even more so; for their worldly sufferings are often independent of their action; but it is wounded pride, disappointed ambition, the anxieties of avarice, envy, jealousy, all the passions, in short, that constitute the torments of the soul.

"Envy and jealousy! Happy are they who know not those two gnawing worms! Where envy and jealousy exist, there can be no calm, no repose. Before him who is the slave of those passions, the objects of his longings, of his hatreds, of his anger, stand like so many phantoms, pursuing him without respite, even in his sleep. The envious and jealous are always in a fever. Is such a state a desirable one? Can you not understand that, with such passions, man creates for himself the most terrible tortures, and that the earth really becomes a hell for him?"

Many of our colloquial expressions present vivid pictures of the effects of the different passions. We say, "puffed up with pride;" "dying with envy;" "bursting with spite;" "devoured by jealousy;" etc.; pictures that are only too true to their originals. In many cases, these evil passions have no determinate object. There are persons, for instance, who are naturally jealous of everyone who rises, of everything that oversteps the common line, even when their own interest is in no way concerned, and simply because they are not able to command a similar success. Every manifestation of superiority on the part of others is regarded by them as an offence to themselves ; for the jealousy of mediocrity would always, if it could, bring everyone down to its own level.

Much of the unhappiness of human life is a result of the undue importance attached by man to the things of this world ; vanity, disappointed ambition, and cupidity, make up no small part of his troubles. If he placed his aims beyond the narrow circle of his outer life, if he raised his thoughts towards the infinitude that is his destiny, the vicissitudes of human existence would seem to him as petty and puerile as the broken toy over the loss of which the child weeps so bitterly.

He who finds his happiness only in the satisfaction of pride and of gross material appetites is unhappy when he cannot satisfy them ; while he who asks for no superfluities is happy under circumstances that would be deemed calamitous by others.

We are now speaking of civilised people, for the savage, having fewer wants, has not the same incitements to envy and anxiety ; his way of looking at things is altogether different. In the civilised state, man reasons upon and analyses his unhappiness, and is therefore all the more painfully affected by it ; but he may also reason upon and analyse the means of consolation within his reach. **This consolation is furnished him by Christianity, which gives him the hope of a better future, and by Spiritism, which gives him the certainty of that future.**

Loss of Those We Love.

934. Is not the loss of those who are dear to us a legitimate source of sorrow, seeing that this loss is both irreparable and independent of our action?

"This cause of sorrow, which acts alike upon rich and poor, is the common law of humanity, for it is either a trial or an expiation; but you have the consolation of holding communication with your friends through the means already possessed by you, *while awaiting other means that will be more direct, and more accessible to your senses.*"

935. What is to be thought of the opinion which regards communication with those who are beyond the grave as a profanation?

"There can be no profanation where there is reverent concentration of thought and sympathy, and when the evocation is made with fitting respect; and the proof of this is found in the fact the spirits who love you take pleasure in coming to you; they rejoice in being remembered by you, and in being able to converse with you. But there would be profanation in this communication if carried on in a spirit of frivolity."

The possibility of entering into communication with spirits is most consoling, since it gives us the means of holding converse with those of our relatives and friends who have quitted the earthly life before us. By our evocation, we draw them nearer to us; they come to our side, hear us, and reply to us; there is, so to say. no longer any separation between them and us. They aid us with their counsels, and assure us of the pleasure afforded them by our remembrance. It is a satisfaction for us to know that they are happy, to learn **from themselves** the details of their new existence, and to acquire the certainty of our rejoining them in our turn.

936. What effect has the inconsolable sorrow of survivors upon the spirits who are the object of that sorrow?

"A spirit is touched by the remembrance and regrets of those he has loved; but a persistent and unreasonable sorrow affects him painfully, because he sees, in this excessive grief, a want of faith in the future and confidence in God, and, consequently, an obstacle to the advancement of the mourner, and, perhaps, to their reunion."

A spirit, when disincarnated, being happier than he was upon the earth, to regret his change of life is to regret his being happy. Two friends are prisoners, shut up in the same dungeon; both of them are some day to be set at liberty, but one of them obtains his deliverance before the other. Would it be kind on the part of him who remains in prison to regret that his friend has been set at liberty before him? Would there not be on his part more selfishness than affection in wishing his friend to remain in captivity and suffering as long as himself? It is the same with two persons who love one another upon the earth; he who quits it first is the first delivered; and the other ought to rejoice in his deliverance, while awaiting with patience the moment when he shall be delivered in his turn.

We may illustrate this subject by another comparison. You have a friend whose situation, while remaining near you, is a painful one; his health or his interests require that he should go to another country, where he will be better off in every respect. He will no longer be near you at every moment, but you will still be in correspondence with him; the separation between you will be only in your daily life. Should you grieve for his removal, since it is for his good?

By the evident proofs which it gives us of the reality of the future life, and of the presence about us and the continued affection and solicitude of those we have loved, as well as by the relations which it enables us to keep up with them, Spiritism offers us the most effectual consolation under the greatest and most painful of earthly sorrows; it does away with solitude and separation, for it shows us that the most isolated of human beings is always surrounded by a host of friends, with whom he can hold affectionate converse.

We are often impatient under the tribulations of life; they seem to us so intolerable that we cannot believe it to be possible for us to bear up under them; and yet, if we have borne them with courage, if we have been able to silence our murmurings, we shall rejoice to have undergone them, when we have finished our earthly career, as the patient rejoices, when convalescent, to have resigned himself to the painful course of treatment that has cured him of his malady.

Disappointments, Ingratitude, Blighted Affections.

937. Are not the disappointments that are caused by ingratitude, and by the fragility of earthly friendships, also a source of bitterness of the human heart?

"Yes; but we teach you to feel pity for the ungrateful, and for faithless friends; their unkindness will do more harm to themselves than to you. Ingratitude comes of selfishness; and he who is selfish will meet, sooner or later, with hearts as hard as his own has been. Think of all those who have done more good than you have done, who are more worthful than you are, and whose kindness has been repaid with ingratitude. Remember that Jesus himself, during his life, was scoffed at, despised, and treated as a knave and an impostor; and do not be surprised that you should be treated in the same way. Let the consciousness of the good you have done be your recompense in your present life, and do not trouble yourself about those to whom you have done it. Ingratitude serves to test your persistence in doing good; it will be counted to you hereafter, and those who have been unmindful of your kindness will be punished, and all the more severely, the greater has been their ingratitude."

938. Are not the disappointments caused by ingratitude calculated to harden the heart and render it unfeeling?

"It would be wrong to let them do so; for the generous man is always glad to have done good. He knows that, if those whom he has benefited do not remember his kindness in the present life, they will remember it in a future one, and will then feel shame and remorse for their ingratitude."

— *But this knowledge will not prevent him from being acutely pained by ingratitude in the present life; might not this pain lead him to think that he would be happier if he possessed less sensibility?*

"Yes; if he preferred a selfish happiness; but that sort of happiness is a very pitiable one. Let such a man try to understand that the ungrateful friends who desert him are unworthy of his friendship, and that he has been mistaken in his estimate of them, and he will no longer regret their loss. Their place will by and by be filled by others who are better able to understand him. You should pity those from whom you have received ill-treatment that you have not deserved, for a heavy retribution will overtake them; but you should not allow yourselves to be painfully affected by their misconduct. Your indifference to their ill-treatment will place you above them."

Nature has implanted in man the need of loving of being loved. One of the greatest enjoyments accorded to him upon the earth is the meeting with hearts that sympathise with his own. This sympathy gives him a foretaste of the happiness that awaits him in the world of perfected spirits, where all is love and kindness ; a happiness that is refused to the selfish.

Antipathetic Unions.

939. *Since spirits who are sympathetic to one another are spontaneously attracted to each other, how is it that, among incarnated spirits, the love is often only on one side; that the most sincere affection is met with indifference or even with repulsion; and that, moreover, the liveliest affection of two persons for one another may be changed into dislike, and even into hatred?*

"Such a contrariety of feeling is a punishment, but only a passing one. Besides, how many are there who imagine themselves to be desperately in love with each other, because they•judge one another from appearances only, but who, when obliged to live together, soon discover that their affection was nothing more than a passing caprice? It is not enough to be taken with some one who pleases you, and whom you imagine to be gifted with all sorts of good qualities; it is only by living together that you can ascertain the worth of the appearances that have captivated you. On the other hand, how many of those unions that seem, at first, as though they never could become sympathetic, grow, in time, into a tender and lasting affection, founded upon the esteem that has been developed between the parties by a better and more complete acquaintance with each other's good qualities? You must not forget that it is the spirit which loves, and not the body, and that, when the illusion of corporeal attractions is dissipated, the spirit perceives the real quality of the union into which it has entered.

"There are two kinds of affection—that of the body, and that of the soul, and these are often mistaken for one another. The affection of the soul, when pure and sympathetic, is lasting; that of the body is perishable: this is why those who fancied that they loved each with an eternal affection often detest one another when their illusion has vanished."

940. *Is not the lack of sympathy between persons destined to live together also a source of sorrow, and one that is all the more bitter because it poisons an entire existence?*

"Very bitter it is, undoubtedly; but it is usually a misfortune of your own causing. In the first place, your laws are in fault; for how can you suppose that those who dislike one another can be intended by God to live together? In the next place, you yourselves are to blame, for you often seek, in those unions, the satisfaction of your pride and ambition rather than the happiness of a mutual affection; and, in such cases, you undergo the natural consequences of your prejudices."

— *But, in such cases, is there not generally an innocent victim?*

"Yes, one for whom it is a heavy expiation; but the responsibility of such unhappiness will, nevertheless, be brought home to those who caused it. If the light of truth have reached the soul of the victim, faith in the future will give consolation under present suffering. But the causes of these private misfortunes will disappear in proportion as your prejudices are dissipated."

Fear of Death.

941. *The fear of death causes perplexity to many persons; whence comes this fear in the case of those who believe in a future life?*

"Such fear is altogether misplaced; but when people have been, in their youth, thoroughly indoctrinated into the belief that there is a hell as well as a heaven, and that they will most likely go to the former, because whatever belongs to human life is a mortal sin for the soul, they are naturally afraid, if they have retained their religious belief, of the fire that is to burn them for ever without destroying them. But most of those who are thus indoctrinated in their childhood, if possessed of judgment, throw aside that belief when they grow up, and, being unable to assent to such a doctrine, become atheists or materialists; so that the natural effect of such teaching is to make them believe that there is nothing beyond this present life.

"Death has no terrors for the righteous man, because, with *faith*, he has the *certainty* of a future life; *hope* leads him to expect an existence happier than his present one; and *charity*, which has been the law of his action, gives him the assurance that, in the world which he is about to enter, he will meet with no one whose recognition he will have reason to dread." (730.)

The carnally-minded man, more attracted by corporeal life than by the life of the spirit, knows only the pains and pleasures of terrestrial existence. His only happiness is in the fugitive satisfaction of his earthly desires; his mind, constantly occupied with the vicissitudes of the present life, and painfully affected by them, is tortured with perpetual anxiety. The thought of death terrifies him, because he has doubts about his future, and because he has to leave all his affections and all his hopes behind him he leaves the earth.

The spiritually-minded man, who has raised himself above the factitious wants created by the passions, has, even in this lower life, enjoyments unknown to the carnally-minded. The moderation of his desires gives calmness and serenity to his spirit. Happy in the good he does, life has no disappointments for him, and its vexations pass lightly over his consciousness, without leaving upon it any painful impress.

942. *Will not these counsels as to the way to be happy in the present life be considered by many persons as somewhat commonplace; will they not be looked upon as truisms; and will it not be said that, after all, the true secret of happiness is to be able to bear up under one's troubles?*

"A good many people will take this view of the matter; but, of these, not a few will be like the sick man, for whom the physician prescribes dieting, but who demands to be cured without changing his habits, and while continuing the indulgences of the table that keep up his dyspepsia."

Weariness of Life — Suicide

943. *What is the cause of the weariness of life which sometimes takes possession of people without any assignable reason?*

"Idleness; lack of conviction; sometimes, satiety. For him who employs his faculties in the pursuit of some useful aim *in harmony with his natural aptitudes*, exertion is not disagreeable: his time passes quickly in congenial occupation; and he is able to bear the

vicissitudes of life with patience and resignation, because he looks
forward to a more solid and lasting happiness in the future."

944.   Has a man the right to dispose of his life?
"No; that right belongs to God alone. He who voluntarily
commits suicide contravenes the providential ordering which sent
him into the earthly life."
— *Is not suicide always voluntary?*
"The madman who kills himself does not know what he is
doing."

*945.   What is to be thought of those who commit suicide because
they are sick of life?*
"Fools! why did they not employ themselves in some useful
work? Had they done so, life would not have been a weariness
to them."

*946.   What is to be thought of those who resort to suicide in
order to escape from the troubles and disappointments of this
world?*
"They are weaklings who lack courage to bear the petty annoyances of existence. God helps those who suffer bravely, but
not those who have neither strength nor courage. The tribulations
of life are trials or expiations; happy are those who bear them without murmuring, for great will be their reward! Unhappy, on the
contrary, are those who expect their well-being from what they
impiously call 'chance' or 'luck'! Chance, or luck, to borrow
their own expressions, may favour them for a time; but only to
make them feel, afterwards, and all the more bitterly, the emptiness
of those words."
— *Will not those who have driven an unhappy fellow-creature
to this deed of despair be held responsible for the consequences of
their action?*
"Yes; and heavy indeed will be their punishment, for *they will
have to answer for those consequences as for a murder."*

*947.   Can we consider as having committed suicide the man
who, becoming disheartened in his struggle with adversity, allows
himself to die of despair?*
"Such self-abandonment is suicide; but those who had caused
the crime, or might have prevented it, would be more to blame
for it than the one by whom it had been committed, and the latter
would therefore be judged leniently. But, nevertheless, you must

not suppose that he would be entirely absolved if he had been wanting in firmness and perseverance, or had failed to make the best use of his intelligence to help himself out of his difficulties. And it would go still harder with him if he had been one of those whose intelligence is paralysed by pride, who would blush to earn their living by manual labour, and would rather die of starvation than derogate from what they call their "social position." Is there not a hundredfold more nobleness and true dignity in bearing up against adversity, in braving the ill-natured remarks of the futile and selfish, whose goodwill is only for those who are in want of nothing, and who turn the cold shoulder to all who are in need of help? To throw away one's life on account of such people is doubly absurd, seeing that they will be perfectly indifferent to the sacrifice."

948. *Is suicide as blamable, when committed in order to escape the disgrace of having done wrong, as when it is prompted by despair?*

"A fault is not effaced by suicide, which, on the contrary, is a second fault added to the first. He who has had the courage to do wrong should have the courage to bear the consequences of his wrong-doing. God is the sole judge, and sometimes diminishes the penalty of wrong-doing in consideration of the circumstances which led to it."

949. *Is suicide excusable when committed in order to avoid bringing disgrace on one's children or family?*

"He who has recourse to such an expedient does wrong; but, as he believes his action to be for the best, God takes note of his intention, for his suicide is a self-imposed expiation; his fault is extenuated by his intention, but it is none the less a fault. But when you have got rid of your social prejudices and abuses, you will have no more suicides."

He who takes his own life, in order to escape the disgrace of a bad action, proves that he attaches more value to the estimation of men than to that of God; for the goes back into the spirit-world laden with his iniquities, of the means of atoning for which, during his earthly life, he has thus deprived himself. God is less inexorable than men · often are ; He pardons those who sincerely repent, and takes account of all our efforts to repair what we have done amiss ; but nothing is repaired by suicide.

950. *What is to be thought of him who makes away with himself in the hope of arriving sooner at a happier state of existence?*

"Another piece of folly! Let a man do good, and he will be much more sure of reaching such a state. His suicide will delay his entrance into a better world; for he himself will ask to be allowed to come back to the earth, in order to *complete the life* that he has cut short in pursuit of a mistaken idea. The sanctuary of the good is never opened by a fault, no matter what may have been its motive."

951. Is not the sacrifice of one's life meritorious when it is made in order to save the lives of others, or to be useful to them?

"Incurred for such an end, it is sublime; but such a voluntary sacrifice of life is not suicide. It is the *useless* sacrifice that is displeasing to God, and also that which is tarnished by pride. A sacrifice is only meritorious when disinterested; if accomplished in view of a selfish end, its value is proportionally lessened in the sight of God."

Every sacrifice of our interest or enjoyment made for the sake of others is supremely meritorious in the sight of God; for it is the fulfilling of the law of charity. Life being, of all earthly possessions, the one to which men attach the greatest value, he who renounces it for the good of his fellow-creatures does not commit a crime; he accomplishes a sacrifice. But, before accomplishing it, he should consider whether his life might not be more useful than his death.

952. Does he commit suicide who falls a victim to the excessive indulgence of passions which he knows will hasten his death, but which habit has converted into physical necessities that he is unable to control?

"He commits moral suicide. Do you not see that a man, in such a case, is trebly guilty? For he is guilty of a want of firmness, of the sin of bestiality, and of forgetfulness of God."

— *Is such a man more or less guilty than he who kills himself from despair?*

"He is more guilty, because he has had time to reflect on the suicidal nature of the course he was pursuing. In the case of him who commits suicide on the spur of the moment, there is sometimes a degree of bewilderment not unallied to madness. The former will be punished much more severely than the latter; for the retributive penalties of crime are always proportioned to the consciousness of wrong-doing that accompanied its commission."

953. Is it wrong on the part of him who finds himself exposed to some terrible and inevitable death to shorten his sufferings by killing himself?

"It is always wrong not to await the moment of dissolution appointed by God. Besides, how can a man tell whether the end of his life has really come, or whether some unexpected help may not reach him at what he supposes to be his last moment?"

— *We admit that suicide is reprehensible under ordinary circumstances, but we are supposing a case in which death is inevitable, and in which life is only shortened by a few instants?*

"There is always in such a case a want of resignation and of submission to the will of the Creator."

— *What in such a case are the consequences of suicide?*

"The same as in all other cases; an expiation proportioned to the gravity of the fault, according to the circumstances under which it was committed."

954. *Is there guilt in the imprudence which has accidentally caused a loss of life?*

"There is no guilt where there is no positive intention or consciousness of doing harm."

955. *Are the women who, in some countries, voluntarily burn themselves to death with the body of their husband, to be considered as committing suicide, and have they to undergo the punishment of that crime?*

"They obey the dictates of a superstitious prejudice, and, moreover, are often the victims of force rather than of their own free-will. They believe themselves to be accomplishing a duty, and such an act does not partake of the character of suicide. Their excuse is found in the moral nullity and ignorance of the greater number of them. All such barbarous and stupid customs will disappear with the development of civilisation."

956. *Do those persons attain the end they have in view, who, unable to bear the loss of the objects of their affection, kill themselves in the hope of rejoining them in the other life?*

"In such cases the result of suicide is the opposite of what was hoped for. Instead of being reunited to the object of their affection, those who have made this sad mistake find themselves separated, and for a very long time, from the being they hoped to rejoin; for God cannot recompense, by the granting of a favour, an act which is at once a proof of moral cowardice, and an insult offered to Himself in distrusting His Providence. They will pay for their folly with sorrows still greater than those they fancied they were about to shorten, and for which they will not be compensated by the satisfaction they hoped do obtain." (934 *et seq.*)

957. What are in general the effects of suicide on the state of the spirit by whom it has been committed?

"The consequences of suicide vary in different cases, because the penalties it entails are always proportioned to the circumstances which, in each case, have led to its commission. The one punishment which none can escape who have committed suicide is *disappointment*; the rest of their punishment depends on circumstances. Some of those who have killed themselves expiate their fault at once; others do so in a new earthly life harder to bear than the one whose course they have interrupted."

Observation has confirmed the statement that the consequences of suicide are not the same in all cases; but it has also shown us that some of those consequences, resulting from the sudden interruption of life, are the same in all cases of violent death. Foremost among these is the **greater** tenacity and consequent persistence of the link that unites the spirit and the body, which link, in nearly all such cases, is in its full strength at the moment when it is broken; whereas, when death is the result of natural causes, that link has been gradually weakened, and is often severed before life is completely extinct. The consequences of violent death are, first, the prolongation of the mental confusion which usually follows death, and, next, the illusion which causes a spirit, during a longer or shorter period, to believe himself to be still living in the earthly life. (155, 165.)

The affinity which continues to exist between the spirit and the body produces, in the case of some of those who have committed suicide, a sort of repercussion of the state of the body in the consciousness of the spirit, who is thus compelled to perceive the effects of its decomposition, and experiences therefrom a sensation of intense anguish and horror; a state which may continue as long as the life which he has interrupted ought to have lasted. This state is not a necessary result of suicide; but he who has voluntarily shortened his life can never escape the consequences of his want of courageous endurance; sooner or later, and in some way or other, he is made to expiate his fault. Thus, many spirits who had been very unhappy upon the earth have stated that they had committed suicide in their preceding existence, and that they had voluntarily submitted to new trials in order to try to bear them with more resignation. In some cases the result of suicide is a sort of connexion with terrestrial matter, from which they vainly endeavour to free themselves, that they may rise to happier worlds, access to which is denied to them; in other cases it is regret for having done something useless, and from which they have reaped only disappointment.

Religion, morality, all systems of philosophy, condemn suicide as being contrary to the law of nature; all lay it down as a principle that we have no right to voluntary shorten our life; but why have we not that right? Why are we not at liberty to put an end to our sufferings? It was reserved for Spiritism to show, by the example of those who have succumbed to that temptation, that suicide is not only a fault, as being an infraction of a moral law (a consideration of little weight with some persons), but is also a piece of stupidity, since no benefit is to be gained by it, but quite the contrary. The teachings of Spiritism in regard to this subject are not merely theoretic; for it places the facts of the case before our eyes.

CHAPTER II

FUTURE JOYS AND SORROWS

1. ANNIHILATION ; FUTURE LIFE.—2. INTUITION OF FUTURE JOYS AND SORROWS.—3. INTERVENTION OF GOD IN REWARDS AND PUNISHMENTS.—4. NATURE OF FUTURE JOYS AND SORROWS.—5. TEMPORAL PENALTIES. —6. EXPIATION AND REPENTANCE.—7. DURATION OF FUTURE PENALTIES.—8. PARADISE, HELL, PURGATORY.

Annihilation — Future Life.

958. Why has man an instinctive horror of the idea of annihilation?

"Because there is no such thing as nothingness."

959. Whence does man derive the instinctive sentiment of a future life?

"From the knowledge of that life possessed by his spirit previous to his incarnation; the soul retaining a vague remembrance of what it knew in its spirit-state."

In all ages, man has occupied himself with the question of a future beyond the grave ; and it is natural that he should have done so. Whatever importance he may attach to the present life, he cannot help seeing how brief it is, and how precarious, since it may be cut short at any moment, so that he is never sure of the morrow. What becomes of him after death? The query is a serious one, for it refers, not to time, but to eternity. He who is about to spend many years in a foreign country endeavours to ascertain beforehand what will be his position there ; how, then, is it possible for us not to inquire what will be our state on quitting our present life, since it will be for ever?

The idea of annihilation is repugnant to reason. The most thoughtless of men, when about to quit this life, asks himself what is going to become of him, and involuntarily indulges in hope. To believe in God without believing in a future life would be illogical. The presentiment of a better life is in the inner consciousness of all men. God cannot have placed it there for nothing.

The idea of a nature life implies the preservation of our individuality after death ; for what good would it do us to survive our body, if our moral essence were to be lost in the ocean of infinity? Such a result would be, for us, the same as annihilation.

Intuition of Future Joys and Sorrous

960. Whence comes the belief in future rewards and punishments which is found among all nations?

"It is a presentiment of the reality imparted to each man by the spirit incarnated in him. This internal voice does not speak to him without a purpose; he is wrong in giving so little heed to it. If he listened to it more often and more heedfully, it would be better for him."

961. *What is the predominant sentiment at the moment of death Is it doubt, fear, or hope?*

"Doubt with the sceptical, fear with the guilty, hope with the good."

962. *How is it that there are sceptics, since the soul imparts to each man the sentiment of spiritual things?*

"There are fewer sceptics than you suppose. Many of those who, from pride, affect scepticism during life, are a good deal less sceptical when they come to die."

The doctrine of moral responsability is a consequence of the belief in a future life. Reason and our sense of justice tell us that, in the apportionment of the happiness to which all men aspire, the good and the wicked could not be confounded together. God could not will that some men should obtain, without effort, blessings which others only obtain through persevering exertion.

Our conviction of the justice and goodness of God, as evidenced by the justice and goodness of His laws, forbids us to suppose that the good and the bad can occupy the same place in His sight, or to doubt that, sooner or later, the former will receive a reward, and the latter a chastisement, for the good and the evil they have done. And thus, from our innate sense of justice, we derive our intuition of the rewards and punishments of the future.

Intervention of God in Rewards and Punishments.

963. *Does God concern Himself personally about each man? Is He not too great, and are we not too small, for each individual to be of any importance in His sight?*

"God concerns Himself about all the beings He has created, however small they may be; nothing is too minute for His goodness."

964. *Has God to concern Himself about each of our actions in order to reward or to punish us?*

"God's laws apply to all your actions. When a man violates one of those laws, God does not pronounce sentence on him by saying, for example, 'You have been gluttonous; I shall punish you for it.' But He has traced a limit to appetite. Maladies, and even death, are the consequence of overstepping that limit. Punishment, in all cases, is a result of the infraction of a law."

All our actions are subjected to the laws of God; and any wrong doing en our part, however unimportant it may seem to us, is a violation of those laws. When we undergo the consequences of such violation, we have only ourselves to thank for it ; for we are the sole authors of our happiness or unhappiness, as is shown in the following apologue :—

"A father has educated and instructed his child—that is to say, he has given him the means of knowing how to guide himself in the affairs of life. He makes over to him a piece of land to cultivate, and says to him, 'I have given you the practical directions, and all the necessary implements, for rendering this land productive, and thereby gaining your living. I have given you all the instruction needed for understanding those directions. If you follow them, your land will yield abundant harvests, and will furnish you wherewithal to obtain repose in your old age ; if you do not, it will bear nothing but weeds, and you will die of hunger.' And having said this, he leaves him free to act as he pleases."

Is it not true that the land thus given will produce exactly in the ratio of the skill and care bestowed on its cultivation, and that any mistake or negligence on the part of the son will have an injurious effect on its productiveness? The son will therefore be well or ill off in his old age, according as he has followed or neglected the directions given to him by his father. God is still more provident than the earthly father, for He tells us, every moment, whether we are doing right or doing wrong, through the spirits whom He constantly sends to counsel us, though we do not always heed them. There is also this further difference—viz., that, if the son of whom we have been speaking has misemployed or wasted his time, he has no opportunity of repairing his past mistakes, whereas, God always gives to man the means, through new existences, of doing this.

Nature of Future Joys and Sorrows.

965. Is there anything of materiality in the joys and sorrows of the soul after death?

"Common-sense tells you that they cannot be of a material nature, because the soul is not matter. There is nothing carnal in those joys and sorrows; and yet they are a thousand times more vivid than those you experience upon the earth; because the spirit when freed from matter is more impressionable; matter deadens its sensibility." (237-257.)

966. Why does man often form to himself so gross and absurd an idea of the joys and sorrows of the future life?

"Because his intelligence is still but imperfectly developed. Does the child comprehend as does the adult? Besides, his idea of a future life is often a result of the teachings to which he has been subjected—teachings that are urgently in need of reform.

"Your language being too incomplete to express what lies beyond the range of your present existence, it has been necessary to address you through comparisons borrowed from that existence, and you have mistaken the images and figures thus employed for realities; but, in proportion as man becomes enlightened, his thought comprehends much that his language is unable to express."

967. In what does the happiness of perfected spirits consist?

"In knowing all things; in feeling neither hatred, jealousy, envy, ambition, nor any of the passions that make men unhappy. Their mutual affection is for them a source of supreme felicity. They have none of the wants, sufferings, or anxieties of material life; they are happy in the good they do, for the happiness of spirits is always proportioned to their elevation. The highest happiness, it is true, is enjoyed only by spirits who are perfectly purified; but the others are not unhappy. Between the bad ones and those who have reached perfection, there is an infinity of gradations of elevation and of happiness; for the enjoyments of each spirit are always proportioned to his moral state. Those who have already achieved a certain degree of advancement have a presentiment of the happiness of those who are further on than themselves; they aspire after that higher happiness, but it is for them an object of emulation, and not of jealousy. They know that it depends on themselves to attain to it, and they labour to that end, but with the calmness of a good conscience; and they are happy in not having to suffer what is endured by evil spirits."

968. *You place the absence of material wants among the conditions of happiness for spirits; but is not the satisfaction of those wants a source of enjoyment for mankind?*

"Yes, of animal enjoyment; but when men cannot satisfy those wants, they are tortured by them."

969. *What are we to understand when it is said that the purified spirits are gathered into the bosom of God, and employed in singing His praises?*

"The statement is an allegorical picture of the knowledge they possess of the perfections of God, because they see and comprehend Him; but you must not take it literally, any more than other statements of a similar character. Everything in nature, from the grain of sand upwards, 'sings'—that is to say, *proclaims* the power, wisdom, and goodness of God; but you must not suppose that spirits of the highest order are absorbed in an eternal contemplation, which would be a monotonous and stupid would be a perpetual uselessness. They have no longer to undergo the tribulations of corporeal life, an exemption which is itself an enjoyment; and, besides, as we have told you, they know and comprehend all things, and make use of the intelligence they have acquired in aiding the progress of other spirits; and they find enjoyment in this order of occupation."

970. In what do the sufferings of inferior spirits consist?

"Those sufferings are as various as are the causes by which they are produced, and are proportioned to the degree of inferiority of each spirit, as the enjoyments of the higher spirits are proportioned to their several degrees of superiority. They may be summed up thus:—The sight of happiness to which they are unable to attain; envy of the superiority which renders other spirits happy, and which they see to be lacking in themselves; regret, jealousy, rage, despair, in regard to what prevents them from being happy; remorse and indescribable moral anguish. They long for all sorts of enjoyments; and are tortured by their inability to satisfy their cravings."

971. Is the influence exercised by spirits over one another always good?

"It is always good on the part of good spirits; but perverse spirits endeavour to draw aside from the path of repentance and amendment those whom they think are susceptible of being misled, and whom they have often led into evil during their earthly life."

— *Death, then, does not deliver us from temptation?*

"No, but the action of evil spirits is much less powerful over other spirits than over men, because they no longer have the material passions of the tempted for auxiliaries." (996.)

972. In what way do evil spirits bring temptation to bear upon other spirits, since they have not the passions to work upon?

"If the passions no longer exist materially, they still exist in thought, on the part of spirits of slight advancement; and the evil ones keep up impure thoughts in their victims by taking them to places where they witness the exercise of those passions, and whatever tends to excite them."

— *But what end do those passions subserve, since they have no longer any real object?*

"That is just what constitutes the tortures of the spirit-life. The miser sees gold which he cannot possess; the debauchee, orgies in wich he can take no part; the haughty, honours which he envies, but cannot share."

973. What are the greatest sufferings that can be endured by wicked spirits?

"It is utterly impossible to describe the mental tortures that are the punishment of some crimes; even those by whom they are experienced would find it difficult to give you an idea of them.

But, assuredly, the most frightful of them all is the sufferer's belief that his condemnation is unchangeable and for all eternity."

Men form to themselves, in regard to the joys and sorrows of the soul after death, a conception more or less elevated according to the state of their intelligence. The greater a man's degree of development, the more refined and the more divested of materiality is his idea of them ; the more rational is the view he takes of the subject, and the less literally does he understand the images of figurative language in regard to them. Enlightened reason, in teaching us that the soul is an entirely spiritual being, teaches us also that it cannot be affected by impressions that act only upon matter; but it does not follow there from that is exempt from suffering, or that it does not undergo the punishment of its wrong-doing. (237.)

The communications made to us by spirits show us the future state of the soul, no longer as a matter of theory, but as a reality. They bring before us all the incidents of the life beyond the grave ; but they also show us that they are the natural consequences of the terrestrial life, and that, although divested of the fantastic accompaniments created by the imagination of men, they are none the less painful for those who, in this life, have made a bad use of their faculties. The diversity of those consequences is infinite, but may be summed up by saying that **each soul is punished by that wherein it has sinned.** It is thus that some are punished by the incessant sight of the evil they have done ; others, by regret, fear, shame, doubt, isolation, darkness, separation from those who are dear to them, etc.

974. Whence comes the doctrine of eternal fire?

"From taking a figure of speech for a reality, as men have done in so many instances."

— *But may not this fear lead to a useful result?*

"Look around you, and see whether there are many who are restrained by it, even among those by whom it is inculcated. If you teach what is contrary to reason, the impression you make will be neither durable nor salutary."

Human language being powerless to express the nature of the sufferings of spirit-life, man has been unable to desvise any more appropriate comparison for them than that of **fire,** because, for him, fire is at once the type of the most excruciating torture, and the symbol of the most energetic action. It is for this reason that the belief in "everlasting burning" has been held from the earliest antiquity and transmitted by succeeding generations to the present day ; and it is for this reason, also, that all nations speak, in common parlance, of "fiery passions," of "burning love," "burning hate," "burning with jealousy," etc.

975. Do inferior spirits comprehend the happiness of the righteous?

"Yes; and that happiness is a source of torment for them, for they understand that they are deprived of it through their own fault; but it also leads a spirit, when freed from matter, to aspire after a new corporeal existence, because every such existence, if well employed, will shorten the duration of that torment. It is thus that he makes choice of the trials through which he will be enabled to expiate his faults; for you must remember that each spirit suffers for all the evil he has done or of which he has been the voluntary cause, for all the good which he might have done and which he did not do, *and for all the evil that has resulted from his having failed to do the good he might have done.*"

"In the state of erraticity, a spirit's sight is no longer veiled; it is as though he had *emerged from a fog* and saw the obstacles that intervene between him and happiness, and he therefore suffers all the more, because he understands the full extent of his culpability. For him, *illusion is no longer possible*; he sees things as they really are."

A spirit, when errant, embraces, on the one hand, all his past existences at a glance; on the other, he foresees the future promised to him, and comprehends what he lacks for its attainment. He is like a traveller who, having reached the top of a hill, beholds both the road over which he has already travelled, and that by which he has still to go in order to reach the end of his journey.

976. Is not the sight of spirits who suffer a cause of affliction for the good ones? And, if so, what becomes of the happiness of the latter, that happiness being thus impaired?

"Good spirits are not distressed by the suffering of those who are a lower point than themselves, because they know that it will have an end; they aid those who suffer to become better, and lend them a helping hand. To do this is their occupation, and is a joy for them when they succeed."

— This is comprehensible on the part of spirits who are strangers to them, and who take no special interest in them; but does not the sight of their sorrows and sufferings disturb the happiness of the spirits who have loved them upon the earth?

"If spirits did not see your troubles, it would prove that they become estranged from you after death, whereas all religions teach you that the souls of the departed continue to see you; but they regard your afflictions from another point of view. They know that those sufferings will aid your advancement if you bear them with resignation; and they are consequently more pained by the want of fortitude which keeps you back, than by sufferings which they know to be only temporary."

977. Spirits being unable to hide their thoughts from one another, and all the acts of their lives being known, does it follow that those who have wronged their fellows are always in presence of their victims?

"Common sense might suffice to tell you that it cannot be otherwise."

— *Is this divulging of all his evil deeds,and the perpetual presence of those who have been the victims of them, a chastisement for the guilty spirit?*

"Yes, and a heavier one than you may suppose it to be; but it only lasts until he has expiated his wrong-doing, either as a spirit, or as a man in new corporeal existences."

When we find ourselves in the world of spirits, all our past will be brought into view, and the good, the evil that we have done will be equally known. In vain would the malefactor seek to avoid the sight of his victims; their presence, from which he cannot possibly escape, will be for him a punishment and a source of remorse until he has expiated the wrongs he has done them, while the spirit of the upright man will find himself constantly surrounded by kindness and good-will.

Even upon the earth there is no greater torment for the wicked man than the presence of his victims, whom he does his utmost to avoid. What will it be when, the illusions of the passions being dissipated, he comprehends the evil he has done, sees his most secret actions brought to light and his hypocrisy unmasked, and perceives that he cannot hide himself from the sight of those he has wronged? But, while the soul of the wicked is thus a prey to shame, regret, and remorse, that of the righteous enjoys perfect peace.

978. Does not the remembrance of the faults committed by the soul, during its state of imperfection, disturb its happiness even after it has attained to purity?

"No, because it has redeemed its faults, and has come forth victorious from the trials to which it had submitted *for that purpose.*"

979. Does not the prevision of the trials it has still to undergo, in order to complete its purification, excite in the soul a painful apprehension that must lessen its happiness?

"Yes, in the case of a soul who is still soiled by evil, and therefore it can only enjoy perfect happiness when it has become perfectly pure. But for souls who have attained to a certain degree of elevation, the thought of the trials they have still to undergo has in it nothing painful."

The soul, arrived at a certain degree of purification, has already a foretaste of happiness. It is pervaded by a feeling of satisfaction, and is happy in all that it sees, in all that surrounds it. The veil which covers the marvels and mysteries of creation being already partially raised for it, the divine perfections begin to be perceived by it in their splendour.

980. Is the sympathic link which unites spirits of the same order a source of felicity for them?

"The union of spirits who sympathise in the love of goodness is one of their highest enjoyments, for they have no fear of seeing that union disturbed by selfishness. In worlds altogether spiritual, they form families animated by the same sentiment, and this union constitutes the happiness of those worlds, as in your world you group yourselves into categories, and experience pleasure in being thus brought together. The pure and sincere affection felt by elevated spirits, and of which they are the object, is a source of felicity, for there are neither false friends nor hypocrites among them."

Man enjoys the first-fruits of this felicity upon the earth when he meets with those with whom he can enter into cordial and noble union. In a life of greater purity than that of the earth, this felicity becomes ineffable and unbounded, because their inhabitants meet only with sympathetic souls **whose affection will not be chilled by selfishness.** For love is life; it is selfishness that kills.

981. Is there, as regards the future state of spirits, any difference between him who, during his earthly life, was afraid of death, and him who looked forward to it with indifference, or even with joy?

"There may be a very considerable difference between them, though this is often obliterated by the causes which gave rise to that fear or that desire. Those who dread death, and those who desire it, may be moved by very different sentiments, and it is those sentiments which determine the state of a spirit. For instance, it is evident that, if a man only desires death because it will put an end to his tribulations, that desire is, in reality, a sort of murmuring against Providence, and against the trials which he has to undergo."

982. Is it necessary to make a profession of Spiritism, and to believe in spirit-manifestations, in order to ensure our well-being in the next life?

"If it were so, it would follow that those who do not believe in them, or who have not even had the opportunity of learning anything about them, will be disinherited, which would be absurd. It is right-doing that ensures future well-being; and right-doing is always right-doing, whatever may be the path that leads to it." (165-799.)

Belief in Spiritism aids our self-improvement by clearing our ideas in regard to the future; it hastens the progress and advancement of individuals and of the masses, because it enables us to ascertain what we shall some day be, and is at once a beacon and a support. Spiritism teaches us to bear our trials with patience and resignation, turns us from the wrong-doing that would delay our future happiness, and contributes to our attainment of that happiness; but it does not follow that we may not attain to that happiness without it.

Temporal Sorrows.

983. Does not a spirit, when expiating its faults in a new existence, undergo material suffering, and, that being the case, is it correct to say that, after death, the soul experiences only moral sufferings?

"It is very true that, when the soul is reincarnated, it is made to suffer by the tribulations of corporeal life; but it is only the body that undergoes material suffering.

"You often say, of one who is dead, that he is released from suffering; but this is not always true. As a spirit, he has no more physical sufferings; but, according to the faults he has committed, he may have to bear moral sufferings still more severe, and, in a new existence, he may be still more unhappy. He who has made a selfish use of riches will have to beg his bread, and will be a prey to all the privations of poverty; the proud will undergo humiliations of every kind; he who has misused his authority, and treated his subordinates with disdain and harshness, will be forced to obey a master still harder than himself. All the tribulations of life are the expiation of faults committed in a preceding existence, when they are not the consequence of faults committed in the present one. When you have quitted your present life, you will understand this. (273, 393, 399.)

"He who, in the earthly life, esteems himself happy because he is able to satisfy his passions, makes few efforts at self-improvement. Such ephemeral happiness is often expiated in the present life, but will certainly be expiated in another existence equally material."

984. Are the troubles of our earthly life always the punishment of faults committed by us in our present lifetime?

"No; we have already told you that they are trials imposed on you by God, or chosen by you in the spirit-state, and before your reincarnation, for the expiation of faults committed by you in a former existence; for no infraction of the laws of God, and especially of the law of justice, ever remains unpunished, and if it be not expiated in the same life, it will certainly be so in another. This is why persons whom you regard as excellent are so often made to suffer; they are stricken in their present life for the faults of their past existences." (393.)

985. When a soul is reincarnated in a world less gross than the earth, is such a reincarnation a reward?

"It is a consequence of its higher degree of purification; for, in proportion as spirits become purified, they reincarnate themselves in worlds of progressively higher degrees, until, having divested themselves of all materiality and washed themselves clean of all stains, they enter on the eternal felicity of the fully purified spirits in the presence of God."

In worlds in which the conditions of existence are less material than in ours, the wants of their inhabitants are less gross, and their physical sufferings are less acute. The men of those worlds no longer possess the evil passions which, in lower worlds, make them each other's enemies. Having no motives for hatred or jealousy, they live in peace with one another, because they practise the law of justice, of love, and of charity ; and they therefore know nothing of the worries and anxieties that come of envy, pride, and selfishness, and that make the torment of our terrestrial existence. (172, 182.)

986. Can a spirit who has progressed in his terrestrial existence be reincarnated in the same world?

"Yes; and if he have not been able to accomplish his mission, he may himself demand to complete it in a new existence; but, in that case, it is no longer an expiation for him." (173.)

987. What becomes of the man who, without doing evil, does nothing to shake off the influence of matter?

"Since he has made no progress towards perfection, he has to begin a new existence of the same nature as the one he has quitted. He remains stationary; and thus prolongs the sufferings of expiation."

988. There are persons whose life flows on in a perfect calm; who, having nothing to do for themselves, are exempt from all cares. Is their good fortune a proof that they have nothing to expiate from any former existence?

"Do you know many such? If you think you do, you are mistaken. Such lives are often only calm in appearance. A spirit may have chosen such an existence; but he perceives, after quitting it, that it has not served to bring him on, and he then regrets the time he has wasted in idleness. Bear well in mind that a spirit can only acquire knowledge and elevation through activity; that, if he supinely falls asleep, he does not advance. He is like one who (according to your usages) needs to work, but who goes off for a ramble, or goes to bed, with the intention of doing nothing. *Bear well in mind, also, that each of you will have to answer for voluntary uselessness on your part, and that such uselessness is always fatal to your future happiness.* The sum of that happiness is always exactly proportioned to the sum of the good that you have done; the sum of your unhappiness is always proportioned to the sum of the evil that you have done, and to the number of those whom you have rendered unhappy."

989. There are persons who, without being positively wicked, render all about them unhappy by their ill-temper; what is, for them, the consequence of this?

"Such persons are assuredly not good, and they will expiate this wrong by the sight of those whom they have rendered unhappy, which will be a constant reproach for them; and then, in another existence, they will endure all that they have caused to be endured by others."

Expiation and Repentance

990. Does repentance take place in the corporeal state, or in the spiritual state?

"In the spiritual state; but it may also take place in the corporeal state, when you clearly comprehend the difference between good and evil."

991. What is the consequence of repentance in the spiritual state?

"The desire for a new incarnation, in order to become purified. The spirit perceives the imperfections which deprive him of happiness; and he therefore aspires after a new existence in which he will be able to expiate his faults." (332, 975).

992. What is the consequence of repentance in the corporeal state?

"*The spirit will advance even in his present life,* if he have the time to repair his faults. Whenever your conscience reproaches you, or shows you an imperfection, you may always become better."

993. Are there not men who have only the instinct of evil, and are inaccessible to repentance?

"I have told you that progress must be incessant. He who, in his present life, has only the instinct of evil, will have the instinct of goodness in another one, *and it is to effect this end that he is re-born many times.* For all must advance, all must reach the goal; but some do this more quickly, others more slowly, according to the energy of their desire. He who has only the instinct of good is already purified, for he may have had that of evil in an anterior existence." (804.)

994. Does the perverted spirit who has not recognised his faults during his life always recognise them after his death?

"Yes; he always does so, and he then suffers all the more, for he feels all the evil he has done, or of which he has been the voluntary cause. Nevertheless, repentance is not always immediate. There are spirits who obstinately persist in doing wrong, notwithstanding their sufferings; but, sooner or later, they will see that have taken the wrong road, and repentance will follow this discovery. It is to their enlightenment that the efforts of the higher spirits are directed, and that you may usefully direct your own."

995. *Are there spirits who, without being wicked, are indifferent about their own fate?*

"There are spirits who do not occupy themselves with anything useful, but are in a state of expectancy. In such cases they suffer in proportion to their inactivity; for all states and conditions must conduce to progress, and with them, this progress is effected by the suffering they experience."

— *Have they no desire to shorten their sufferings?*

"They have that desire, undoubtedly; but they have not sufficient energy to do what would give them relief. Are there not among you many who prefer to starve rather than to work?"

996. *Since spirits see the harm that is done them by their imperfections, how is it that any of them persist in aggravating their position, and prolonging their state of inferiority, by doing evil, as spirits, in turning men aside from the right road?*

"It is those whose repentance is tardy that act thus. A spirit who repents may afterwards allow himself to be drawn back into the wrong road by other spirits still more backward than himself." (971.)

997. *We sometimes find that spirits, who are evidently of very* he who, urged on by pride, revolts against God, persisting in his *touched by the prayers offered for them. How is it that others, whom we have reason to believe are more enlightened, show a hardness and a cynicism that no efforts can vanquish?*

"Prayer is only efficacious in the case of spirits who repent; he who, urged on by pride, revolts against God, persisting in his wrong-doing, and perhaps going even more widely astray, cannot be acted upon by prayer, and can only derive benefit therefrom when a glimmering of repentance shall have shown itself in him." (664.)

We must not lose sight of the fact that a spirit, after the death of his body, is not suddenly transformed. If his life have been reprehensible, it has been so because he was imperfect. But death does not render him perfect all at once ; he may in his wrong-doing, his false ideas, his prejudices, until he has become enlightened by study, reflection, and suffering.

998. Is expiation accomplished in the corporeal state, or in the spirit-state?

"Expiation is accomplished during the corporeal existence, through the trials to which the spirit is subjected; and, in the spirit-state, through the moral sufferings belonging to the spirit's state of inferiority."

999. Does sincere repentance during the earthly life suffice to efface the faults of that life, and to restore the wrong-doer to the favour of God?

"Repentance helps forward the amelioration of the spirit, but all wrong-doing has to be expiated."

— *That being the case, if a criminal should say, "Since I must necessarily expiate my past, I have no need to repent," what effect would it have upon him?*

"If he harden himself in the thought of evil, his expiation will be longer and more painful."

1000. Can we, in the present life, redeem our faults?

"Yes, by making reparation for them. But do not suppose that you can redeem them by a few trifling privations, or by giving, after your death, what you can no longer make use of. God does not value a sterile repentance, a mere smiting of the breast, easily done. The loss of a little finger in doing good to others effaces more wrong doing than any amount of self-torture undergone solely with a view *to one's own* interest. (726.)

"Evil can only be atoned for by good ; and attempts at reparation are valueless if they touch neither a man's *pride* nor his *worldly interests*.

"How can his rehabilitation be subserved by the restitution of ill-gotten wealth after his death, when it has become useless to him, and when he has already profited by it?

"What benefit can he derive from the privation of a few futile enjoyments and of a few superfluities, if the wrong he has done to others is not undone?

"What, in truth, is the use of his humbling himself before God, if he keeps up his pride before men?" (720, 721.)

1001. Is there no merit in ensuring the useful employment, after our death, of the property possessed by us?

"To say that there is no merit so doing would not be correct; it is always better than doing nothing. But the misfortune is, that he who only gives after his death is often moved rather by selfishness than by generosity; he wishes to have the honour of doing good without its costing him anything. He who imposes privation upon himself during his life reaps a double profit—the merit of his sacrifice, and the pleasure of witnessing the happiness he has caused. But selfishness is apt to whisper, 'Whatever you give away is so much cut off from your own enjoyments;' and as the voice of selfishness is usually more persuasive than that of disinterestedness and charity, it too often leads a man to keep what he has, under pretext of the necessities of his position. He is to be pitied who knows not the pleasure of giving; for he is deprived of one of the purest and sweetest of enjoyments. In subjecting a man to the trial of wealth, so slippery, and so dangerous for his future, God placed within his reach, by way of compensation, the happiness which generosity may procure for him, even in his present life." (814.)

1002. What will become of him who, in the act of dying, acknowledges his wrong-doing, but has not time to make reparation? Does repentance suffice in such a case?

"Repentance will hasten his rehabilitation, but it does not absolve him. Has he not the future, which will never be closed against him?"

Duration of Future Penalties.

1003. Is the duration of the sufferings of the guilty, in the future life, arbitrary or subordinate to a law?

"God never acts from caprice; everything in the universe is ruled by laws which reveal His wisdom and His goodness."

1004. What decides the duration of the sufferings of the guilty?

"The length of time required for his amelioration. A spirit's state of suffering or of happiness being proportioned to the degree of his purification, the duration of his sufferings, as well as their nature, depends on the time it takes him to become better. In proportion as he progresses, and his sentiments become purified, his sufferings diminish and change their nature."

1005. Does time appear, to the suffering spirit, longer or shorter than in the earthly life?

"It appears longer: sleep does not exist for him. It is only for spirits arrived at a certain degree of purification that time is merged, so to say with infinity." (240)

1006. Could a spirit suffer eternally?

"Undoubtedly, if he remained eternally wicked; that is to say, if he were never to repent nor to amend, he would suffer eternally: But God has not created beings to let them remain for ever a prey to evil; He created them only in a state of simplicity and ignorance, and all of them must progress, in a longer or shorter time, according to the action of their will. The determination to advance may be awakened more or less tardily, as the development of children is more or less precocious; but it will be stimulated, sooner or later, by the irresistible desire of the spirit himself to escape from his state of inferiority, and to be happy. The law which regulates the duration of a spirit's sufferings is, therefore, eminently wise and beneficent, since it makes that duration to depend on his own efforts; he is never deprived of his free-will, but, if he makes a bad use of it, he will have to bear the consequences of his errors."

1007. Are there spirits who never repent?

"There are some whose repentance is delayed for a very long time; but to suppose that they will never improve would be to deny the law of progress, and to assert that the child *will never become a man.*"

1008. Does the duration of a spirit's punishment always depend on his own will, and is it never imposed on him for a given time?

"Yes; punishment may be imposed on him for a fixed time, but God, who wills only the good of His creatures, always welcomes his repentance, and the desire to amend never remains sterile."

1009. According to that, the penalties imposed on spirits are never eternal?

"Interrogate your common sense, your reason, and ask yourself whether an eternal condemnation for a few moments of error would not be the negation of the goodness of God? What, in fact, is the duration of a human life, even though prolonged to a hundred years, in comparison with eternity? ETERNITY! Do you rightly comprehend the word? sufferings, tortures, without end, without hope, for a few faults! Does not your judgment reject such an idea? That the ancients should have seen, in the Master of the Universe, a terrible, jealous, vindictive God, is conceivable, for, in their ignorance, they attributed to the Divinity the passions of men; but such is not the God of the Christians, who places love, charity, pity, the forgetfulness of offences, in the foremost rank of virtues, and who could not lack the qualities which He has made it the duty of His creatures to possess. Is it not a contradiction to attribute to Him infinite love and infinite vengeance? You say that God's justice is infinite, transcending the limited understanding of mankind; but justice does not exclude kindness, and God would not be kind if He condemned the greater number of His creatures to horrible and unending punishment. Could He make it obligatory on His children to be just, if His own action towards them did not give them the most perfect standard of justice? And is it not the very sublimity of justice and of kindness to make the duration of punishment to depend on the efforts of the guilty one to amend, and to mete out the appropriate recompense, both for good and for evil, 'to each, according to his works'?"

SAINT AUGUSTINE

"Set yourselves, by every means in your power, to combat and to annihilate the idea of eternal punishment, which is a blasphemy against the justice and goodness of God, and the principal source of the scepticism, materialism, and indifferentism that have invaded the masses since their intelligence has begun to be developed. When once a mind has received enlightenment, in however slight a degree, the monstrous injustice of such an idea is immediately perceived; reason rejects it, and rarely fails to confound, in the same ostracism, the penalty against which it revolts and the God to whom that penalty is attributed. Hence the numberless ills which have burst upon you, and for which we come to bring you a remedy. The task we point out to you will be all the easier because the defenders of this belief have avoided giving a positive opinion in regard to it; neither the Councils nor the Fathers of the Church have definitely settled this weighty question. If Christ, according to the Evangelists and the literal interpretation of His allegorical utterances, threatens the guilty with *a fire that is unquenchable*, there is absolutely nothing in those utterances to prove that they are condemned *to remain inthat fire eternally*.

"Hapless sheep that have gone astray! behold, advancing towards you, the Good Shepherd, who, so far from intending to drive you

for ever from His presence, comes Himself to seek you, that
He may lead you back to the fold! Prodigal children! renounce
your voluntary exile, and turn your steps towards the paternal
dwelling! Your Father, with arms already opened to receive you,
is waiting to welcome you back to your home!"

LAMENNAIS

"Wars of words! wars of words! has not enough blood been
already shed for words, and must the fires of the stake be
rekindled for them? Men dispute about the words 'eternal punishments,' 'everlasting burnings;' but do you not know that what
you now understand by *eternity* was not understood in the same
way by the ancients? Let the theologian consult the sources of
his faith, and he, like the rest of you, will see that, in the Hebrew
text, the word which the Greeks, the Latins, and the moderns,
have translated as *endless and irremissible punishment,* has not
the same meaning. Eternity of punishment corresponds to *eternity
of evil.* Yes; so long as evil continues to exist among you, so
long will punishment continue to exist; it is in this relative sense
that the sacred texts should be interpreted. The eternity of
punishments, therefore, is not absolute, but relative. Let a day
come when all men shall have donned, through repentance, the
robe of innocence, and, on that day, there will be no more weeping,
wailing, or gnashing of teeth. Your human reason is, in truth,
of narrow scope; but, such as it is, it is a gift of God, and there
is no man of right feeling who, with the aid of that reason, can
understand the eternity of punishment in any other sense. If we
admit the eternity of punishment, we must also admit that evil
will be eternal; but God alone is eternal, and He could not have
created an eternal evil, without plucking from His attributes the
most magnificent of them all, viz., His sovereign power; for he
who creates an element destructive of his works is not sovereignly
powerful. Plunge no more thy mournful glance, O human race!
into the entrails of the earth, in search of chastisements! Weep,
but hope; expiate, but take comfort in the thought of a God who
is entirely loving, absolutely powerful, essentially just." PLATO

"Union with the Divine Being is the aim of human existence.
To the attainment of this aim three things are necessary—knowledge, love justice: three things are contrary to this aim—ignorance,
hatred, injustice. You are false to these fundamental principles
when you falsify the idea of God by exaggerating His severity;
thus suggesting to the mind of the creature that there is in it

more clemency, long-suffering, love, and true justice, than you attribute to the Creator. You destroy the very idea of retribution by rendering it as inadmissible, by your minds, as is, by your hearts, the policy of the Middle Ages, with its hideous array of torturers, executioners, and the stake. When the principle of indiscriminating retaliation has been banished for ever from human legislation, can you hope to make men believe that principle to be the rule of the Divine Government? Believe me, brothers in God and in Jesus Christ, you must either resign yourselves to let all your dogmas perish in your hands rather than modify them, or you must revivify them by opening them to the beneficent action that good spirits are now bringing to bear on them. The idea of a hell full of glowing furnaces and boiling cauldrons might be credible in an age of iron; in the nineteenth century it can be nothing more than an empty phantom, capable, at the utmost, of frightening little children, and by which the children themselves will no longer be frightened when they are a little bigger. By your persistence in upholding mythic terrors, you engender incredulity, source of every sort of social disorganisation; and I tremble at beholding the very foundations of social order shaken, and crumbling into dust, for want of an authoritative code of penality. Let all those who are animated by a living and ardent faith, heralds of the coming day, unite their efforts, not to keep up antiquated fables now fallen into disrepute, but to resuscitate and revivify the true idea of penality, under forms in harmony with the usages, sentiments, and enlightenment of your epoch.

"What, in fact, is 'a sinner'? One who, by a deviation from the right road, by a false movement of the soul, has swerved from the true aim of his creation, which consists in the harmonious worship of the Beautiful, the Good, as embodied in the archetype of humanity, the Divine Exemplar, Jesus Christ.

"What is 'chastisement'? The natural, derivative consequence of that false movement; the amount of pain necessary to disgust the sinner with his departure from rectitude, by his experience of the suffering caused by that departure. Chastisement is the goad which, by the smarting it occasions, decides the soul to cut short its wanderings, and to return into the right road. *The sole aim of chastisement is rehabilitation; and therefore, to assume the eternity of chastisement is to deprive it of all reason for existing.*

"Cease, I beseech you, the attempt to establish a parallellism of duration between good, essence of the Creator, and evil, essence of the creature; for, in so doing, you establish *a standard of penality* that is utterly without justification. Affirm, on the contrary, the gradual diminution of imperfections and of chastisements through successive existences, and you consecrate the doctrine of the union of the creature with the Creator by the reconciliation of justice with mercy."   PAUL, APOSTLE

It is desired to stimulate men to the acquisition of virtue, and to turn them from vice, by the hope of reward and the fear of punishment ; but, if the threatened punishment is represented under conditions repugnant to reason, not only will it fail of its aim, but it will lead men, in rejecting those conditions, to reject the very idea of punishment itself. But let the idea of future rewards and punishments be presented to their mind under a reasonable form, and they will not reject it. This reasonable explanation of the subject is given by the teachings of Spiritism.

The doctrine of eternal punishment makes an implacable God of the Supreme Being. Would it be reasonable to say of a sovereign that he is very kind, very benevolent, very indulgent, that he only desires the happiness of all around him, but that he is, at the same time, jealous, vindictive, inflexibly severe, and that he punishes three-quarters of his subjects with the most terrific tortures, for any offence, or any infraction of his laws, even when their imputed fault has resulted simply from their ignorance of the laws they have transgressed? Would there not be an evidente contradiction in such a statement of the sovereign's character? And can God's action be less consistent than that of a man?

The doctrine in question presents another contradiction. Since God foreknows all things, He must have known, in creating a soul, that it would transgress His laws, and it must therefore have been, from its very formation, predestined by Him to eternal misery ; but is such an assumption reasonable or admissible? The doctrine of **punishment proportioned to wrong-doing** is, on the contrary, entirely consonant with reason and justice. God undoubtedly foresaw, in creating a given soul, that, in its ignorance, it would do wrong ; but He has ordained that its very faults themselves shall furnish it with the means of becoming enlightened, through its experience of the painful effects of its wrong-doing : He will compel it to expiate that wrong-doing, but only in order that it may be thereby more firmly fixed in goodness ; thus the door of hope is never closed against it, and the moment of its deliverance from suffering is made to depend on the amount of effort it puts forth to achieve its purification. If the doctrine of future punishment had always been presented under this aspect, very few would ever have doubted its truth.

The word **eternal** is often figuratively employed, in common parlance, to designate any long period of duration of which the end is not foreseen, although it is known that it will come in course of time. We speak, for instance, of "the eternal snows" of mountain-peaks and polar regions, although we know, on the one hand, that our globe will come to an end, and, on the other hand, that the state of those regions may be changed by the normal displacement of the earth's axis, or by some cataclysm. The word **eternal**, therefore, in this case, does not mean **infinitely perpetual.** We say, in the suffering of some long illness, that our days present the same "eternal round" of weariness ; is it strange, then, that spirits who have suffered for years, centuries, thousands of ages even, should express themselves in the same way? Moreover, we must not forget that their state of backwardness prevents them from seeing the other end of their road, and that they therefore believe themselves to be destined to suffer **for ever ;** a belief which is itself a part of their punishment.

The doctrine of material fire, of furnaces, and tortures, borrowed from the pagan Tartarus, is completely given up by many of the most eminent theologians of the present day, who admit that the word "fire" is employed figuratively in the Bible, and is to be understood as meaning **moral** fire. (974). Those who, like ourselves, have observed the incidents of the life beyond the grave, as presented to our view by the communications of spirits, have had ample proof that its sufferings are none the less excruciating for not being of a material nature. And even as regards the duration of those sufferings, many theologians are beginning to admit the restriction indicated above, and to consider that the word **eternal** may be considered as referring to **the principle of penality in itself,** as the consequence of an immutable law, and **not** to its application to each individual. When religious teaching shall openly admit this interpretation, it will bring back to a belief in God and in a future life many who are now losing themselves in the mazes of materialism.

Resurrection of the Body.

1010. Is the doctrine of the resurrection of the body an implication of that of reincarnation, as now taught by spirits?

"How could it be otherwise? It is with regard to that expression as to so many others, that only appear unreasonable because they are taken literally, and are thus placed beyond the pale of credibility; let them only be rationally explained, and those whom you call free-thinkers will admit them without difficulty, precisely because they are accustomed to reflect. Free-thinkers, like the rest of the world, perhaps even more than others, thirst for a future; they ask nothing better than to believe, but they cannot admit what is disproved by science. The doctrine of the plurality of existences is conformable with the justice of God; it alone can explain what, without it, is inexplicable; how can you doubt, then, that its principle is to be found in all religions?"

1011. The Church, then, in the dogma of the resurrection of the body, really teaches the doctrine of reincarnation?

"That is evident; but it will soon be seen that reincarnation is implied in every part of Holy Writ. Spirits, therefore, do not come to overthrow religion, as is sometimes asserted; they come, on the contrary, to confirm and sanction it by irrefragable proofs. But, as the time has arrived to renounce the use of figurative language, they speak without allegories, and give to every statement a clear and precise meaning that obviates all danger of false interpretation. For this reason there will be, ere long, a greater number of persons sincerely religious and really believing than are to be found at the present day."

Physical science demonstrates the impossibility of resurrection according to the common idea. If the relics of the human body remained homogeneous, even though dispersed and reduced to powder, we might conceive the possibility of their being reunited at some future time ; but such is not the case. The body is formed of various elements, oxygen, hydrogen, azote, carbon, etc., and these elements, being dispersed, serve to form new bodies, so that the same molecule of carbon, for example, will have entered into the composition of many thousands of different bodies (we speak only of human bodies, without counting those of animals); such and such an individual may have, in his body, molecules that were in the bodies of the men of the earliest ages; and the very same organic molecules that you have this day absorbed in your food may have come from the body of some one whom you have known ; and so on. Matter being finite in quantity, and its transformations being infinite in number, how is it possible that the innumerable bodies formed out of it should be reconstituted with the same elements? Such a reconstruction is a physical impossibility. The resurrection of the body can, therefore, be rationally admitted only as a figure of speech, symbolising the fact of reincarnation ; thus interpreted, it has in it nothing repugnant to reason, nothing contrary to the data of physical science.

It is true that, according to theological dogma, this resurrection is not to take place until the "Last Day," while, according to spiritist doctrine, it takes place every day ; but is not this picture of the "Last Judgement" a grand and noble metaphor, implying, under the veil of allegory, one of those immutable truths that will no longer be met with incredulity when restored to their true meaning? To those who carefully ponder the spiritist theory of the future destiny of souls, and of the fate that awaits them as the result of the various trials they have to undergo, it will be apparent that. with the exception of the condition of simultaneousness, the judgement which condemns or absolves them is not a fiction, as is supposed by unbelievers. It is also to be remarked that the judgement which assigns to each soul its next place of habitation is the natural consequence of the plurality of worlds, now generally admitted ; while, according to the doctrine of the "Last Judgment," the earth is supposed to be the only inhabited world.

Paradise, Hell and Purgatory.

1012. Are there, in the universe, any circumscribed places set apart for the joys and sorrows of spirits, according to their merits?

"We have already answered this question. The joys and sorrows of spirits are inherent in the degree of perfection at which they have arrived. Each spirit finds in himself the principle of his happiness or unhappiness; and, as spirits are everywhere, no enclosed or circumscribed place is set apart for either the one or the other. As for incarnated spirits, they are more or less happy or unhappy, according as the world they inhabit is more or less advanced."

— *"Heaven" and "hell," then, as men have imagined them, have no existence?*

"They are only symbols; there are happy and unhappy spirits everywhere. Nevertheless, as we have also told you, spirits of the same order are brought together by sympathy; but, when they are perfect, they can meet together wherever they will."

The localisation of rewards and punishments in fixed places exists only in man's imagination ; it proceeds from his tendency to **materialise** and to **circumscribe** the things of which he cannot comprehend the essential infinitude.

1013. What is to be understood by Purgatory?

"Physical and moral suffering; the period of expiation. It is almost always upon the earth that you are made by God to undergo your purgatory, and to expiate your wrong-doing."

What men call **purgatory** is also a figure of speech, that should be understood as signifying, not any determinate place, but **the state** of imperfect spirits who have to expiate their faults until they have attained the complete purification that will raise them to the state of perfect blessedness. As this purification is effected by means of various incarnations, purgatory consists in the trials of corporeal life.

1014. How is it that spirits who, by their language, would seem to be of high degree, have replied according to the commonly-received ideas to those who have questioned them in the most serious spirit concerning hell and purgatory?

"They speak according to the comprehension of those who question them, when the latter are too fully imbued with pre-conceived ideas, in order to avoid any abrupt interference with their convictions. If a spirit should tell a Mussulman, without proper precautions, that Mahomet was not a true prophet, he would not be listened to with much cordiality."

— *Such precautions are conceivable on the part of spirits who wish to instruct us; but how is it that others, when questioned as to their situation, have replied that they were suffering the tortures of hell or of purgatory?*

"Spirits of inferior advancement, who are not yet completely dematerialised, retain a portion of their earthly ideas, and describe their impressions by means of terms that are familiar to them. They are in a state that allows of their obtaining only a very imperfect foresight of the future; for which reason it often happens that spirits in erraticity, or but recently freed from their earthly body, speak just as they would have done during their earthly life. *Hell* may be understood as meaning a life of extremely painful trial, with *uncertainty* as to the future attainment of any better state; and *purgatory* as a life that is also one of trial, but with the *certainty* of a happier future. Do you not say, when undergoing any very intense physical or mental distress, that you are suffering 'the tortures of the damned'? But such an expression is only a figure of speech, and is always employed as such."

1015. What is to be understood by the expression, "a soul in torment"?

"An errant and suffering soul, uncertain about its future, and to whom you can render, in its endeavour to obtain relief, an assistance that it often solicits at your hands by the act of addressing itself to you." (664.)

1016. In what sense is the word heaven *to be understood?*

"Do you suppose it to be a place like the Elysian Fields of the ancients, where all good spirits are crowded together pell-mell, with no other care than that of enjoying, throughout eternity, a passive felicity? No; it is universal space; it is the planets, the stars, and all the worlds of high degree, in which spirits are in the enjoyment of all their faculties, without having the tribulations of material life, or the sufferings inherent in the state of inferiority."

1017. Spirits have said that they inhabited the third, fourth, and fifth heaven, etc.; what did they mean in saying this?

"You ask them which heaven they inhabit, because you have the idea of several heavens, placed one above the other, like the storeys of a house, and they therefore answer you according to your own ideas; but, for them, the words 'third,' 'fourth,' or 'fifth' heaven, express different degrees of purification, and consequently of happiness. It is the same when you ask a spirit whether he is in hell; if he is unhappy, he will say 'yes,' because, for him, *hell* is synonymous with *suffering*; but he knows very well that it is not a furnace. A Pagan would have replied that he was in Tartarus."

The same may be said in regard to other expressions of a similar character, such as "the city of flowers," "the city of the elect," the first, second, or third "sphere," etc., which are only allegorical, and employed by some spirits figuratively, by others from ignorance of the reality of things, or even of the most elementary principles of natural science.

According to the restricted idea formerly entertained in regard to the **localities** of rewards and punishments, and to the common belief that the earth was the centre of the universe, that the sky formed a vault overhead, and that there was a specific region of stars, men placed heaven up above, and hell down below; hence the expressions to "ascend into heaven," to be in "the highest heaven," to be "cast down into hell," etc. Now that astronomy, having traced up the earth's history and described its constitution, has shown us that it is one of the smallest worlds that circulate in space and devoid of any special importance, that space is infinite, and that there is neither "up" nor "down" in the universe, men have been obliged to ceasse placing heaven above the clouds, and hell in the "lower parts of the earth." As for purgatory. no fixed place was ever assigned to it.

It was reserved for Spiritism to give, in regard to all these points, an explanation wnicn is at once, and in tne nignest degree, rational and consoling, by showing us that we have **in ourselves** our "hell" and our "heaven," and that we find our "purgatory" in **the state of incarnation, in our successive corporeal or physical lives.**

1018. In what sense should we understand the words of Christ, "My kingdom is not of this world"?

"Christ, in replying thus, spoke figuratively. He meant to say that He reigned only over pure and unselfish hearts. He is wherever the love of goodness holds sway; but they who are greedy for the things of this world, and attached to the enjoyments of earth, are not with Him."

1019. Will the reign of goodness ever be established upon the earth?

"Goodness will reign upon the earth when, among the spirits who come to dwell in it, the good shall be more numerous than the bad; for they will then bring in the reign of love and justice, which are the source of good and of happiness. It is through moral progress and *practical conformity with the laws of God*, that men will attract to the earth good spirits, who will keep bad ones away from it; but the latter will not definitively quit the earth until its people shall be completely purified from pride and selfishness.

"The transformation of the human race has been predicted from the most ancient times, and you are now approaching the period when it is destined to take place. All those among you who are labouring to advance the progress of mankind are helping to hasten this transformation, which will be effected through the incarnation, in your earth, of spirits of higher degree, who will constitute a new population, of greater moral advancement than the human races they will gradually have replaced. The spirits of the wicked people who are mowed down each day by death, and of all who endeavour to arrest the onward movement, will be excluded from the earth, and compelled to incarnate themselves elsewhere; for they would be out of place among those nobler races of human beings, whose felicity would be impaired by their presence among them. They will be sent into never worlds, less advanced than the earth, and will therein fulfil *hard and laborious missions*, which will furnish them with the means of advancing, while contributing also to the advancement of their brethren of those younger worlds, less advanced than themselves. Do you not see, in this exclusion of backward spirits from the transformed and regenerated earth, the true significance of the sublime myth of the driving out of the first pair from the garden of Eden? And do you not also see, in the advent of the human race upon the earth, under the conditions of such an exile, and bringing within itself the germs of its passions and the evidences of its primitive inferiority, the real meaning of that other myth, no less sublime, of the fall of those first parents, entailing the sinfulness of their descendants? 'Original sin,' considered from this point of view, is seen to consist in the imperfection of human nature; and each of the spirits subsequently incarnated in the human race is therefore responsible only for his own imperfection and his own wrong-doing, and not for those of his forefathers.

"Devote yourselves, then, with zeal and courage to the great work of regeneration, all you who are prossessed of faith and good will; you will reap a hundredfold for all the seed you sow. Woe to those who close their eyes against the light; for they will have condemned themselves to long ages of darkness and sorrow! Woe to those who centre their enjoyment in the pleasures of the earthly life; for they will undergo privations more numerous than their present pleasures! And woe, above all, to the selfish; for they will find none to aid them in bearing the burden of their future misery!"

CONCLUSION

I

HE who, in regard to terrestrial magnetism, knows only the little figures of ducks which, with the aid of a magnet, are made to swim about in a basin of water, would find it difficult to understand that those toy-figures contain the secret of the mechanism of the universe and of the movement of worlds. He, whose knowledge of Spiritism is confined to the table- turning which was the starting-point of the modern manifestations, is in a similar position; he regards it merely as an amusement, a social pastime, and cannot understand how a phenomenon so simple and so common, known to antiquity and even to savage tribes, can be connected with the weightiest questions of psychology and of human life. For the superficial observer, what connection can exist between a table that turns and the morality and future destiny of the human race? But as, from the simple pot which, in boiling, raises its lid (a pot, too, which has boiled from the remotest antiquity), there has issued the potent motor with whose aid man transports himself through space and suppresses distance, so, be it known to you, O ye who believe in nothing beyond the material world! there has issued, from the table-turning which provokes your disdainful smiles, a new philosophy that furnishes the solution of problems which no other has been able to solve. I appeal to all honest adversaries of Spiritism, and I adjure them to say whether they have taken the trouble to study what they criticise; reminding them that criticism is necessarily of no value unless the critic knows what he is talking about. To ridicule that of which we know nothing, which we have not made the subject of conscientious examination, is not to *criticise*, but to give proof of frivolity and want of judgment. Assuredly, if we had present this philosophy as being the product of a human brain, it would have met with less disdain, and would have had the honour of being examined by those who profess to be the leaders of opinion: but it claims to be derived from spirits; what an absurdity! It is scarcely held to deserve a single glance by those who judge it merely by its title, as the monkey in the fable judged of the nut by its husk. But put aside all thought of the origin of this book; suppose it to be the work of a man, and say, in truth and honesty, whether, after having carefully read it, you find in it anything to laugh at?

II

Spiritism is the most formidable opponent of materialism, and it is therefore not surprising that it should have the materialists for adversaries; but as materialism is a doctrine which many of those who hold it hardly dare to avow, they cover their opposition with the mantle of reason and science. Their shafts are especially aimed at the *marvellous* and the *supernatural,* which they deny; and as, according to them, Spiritism is founded on the marvellous and the supernatural, they declare that it can be nothing more than a ridiculous delusion.

Strange to say, some of those who are most incredulous in regard to Spiritism deny the possibility of its phenomena in the name of religion, of which they often know as little as they do of Spiritism. They do not reflect that, in denying, without restriction, the possibility of the "marvellous" and the "supernatural," they deny religion, for religion is founded on revelation and miracles; and what is revelation if not extra-human communications? All the sacred writers, from Moses downwards, have spoken of this order of communications. And what are miracles if not facts of a character emphatically marvellous and supernatural, since they are, according to liturgical acceptation, derogations from the laws of nature, so that, in rejecting the marvellous and the supernatural, they reject the very basis of all religions? But it is not from this point of view that we have to consider the subject. Belief in spirit-manifestation does not necessarily settle the question of miracles; that is to say, whether God does, or does not, in certain cases, derogate from the eternal laws that regulate the universe; it leaves, in regard to this question, full liberty of belief to all. Spiritism says, and proves, that the phenomena on which it is based are supernatural only in appearance, that they only appear to some persons to be such, because they are unusual, and out of the pale of facts hitherto known; and that they are no more supernatural than all the other phenomena which the science of the present day is explaining, though they appeared to be "miraculous" in the past. All spiritist phenomena, *without exception*, are the consequence of general laws; they reveal to us one of the powers of nature, a power hitherto unknown, or rather that has not hitherto been understood, but which observation shows us to be included in the scheme of things. Spiritism, therefore, is founded less on the marvellous and the supernatural than is religion itself; and those who attack it on this score do so because they know not what it really is. As for those who oppose it in the name of science, we say to them, be they ever so learned, "If your science, which has taught you so many things, has not taught you that the domain of nature is infinite, you are scientific to very little purpose."

III

You say that you wish to cure your age of a malady of credulity that threatens to invade the world. Would you prefer to see the world invaded by the incredulity that you seek to propagate? Is it not to the absence of all belief that are to be attributed the relaxing of family-ties and the greater part of the disorders that are undermining society? By demonstrating the existence and immortality of the soul, Spiritism revives faith in the future, raises the courage of those who are depressed, and enables us to bear the vicissitudes of life with resignation. Do you call this an evil? Two doctrinal theories are offered for our acceptance; one of them denies the existence of a future life, the other proclaims and proves it; one of them explains nothing, the other explains everything, and, by so doing, appeals to our reason; one of them is the justification of selfishness, the other gives a firm basis to justice, charity, and the love of one's fellow-creatures; one of them shows only the present and annihilates all hope, the other consoles us by showing the vast field of the future; which of the two is the more pernicious?

There are some, among the most sceptical of our opponents, who give themselves out as apostles of fraternity and progress; but fraternity implies disinterestedness and abnegation of one's own personality, and by what right do you impose such a sacrifice on him to whom you affirm that, when he is dead, everything will be over for him, that soon, perhaps to-morrow, he will be nothing

more than a worn-out machine, out of gear, and thrown aside as
so much rubbish? Why, in that case, should he impose on himself
any privation? Is it not more natural that he should resolve to
live as agreeably as possible during the few brief instants you
accord to him? And would not such a resolve naturally suggest
to him the desire to possess largely in order to secure the largest
amount of enjoyment? And would not this desire naturally give
birth to jealousy of those who possess more than he does? And,
from such jealousy to the desire to take from them what they
possess, is there more than a single step? What is there, in fact,
to restrain him from doing so? The law? But the law does not
reach every case. Conscience? the sense of duty? But what,
from your point of view, is conscience? and upon what do you
base the sense of duty? Has that sense any motive or aim if it
be true that everything ends for us with our present life? In
connection with such a belief, only one maxim can be reasonably
admitted—viz., "Every man for himself." Fraternity, conscience,
duty, humanity, progress even, are but empty words. Ah! you
who proclaim such a doctrine, you know not how much harm you
do to society, nor of how many crimes you incur the responsibility!
But why do we speak of responsibility? Nothing of the kind
exists for the materialist; he renders homage only to matter.

IV

The progress of the human race results from the practical
application of the law of justice, love, and charity. This law is
founded on the certainty of the future; take away that certainty,
and you take away its corner-stone. It is from this law that all
other laws are derived, for it comprises all the conditions of·
human happiness; it alone can cure the evils of society; and the
improvement that takes place in the conditions of social life, in
proportion as this law is better understood and better carried out
in action, becomes clearly apparent when we compare the various
ages and *peoples* of the earth. And if the partial and incomplete
application of this law have sufficed to produce an appreciable
improvement in social conditions, what will it not effect when
it shall have become the basis of all social institutions? Is such
a result possible? Yes; for as the human race has already accomplished ten steps, it is evident that it can accomplish twenty,
and so on. We can infer the future from the past. We see that

the antipathies between different nations are beginning to melt away; that the barriers which separated them are being overthrown by the progress of civilisation, and that they are joining hands from one end of the world to the other. A larger measure of justice has been introduced into international law; wars occur less frequently, and do not exclude the exercise of humane sentiments; uniformity is being gradually established in the relations of life; the distinctions of races and castes are being effaced, and men of different religious beliefs are imposing silence on sectional prejudices, that they may unite in adoration of one and the same God. We speak of the nations who are at the head of civilisation (789-793). In all these relations, men are still far from perfection, and there are still many old ruins to be pulled down before the last vestiges of barbarism will have been cleared away; but can those ruins withstand the irresistible action of progress, that living force which is itself a law of nature? If the present generation is more advanced than the last, why should not the next be more advanced than the present one? It will necessarily be so through the force of things; in the first place, because each generation, as it passes away, carries with it some of the champions of old abuses, and society is thus gradually reconstituted with new elements that have thrown aside antiquated prejudices; in the second place, because, when men have come to desire progress, they study the obstacles which impede it, and set themselves to get rid of them. The fact of the progressive movement of human society being incontestible, there can be no doubt that progress will continue to be made in the future.

Man desires to be happy; it is in his nature so to do. He only he has not obtained complete happiness, and that this happiness but for which result progress would have no object; for where would be the value of progress for him if it did not improve his position? But when he shall have obtained all the enjoyments that can be afforded by intellectual progress, he will perceive that he has not obtained complete happiness, and that this happiness is impossible without security in the social relations; and as he can only obtain this security through the moral progress of society in general, he will be led, by the force of things, to labour for that end, to the attainment of which, Spiritism will furnish him with the most effectual means.

V

Those who complain that spiritist belief is spreading in all directions and threatening to invade the world, thereby proclaim its power; for no opinion that is not founded on reason and on fact could become general. Therefore, if Spiritism is taking root everywhere, making converts in every rank of society, and especially among the educated classes, as is admitted by all to be the case, it is evident that it must founded in truth. That being so, all the efforts of its detractors will be made in vain; an assertion borne out by the fact that the ridicule attempted to be heaped upon it by those who have hoped thereby to arrest its march seems only to have given it new life. This result fully justifies the assurances that have been so constantly given us by our spirit-friends, who have repeatedly said to us, "Do not allow yourself to be made uneasy by opposition. Whatever is done against you will turn to your advantage, and your *bitterest opponents will serve you in spite of themselves.* Against the will of God, the ill-will of men is of no avail."

Through the moral teachings of Spiritism, the human race will enter upon a new phase of its destiny; that of the moral progress which is the inevitable consequence of this belief. The rapid spread of spiritist ideas should cause no surprise, being due to the profound satisfaction they give to those who adopt them with intelligence and sincerity; and as happiness is what men desire above all things, it is not surprising that they should embrace ideas which impart so much happiness to those who hold them.

The development of these ideas presents three distinct periods. The first is that of *curiosity*, excited by the strangeness of the phenomena produced; the second, that of *reasoning and philosophy*; the third, that of *application and consequences.* The period of curiosity is gone by, for curiosity has only a brief existence; the mind, when satisfield in regard to any novelty, quitting it at once for another, as is not its habit in regard to subjects that awaken graver thought and that appeal to the judgment. The second period has already begun; the third will certainly follow. The progress of Spiritism has been specially rapid since its essential nature and its scope have been more correctly understood, because it touches the most sensitive fibre of the human heart, viz., the desire of happiness, which it augments immeasurably, even in the present world; this, as previously remarked, is the cause of its wide acceptance, the secret of the force that will make it triumph. It renders happy those who understand it, while awaiting the extension of its influence over the masses. How many a spiritist, who has never witnessed any of the physical phenomena of spirit-manifestation, says to himself, "Besides the phenomena of Spiritism, there is its philosophy, which explains what NO OTHER has ever explained. That philosophy furnishes me, through arguments drawn from reason only and independently of any sanction but that of reason, with a *rational* solution of problems that are of the most vital importance to my future; it gives me calmness, security, confidence; it delivers me from the torments of uncertainty. In comparison with results so valuable, the question of the physical phenomena is of secondary importance."

To those who attack this philosophy, we reply, "Would you like to have a means of combating it successfully? If so, here it is: Bring forward something better in its place; find a more philosophic solution of the problems it solves: give to man ANOTHER CERTAINTY that shall render him still happier. But you must thoroughly understand the meaning of the word *certainty*, for man only accepts as *certain* what apears to him to be reasonable. You must not content yourselves with saying that the thing is not so, which is a mode of proceeding altogether too easy. You must prove, not by negation, but by facts, that what we assert to exist has no existence, has never been, and CANNOT BE, and above all, having shown that it has no existence, you must show what you have to offer in its place; and you must prove that the tendency of Spiritism is not to make men better, and consequently happier, by the practice of the purest morality—that sublime and simple morality of the Gospels, which men praise so much, and practise so little. When you have done all this, you will have a right to attack it."

Spiritism is strong because its bases are those of religion itself, viz., God, the soul, the rewards and punishments of the future; because it shows those rewards and punishments to be the natural consequences of the earthly life; and because, in the picture it presents of the future, there is nothing which the most logical mind could regard as contrary to reason. What compensation can you offer for the sufferings of the present life, you whose whole doctrine consists in the negation of the future? You base your teachings on incredulity; Spiritism is based on confidence in God: while the latter invites all men to happiness, to hope, to true fraternity, you offer them, in prospect, ANNIHILATION, and in the present, by way of consolation, SELFISHNESS: it explains everything, and you explain nothing; it *proves* by facts, while your assertions are devoid of proof. How can you expect that the world should hesitate between these two doctrines?

To suppose that Spiritsm derives its strength from the physical manifestations, and that it might therefore be put an end to by hindering those manifestations, is to form to one's self a very false idea of it. Its strength is in its philosophy, in the appeal it makes to reason, to common sense. In ancient times it was the object of mysterious studies, carefully hidden from the vulgar; at the present day it has no secrets, but speaks clearly, without ambiguity, mysticism, or allegories susceptible of false interpretations. The time having come for making known the truth, its language is such as all may comprehend. So far from being opposed to the diffusion of the light, the new revelation is intended for all mankind; it does not claim a blind acceptance, but urges every one to examine the grounds of his belief, and as its teachings are based upon reason, it will always be stronger than those who base their arguments upon annihilation. Would it be possible to put a stop to spirit-manifestations, by placing obstacles in the way of their production? No; for such an attempt would have the effect of all persecutions, viz., that of exciting curiosity, and the desire of making acquaintance with a forbidden subject. Were spirit-manifestations the privilege of a single individual, it would undoubtedly be possible, by preventing his action, to put an end to them; but unfortunately for our adversaries, those manifestations are within everybody's reach, and are being obtained by all, from the highest to the lowest, from the palace to the cottage. It might be possible to prevent their production in public, but, as is well known, it is not in public, but in private, that they are most successfully produced; and as any one may be a medium, how would it be possible to prevent each family in the privacy of its home, each individual in the silence of his chamber, each prisoner, even, in his cell, from holding communication with the invisible beings around them, in the very presence of those who should endeavour to prevent them from doing so? If mediums were forbidden to exercise their faculty in one country, how would it be possible to hinder them from doing so elsewhere throughout the rest of the world, since there is not a single country, in either continent, in which mediums are not to be found? In order to shut up all the mediums, it would be necessary to incarcerate half the human race; and even if it were possible, which would scarcely be easier, to burn all the spiritist books in existence, they would at once be reproduced, because the source from which they emanate is beyond the reach of attack, and it is impossible to imprison or to burn the spirits who are their real authors.

Spiritism is not the work of any man; no one can claim to have created it, for it is as old as creation itself. It is to be found everywhere, in all religions, and in the Catholic religion even more than in the others, and with more authoritative inculcation, for the Catholic dogma contains all that constitutes Spiritism;—admission of the existence of spirits of every degree; their relations, occult and patent, with mankind; guardian-angels, reincarnation, the emancipation of the soul during the present life, second-sight, visions, and manifestations of every kind, including even tangible apparitions. As for demons, they are nothing else than bad spirits; and with the exception of the belief that the former are doomed to evil for ever, while the path of progress is not closed against the others, there is, between them, only a difference of name.

What is the special and peculiar work of modern Spiritism? To make a coherent whole of what has hitherto been scattered; to explain, in clear and precise terms, what has hitherto been wrapped up in the language of allegory; to eliminate the products of superstition and ignorance from human belief, leaving only what is real and actual: this is its mission, but that of a founder does not belong to it. It renders evident that which already exists; it coordinates, but it creates nothing, for its elements are of all countries and of every age. Who, then, could flatter himself with the hope of being able to stifle it, either by ridicule or by persecution? If it were possible to proscribe it in one place, it would reappear in another, or on the very spot from which it had been banished, because it exists in the constitution of things, and because no man can annihilate that which is one of the powers of nature, or veto that which is in virtue of the Divine decrees.

But what interest could any Government have in opposing the propagation of spiritist ideas? Those ideas, it is true, are a protest against the abuses that spring from pride and selfishness; but although such abuses are profitable to the few, they are injurious to the many, and Spiritism would therefore have the masses on its side, while its only adversaries would be those who profit by the abuses against which it protests. So far from Governments having anything to dread from the spread of spiritist ideas, the tendency of those ideas being to render men more benevolent towards one another, less greedy of material things, and more resigned to the orderings of Providence, they constitute, for the State, a guarantee of order and of tranquillity.

VII

Spiritism presents three different aspects, viz., the facts of spirit-manifestation, the philosophic and moral principles deducible from those facts, and the practical applications of which those principles are susceptible; hence three classes into which its adherents are naturally divided, or rather, three degrees of advancement by which they are distinguished: 1st, Those who believe in the reality and genuineness of the spirit-manifestations, but confine themselves to the attestation of these, and for whom Spiritism is merely an experimental science; 2d, Those who comprehend its moral bearings; 3d, Those who put in practice, or, at least, endeavour to put in practice, the system of morality which it is the mission of Spiritism to establish. Whatever the point of view, experimental, scientific, or moral, from which these strange phenomena are considered, every one perceives that they are ushering in an entirely novel order of ideas, which must necessarily produce a profound modification of the state of the human race; and every one who understands the subject also perceives that this modification can only be for good.

As for our adversaries, they may also be grouped into three categories: 1st, Those who systematically deny whatever is new, or does not proceed from themselves, and who speak without knowing what they are talking about. To this class belong all those who admit nothing beyond the testimony of their senses; they have not seen anything, do not wish to see anything, and are still more unwilling to go deeply into anything; they would, in fact, be unwilling to see too clearly, for fear of being obliged to confess that they have been mistaken; they declare that Spiritism is chimerical, insane, utopian, and has no real existence, as the easiest way of settling the matter; they are the wilfully incredulous. With them may be classed those who have condescendend to glance at the subject, in order to be able to say, "I have tried to see something of it, but I have not been able to succeed in doing so;" and who do not seem to be aware that half an hour's attention is not enough to make them acquainted with a new field of study; 2d, Those who, although perfectly aware of the genuineness of the phenomena, oppose the matter from interested motives. They know that Spiritism is true; but being afraid of consequences, they attack it as an enemy. 3d, Those who dread the moral rules of Spiritism as constituting too severe a censure of their acts and tendencies. A serious admission of the truth of Spiritism would be in their way; they neither reject nor accept it, but prefer to close their eyes in regard to it. The first class is swayed by pride and presumption; the second by ambition; the third by selfishness. We should seek in vain for a fourth class of antagonists, viz., that of opponents who, basing their opposition on a careful and conscientious study of Spiritism, should bring forward positive and irrefutable evidence of its falsity.

It would be hoping too much of human nature to imagine that it could be suddenly transformed by spiritist ideas. The action of these undoubtedly is not the same, nor is it equally powerful, in the case of all those by whom they are professed; but their result, however slight it may be, is always beneficial, if only by proving the existence of an extra-corporeal world, and thus disproving the doctrines of materialism. This result follows from a mere observation of the phenomena of Spiritism; but, among those who, comprehending its philosophy, see in it something else than phenomena more or less curious, it produces other effects. The first and most general of these is the development of the religious sentiment, even in those who, without being materialists, are indifferent to spiritual things; and this sentiment leads to contempt of death—we do not say to a *desire* for death, for the spiritist would defend his life like anyone else, but to an indifference which causes him to accept death, when inevitable, without murmuring and without regret, as something to be welcomed rather than feared, owing to his certainty in regard to the state which follows it. The second effect of spiritist convictions is resignation under the vicissitudes of life. Spiritism lead us to consider everything from so elevated a point of view that the importance of terrestrial life is proportionally diminished, and we are less painfully affected by its tribulations; we have consequently more courage under affliction, more moderation in our desires, and also a more rooted repugnance to the idea of shortening our days, Spiritism showing us that suicide always causes the loss of what it was intended to obtain. The certainty of a future which it depends on ourselves to render happy, the possibility of establishing relations with those who are dear to us in the other life, offer the highest of all consolations to the spiritist; and his field of view is widened to infinity by his constant beholding of the life beyond the grave, and his growing acquaintance with conditions of existence hitherto veiled in mystery. The third effect of spiritist ideas is to induce indulgence for the defects of others; but it must be admitted that, selfishness being the most tenacious of human sentiments, it is also the one which it is most difficult to extirpate. We are willing to make sacrifices provided they cost us nothing, and provided especially that they impose on us no privations; but money still exercises an irresistible attraction over the greater number of mankind, and very few understand the word "superfluity" in connection with their own personality.

The abnegation of our personality is, therefore, the most eminent sign of progress.

VIII

"Do spirits," it is sometimes asked, "teach us anything new in the way of morality, anything superior to what has been taught by Christ? If the moral code of Spiritism be no other than that of the gospel, what is the use of it?" This mode of reasoning is singularly like that of the Caliph Omar, in speaking of the Library of Alexandria:—"If," said he, "it contains only what is found in the Koran, it is useless, and in that case must be burned; if it contains anything that is not found in the Koran, it is bad, and in that case, also, it must be burned." No; the morality of Spiritism is not different from that of Jesus; but we have to ask, in our turn, whether, before Christ, men had not the law given by God to Moses? Is not the doctrine of Christ to be found in the Decalogue? But will it therefore be contended that the moral teaching of Jesus is useless? We ask, still further, of those who deny the utility of the moral teachings of Spiritism, why it is that the moral teachings of Christ are so little practised, and why it is that those who rightly proclaim their sublimity are the first to violate the first of His laws, viz., that of *universal charity?* Spirits now come not only to confirm it, but also to show us its practical utility; they render intelligible, patent, truths that have hitherto been taught under he form of allegory; and, with this reinculcation of the eternal truths of morality, they also give us the solution of the most abstract problems of psychology.

Jesus came to show men the road to true goodness. Since God sent Him to recall to men's mind the divine law they had forgotten. why should He not send spirits to recall it to their memory once again, and with still greater precision, now that they are forgetting it in their devotion to pride and to material gain? Who shall take upon himself to set bounds to the power of God, or to dictate His ways? Who shall say that the appointed time has not arrived, as it is declared to have done by spirits, when truths hitherto unknown or misunderstood are to be openly proclaimed to the human race, in order to hasten its advancement? Is there not something evidently providential in the fact that spirit-manifestations are being made on all points of the globe? It is not a single man, an isolated prophet, who comes to arouse us; light is breaking forth on all sides, and a new world is being opened out before our eyes. As the invention of the microscope has revealed to us the world of the infinitely little, the existence of which was unsuspected by us, and as the telescope has revealed to us the myriads of worlds the existence of which we suspected just as little,—so the spirit-communications of the present day are revealing to us the existence of an invisible world that surrounds us on all sides, that is incessantly in contact with us, and that takes part, unknown to us, in everything we do. Yet a short time, and the existence of that world, *which is awaiting every one of us*, will be as incontestible as is that of the microscopic world, and of the infinity of globes in space. Is it nothing to have made known that new world, to have initiated us into the mysteries of the life beyond the grave? It is true that these discoveries, if such they can be called, are contrary to certain received ideas; but have not all great scientific discoveries modified, and even overthrown, ideas as fully received by the world, and has not our pride of opinion had to yield to evidence? It will be the same in regard to Spiritism, which ere long will have taken its place among the other branches of human knowledge.

Communication with the beings of the world beyond the grave enables us to see and to comprehend the life to come, initiates us into the joys and sorrows that await us therein according to our deserts, and thus brings back to *spiritualism* those who had come to

see in man only matter, only an organised machine; we are therefore justified in asserting that *the facts of Spiritism have given
the death-blow to materialism.* Had Spiritism done nothing more
than this, it would be entitled to the gratitude of all the friends
of social order; but it does much more than this, for it shows *the
inevitable results of evil,* and, consequently, *the necessity of goodness.* The number of those whom it has brought back to better
sentiments, whose evil tendencies it has neutralised, and whom it
has turned from wrong-doing, is already larger than is usually
supposed, and is becoming still more considerable every day;
because the future is no longer for them a vague imagining, a
mere hope, but a *fact,* the reality of which is felt and understood
when they *see* and *hear* those who have left us lamenting or
rejoicing over what they did when they were upon the earth.
Whoever witnesses these communications begins to reflect on the
reality thus brought home to him, and to feel the need of self-
examination, self-judgment, and self-amendment.

IX

The fact that differences of opinion exist among spiritists in
regard to certain points of doctrine has been used by opponents as
a handle against it. It is not surprising that, in the beginning of
a new science, when the observations on which it is based are still
incomplete, the subjects of which it treats should have been
regarded by its various adherents from their own point of view,
and that contradictory theories should thus have been put forth.
But a deeper study of the facts in question has already overthrown
most of those theories, and, among others, that which attributed
all spirit-communications to evil spirits, as though it were impossible for God to send good spirits to men; a supposition that
is at once absurd, because it is opposition to the facts of the case,
and impious, because it is a denial of the power and goodness of
the Creator. Our spirit-guides have always advised us not to
trouble ourselves about divergences of opinion among spiritists,
assuring us that unity of doctrine will eventually be established;
and we accordingly see that this unity has already been arrived at
in regard to the major part of the points at issue, and that
divergences of opinion, in regard to the others, are disappearing
day by day.

To the question, "While awaiting the establishment of doctrinal unity, upon what basis can an impartial and disinterested inquirer arrive at a judgment as to the relative merits of the various theories put forth by spirits?" the following reply was given:—

"The purest light is that which is not obscured by any cloud; the most precious diamond is the one which is without a flaw; judge the communications of spirits, in like manner, by the purity of their teachings. Do not forget that there are, among spirits, many who have not yet freed themselves from their earthly ideas. Learn to distinguish them by their language; judge them by the sum of what they tell you; see whether there is logical sequence in the ideas they suggest, whether there is, in their statements, nothing that betrays ignorance, pride, or malevolence; in a word, whether their communications always bear the stamp of wisdom that attests true superiority. If your world were inaccessible to error, it would be perfect, which it is far from being; you have still to learn to distinguish error from truth; you need the lessons of experience to exercise your judgment and to bring you on. The basis of unity will be found in the body of doctrine among the adherents of which good has never been mixed with evil; men will rally spontaneously to that doctrine, because they will judge it to be the truth.

"But what matter a few dissidences of opinion, more apparent than real? The fundamental principles of Spiritism are every-where the same, and should unite you all in a common bond; that of the love of God and the practice of goodness. Whatever you suppose to be the mode of progression and the normal conditions of your future existence, the aim proposed is still the same, viz., *to do right*; and there is but one way of doing *that*."

If there be, among spiritists, differences of opinion in regard to some points of theory, all of them are agreed in regard to the fundamentals of the matter; unity, therefore, already exists among them, with the exception of the very small number of those who do not yet admit the intervention of spirits in the manifestations, and who attribute these either to purely physical causes, which is contrary to the axiom, "Every intelligent effect must have an in-telligent cause," or to a reflex action of our own thought, which is disproved by the facts of the case. There may, then, be *different schools*, seeking light in regard to the points of spiritist doctrine that are still open to controversy; there ought not to be *rival sects*, making opposition to one another. Antagonism should only exist between those who desire goodness, and those who desire, or do, evil; but no one who has sincerely adopted the broad principles of morality laid down by Spiritism can desire evil or wish ill to his neighbour, whatever may be his opinions in regard to points of secondary importance. If any school be in error, it will obtain light, sooner or later, if it seeks honestly and without prejudice; and all schools possess, meanwhile, a common bond that should unite them in the same sentiment. All of them have a common aim; it matters little what road they take, provided it leads to the common goal. None should attempt to impose their opinion by force, whether physical or moral; and any school that should hurl its anathema at another would be clearly in the wrong, for it would evidently be acting under the influence of evil spirits. The only force of an argument is its intrinsic reasonableness; and moderation will do more to ensure the triumph of the truth than diatribe envenomed by envy and jealousy. Good spirits preach only union and the love of the neighbour; and nothing malevolent or uncharitable can ever proceed from a pure source.

As bearing on the subject of the foregoing remarks, and also as a fitting termination of the present work, we subjoin the following message from the spirit of Saint Augustine—a message conveying counsels well worthy of being laid to heart by all who read it:—

"Long enough have men torn one another to pieces, anathematising each other in the name of a God of peace and of mercy, whom they insult by such a sacrilege. Spiritism will eventually constitute a bond of union among them, by showing what is truth and what is error; but there will still be, and for a long time to come, scribes and pharisees who will reject it, as they rejected Christ. Would you know the quality of the spirits who influence the various sects into which the world is divided? Judge them by their deeds and by the principles they profess. Never did good spirits instigate to the commission of evil deeds; never did they counsel or condone murder or violence; never did they excite party-hatreds, the thirst for riches and honours, or greed of earthly things. They alone who are kind, humane, benevolent, *to all*, are counted as friends by spirits of high degree; they alone are counted as friends by Jesus, for they alone are following the road which He has shown them as the only one which leads to Him."

SAINT AUGUSTINE

INDEX

INDEX

———

CHAPTER II

CHAPTER III

CHAPTER IV

CHAPTER V

CHAPTER VI

CHAPTER VII

CHAPTER VIII

CHAPTER IX

PRINTED IN BRAZIL
(JULY/2003)
BY

EDITORA e GRÁFICA
VIDA & CONSCIÊNCIA

R. Agostinho Gomes, 2312 • Ipiranga • SP
Fonefax: (11) 6161-2739 / 6161-2670
e-mail:grafica@vidaconsciencia.com.br
site: www.vidaeconsciencia.com.br